American investment in British manufacturing industry

American Investment in British Manufacturing Industry was first published in 1958 and is now widely regarded as a seminal work in international business. The book was the first to analyse the impact of foreign direct investment on a host country.

To commemorate the fortieth anniversary of its original publication Emeritus Professor Dunning has revised and updated this classic work. This new edition includes:

- a new introduction
- a comparison of US MNE activity in the UK in the 1990s with the 1950s
- a new concluding chapter revisiting American investment from a contemporary perspective
- an updated appendix analysing US direct investment in UK manufacturing from 1950 to 1995
- analysis of significant changes such as the European Union, new technology and the growth of non-US and Japanese foreign investment in the UK

This volume will be essential reading for all those interested in international business, business history and the contribution of foreign direct investment to UK industrial competitiveness.

Professor John H. Dunning is Professor Emeritus of International Business at the University of Reading, UK. He is past President of the International Trade and Finance Association, and of the Academy of International Business. He has published extensively on international direct investment and the multinational enterprise, and on industrial and regional economics.

American investment in British manufacturing industry

Revised and updated edition

John H. Dunning

London and New York

338.47670941
D92aa

First published in 1958 by George Allen & Unwin Ltd.
New revised and updated edition 1998 by Routledge
11 New Fetter Lane, London EC4P 4EE

Simultaneously published in the USA and Canada
by Routledge
29 West 35th Street, New York, NY 10001

© 1998 John H. Dunning

Typeset in Baskerville by
J&L Composition Ltd, Filey, North Yorkshire
Printed and bound in Great Britain by
Creative Print and Design (Wales), Ebbw Vale

All rights reserved. No part of this book may be reprinted or
reproduced or utilized in any form or by any electronic,
mechanical, or other means, now known or hereafter
invented, including photocopying and recording, or in any
information storage or retrieval system, without permission in
writing from the publishers.

British Library Cataloguing in Publication Data
A catalogue record for this book is available from the British Library

Library of Congress Cataloging in Publication Data
Dunning, John H.
   American investment in British manufacturing industry/John
   Dunning.—New rev. and updated ed.
   p.   cm.
   Includes bibliographical references and index.
   1. Manufacturing industries—Great Britain.   2. Investments,
   American—Great Britain.   I. Title.
   HD9731.5.D8   1998
   338.4'767'0941—dc21   97–47604

ISBN 0–415–18411–8 (hbk)
ISBN 0–415–18412–6 (pbk)

Contents

University Libraries
Carnegie Mellon University
Pittsburgh, PA 15213-3890

Appendices

Figure and tables

Preface to 1958 edition

This book is the result of a three-year research project financed by a grant from the Board of Trade under the Conditional Aid Scheme for the use of counterpart funds derived from US economic aid. Though appearing under my name, its preparation has involved the co-operation of a large number of people, foremost among whom are the senior executives of more than 200 American-financed firms in this country who gave liberally of their time, understanding and patience, and without whose assistance this study could not have been completed. I can only hope that the results of my researches might be some small recompense for the kindness they have shown towards me.

I have also been fortunate to benefit from the able research assistance of, first, Dr A. McKee and, second, Mr W. A. Stearn; in addition, Miss S. Mitchell helped me visit a number of firms in the summer of 1955. Miss D. Marshallsay has been responsible for the preparation of the Index and has also lightened my task of proofreading; to her too I should like to offer my thanks. Professor P. Ford has been a source of encouragement throughout the project and has suggested a number of valuable improvements to the manuscript. I have also appreciated the kindly interest shown by Mr Francis Rogers, one-time head of the US productivity and technical co-operation activities in the UK, and by Mr D. Gill, OBE, secretary of the American Chamber of Commerce in London. Finally, I should like to record the very real debt which I owe to Ida Dunning, who, as well as acting as my secretary for most of the three years, has nobly shared with me the burden of preparing this work for publication.

To the editor of the *Manchester School of Economic and Social Studies*, I gratefully acknowledge permission to reproduce the substance of an article which I wrote for that journal in September 1956, and to the District Bank Ltd for permission to make use of material which first appeared in the September 1955 and June 1956 issues of its quarterly review.

JHD
Southampton
July 1957

Preface to 1998 edition

The forty years since the date of the original publication of *American Investment in British Manufacturing Industry* have seen a wide range of analytical and empirical studies on the impact of the foreign direct investment (fdi) on the economic efficiency and welfare of recipient countries.[1] While the emphasis given by these studies to particular costs and benefits associated with such capital flows has varied over time and between countries, the distinctive contribution of foreign, as opposed to domestically, owned investment has changed little. However, because those sectors in which fdi is likely to concentrate are also those which tend to be dominated by multinational enterprises (MNEs) of all nationalities, and these compete with each other in global markets, foreignness *per se* may well becoming rather less important than once it was.

Clearly, however, the economic and political scenario of the 1990s facing US corporations contemplating foreign production in the UK is very different from that of the 1950s. For much of the first two decades after the Second World War, virtually all the European economies exercised foreign exchange constraints, and/ or direct control over the amount of imports they allowed. Moreover, intra-European trade was severely constrained by high tariff and non-tariff barriers. In consequence, not only did US firms need to invest in Europe, or engage in licensing with European firms to sell their goods in European markets; for the most part, such import-substituting investment tended to service national, rather than European markets. In the 1990s, the situation is totally different. There are virtually no foreign exchange constraints – except in parts of Central and Eastern Europe – while the European Union (EU), which now consists of fifteen countries with a population of 340 million, has substantially abolished tariff and non-barriers among its member states. US exports to, and fdi in, the EU now tend to be complementary, rather than substitutable, modes in supplying European markets;[2] while between one-third to one-half of all manufacturing sales of US subsidiaries in the EU are sold to other countries in Europe.[3]

These developments in Europe are, in many respects, a microcosm of those occurring in the rest of the world, particularly, since the late 1980s, as the liberalization of markets and international commerce have gathered pace. The results of the growing internationalization of the world economy is best shown by the fact that, since the mid-1970s, international trade has grown at $1\frac{1}{2}$ times the rate of that of the world's gross domestic product (gdp), and fdi at more than twice the rate.[4] The total manufacturing sales of the foreign affiliates of MNEs[5] now comfortably exceed those of manufacturing exports,[6] while it is further estimated that between one-third and two-fifths of all trade in manufactured products is conducted within MNEs.[7]

In the mid-1950s, it is doubtful whether the world's stock of outward foreign direct investment was more than 3 per cent of its gross domestic product. By 1973, this figure had risen to 4.2 per cent, by 1980 to 4.9 per cent, by 1990 to 8.1 per cent and by 1994 to 9.7 per cent.[8] In 1993, the foreign assets and employment of the leading industrial MNEs accounted for two-fifths of their global assets and employment, while more than one-fifth of the research and development of these same companies was undertaken outside their home countries.[9]

Over the past forty years, the geographical distribution of fdi has also changed. Taking US data as an example, in 1950 69.5 per cent of the foreign direct assets of US companies was in the rest of the Americas and the Western Hemisphere, 14.4 per cent in Europe and 16.1 per cent in the rest of the world. In 1994, the corresponding percentages were 30.1, 50.0, 19.9. Other data show that, whereas in the period 1975–80, 76.6 per cent of the fdi flows of all countries were directed to developed countries (43.1 per cent to Western Europe), in the years 1990–4 68.4 per cent were so directed (43.4 per cent to Western Europe).[10] In the intervening years, many countries had opened their boundaries to foreign capital; in the 1990s, for example, China has been the largest recipient of fdi among developing countries, whereas it was not even in the top ten of recipients in the later 1970s. Central and Eastern Europe, which attracted just a few million dollars of inbound fdi before 1979, accounted for 2.0 per cent of the world's new fdi investment flows between 1990 and 1995.[11]

The emergence of new industrial producers on the world economic scene has also meant a widening of the range of investing companies engaging in fdi. When I wrote *American Investment* most of Europe was still recovering from the Second World War, the Japanese industrial machine was still in a sorry state, and Third World fdi was almost exclusively confined to a handful of Latin American countries. Even in 1973, the share of the world stock of fdi accounted for by Germany, Japan and the developing countries was only 12.0 per cent, while the combined share of the US and UK was 61.9 per cent. However, in 1993, the corresponding figures were 27.6 per cent and 37.5 per cent. The US, which in 1967 was alone responsible for 50.4 per cent of the world's stock of outward direct investment, accounted for only 25.8 per cent of that stock in 1995.

One should perhaps not be unduly surprised by these figures; after all, they are following a similar historical trajectory to that of international trade, and largely reflect the spread of economic development and industrialization throughout the world. But, as far as the updating of material contained in this volume is concerned, they do have three important implications which are examined in some detail in Chapter 11 and in Appendix 3.

The first is that in the 1950s the world was in a stage of economic transition, and the significance of the UK economy – relative to that of other countries – to

US direct investors, and that of US fdi – relative to that of other foreign countries – to the UK economy, was at its peak. At the same time, and second, the 1950s witnessed the beginning of a major upsurge in fdi, as a form of international economic involvement, which has gathered momentum throughout the last forty years. The UK – perhaps more than any other developed country – has been at the forefront of this surge in MNE activity. In 1994, for example, the combined share of the outward and inward direct investment stock as a percentage of her gdp was a staggeringly high 48.4 per cent, compared with an average of all developed countries of 19.8 per cent and for the European Union of 18.9 per cent. And although, as the data set out in Appendix 3 will show, the share of US affiliates as compared with that of all foreign affiliates of UK manufacturing output has fallen, its share of all UK manufacturing sales rose quite dramatically from 4.8 per cent in 1953 to 14.7 per cent in 1994.

The third implication concerns the nature of US fdi in the UK. In the 1950s, such investment was mainly in pursuance of a multi-domestic organizational strategy of the investing companies in which the various entities of the global operations of US MNEs largely acted independently of each other. In the 1990s, the situation is totally different in that the great majority of the 650 or so US affiliates in UK manufacturing industry (cf. 246 in 1953 and 1,234 in 1979) are part of a global or regional (i.e. European) integration strategy of their parent companies.[12] *Inter alia*, this change in strategy, which has been brought about by the liberalization of markets, a substantial fall in transport and communication costs, and the widening of geographical portfolio of investments by MNEs, has not only changed the industrial composition of US fdi in the UK but the extent to, and the ways in, which the economic fortunes of the UK are related to those of other countries in which US subsidiaries are located. Added to this, the more recent growth of fdi by US firms to augment, rather than exploit, their competitive advantages, we are observing a very different scenario for US fdi in the UK than that in the 1950s.

When it was first published, *American Investment* was a contemporary commentary on a relatively new phenomenon in the British economy. Now it is part of the UK's economic history. Yet, as the reader will discover, most of the analyses and findings of the following 300 pages are no less pertinent in 1998 than they were in 1958. Most of the benefits and costs, and of the welcome and less welcome features expressed in this volume, are still voiced by governments, academics, business leaders, trade unions and consumer groups in both developed and developing countries in the 1990s. The tune may vary somewhat – but the song remains the same!

It is to be hoped, then, that a new generation of scholars who now have a chance to read this monograph – which has been out of print for the last fifteen years or more – will view it both as a historical record of events at a particular time and in a particular place, and also as a reminder that even forty years ago it was possible to draw some general conclusions about the impact of fdi on the economic welfare of host countries which have well stood the test of time.

In the pages which follow, we have made only minor editorial changes to the original text. The only exception is in Chapter 1 (p. 6 and p. 20), where, in the light of more recent historical research, we have corrected a couple of paragraphs. Very occasionally, however, we do refer the reader to contemporary writings on the subject being discussed. In such cases we have bracketed the citations.

Introduction

In a study of the role which private American investment had so far played in assisting the post-war economic recovery of Western Europe, an OEEC report published in 1954 said:

> The first function of United States capital is fulfilled by direct investment in manufacturing or merchandising when it carries with it improved technology, efficient production and sales methods, patents, management, skilled personnel and fresh ideas, all elements from which even the economies of the most advanced European countries can derive higher productivity. The contribution of such investment to economic progress in Europe may be very large indeed and out of proportion to the amount of money involved in the original investment and ensuing service charges.[1]

The main purpose of this study is to enlarge upon the theme of the above quotation, and assess its relevance and implications from the viewpoint of the British economy; to evaluate the extent to which United States business investment in British manufacturing industry – now (1953) valued at close on $1,200 million and growing at the rate of 10–12 per cent per annum – has affected in the past, and is affecting today, the course and efficiency of British industrial development. With the American economy being particularly well endowed with those resources necessary to meet the demands of this increasingly scientific and technological age, yet with the need for the same resources nowhere more keenly felt than in the United Kingdom as she seeks to maintain and expand her export markets, the case for a close Anglo-American relationship is a very strong one. With, too, the UK's dollar problem still largely unsolved, yet with the external commitments of the United States likely to make heavier demands on her foreign earnings in the future, this would seem an opportune moment to pause and reflect on some of the ways in which US manufacturing subsidiaries and Anglo-American companies operating in the UK have promoted indigenous industrial expansion and aided America's search for new sales outlets.

To the best of our knowledge, no comprehensive study of the scope of American corporate investment in British manufacturing industry has yet been made. In 1931, an American economist – F. A. Southard – concluded an elaborate survey of the extent and character of American business interests in Europe,[2] and Cleona

Lewis's *America's Stake in International Investment*[3] is still a standard text on the wider aspects of the subject. More recently, Professor E. R. Barlow has published an account of some of the problems associated with the operation and administration of US manufacturing units in Mexico,[4] but the only information relating to American business investment in the United Kingdom is that which is incorporated in the periodic surveys of US overseas assets issued by the US Department of Commerce.[5] In any event, all these studies approach their subject matter principally from the viewpoint of the *investing* country and not the country in which the investment is being made.

It is hoped that this work will serve a useful purpose both in helping to bridge this gap in our knowledge and in stimulating interest in Anglo-American investment relationships as a whole. At the same time, we would emphasize that the book was written neither to prove or support any preconceived thesis, nor as a practical guide to the problems facing US businessmen overseas. Its purpose is less ambitious: to assess, as objectively as possible, the role occupied by American-financed firms in the British economy and their contribution to industrial development and economic welfare. This being so, our analysis is essentially descriptive rather than analytical in character. As has been acknowledged in the preface, our debt is considerable to a large number of firms, organizations and individuals who have provided us with the greater part of the raw material for our study. For the reader who likes his future pattern of reading set out before him, the study which follows is divided into three main parts.

First, the background picture. Chapter 1 traces the growth and development of US business investment in British manufacturing industry from its genesis in 1858, and Chapter 2 considers its present-day scope and significance. Chapter 3 analyses the geographical location, size distribution, and ownership pattern of American-controlled firms in this country, and Chapter 4 their financial, administrative and managerial structures.

The object of Chapter 5 – the second part of the book – is more normative in character. It aims to compare and contrast the operating and managerial methods adopted in US parent factories with those practised by branch units in the UK, with the purpose of assessing the extent to which the former (the superiority of which, in their wider context, have been put forward as the major cause of America's high productivity) can be economically transferred across the Atlantic. To what extent, for example, are such productivity differences between US parent companies and their UK affiliates *avoidable*, or within the power of the individual businessman to avoid, and to what extent *unavoidable*, or a reflection of circumstances outside the control of any one firm?

The third part of our study, from Chapter 6 onwards, deals with the implications of the data contained in the preceding chapters to British industrial development. Chapter 6 first outlines the impact made by American manufacturing subsidiaries on the competitive structure of the industries in which they produce, and then assesses the extent and significance of the transatlantic research, manufacturing and managerial expertise which such firms are able to draw upon. In particular, how far and in what way has the efficiency of the UK competitors of

American firms been affected? In Chapter 7 we consider the relationships between US-affiliated firms and their British component and raw material suppliers, and in so doing examine both the nature of the former's purchasing techniques *vis-à-vis* those adopted by comparable UK firms, and the extent to which new ideas and knowledge have been made available as a result. Chapter 8 discusses the implications of US investment as seen through the eyes of the industrial or domestic UK consumer. In what fields, for example, and by how much, have US-designed products helped to raise the level of industrial efficiency? What are the advantages which the presence of American firms in this country offer over any alternative means of acquiring competitive enhancing techniques?

Chapter 9 supplements these earlier chapters with a more detailed study of the managerial techniques practised by US-controlled firms, and Chapter 10 briefly analyses some of the wider economic implications of recent US investment trends in the United Kingdom, from the viewpoint of both the investing and receiving countries. Here we are concerned with such questions as the effects of the $1,200 million US investment on the British balance of payments, and the value of these business interests to the American economy. The function of this book has been both to consolidate existing knowledge and to open up new lines of inquiry.

As will be appreciated from the footnotes of acknowledgements, most of the information contained in Chapters 1 and 2 has been derived from already-published sources. The majority of the data for the original part of the study, which is to be found in Chapter 3 and subsequent chapters, was obtained from information directly provided by a large number of individual firms. Some 115 US subsidiaries and 45 Anglo-American companies located in Great Britain with a 25 per cent or more American equity capital interest in them were visited between January 1954 and December 1955. A further 45 firms gave postal information. The global statistics contained in Chapters 3–5 are based entirely on data received from these firms.

In all, 245 US-affiliated companies engaged in British manufacturing industry in December 1953 were invited to co-operate in our survey. This number were believed to include all firms of this kind which employed more than 100 workers at that time; of these 40 either failed to reply, or were unwilling to assist us in any way. To the best of our knowledge, however, the remaining firms which comprise our sample at present employ between 90 per cent and 95 per cent of the total labour force of US-financed manufacturing units in the UK. In this respect, therefore, our statistical coverage is very nearly complete. In addition, visits were paid to the parent companies of twenty of these subsidiaries in the autumn of 1954.

The information given by the top management whom we interviewed was cross-checked as far as possible by referring to other sources of information. For example, in connection with that part of our enquiry which studied the impact made by US firms on their British suppliers, we visited fifty UK subcontractors to gain their views at first hand. Much of the data presented on new products and managerial techniques in Chapters 8 and 9 may be readily confirmed in one way or another. Competitors and consumers of US firms, trade associations, official and semi-official bodies, technical, trade and business publications were also freely consulted in an attempt to obtain a balanced viewpoint.

Since financial exigencies imposed a time limit of two years' field research, the character of our survey has necessarily been *extensive* rather than *intensive*. As it is the first survey of its kind, this is probably an advantage. At the same time, we have been conscious of the dangers of superficial reasoning and generality of approach. This being so, wherever possible, we have tried to corroborate any arguments or conclusions by drawing on actual case studies cited to us. We have deliberately confined the scope of our enquiry to the field of manufacturing industry, though there are also important US financial interests in UK trade, banking, public utilities and business services.

Understandably, not all the firms who took part in our investigations were able, or willing, to answer all the questions asked. In brief, our method of approach took the following form. At an initial interview we aimed to obtain as much background information and as many general statistics as possible, together with the impressions of the firms themselves as to the role which they were playing in the British economy. In about one-half of these cases, this interview was followed up by a second visit, in which we confined ourselves to asking questions on those particular aspects of our enquiry about which the firms in question seemed to be best informed. Thus, while one subsidiary might have made a thorough study of Anglo-American productivity and operation costs, another might have helpful observations on managerial techniques, and a third on its relationship with its UK raw material component suppliers, and so on. Most of the individual examples quoted in Chapters 5, 7, 8 and 9 were derived from these interviews or from subsequent postal communication.

We believe that in all cases we obtained a sufficiently representative body of opinion to form a reasonable judgement of the situation as a whole. There is, however, one important qualification which we should make at this stage. That is, that in no instance did we examine the internal documents of the firm visited. Our feeling was that the width of the ground covered precluded the spending of time which such a course of action would have entailed. In the last resort, then, while taking the utmost care to avoid biased statements and rash judgements, much of the analysis contained in Chapters 3–9 is *our* interpretation of a mixture of facts, impressions and opinions put forward by a large number of businessmen and members of various organizations.

Finally, it should be mentioned that the scope of our enquiry has been partially determined by the fact that concurrently with this research project have been proceeding others which, in part at least, have bordered in content on our own subject. In effect this has meant that, to avoid duplication of time and energy and causing unnecessary inconvenience to firms, our analysis has been limited in two respects. First, the Department of Applied Economics at Cambridge is making a detailed comparison of productivity and operational costs within manufacturing plants in different countries. Within this study are incorporated case-histories of a number of Anglo-American affiliated companies. Partly, in view of this, the data presented in Chapter 5 are rather more generalized than they might otherwise have been. Second, both University College London and the newly formed Science and Industry Committee[6] have been examining certain aspects affecting growth and technical innovation in British industry. The former enquiry has concerned itself with two industries – the rubber products and synthetic detergent industries – in which there are important American interests in this country;[7] the latter, though less restricted in scope, is also concerned with the main determinants of the speed and direction at which new products and manufacturing techniques are introduced into the economy, and once again interest has been directed to certain US-financed firms. While neither of these projects is viewing the problem from the same aspect as ourselves, we decided it best to avoid covering the same ground wherever possible.

In the main then, our conclusions are *qualitative* rather than *quantitative* in character. This is not to imply that there is a lack of any kind of numerical confirmation. But in answer to the question 'What has been the impact made by US firms on the development of such and such an industry . . .?' the writer is neither technologically competent to evaluate the true significance of certain manufacturing processes, nor sufficiently well acquainted with the extent to which they already applied in this country to assess the validity of any claim to originality.

Such indefiniteness may be disappointing to some readers, but it is largely unavoidable in a study of this kind; in a measure the writer shares this disappointment, but would like to feel that his own analysis has paved the way for a more detailed and thorough examination of particular aspects of the subject to be dealt with by people better informed than himself.

This research project will, however, have achieved its purpose if it brings with it a greater realization, on both sides of the Atlantic, of some of the reciprocal benefits which properly planned Anglo-American investment may bring to the investing and receiving countries. We live in a world of political alliances, yet at root, economic co-operation between the free countries is as vital a factor influencing peace. Much has already been accomplished in this direction as exemplified by the work of such organizations as the United Nations, the Organization for European Economic Co-operation and the Commonwealth Economic Committee, and by such projects as the Colombo Plan, the European Coal and Steel Cartel and the proposed European Industrial Free Trade Area. It is hoped, however, that from what follows in this book the significance of Anglo-*American* co-operation will be better appreciated. Each country is inseparably linked to the economic prosperity of the other. Each operates within a world economic environment which makes their economies more complementary to each other than competitive. It is our belief that in the exploitation of this relationship and the mutual gains which follow from it, US direct investment in Britain has an important – indeed, an indispensible – role to play.

1 The growth of US investment in British manufacturing industry

Though a handful of US firms had established sales agencies and banking houses in this country during the late eighteenth and early nineteenth centuries[1] not until 1852 was there any direct American participation in British manufacturing industry. At that date, Samuel Colt, an American gun manufacturer, decided to set up a branch plant in Pimlico, London 'to protect himself from the destructive effects which would follow the introduction of . . . spurious arms into use in England, where he had no patent'.[2] According to his biographers, Colt would have preferred to license the right to produce pistols to a British manufacturer, but at the time 'no machinery made in England was exact enough for the work necessary to turn out the revolvers'.[3] However, the venture was not a financial success, and in 1857 Colt sold his UK interests to a group of Englishmen.

The next recorded US manufacturing investment in the UK was that by J. Ford and Company of New Brunswick, New Jersey, who, in 1856, set up a vulcanized rubber factory in Edinburgh, Scotland.[4] The belief that higher profits could be earned by investing in the United Kingdom than by expanding in the United States was the chief reason for this initial venture, though the choice of location within the UK was strongly influenced by the fact that, at that time, English patents were not protected in Scotland, and could be exploited there without the payment of royalties. The new factory was entirely American designed and managed; and, with the aid of specialized machinery and a nucleus of key workers especially shipped over from the parent plant, early production was facilitated.

Later in the same year, the partnership was incorporated into a limited company – The North British Rubber Co. Ltd – and the original capital of £100,000 was increased. By 1861, the company was employing 300 people, and supplying 10 per cent of the UK market for rubber products.[5] However, in the second half of the 1860s, partly because of unfavourable European trading conditions, and partly because the parent company wished to enlarge its own manufacturing facilities, the entire US shareholding was repatriated. Between that time and 1946, at which date the US Rubber Company purchased part of its equity share capital, the British concern had no American financial connections.

Yet perhaps the first exclusively American innovation to be successfully introduced in the UK by way of a foreign direct investment, was the sewing machine.

Here the Singer Company led the way with the establishment of its first UK manufacturing unit at Bridgeton, near Glasgow, in 1867. For some years previously, imports of sewing machines from America had been growing – especially since 1864, at which date the now world-renowned sales and servicing facilities of the Singer Company had been first introduced.[6] With the expansion of home production – in 1902 the UK subsidiary produced its 10 millionth machine – these now gradually diminished: by 1899, US imports were valued at only £92,894, and by the beginning of the First World War, the UK had substantially replaced its former dependence on imported sewing machines by an export trade of nearly £2½ million.[7] Moreover, even as early as 1875, the Glasgow factory was supplying two-fifths of the UK market, and about the same proportion of Singer's global sales.[8]

In the same year as Singer commenced production at Glasgow, R. Hoe and Company of New York set up a British subsidiary in London to manufacture its newly designed revolving printing press. Replacing the much slower steam and hand methods of printing, the American machine, with an output of 20,000 impressions an hour, in effect brought about a revolution in newspaper printing.[9] Earlier, a variation of this machine had been imported by Lloyd's of London for the production of its weekly newspaper, and this had so impressed the publishers of *The Times* that they ordered two presses from Hoe on condition that they were made in the UK. In due course, the equipment was produced by a British firm, manufacturing under licence to the American company, but shortly afterwards, the latter set up its own production unit, and from 1867 onwards it flourished practically unworried by competition, supplying almost all the leading newspapers in Great Britain and Ireland with its machines.[10]

The effects of this investment were both widespread and cumulative. First, it hastened the decline of the small hand-printer and concentrated output in the hands of a reduced number of firms who could afford the high initial outlay. Second, with the increased speeds in newspaper production now made possible, and the expansion of the UK market brought about by (i) the abolition of tax on newspapers in 1855 and that of the duty on paper in 1861; (ii) the rapid growth of population, and (iii) the beginning of compulsory education in 1870, there arose the complementary need for new and faster methods of typesetting and line adjustment. Here, too, American capital invested in a British-originated company – the Linotype and Machinery Co. Ltd – played a major role. During the 1880s, the Mergenthaler Linotype Company of New York had commercialized the patents of the German, Ottmar Mergenthaler, by which typesetting could be carried out both mechanically and a line at a time. Such machines were then produced in the United Kingdom by the Linotype Co. Ltd under licence, but later, after that concern had merged its interests with those of the Machinery Trust Co. Ltd, the American corporation gained complete financial control. By the early 1900s, the new subsidiary, which retained its original name, was assembling American-designed machines from parts imported from the United States. After this, growth was steady in spite of design and manufacturing problems, with the subsidiary gradually becoming more self-sufficient in its production. By 1914 virtually all the national and many of the provincial newspapers had mechanized their typesetting methods and were using linotype machines. Even today (1958), many years after the expiration of its original patents, the British Linotype Company remains largely pre-eminent in this field.

1870–1914 – THE FORMATIVE YEARS

Such were the beginnings of American business investment in British manufacturing industry. They took place at a time when the United States was on the threshold of the most formative period in her industrial development. For industrial nations as a whole, the years which followed were rich in the discovery and exploitation of new sources of energy, new materials, new products, new manufacturing methods, and new organization structures. For America, in particular, they signified an era of unprecedented economic expansion. Between 1869 and 1909 the annual value of that country's industrial output rose from $3.4 million to $20 million;[11] and by the turn of the century, the US had surpassed, both in scale and technique, its two main manufacturing competitors – the United Kingdom and Germany. At the same time, faced with a then unique factor-supply position of acute scarcity of labour, an abundance of land, easily accessible energy resources and a plentiful supply of capital, the pattern and character of her industrial growth broke away from that established by the older industrialized nations and assumed an individuality of its own.

In her formative development, the United States was fortunate in as much as the era in question was directly coincident with the discovery of new sources of energy and power – which were later to prove ideally suited to her particular economic environment. While benefiting from the manufacturing experiences (and mistakes) of her European forerunners, her industrial trajectory was hampered neither by an institutional structure unfavourable to mechanization and new production methods, nor by the tradition of inherited ideas. Her patent laws were liberal, and innovations were highly rewarded. At the time under discussion, she had virtually no industrial relations problems, venture capital was easy to come by, and her manpower (often recruited from Europe's best) was still young, dynamic, flexible, fresh from pioneering a frontier settlement, and eager to raise its living standards. Much wealth had already been accumulated from earlier industrial and agricultural expansion, while incomes were sufficiently high and equitably distributed to give the necessary stimulus to capital growth and fully mechanized manufacturing techniques. And all this the American industrialist could exploit in the knowledge that he was protected from external competition by a high tariff wall, while being able to take advantage of one of the largest free-trade areas in the world within the United States' borders.

Yet in the last resort, the key to America's rise to industrial greatness was to be found in the adventurous spirit and inventive genius of a small group of men with scientific and business acumen. While the highly capitalized modern business corporation was gradually assuming more importance and influence, the real shape and course of the US's destiny still lay in the hands of the individual entrepreneur – at that time, a combination of engineer, scientist, inventor and businessman – with his limited workshop and laboratory facilities. Men such as Thomas Edison, George Westinghouse, John D. Rockefeller and Philip Armour in manufacturing industry, and J. P. Morgan in finance, were all pioneers in their respective fields and, like their earlier counterparts in British industry, international in outlook and eager to exploit their discoveries wherever possible. Moreover in many cases they could foresee the likelihood of their inventions, tried and proved successful in the United States, being equally suited to the industrial structure and markets of other economies. In consequence, attention was soon focused on building up adequate export outlets, and later to the conclusion of cross-border licensing agreements, or the establishment of branch manufacturing units in the countries concerned.

This, undoubtedly, was one of the earliest driving forces behind the flow of direct American investment to the United Kingdom. The UK economic historian J. R. Clapham also recalls that the period in question was one of the disappearance of frontier settlements, and that only partially was the capital accumulated from this movement taken up by new industrial ventures.[12] As a result, he argues, wider avenues were sought to absorb these surplus savings, and with the UK offering particularly favourable opportunities for investment in manufacturing industry, the 1880s saw the first large-scale export of American business capital to that country.

It would, of course, be wrong to suppose that there were not equally important industrial advances taking place in the United Kingdom during these years. For in this era the basic electrical discoveries of Faraday, Wheatstone and Kelvin were made, and there were innovations, often of considerable significance, if less spectacular, in certain sections of the iron and steel, non-electrical engineering and chemical industries. The origins of the rubber, artificial silk, synthetic chemical, motor-car and cycle trades all date back to this time: industrial output doubled between 1880 and 1913.[13] Yet the fact remains that, in the commercial application of new inventions and the development of complementary industries, e.g. machine tools, non-ferrous metals, etc. and new organizational structures, the United Kingdom lagged well behind her international competitors.

There were many and varied reasons for this – some avoidable, some unavoidable; all, however, stemmed from a common cause – the comparative reluctance of manufacturers to adopt and exploit the basic inventions of the period. First, for example, there was not the same coincidence between the pace of industrial expansion and the discovery of new sources of power in the UK as there was in Germany – a rejuvenated and unified Germany since 1871 – and in the United States after the Civil War. Second, Britain's industrial structure was less adaptable and, *prima facie* at least, economically less well-suited to the commercial exploitation of the product discoveries and the manufacturing innovations of the latter nineteenth century. Certainly any movement towards large-scale business units by way of amalgamation or combination, such as was taking place in the USA at this time, was officially discouraged and viewed with considerable suspicion. Third, in many cases, e.g. in the motor-car and electrical industries, restrictive and misguided legislation, coupled with indifferent and expensive patent procedure, severely hampered, and in some cases completely paralysed, the exploitation of new inventions and techniques. Fourth, vested private interests were sometimes powerful enough to stifle new developments, while the political philosophy of the day precluded any action being taken by the state which involved the 'infringement of conventional conception of public privileges',[14] for example such as was inevitable in the laying of cables for electricity distribution. Fifth, the industrial prosperity of the British economy, then largely dependent on the basic, yet still expanding trades of cotton, coal, iron and steel and shipbuilding, was hardly in question. Why then launch out on the development of new products and manufacturing methods, with their associated uncertainty, when the old ones were serving the country so well? Sixth, there was neither the same incentive to use highly capitalized production techniques, because of the abundance of inexpensive labour, nor to substitute steam power by electrical power as coal was so cheap and easily accessible. Seventh, between 1870 and 1913, a substantial amount of British capital was invested overseas in the Dominions, South America and the United States. The fact that over 40 per cent of the United Kingdom's total investment (i.e. home and foreign) during this period was exported at least suggests a measure of neglect in domestic capital formation.[15]

While then it is true that Britain made available to the world many new and important inventions during this period, there can be little room for doubt that her powers of application and commercialization fell seriously behind those of her major competitors. The gap between the discovery of an idea, its acceptance and its full exploitation, was gradually widening, both in terms of the resources and time involved. The risks, when viewed in the light of the circumstances of the time, were judged too great. Gradually the United Kingdom surrendered her industrial leadership to the United States and, to a lesser extent, Germany.

In the period between 1870 and 1914 a well-defined pattern of US investments was evolved in the UK, the interest being centred principally in what were then the newer British industries, and which were also those, for one reason or another, in which the United States had already established a competitive advantage. Substantially the same characteristics have manifested themselves up to this day. The actual capital invested during these years, and the number of American firms establishing branch subsidiaries, was not large, but the resulting impact on British industrial development was both widespread and of unquestionable significance. Indeed, it is not too much to claim that in certain branches of industry at this time US capital, know-how and experience combined to provide the vital impetus to indigenous growth.

Such, for example, might well be said of the development of the electrical equipment industry before 1914. In particular the lighting, traction and telecommunication sections were each strongly influenced both by the establishment of American branch manufacturing units and by the conclusion of licensing agreements between UK and US concerns. And on the basis of these three applications, the whole complex structure of the present-day electrical industry was built.

Today (1958), the Standard Telephones and Cables Co. Ltd is the last of the major UK electrical manufacturing concerns in which there is still a substantial American shareholding. Yet, at one time or another, over the past seventy years, nearly all the modern electrical giants have had direct or portfolio US capital invested in them. Right up to 1953, for example, the International General Electric Company of New York owned a $22 million shareholding in the Associated Electrical Industries Ltd, a UK holding company which today employs over 60,000 people, and the constituent firms of which are all of American or Anglo-American origin.

American investment in the lighting industry first showed itself with the formation of the Edison Swan Electric Co. Ltd in 1883. Three years previously, the Anglo-American Brush Electric Light Corporation Ltd had concluded a licensing arrangement with the American Brush Company to manufacture arc lamps and arc lamp apparatus, but, notwithstanding the British firm's name, no United States capital was involved.[16] The purpose of this new company was to exploit the patents, and take over most of the business, of the Edison Electric Light Co. Ltd – the British licensee of the American Edison Company – a purely British concern. For some years prior to this merger, developments in incandescent lamp production had been proceeding more or less concurrently in the two countries – Edison having applied for a UK patent for his invention in 1879, and Swan in 1880.[17] The amalgamation was, in fact, a reflection of the two firms' desire to avoid possible patent litigation in the future. The Edison shareholding in the new venture was 40 per cent, but this quickly diminished as the capital was redistributed amongst American individuals, and as subsequent issues were taken up in the United Kingdom. Yet, in effect, the merger meant that for a period of ten years, until the Edison patents expired in 1893, the new company had virtually a complete monopoly in the production of incandescent lamps in this country.

After 1893, the pace of electric lighting development quickened – especially in the United States and Germany. In 1896, a second major development occurred in this country with the formation of the British Thomson-Houston Co. Ltd (BTH). This company was granted exclusive rights to make and sell a wide range of equipment, including lamps, lamp machinery, railway electrification equipment, generating capacity, switchgear, etc., under licence to the American Thomson-Houston Company. At first, only a nominal US financial interest was envisaged, but in 1897, as a result of a patent agreement made with the General Electric Company, New York (GEC), the American shareholding increased considerably. In 1901, the GEC acquired the American Thomson-Houston Company (and also the Edison Electric Light Company (US)) and changed its name to International General Electric Company (IGEC). This transaction gave it a majority interest in the equity capital of BTH, and four years later US ownership became complete.[18]

During these latter years, a considerable managerial and technical reorganization took place at the BTH Rugby factory. Administrative and engineering personnel were brought over from America to take over all the senior executive posts and the latest US manufacturing techniques and equipment were installed.

Yet the period of US management was (purposely) short-lived; without question – as in the Edison–Swan merger – the most valuable benefits which the British company derived from its American associate during the years of partnership took the form of research, development and manufacturing expertise. To quote a senior executive of the British company:

> Up to 1914, the benefits derived by our firm from its US associations were very great, and most of our products were based on IGEC designs modified to suit British conditions. For example, the drawn tungsten lamp of 1909 and the gas-filled lamp of 1913 both originated from the research laboratories of the American concern, and likewise product design and manufacturing know-how in respect of turbines, batteries, lamp-making machinery, railway electrification, telephones and dictographs. Anglo-American co-operation also succeeded in our company pioneering, or helping to pioneer the application of electric power to textile and rolling mills, the electrification of Tyneside shipyards, and the introduction of electric travelling cranes into engineering workshops.

On the other hand, it would appear that by 1910 an increasing proportion of the knowledge being transferred to the UK by the IGEC was only of limited practical value – partly because American designs and production techniques were increasingly reflecting the high labour costs and large markets faced by the US industrialist, and partly because during these years the markets served by the UK company were developing their own specialist requirements and demanding a large amount of product and process adaptation. Even then, the exchange of information was by no means only one-way. Specialized design knowledge in connection with turbo-alternators was being sent back to the parent company as early as 1908.

Yet, in spite of its American associations, the lighting section of the British electrical industry lost ground to its international competitors in the closing years of the nineteenth century. Up to 1882, it had been reported that British engineers were 'if anything, more active and advanced than their fellows abroad',[19] but in that year, the Electrical Lighting Act was passed. Among its provisions, it assigned local authorities compulsory purchase rights over electricity generating stations erected by private undertakings after a period of twenty-one years (or seven-year intervals thereafter), at a compensation price which made no allowance for the 'goodwill' built up in the interim period. Earlier, the Tramways Act of 1870 had given similar powers in respect of privately constructed tramways and these, too, were to have a paralysing effect on the development of electric traction. There is no doubt that both Acts were a considerable disincentive to electrical progress, and only when an amended Lighting Act was passed in 1888 (which increased the time which must elapse before compulsory purchase could take place to forty-two years) was the difficulty in any way resolved – and then not wholly so, for local authorities still had the right to oppose any new electrical project.[20] In the meantime, six vital years of experience in the development of the means of production had been lost by the United Kingdom to its American and Continental

European competitors. This apathy appears to have continued well into the twentieth century with the British making little or no technical contribution to the development of metal filament lamps. Indeed, it was not until 1912 that the first lamp research laboratory was established in the United Kingdom, all important innovations having been previously imported from Germany and the United States.[21]

The application of electricity for traction and generating purposes was even more delayed, though here too, US capital was attracted at the turn of the century. Mention has already been made of the part played by BTH in this connection. Suffice it to note that this company also supplied a major part of electrical equipment for the Central London Railway (1900), the London Underground Railway (1905)[22] and more than fifty tramway systems throughout the country.

Then, in 1899, a wholly-owned subsidiary of the US Westinghouse Electric Company was set up in the United Kindgom, eighteen years after the first Westinghouse factory had been established at King's Cross, London, for the manufacture of air-brakes. In fact, it was during the course of his work as a railway engineer that George Westinghouse first recognized the possibilities offered by electric traction and particularly for the United Kingdom, with its compact and strongly localized industrial population. Five years after the formation of the new company, manufacturing started in a huge new factory at Trafford Park, Manchester. Like the King's Cross plant, it was designed and constructed on US lines, and under the supervision of American managers. The report issued at the time reads like the comments on the erection of the Fawley oil refinery fifty years later, for it said 'the construction of the works was a speed record for British workmen under American contractors . . . due to good wages, good supervision and the use of new mechanical devices'.[23] Most of the original machinery and fixtures were imported from the United States, and at the beginning all senior posts, including works foremen, were held by American nationals. At the same time, forty British personnel were sent over to the parent company to study engineering and managerial methods, and it was these men who on their return gradually assumed executive control. Right up to 1917, however, when the UK subsidiary was purchased by Metropolitan-Vickers Co. Ltd, the Managing Director, Works Manager and Chief Electrical Engineer continued to be American nationals.

For the American company, this new venture, though providing a valuable lesson in the problems of branch plant management, brought with it many problems. First, the anticipated demand for electric traction failed to materialize, and much of the equipment at the Trafford Park factory remained idle right up to the First World War. Second, certain American managerial and administrative practices proved unpopular when introduced into a UK industrial environment. In retrospect, it is clear that the US company allowed its subsidiary too little flexibility in the designs and standards laid down which, while on occasions it helped 'to force the pace of development',[24] were, in general, quite impracticable when viewed in the light of the materials supply position and industrial framework of the age. This lack of appreciation of the inherent differences in the UK and US economic and technological environment also reflected itself in the labour policies adopted, e.g. at first a corps of works police patrolled the Manchester workshops according to Pittsburgh's practice, seeing that everyone was kept hard at work, and each week stood by as wages were drawn from a series of pay-boxes. It is, therefore, hardly surprising that, in early days, industrial relations were poor, and turnover and absenteeism high. At the annual general meeting of the UK subsidiary in 1905 'a little commonsense and economical management'[25] was called for: in fact, however, matters only improved after a change in management in 1906.

Once again, however, American research and manufacturing experience helped to speed up the pace of UK industrial development, and, up to a point, as the US company developed and widened its scope, so did its subsidiary. Certainly, the new engineering methods utilized at Trafford Park provoked much national interest at that time. By the beginning of the First World War, the Westinghouse organization had helped introduce into the UK a variety of products, including gas and steam turbines, electric locomotives, transformers and voltage regulators, though it was not until several years later that the original purpose of the company's founder could be said to be achieved, viz. 'the establishment of a works for the production of every description of electrical machinery and telephone appliances'.[26]

Finally, American influence played an important role in the early development of the UK telecommunications industry. In March 1876, Graham Bell patented his invention 'which in essence covered all the principles of telephone transmission'[27] in the United States, and two years later, with a view to exploiting these patents, the first telephone company in Great Britain was registered under the title Telephone Co. Ltd (Bell Patents). The following year saw the formation of the Edison Telephone Company of London Ltd to work the American patents of Thomas Edison's electrochemical telephone. For ten months, the two concerns competed fiercely with each other, but in 1880 faced by threatened litigation from the General Post Office (GPO) which was claiming, under the Telegraph Act of 1868, the sole authority to acquire, maintain and work the electric telegraph – and this included the telephone – they merged forces to become the United Telephone Co. Ltd. In December 1880, a High Court ruling upheld the GPO's claim, but because the Bell and Edison patents did not expire until 1891, a compromise was made. The GPO licensed the United Telephone Company and its subsidiaries to operate in certain restricted areas, but reserved the right to purchase the exchanges for themselves in 1890 or at seven-year periods thereafter.

As the years passed, however, and the Post Office's telegraph revenue fell off, the restrictions became more stringent. Undecided in policy, wavering between encouraging competition amongst private telephone companies on the one hand, and preserving its own monopoly on the other, yet all the time trying to protect its other sources of income, it is not surprising that the GPO has been held largely responsible for the slow, unsystematic and piecemeal telephonic development which followed during the next thirty years. In 1884, there were only 12,800 UK telephone subscribers compared with 135,000 in the United States. In 1889, a speaker in the House of Lords, commenting on the London exchange system, said 'no city in civilized Europe is so far behind'.[28] Not until 1894 was the National Telephone Company Ltd – a subsequent merger of the United Telephone Company and other (mostly licensee) interests – allowed wayleave by local authorities for its underground wiring. Municipal telephone ventures, with the exception of Hull, were unsuccessful, and when the GPO and the National did eventually come to an understanding over the operation of the London exchanges, they were accused of keeping up prices to an excessive and non-competitive level. In 1898, a Select Committee reported that the British telephone service, as it was then operated, was neither to the benefit of the country at large, nor even to the most limited portions of it where exchanges existed.[29] Eventually, however, an agreement was reached in 1904 between the main competing interests, by which, in exchange for a lump sum payment, the complete telephone system of the United Kingdom was to be transferred to the state: this finally became effective on 1 January, 1912.

From its outset, it has been a unique feature of the UK telephone industry that those firms manufacturing telephone equipment and those responsible for its installation and operation have been separate from each other. Even the early Bell and Edison companies were simply agents for selling instruments and telephonic systems, and all equipment, including that for the first telephone exchange installed in 1879, was of American origin. Right up to the First World War, in fact, a very large proportion of the telephone equipment used in the UK was imported from the US. The main UK producers at this time were (i) the Western Electric Co. Ltd (an American subsidiary which had purchased the important Fowler Waring Cable Company in North Woolwich in 1897), (ii) the Peel-Conner Telephone Works (a subsidiary of the General Electric Co. Ltd (UK) which was managed by an American national who had had considerable experience in US telephone development) and (iii) the Automatic Telephone and Electric Co. Ltd – a British firm – the subsequent history of which will be traced in a later section of this chapter.

Such were the main features of the early American investment in the UK electrical equipment industry, which, possibly because of the character of the products themselves and their newness to the United Kingdom economy, attracted particular comment at the time. However, during the closing years of the nineteenth century, American capital also made important infiltrations into the well-established branches of British industry. Here, in most cases, the *raison d'être* was not so much to introduce a new product as a new technique or method of manufacturing, though, in selected instances, a deliberate attempt was made to gain control of the British and European product markets.

Three case studies may serve to illustrate these points. First, in 1896, the Diamond Match Company of New York set up its own manufacturing unit at Liverpool, after failing to find a purchaser for the UK rights of its new continuous match-making machine. At that time, British match production was largely in the hands of Bryant and May Ltd who were still dipping and drying matches by hand, and who – so it was reported in 1902 – had not improved their match-making machinery for sixteen years.[30] The impact made by the Diamond Company on match production in this country was both immediate and marked. Cheaper, better quality and a wider range of matches were produced than heretofore, and within five years the American subsidiary had built up a market equivalent to that previously held by Bryant and May – whose dividends had fallen in the meantime from 20 per cent to 14 per cent. Eventually, in 1901, an agreement was reached between the two firms: in exchange for the goodwill, property rights and assets of the Diamond Match Company (UK), Bryant and May surrendered 54.5 per cent of its own capital and virtually its entire voting power. Various market-sharing arrangements were then concluded between the two firms, but the effectiveness of the partnership was short-lived as the greater part of the US shareholding was soon repatriated and new capital issues were entirely taken up in the United Kingdom. Today (1958), Bryant and May is a wholly-owned subsidiary of the British Match Corporation Ltd, and only 5 per cent of its equity stock is held by the nominees of the US Diamond Company, who, at the time of the transfer, received these shares in exchange for their holding in Bryant and May.

Second, at the turn of the century, the British tobacco industry was literally invaded by American capital. Restricted in its sales by a high tariff wall imposed on US cigarettes, the American Tobacco Company acquired, for over £1 million, the young and prosperous British firm of Ogden's Ltd in September 1901, and straight away launched an extensive publicity campaign to sell cheap cigarettes. The Chairman of the US company at the time made no secret of his intentions, viz.: 'to obtain a large share of the tobacco trade both of England and the Continent',[31] and he threatened to spend up to £6 million in doing so. The reaction of the British producers was prompt, within a month of the purchase of Ogden's, thirteen of the leading tobacco companies had amalgamated and formed themselves into the Imperial Tobacco Company, with an issued capital of £14½ million.[32] Then followed several months of cut-throat competition between the two concerns. Ogden's cut their prices up to 45 per cent; Imperial retaliated by trying to gain exclusive control of retail outlets.[33] Eventually, a market-sharing agreement was reached in September 1902; Ogden's became part of the Imperial Tobacco Group, which was given the monopoly of the British and Irish markets, while the United States and its dependencies were to be supplied by the American Tobacco Company. A new firm, the British–American Tobacco Co. Ltd was set up to handle the remainder of the export business and was allocated factories both in the United States and in the United Kingdom. In 1911, an anti-trust action in the United States broke up this arrangement, and the American shareholding in the British American Tobacco Company gradually fell, until, by the early 1950s, it was only 5 per cent of the firm's total capital. There is little evidence to suggest that American methods of cigarette manufacturing had much effect in this country during these early years, but there is no doubt of the marked impact which was made on the market structure of the tobacco industry. As Clapham points out, 'with their assured markets and immense power, the Imperial and the B.A.T. were successful. . . . It was the nearest thing in Britain to a free monopoly.'[34]

The third US foothold gained in this period was in the boot and shoe industry. In America, the high cost of labour had led that country to mechanize the production of boots and shoes in the early stages of her industrial growth. By contrast, in the UK the industry had grown up on a craft basis; in 1892, for instance, the large majority of boots and shoes were still being made by hand, and contracted out to home workers. Gradually, however, between 1890 and 1914, US manufacturing techniques were adopted, the acceptance of which was made easier by the availability of American-designed boot and shoe machinery in the UK. This was manufactured by the British United Shoe Machinery Co. Ltd – an offshoot of the United Shoe Machinery Corporation of Boston, USA – formed in 1899 by amalgamation of the English businesses of two American companies, and by the outright purchase of the British concern, Pearson and Benyon Ltd. As a result of this merger, which followed a similar movement in the United States, 'one company was now able to supply the shoe manufacturer with a complete installation of the most modern machines for the whole of his business'.[35] From the start, the BUSM, which in the early 1950s supplied 80 per cent of the shoe machinery used in the UK, adopted the policy of leasing rather than selling its equipment – a factor which greatly helped the small manufacturer and domestic producer. Soon the effect on boot and shoe production methods was evident. In 1902 it was reported that 'the superiority of their machines compelled manufacturers to use them',[36] and – over forty years afterwards – a Board of Trade Working Party on the Boot and Shoe Industry held that 'there is no doubt whatever that the British United Shoe Machinery Company is a most efficient concern, and that their service departments are of very great benefit to all users of their machines'.[37]

By 1900 is was estimated that over $10 million had been invested by the seventy-five American subsidiaries, or jointly owned Anglo-American enterprises, then operating in the United Kingdom.[38] Of these firms, only a dozen or fifteen were actually manufacturing, though many of the sales and distributive agencies being established by US concerns at the time were deliberately preparatory to manufacturing in the UK. No doubt, this latter movement was hastened by the extreme nationalistic feeling of the period (e.g. engendered by the Boer War, etc.) and US firms, finding their exports reduced, attempted to circumvent this difficulty by investing in the United Kindgom and becoming naturalized as quickly as possible. At the same time, Great Britain appeared to be the only major country where foreign capitalists were treated in the same way as residents.[39] Finally, in addition to those already mentioned, other well-known US names to establish production units in the last three decades of the nineteenth century included Kodak Ltd – cameras and sensitized films, American Arithmometer Ltd (later to become Burroughs Adding Machine Co. Ltd) – office machinery (1896), Babcock and Wilcox Ltd – boilers and heavy engineering products (1881), The American

Pullman Car Company – railway cars (1874), Maguire Tramways – tramcars (1897), and American Radiator – radiators (1896).

The pace of American investment in British manufacturing industry quickened with the turn of the present century. In 1902 *The Scotsman* viewed the invasion of British industry by US capital as the most remarkable commercial development of that year.[40] In the previous years, J. A. McKenzie had written that US industrial interests had 'acquired control of almost every new industry created during the past fifteen years'.[41] Certainly, such investments as those already mentioned attracted particular comment at the time, not only because the amount of capital involved was considerable (i.e. in relationship to comparative British investments), but also because, however hard a US firm might try to conform to national habits, it appeared that it was never able to disguise its identity completely.[42]

Between 1901 and 1914, some seventy US manufacturing subsidiaries, or jointly owned Anglo-American concerns, were set up in the United Kingdom, during which time both the character of, and the motives behind, the investment widened considerably. First, in the early years of the century, a flood of patent medicine companies invaded the British market. Most of these were sales concerns, but a number of important manufacturing units, including the Parke Davis Co. Ltd, also established themselves. In retrospect, a Select Committee on Patent Medicines in 1914 argued that the tightening-up of American legislation concerning publicizing the contents of certain medicines was the main factor responsible for the majority of these firms coming to the United Kingdom.[43] Second, the Patents and Design Act, 1907, in providing for the revocation of patents not actually worked in the United Kingdom, is credited with having persuaded several American firms to manufacture in this country, e.g. in the cinematic film, safety razor, and cash register industries.[44] Probably, however, the strength of this motive has been over-emphasized. Third, a number of well-known food and drink companies, including H. J. Heinz and Horlick, set up manufacturing units in the United Kingdom during this time. Here, the motive was obvious enough – to save transport costs and reduce breakage losses; moreover, in many cases the product was perishable.[45] Substantial savings of this kind also attracted farm machinery and motor vehicles firms; it was, for example, estimated some years ago that ten 'knocked-down' cars occupied the cargo space of one completely assembled car.[46] Fourth, differences in British and American labour costs were already becoming apparent, and leading to the establishment of a number of branch plants in the engineering and machinery industries: generally, however, these differences were a secondary, rather than a primary reason for foreign investment, and sometimes, where US companies translated their high wage policies to the UK, of negligible importance.[47] Lastly, the need to cater for a market's national idiosyncrasies and to supply adequate after-sales and servicing facilities led numerous firms in the chemical, electrical equipment, foundation garment and musical instrument industries to establish manufacturing outlets in the UK in these years. In most cases, however, the inducements to invest were a combination of the above factors, and the general desire to expand business overseas. Import tariffs were practically non-existent at this time.

In 1903 the first Ford car was sold in the United Kingdom. As in the electrical equipment industry, restrictive legislation – e.g. the red flag regulations were not repealed until 1896 – hampered growth, though, perhaps, more important was the fact that the structure of Britain's engineering industry was less suited to the techniques of production demanded by the motor industry than was that of the US.[48] In 1911, the Ford Motor Co. (Eng.) Ltd – a new company – started to assemble imported components in an American-designed factory at Trafford Park, Manchester. From the very beginning, use was made of the semi-automatic principle of large-scale production as adopted by the parent plant, and American executives employed. The stated aim of this new venture was to supply the British market with low-priced standardized cars; its success was such that by 1913 Ford was the largest UK producer, and the Model T had become the best-selling car in England. In that same year the Manchester plant turned out an output of 6,000 vehicles out of a total domestic production of 25,000 vehicles.[49]

The inflow of American capital was by no means restricted to manufacturing industry in these years. The development of selected branches of trade and commerce was also strongly influenced by such investment. Foremost in this respect might be mentioned the formation of J. Pierpoint Morgan's Shipping Trust – the International Mercantile Marine Co. Ltd – in 1902, with a capital of $120 million. With the subsequent interest shown by American companies in British shipping, this development caused much comment and some alarm at the time. Indeed, with the outright purchase of the White Star, Dominion and Atlantic Transport lines, and a $11.7 million shareholding in the Leyland Line, it was thought that the object of the Trust was to Americanize the UK shipping companies it controlled, and gain authority over the Atlantic service.[50] In retrospect, it seems that this was not the case, though how far an agreement with the Board of Trade, signed in 1902,[51] which forbade United Kingdom companies from transferring their vessels to the United States' flag without prior permission, was itself responsible for this, it is difficult to say. Certainly, in most cases the ships of the above lines continued to be manned by British officers and crew.[52]

In meat distribution, too, American interests were well in evidence. A Departmental Committee set up to study combinations in the meat trade in 1909 found that the United States Beef Trust (then consisting of Armour and Co., Swift Beef Co., Morris Beef Co. and Hammond Beef Co.) was exerting strong control over the distribution, quality and price of the meat in London and the South, and a considerable influence in the Midlands.[53] Moreover, it reported that by establishing their own wholesale and retail outlets, US subsidiaries 'were driving their competitors out of business or forcing them to come to an agreement with the combination'.[54] On the other hand, the committee concluded that in spite of this tendency towards monopoly, many managerial and manufacturing practices imported by these concerns had influenced trading methods to the benefit of the consumer.

In the banking sector, there was only a limited US presence in the United Kingdom. Indeed, until the end of 1913, US national banks were prohibited by law from engaging in foreign banking. However, several private banking houses, such as J. P. Morgan, American Express and Lazard Frères had set up branches in the UK in the late nineteenth and early twentieth centuries to provide banking and financial services for American individuals and companies abroad. By the early 1900s, too, a number of US insurance companies were doing business in the UK; but, for the most part, fdi in this sector flowed from the opposite direction across the Atlantic.

Finally, US techniques were increasingly influencing merchandizing methods as such. For example, Selfridges Ltd was formed on American business practice, theories and ideals in 1909, and in the following year the first of the 950 Woolworth stores was opened. From their experience and study of US salesmanship and marketing techniques, men such as Thomas Lipton and William Dibben were pioneering the department and chain store in this country, while mail order, hire purchase and advertising methods increasingly reflected American influence at this time.[55]

By the outbreak of the First World War, then, American business interests had permeated – and for the most part successfully – a wide section of British industry and commerce. At the same time, continuing its earlier pattern of selectivity, the investment was almost entirely confined to the newer fields of production where the commercial supremacy of the United States was at that time most pronounced. Only to a very limited extent, for instance, had any American capital infiltrated the basic industries, which still then accounted for the greater proportion of Britain's economic wealth. The same applied to portfolio investments; in total these were very small since US interest rates were comparatively more attractive than those in the United Kingdom during this period, but what little there was, was directed towards the newer industrial ventures, and notably the various London underground railway projects.

No official figure of the amount or value of American direct investments in British manufacturing industry in 1914 is available. Our own estimate is that about seventy firms with a combined capital holding of close on $100 million and a labour force of 20,000–25,000 people were operating manufacturing units at this time.[56] Though the US was most certainly the leading foreign investor before the First World War, there were several significant investments by continental European companies. Most noticeable of these were Siemens – electrical equipment (Germany), Hoescht – dyestuff (Germany), Bayer – pharmaceuticals (Germany), SKF – ball bearings (Sweden), and Anglo-Swiss and Nestlé – condensed milk (Switzerland).[57]

Concerning the profitability of these early investments, some US firms would appear to have been proud of their achievements, and others not. While it seems there were very few actual failures,[58] a number of companies had extremely shaky beginnings, and were only kept on their feet by financial help from America; others sold out to British interests within a comparatively short time of the original

US investment. For the most part, those enterprises which made a bid to gain control of a particular industry failed, being forced, sooner or later, to come to some sort of agreement with their British competitors. Yet, the influence exerted by American capital on the structure of UK industrial development was mainly for the good. For example, had it not been for the large amount of US capital invested in it, the electrical equipment industry might have developed less efficiently by following the traditional but rather more haphazard pattern of growth experienced by Britain's basic industries. Without doubt, too, the considerable interest aroused by such firms in American production and managerial methods during these years was, in no small measure, responsible for the receptivity of the newer industries. On the applicability of these latter in this country, opinions varied; in most subsidiaries, e.g. the Diamond Match, Kodak, Dennison and Linotype companies, American labour and administration techniques were well received, but in one or two important cases, e.g. Westinghouse, they met with not a little local resistance.

1919–1929 – A PERIOD OF CONSOLIDATION AND STEADY EXPANSION

Between 1919 and 1929 the value and scope of US direct investments in British industry steadily increased. Probably as many *new* businesses were set up in these years as in any similar length of time before or since, and the great majority of those manufacturing units established prior to 1914 increased their production as well. In addition to those reasons already cited, there were two new factors which led to this increased flow of investment. First, as a result of the war, much of British industry was seeking to replace its capital and to re-equip itself with the latest production methods. But unfortunately, domestic savings were insufficient while many overseas assets had recently been liquidated: hence foreign – and more particularly American – capital was doubly welcome. On the other hand, the United States, which had now assumed the role of a major overseas lender, was increasing her capital exports each year, and though these were principally directed to short-term portfolio investment – of the $10,000 million invested in Europe between 1919 and 1929, 70 per cent took this form[59] – the offers made by some British firms to exchange part of their share capital for the latest research and manufacturing expertise proved very attractive.

Second, and more directly, many US branch manufacturing units were set up in the United Kingdom during this period because of the growing import duties and quota restrictions imposed upon their parent firms' products. Prior to 1914, the graet majority of American goods had come into the UK free of tariffs, but the McKenna Duties (1915), the Safeguarding of Industry Acts (1921 and 1927) and the Cinematograph Act (1927) each had the effect of virtually driving a certain class of American imports out of the market. This, in effect, meant that US companies, if they wished to retain their United Kingdom markets, had to manufacture for themselves in this country, or conclude licensing agreements with UK firms. Furthermore, the tariffs undoubtedly had the effect of hastening the decisions of other firms who were undecided about the relative merits of establishing an overseas manufacturing unit compared with expanding domestic exports.

Most certainly this was an important factor influencing the growth of US investment in the British motor-car industry at the time – the duties on vehicles and their components since 1915 being as much as 33 per cent *ad val.* American imports which in 1913 accounted for 80 per cent of home production dropped to 40 per cent by 1930. Though the Ford Motor Company was already a leading UK manufacturer, several new motor-car companies and component suppliers set up branch units in the 1920s. Most noticeable of these was the purchase of Vauxhall Ltd by the General Motors Corporation of New York, in 1927. Explaining the reasons for seeking this investment, the President of the American concern said that in England he found 'the general elements that provide a sound basis for investment in the motor industry, viz.: (1) high character values (2) the amount and character of labour needed (3) fundamental production facilities and (4) an expanding market'.[60] In the same year, the two largest United States' tyre companies – the Goodyear Rubber Company and Firestone Rubber Company – commenced manufacturing operations in the UK: both firms had been importing from their parent company for some years previously. At the opening of the Firestone factory in London in 1928, Sir William Joynson-Hicks – the then Home Secretary – commented 'that by imposing a $33\frac{1}{3}$ per cent tariff on tyres the Government had extended an invitation to Mr Firestone to manufacture tyres in England rather than pay \$1,000 per day in import duties'.[61]

In 1919, the Ford subsidiary enlarged its activities to include the production of agricultural tractors – just two years after the first Fordson tractor had been imported from America – in an effort to beat the German blockade by increasing home food production. A foundry and machine-shop was established at Cork, Ireland, which first assembled and serviced tractors imported from the parent company, but later relied to an increasing extent on UK suppliers.[62] In 1928, however, there came a major experiment when the whole of the American tractor plant was shipped complete from Rouge River (USA), through the Great Lakes across the Atlantic to Cork. Between this time and 1939, the entire world output of Fordson tractors was supplied from the United Kingdom. In the same year as the Cork experiment – by which time the Manchester factory was producing over 26,000 cars per year – the Ford Motor Co. Ltd was incorporated as a public company with assets totalling \$35 million, 40 per cent of which were British-owned. This concern acquired both the stock of the old Ford Motor Co. (Eng.) Ltd and that of each Continental European subsidiary operating at the time. A year later saw the start of a huge new factory at Dagenham – with a capacity of 200,000 vehicles per annum – from which it was planned to supply the whole European market with cars and tractors.[63]

During the 1920s, the ramifications of the electrical equipment industry greatly increased in complexity.[64] In 1921, BTH and GEC (UK) licensed each other to the use of their respective patents. Such patent-sharing, cross-licensing agreements and international pooling schemes were numerous in this era, though the actual amount of US capital involved was small. Indeed, direct participation by American companies in this field probably fell, as the Westinghouse Electric Co. Ltd was purchased by a British company – Metropolitan Vickers Co. Ltd – in 1917. In 1928, however, an important structural reorganization occurred when Metropolitan Vickers gained financial control of both the British-Thomson-Houston Co. Ltd and the Edison Swan Electric Light Co. Ltd while at the same time, it surrendered a minority share of its own capital to the IGEC (New York). The new company was then reincorporated as the Associated Electrical Industries Ltd (capital $75 million) which gave it financial control of BTH, Metropolitan Vickers and Edison Swan. Between this date and 1953, when the US capital was repatriated in full, the actual proportion of the IGEC's shareholding in AEI varied from 25–40 per cent.

In the telephone industry, American interests widened in 1919 with the purchase of a substantial interest in the Automatic Telephone Manufacturing Co. Ltd (UK), by the Theodore Gary Group (US). As a direct result of this association, the Strowger system of automatic telephoning was introduced into the United Kingdom and accepted by the General Post Office as standard equipment. At the same time, because the Post Office refused to deal with a private monopolist, yet wanted to avoid wasteful competition, patents had to be cross-licensed to the other main telephone apparatus suppliers[65] – at that time, Standard Telephones and Cables Ltd, Siemens Brothers and GEC. In 1935 the Automatic Telephone Company became wholly British again, the Gary Group selling out its interests owing to the unfavourable economic situation in America. The other American company, Standard Telephones and Cables Ltd,[66] which changed hands in 1925 when the US Western Electric Company was bought out by the International Telephone and Telegraph Co. Ltd, is still (1958) the largest telephone and cable manufacturer in Europe.

Finally, mention should be made of the interest shown by US investors in electric supply distribution. Here, the Utilities Power and Light Corporation Ltd, through the Greater London and Counties Trust Ltd, which was formed in 1925, played a leading role in fostering the development of electricity supply, particularly in rural and semi-rural areas in southern England. This it did both by the promotion of special Acts of Parliament to establish new power companies, e.g. Wessex Electricity Company and the East Anglian Electric Supply Company, and by the acquisition of established authorized undertakings such as those in Oxford, Reading and Cookham. In February 1928, an offer was made to the shareholders of Edmundsons Electricity Corporation Ltd, the result of which more than 95 per cent of the ordinary capital of that company passed into the hands of the Greater London and Counties Trust Ltd. Further acquisitions continued to be made by the Trust, but ultimately the control and management of all the companies was placed in the hands of Edmundsons by the transfer of all the shareholdings to that company. A policy of integration was then pursued and the great majority of the smaller undertakings were absorbed by the larger power companies within whose territory they were situated. In July 1936, the American owners decided to withdraw from active participation in the electricity supply industry, and the Greater London and Counties Trust Ltd sold its entire holding in Edmundsons. Once more the group became entirely British-owned and, in turn, the Greater London and Counties Trust Ltd was placed in liquidation.[67]

During the 1920s, the flow of US portfolio investment also began to increase rapidly and was soon causing some apprehension. Eventually, discriminatory measures were taken. In September 1928, at the annual shareholders' meeting of GEC (UK) it was agreed that foreigners be prohibited from voting. Yet, in January of the following year, heavy American buying drove the company's £1 shares from 45s. to 87s. 6d. as a result of which 60 per cent of the stock gravitated to the United States.[68] In 1929 a proposal was put forward to offer a further issue of shares to UK subscribers only, but this was withdrawn owing to bitter pro-tests.[69] Such antagonism was by no means confined to the electrical industry; similar attempts towards protective action were taken by UK firms in the rubber, aircraft and cable industries, where the size of American investments was also causing anxiety.[70] Certainly, this was another period in which people were encouraged to 'Buy British' – partly because of the difficulty of the external trade position and partly to alleviate internal unemployment which was then approach-ing its post-war peak. Sir Charles Higham, speaking in October 1930, asserted that the former reason was the principal cause of many US firms opening up branch factories in this country.[71] Though disputed at the time, there is little doubt that the US firms then operating in the United Kingdom, and those contemplating new factories, were less eager than previously to publicize their origin or to advertise their production and management methods – an attitude which persisted well into the following decade.

Nevertheless, the infiltration of US capital continued on a wide front. Between seventy and eighty American factories were set up between 1919 and 1929 for the manufacture of such products as boilers and radiators, marine and oil refinery equipment, safety razors and razor-blades, surgical dressings, refrigerating appa-ratus, type-composing machines, cosmetics, pharmaceutical items, food-canning machinery,[72] cinematograph equipment, pencils, office equipment and furniture, chewing gum, heavy chemicals and processed cheese.[73] Three of these develop-ments are worthy of special comment.

First, in the chemical industry, the Monsanto Chemical Company of New York purchased a 50 per cent interest in the old-established Graeson Company in 1920, and aided by tariff protection (this time from German competition) expanded rapidly, introducing many new kinds of phenolic and plastic materials. In 1928, the remaining half interest was bought out, and since that date a number of other companies have been acquired. By the 1950s, this firm had become the largest all-purpose Anglo-American chemical concern in the United Kingdom. Then, in 1926, Du Pont's purchased 48 per cent of the issued share capital of Nobel Chemical Finishes Ltd which it held until the Imperial Chemical Industries acquired control ten years later. The main impact made by the US firm in the intervening period was to introduce and develop a variety of cellulose car lacquers. 'To this extent', commented one executive, 'the Du Pont holding was real and important'.[74]

Second, in 1922, the United States' drug concern – Liggetts International Ltd – purchased the whole of the ordinary share capital of Boots Pure Drug Co. Ltd. The founder of the British firm, Sir Jesse Boot, was by this time an invalid and anxious about the future of his company. At the same time, Liggett – a remarkable American who had built up a powerful chain of drug stores throughout the United States – was looking for further investment outlets. He made Sir Jesse an offer for his business, and a settlement was eventually reached. In this way, the American company (and later the United Drug Company to whom shares were transferred in 1925) gained complete control of Boots, though the American owners made no attempt to direct the business, which continued to grow on the lines initiated by its founder. In 1933 ownership of Boots returned to the United Kingdom when a financial crisis in the affairs of the US company forced the repatriation of its £1 million shareholding.[75]

Third, the 1920s saw a marked expansion in the British gramophone industry. The origin of this industry in the United Kingdom dates back to 1898 when William Owen, an American lawyer, founded the Gramophone Company (later to become HMV) in London. First assembling gramophones from parts made in the United States and importing recordings from Hannover in Germany, though later manufacturing at Hayes, the British company owed much of its early success to American methods of advertising and salesmanship.[76] The Columbia Company of New York also established a British branch in the early twentieth century and, with the Gramophone Company, supplied most of the UK output of gramophones and records up to 1914. During the war, the American gramophone industry grew much faster than its UK counterpart, to such an extent, in fact, that in 1919 the R. C. Victor Company of New York purchased a 50 per cent interest in the Gramophone Company for $9 million. The position was, however, reversed in the early 1920s when the US industry, having apparently reached its zenith, lost ground with the growing competition of the radio. Eventually, the UK Columbia Company, under the directorship of Louis (later, Sir Louis) Sterling, purchased a 93 per cent interest in its parent company. At the same time, it signed a licensing agreement with the Western Electric Company for the electrical recording process which it had earlier introduced into the United Kingdom. An opposite movement took place in 1926 when the British Brunswick Company established a UK subsidiary to manufacture gramophone records, but this venture proved unsuccessful, and was wound up three years later. Finally, in 1931, the HMV and Columbia companies merged to form Electric and Musical Industries Ltd, but four years later the RCA Victor Company disposed of the last of its holdings in this firm to avoid trouble under the Sherman Anti-Trust Acts. Commenting on the impact of American investment in the gramophone industry, the *Economist* concluded in 1928 that it had been particularly important in furthering price competition, in popularizing the instalment system and in the introduction of numerous improvements in the quality of reception and design of cabinets.[77]

In 1929, the first official Census of American Direct Investments in Foreign Countries was carried out by the US Department of Commerce.[78] It was then cstimatcd that there were 169 manufacturing units operating in the United Kingdom in which there was an American equity shareholding of 25 per cent or more. Their combined investment was put at $268 million, or 55 per cent of the total US capital stake in the UK. Sales agencies, trading ventures, banking houses, mining and agricultural enterprises made up the balance. No detailed sectoral breakdown of the manufacturing assets held was given for the United Kingdom separately, save that American interests at the time were primarily concentrated in the electrical goods, machinery, metal products, musical instruments, motor vehicle, chemical and foodstuffs industries. For Europe as a whole, of the total US investment in manufacturing industry, electrical equipment accounted for 25 per cent, motor vehicles 14 per cent, machinery 12 per cent, metal products 8 per cent and chemicals 9 per cent. As to the *form* of the United States' capital holdings, the direct subsidiary was the most popular, though it was found that in Europe 'there were enough large and well-established organizations to attract U.S. capital'.[79] This was mainly put down to the large number of manufacturers who sold part of their share capital to US companies to finance the necessary modernization and expansion of their plants after the First World War.

1930–1939 – TARIFF POLICY INDUCES MORE US FIRMS TO BRITAIN

In 1934, in response to a Senate Resolution, the Department of Commerce conducted a further and more detailed survey on American factories abroad.[80] The survey covered the period up to 31 December 1932, and the definitions and terms used broadly corresponded to their counterparts in the 1929 document. It revealed that in the United Kingdom some 197 American-controlled manufacturing units employing a combined labour force of 66,363 were operating in 1932, and that the amount of US capital invested was $165 million. Of the 141 companies which stated their original date of establishment, 12 (with a capital of $25 million) had commenced production before 1900 (including one firm in 1860 and another in 1862), 33 (with a capital of $38 million) between 1900 and 1919, and 96 (with a capital of $87 million) between 1920 and 1932. Because only some of the companies gave details about the nature of their activities, it was not possible to assess with any accuracy their distribution within manufacturing industry. Undoubtedly, however – as in 1929 – the motor vehicle, chemical, electrical appliance and machinery industries continued to account for the major proportion of US interests, and within these groups it would seem that the major share of the market was supplied by a few comparatively large firms. On the other hand, between the two surveys, the range of products manufactured by US subsidiaries in the UK had widened to include pumps and valves, paints, milk and egg products, buttons, optical goods, soap products, toys, refined petroleum, silver-ware and domestic electrical products. It must, of course, be remembered that this second survey was carried out at a time of world economic depression, and there is no doubt that the values quoted considerably underestimated the true worth of the investments.

The abandonment by the United Kingdom of the gold standard in 1931 and the substitution of a managed currency and exchange control in its place, the Ottawa Agreement and the Imperial Preference Tariff of 1932, the rationalization of industry, and a gradual recovery of trade and commerce, heralded a new economic milieu for the United Kingdom, and prompted an increase in foreign investment – and particularly that of American origin – into the country. On the other hand, the world depression and its crippling effect on the US economy had its own severe repercussions on both the ability and the desire of that country's firms to invest abroad. Overseas lending first contracted in 1928 when domestic speculation became particularly attractive. After the Wall Street crash of the following year, it revived again, but was soon checked by political developments in Europe. Imports of the debtor countries contracted as international trade and investment fell to a shadow of their earlier levels.

In 1929, $7.4 billion was made available to the world by US imports on current account and capital exports; by 1932 the outflow had fallen by 67 per cent to $2.4 million. Defaults by debtor countries became more frequent as prices slumped, and overseas holdings were fast repatriated in spite of capital losses resulting from exchange depreciations, to help parent concerns weather their own economic difficulties. From the United Kingdom's viewpoint, the main effects of these years was shown in the official Census of US Overseas Assets held in 1936.[81] Between 1929 (the date of the previous census) and that time, though the *value* of US capital holdings in British manufacturing industry rose very slightly from $268 million to $271 million, the *number* of such holdings increased substantially from 169 to 224; the average investment had thus fallen from $1.6 million to $1.2 million.

In effect, this meant that, while there had been several large withdrawals of capital, counterbalancing factors, e.g. the Imperial Preference Tariff of 1932, the widening investment outlets offered by British industry and the increasing competitiveness of UK manufacturers to US imports, had, by inducing many new foreign investments, stemmed any absolute decline in the value of capital holdings.[82] Between sixty-five and seventy-five UK manufacturing units were established in the UK between 1930 and 1939. Over half of this number located their factories along the Great West and North Circular Roads, just outside London and on the Slough Trading Estate. There were no really revolutionary developments of the pre-1914 kind, yet the permeation of American manufacturing and managerial methods into UK industry steadily continued. Though some US companies did buy out or invest in existing British firms in these years, for the most part they preferred to set up their own greenfield ventures. Important American firms investing in Britain for the first time during these years included Remington Rand Co. – office equipment (1937), Cincinnati Milling Machines Co. – machine tools (1933), The Hoover Company – domestic electrical appliances (1931), Armstrong Cork Co. – cork manufacturers (1938), Procter and Gamble – soap products (1930), Champion Sparking Plugs Ltd – sparking plugs (1937),

Standard Brands, Inc. – food products (1932), Mars – chocolate confectionery (1934) and Frigidaire – refrigerators (1933).

Taking matters as a whole, the inter-war years were not the best of times for British industrial development. The United Kingdom slipped further behind in her bid for foreign markets, and her share of world manufacturing exports contracted from 27 per cent in the period 1911–13 to 22 per cent in 1938.[83] The costs of some of the indecisions and mistakes of the last quarter of the nineteenth century were now beginning to reveal themselves. On the other hand, with the development of several new industries (e.g. industrial instruments, radio and television, synthetic fibres) and the rejuvenation of others (machine tools, chemicals),[84] with the rapid advancement of several production techniques and the discoveries of new industrial materials, the period could hardly be called one of stagnation. Yet, once again, with her own industries better established, the United States continued to dominate in most of these fields and was responsible for introducing many new ideas and methods into the United Kingdom, either through the establishment of subsidiary manufacturing units or the conclusion of licensing arrangements. For example, the development of the industrial instruments industry was noticeably advanced by the Bristol Instruments Company of New York which set up a subsidiary in the UK in 1932, and by two Anglo-American concerns, Foxborough-Yoxall Co. Ltd and Short and Mason Co. Ltd, which were formed shortly afterwards. Much the same could be said of the British Laundry Machine Co. Ltd and its impact on the expansion of the UK laundry industry, and of York Shippley Ltd in the field of commercial refrigeration.

Within subsidiaries originated earlier, the 1930s saw a steady expansion, though in some cases the proportion of US shareholding fell as public companies were incorporated or the number of British directors increased. Gradually, too, many of the older established US firms were becoming more autonomous in their management and organizational structures. Perhaps the most rapid strides during this period occurred in the motor vehicles industry. While the total number of cars produced by British manufacturers rose from 170,000 in 1930 to 342,000 in 1938, the share of the Ford and Vauxhall companies doubled – the former expanding its output from 22,000 to 77,000. More US subsidiaries to supply components to these two concerns also established manufacturing units in the United Kingdom.

In all then, the field of US business investment in the United Kingdom was much extended during this era. Both new industries were introduced into the economy and others which had been set up earlier consolidated their positions. But counterbalancing this trend, there were cases of American-originated firms losing their identity and becoming, either *de jure* or in practice, British companies. At the same time, Continental European companies continued to increase their stake in UK industry. Among the most noticeable of these were British Enka and Philips of the Netherlands, Hoffman La Roche of Switzerland, Electrolux of Sweden, and the Pirelli tyre company of Italy. More generally, of the 315 new manufacturing subsidiaries set up in the UK between 1919 and 1939, 228 were US-owned and all but 17 of the rest were from Continental Europe.

Approximately two-thirds of all new ventures took the form of greenfield invest-ments, and the balance were acquisitions and mergers.[85]

1940–1955 THE GROWING IMPORTANCE OF AMERICAN INVESTMENT TO THE UK ECONOMY

By 1940, total US business investments in the United Kingdom had risen to $530 million and manufacturing investments to $275 million.[86] At that date, some 233 companies were operating branch units in the UK, the direction of whose interests was substantially the same as that which existed in 1936. In 1943, a survey carried out by the US Treasury Department estimated the value of American manufac-turing investments had then reached $306.6 million.[87]

Since that time, changing economic circumstances have markedly affected the flow of US direct investment to Britain. From many aspects it might be argued that no period has brought with it such a combination of circumstances so conducive to the expansion of American business interests as that between 1939 and 1955.

For, first, the post-war world (and in particular the sterling area) shortage of dollars has, by depriving US firms of their pre-war sales outlets, directly induced them to set up manufacturing units in the United Kingdom so that they might sell their products overseas for sterling. From the United Kingdom's viewpoint such investment has been welcomed for the help it has been able to give to the balance of payments, not only by reducing dollar imports, but also by expanding exports. This has resulted in new companies establishing manufacturing units and pre-war-originated firms expanding their plant capacity to satisfy the demands of overseas markets previously supplied by their parent concerns.

Second, within the United Kingdom, there has been a growing demand for all types of American designed and styled goods. On the one hand, rising labour costs, full employment, the need to replace capital equipment depleted by the war, and a more realistic and dynamic approach adopted by the management of British firms towards new manufacturing methods and raising productivity, have all tended to further the acceptance of American managerial attitudes and production techniques. Hence, for example, one has the rapid expansion of the office equipment, agricultural machinery, excavating and earth-moving machin-ery and industrial instrument industries – to mention just four spheres in which the contribution by US-controlled firms in recent years has been of particular significance. On the other hand, a rising national income, more equitably dis-tributed, together with the increased attention given to, and the prestige value afforded by, American consumer goods, has raised the level of consumers' spend-ing for certain products which, before the war, were largely, if not exclusively, the province of the US market. Among these, high-class cosmetics, kitchen equip-ment, domestic electrical appliances and packaged foods are examples, and once more American capital has been attracted to these fields.

The need to develop specific industries has also encouraged the growth of post-war American investment in Britain. The classic case is that of the emergence of an important petroleum refining industry, the nature and scope of which has also affected the development of many other industries, such as petrochemicals, petroleum refining equipment and shipbuilding. Finally, American capital has also been attracted to those fields in which research and development are of above average significance, and where the United States was able to build up an important lead during the Second World War. The rapid growth of the pharmaceutical, electronics and industrial instruments industries amply illustrates this fact.

The increase of government intervention in industrial affairs during the postwar period has included overall control of both the volume and direction of inward direct investment. In the late 1940s and early 1950s each and every American firm wishing to establish a branch plant in the UK has had to undergo similar scrutiny to that normally exerted on home investors.[88] The three tests have been:

1 Whether the project will reduce the demand for imports and, in particular, whether it will, after remittable profits are taken into account, result in a net saving of desirable currencies.
2 Whether the project will lead to a substantial net increase in the United Kingdom exports to desirable markets.
3 Whether the project will make a significant contribution to the United Kingdom's industrial efficiency by providing foreign 'know-how' and techniques not otherwise available.

Hence, the specialized character of the new firms established. Of sixty British firms which started manufacturing between 1945 and 1953, forty-two were capital equipment producers, most of which directly satisfy condition 3 above in their labour-saving or efficiency-raising functions, and the average amount exported by a post-war subsidiary was 52 per cent, compared with 35 per cent by those firms set up before the war.[89]

It is, of course, true that many of the American subsidiaries which have recently set up manufacturing units in the UK, were already well known to the British consumer before the war. Firms such as National Cash Register, Remington Rand, IBM and International Harvester were all distributing US products in this country prior to 1939. At the same time, there is little doubt that in the last decade US managerial and manufacturing methods have been more welcomed and better publicized than heretofore, e.g. as epitomized by the £65 million Esso Refinery project at Fawley, and a £100 million expansion programme of the Ford and Vauxhall Motor companies. Since 1945, the number of British firms which have been aided in their expansion by US business capital has also grown. Once again, this has been partly due to a shortage of internal investment funds, but more particularly to the realization of the possible gains offered by the latest American production techniques. On the other hand, there have been a number of important capital repatriations as pre-war-established US firms have sold out to British interests. The war years did much to sever relationships between many subsidiaries and their parent concerns; in 1940, for example, practically without exception American business executives in the UK returned home. In other cases, doubt regarding future political and economic events in the United Kingdom has been responsible for a withdrawal of funds.[90]

Certainly, the last decade has brought its obstacles to US direct investment in the UK as well as its incentives. Both the fear of nationalization and expropriation of foreign-held assets by the UK government, and the memories of capital losses experienced in the inter-war period, have discouraged some US firms from producing in Britain. At the same time, foreign exchange restrictions, as reflected in the difficulties associated with capital repatriation and profit remittances, have prompted many potential investors to conclude licensing agreements with UK firms. Complicated and lengthy administrative procedures, the absence of any one-stop negotiating institution in the UK and indifferent publicity by the UK authorities have also deterred the inflow of American capital,[91] while, for its part, the US government has done little to aid overseas investment by its taxation policy and interpretation of the Sherman Anti-Trust Acts. Finally, the extremely bouyant conditions of the American and Canadian economies since the war have been such as to assure the US businessman a safe return on his capital at home without having to look overseas.

The increasing participation of US firms in British manufacturing industry over the past century has been but one aspect of the pattern of demand and supply conditions in the United Kingdom, coming more closely into line with those created in the United States a decade or two decades previously. Both American-styled capital and consumer goods have been increasingly favoured by the British consumer, while more recently, due mainly to external trade difficulties, there has been a growing desire of the UK economy to be independent of dollar-originated supplies. In consequence, US investment capital has been attracted to the UK, and particularly to those industries which help to raise the level of UK industrial competitiveness and to improve the balance of payments.

The following chapter now turns to consider the present-day (mid-1950s) scope and significance of US participation.

2 The present-day scope of American participation in British industry

By 1955, the value of the US foreign direct investment stake in manufacturing industry had reached the record figure of $6,322 million or 32.9 per cent of all that country's foreign capital holdings. Of this amount, Canada claimed the largest share of $2,834 million, and the United Kingdom the second largest of $941 million, or 57.7 per cent of US manufacturing investments in Europe as a whole. Including trading, banking, public utility and mining interests, the total US investment stake in UK industry in 1955 was $1,420 million, or 7.2 per cent of all American overseas net assets.[1] This proportion had remained remarkably constant since the first official census was taken in 1929. No data are available on other foreign direct investments in the UK in 1955 but in 1962, the first year in which the then UK Board of Trade published figures, US firms accounted for 64.1 per cent of the total inward capital stake and Continental European firms for 20.7 per cent.[2]

As may be seen from Table 2.1, the importance of US manufacturing investments in relationship to all US investments in the United Kingdom has steadily increased over the years. In 1929, such investments accounted for 55.3 per cent of the total US holdings. By 1943 this proportion had risen to 59.0 per cent, by 1950 to 63.8 per cent and by 1955 to 67.7 per cent. The upward trend in petroleum investments has been even more noticeable. Until 1939, the activities of American oil companies were almost entirely confined to the marketing of the finished product imported from overseas, while since the war, investment has been primarily directed to the expansion of refining capacity. Between 1945 and 1955, for example, nearly $200 million was invested by the Standard Oil Company of New Jersey and the Socony Vacuum Company of New York alone, in their British refineries at Fawley and Coryton respectively. Since in our definition of 'manufacturing industry' we have tried to follow that adopted by the (British) Standard Industrial Classification (sic),[3] those companies mainly concerned with petroleum refining have been included within our terms of reference. Using this criterion, the total sum invested by American business interests in foreign manufacturing industry in 1955 was $1,125 million[4] or 79.1 per cent of total US interests, a figure which, it should be noted, includes the value of the US shareholding in all those UK manufacturing concerns where the American equity shareholding is 25 per cent or more.[5] Since, however, in nearly one-third of all American firms so

Table 2.1 Value of the US direct investment stake in the United Kingdom, Europe and all areas, 1929/55

Industry	$ million				
	1929	1936	1943	1950	1955
Agriculture	–	–	–	–	–
Mining and smelting	n.a.	n.a.	14.2	3.2	3
% of inv. in Europe	–	–	(9.7)	(15.2)	(7.5)
% of inv. in all areas	–	–	(1.5)	(negl)	(negl)
Petroleum[1]	21.0	61.0	74.5	123.0	216
% of inv. in Europe	(9.1)	(22.2)	(20.1)	(28.8)	(28.4)
% of inv. in all areas	(1.9)	(5.7)	(5.4)	(3.7)	(3.7)
Manufacturing	268.0	271.0	306.6	541.8	941
% of inv. in Europe	(42.6)	(44.3)	(34.9)	(58.1)	(57.7)
% of inv. in all areas	(14.7)	(15.9)	(13.6)	(14.1)	(14.9)
Public utilities, transport, etc.	n.a.	–	−13.2[3]	10.6	16
% of inv. in Europe	–	–	–	(38.8)	(45.7)
% of inv. in all areas	–	–	–	(0.1)	(negl)
Trade	68.0	81.0[2]	84.9	102.2	141
% of inv. in Europe	(48.9)	(34.5)	(28.6)	(54.5)	(48.3)
% of inv. in all areas	(18.5)	(4.0)	(13.0)	(13.4)	(10.9)
Miscellaneous	128.0	61.0	53.2[4]	66.2	103
% of inv. in Europe	(61.3)	(75.9)	(21.8)	(51.2)	(45.0)
% of inv. in all areas	(23.6)	(16.9)	(6.6)	(10.0)	(2.2)
Total	485.0	474.0	518.8[4]	847.0	1,420.0
% of inv. in Europe	(36.7)	(37.6)	(25.4)	(49.2)	(47.5)
% of inv. in all areas	(6.5)	(7.1)	(6.7)	(7.1)	(7.2)

Sources: US Department of Commerce, Office of Business Economics, *Foreign Investments of the United States and Census of 1950* (1953); S. Pizer and F. Cutler, 'International Investment and Earnings', *Survey of Current Business*, August 1955; US Treasury Department, *Census of American-Owned Assets in Foreign Countries*, 1947.

Notes
n.a. = not available.
negl = negligible.
1 Includes production and distribution.
2 Figure is referred to as 'Distribution' . . . individual figures not available.
3 Represents amount owing by US interests to British interests.
4 Amended figure as given in latest Census Reports.

defined, part of the capital is British-owned – and since, in all but twenty of these, the US interest is a controlling one – it underestimates, probably by about $350 million, the total net assets of those concerns.

The growth of US-owned manufacturing and petroleum investments in the UK has been primarily at the expense of the other main industrial groups, and more particularly public utility and mining investments. These latter have actually declined in value as well as in volume, and while it is true that the number of sales agencies and banking ventures has risen considerably, their average investment stake has remained almost unchanged. This is partly because since 1945 the more important US exporting firms have been forced to set up their own manufacturing units as a result of import restrictions imposed by the UK government. Certainly, in no other country do US manufacturing investments assume such a proportionately important role, though this perhaps is only to be expected in view of the dependence of the United Kingdom economy on her manufacturing industries.

For the first time since the 1932 report on American Factories Abroad,[6] the US Department of Commerce released a detailed industrial breakdown of its manufacturing investments in the United Kingdom in 1955.[7] Of a total American investment of $941 million, motor vehicles and equipment accounted for 22.1 per cent; machinery (except electrical), 19.7 per cent; chemicals and allied products 11.6 per cent; primary and fabricated metals 11.6 per cent; electrical machinery, equipment and supplies 11.3 per cent; food products 6.3 per cent; rubber products 4.4 per cent and miscellaneous products 13.1 per cent.

According to the 1950 Census of Overseas Assets, the number of US enterprises operating in the United Kingdom in that year was 695 – the majority of which were wholly-owned subsidiaries of American parent companies. No classification by type of investment was given, but from our own studies there seems no real reason to suppose that the total number of manufacturing units in Britain substantially increased between 1943 and 1953, at which former date they were stated to be 246. For while in the course of that decade nearly sixty new manufacturing branches were established in the UK,[8] a fair number of American-originated concerns sold out to British interests at the same time. No doubt there was a small net increase, but not as much as might be supposed from the investment figures. Certainly, much the larger part of the growth in investment since the end of the war (which has been increasing at the average rate of 10–12 per cent per annum) has taken the form of profits ploughed back by established American concerns. Unfortunately, official statistics do not give us as much information as we would like on this point. We do know, however, that between 1949 and 1955, of an increased US investment of $677 million, only $98 million represented a net capital outflow from America. The years 1952 and 1953, in fact, saw a movement in the opposite direction, largely as the result of one or two substantial repatriations (e.g. the $22 million US shareholding in the AEI group). We also know that between 1943 and 1949 total holdings rose by only $210 million. Since, during that time, there was considerable foreboding among many US companies about the possibility of the nationalization or expropriation of their UK-based investments, and the general possibility of a Third World War, notwithstanding that many US firms set up new subsidiaries during this period, it is doubtful whether there was any net capital flow from America at all. Indeed, allowing for the rising price level in these years, and the substantial rate at which profits were being ploughed back by the more growth-oriented subsidiaries, there might very well have been some capital repatriation. Certainly, the great proportion of new investment from America between 1945 and 1955 had been to establish completely new subsidiaries: pre-war-originated branch plants have largely financed their own expansion from undistributed earnings, as have most of those sales companies which commenced manufacturing for themselves.

Our own survey is principally concerned with the organization and operation of some 205 United States' manufacturing subsidiaries and Anglo-American concerns, which at 31 December 1953, had a US equity shareholding of 25 per cent or more invested in them. *To the best of our knowledge these firms, at the time of our enquiry employed between them 90–95 per cent of the total labour force of American firms in Great Britain.* No important US company is believed to have been omitted from our analysis,[9] and in each case the number and kind of firms giving information of a kind dealt with in this and subsequent chapters has been sufficiently representative of the total to allow reasonably accurate estimates to be made of the position as a whole.

In an attempt to measure and assess the extent and significance of American participation in British industry, we have taken as our criteria three main variables – (1) total labour force, (2) value of total output and (3) estimated share of UK production – all for the years 1953 and for, where applicable, 1939. We have chosen these criteria rather than data relating to investment and net assets, partly to avoid duplication with data already available, and partly because the kind of detailed information we required did not appear to be readily available from the *subsidiaries* in our survey and, except in a few selected instances, it has not been possible for us to get in touch with the American parent company. Only in the case of public companies, and the larger private companies, have we obtained any details about the capital and financial structure of US affiliates in this country, and these are further analysed in Chapter 4.

Throughout our analysis, the definition of 'American firm' is the same as that used by the US Department of Commerce: no allowance has been made for British firms in which the US financial stake is less than 25 per cent of the equity capital, nor for any of the very large number of British firms which have licensing agreements (but no financial associations) with US companies. Only firms in which there are *direct* American investments were consulted: those enterprises partly financed by *portfolio* capital or by securities subscribed to by American individuals are excluded.[10] Our analysis is also confined to affiliates which were American-owned or partly owned on *31 December 1953*: those US-originated firms, or firms which at one time or another have had American affiliations, but which were, at that date, wholly or substantially British, are omitted. This, it should be noted, is an important exclusion, for many firms which fall within this category, such as Associated Electrical Industries Ltd, Ruberoid Ltd, British Timken Ltd, Blaw Knox Ltd, Kayser Bondor Ltd, still benefit – either directly or indirectly – from the managerial, manufacturing and marketing knowledge earlier made available from their US associates, and thus, through the normal competitive channels, may still exert an important impact on British industrial development.

The 205 firms which make up our sample employed 246,200 people or 2.8 per cent of the total labour force in British manufacturing industry at the end of 1953. The value of their combined output for that year could not be assessed with the same accuracy, as not all firms were willing to divulge the relevant information. But, on the basis of the 75 per cent who did give their sales turnover, the total *value of the goods and services supplied by US-financed firms in 1953 was between £700 and £725 million, or about 4 per cent of the estimated value for all UK manufacturing industry.*[11] By 'total value' is meant 'value of gross output' as defined in the Census of Production returns,[12] a figure which excludes distribution margins and indirect taxes.

Perhaps of greater significance is the fact that of the American-styled and designed products consumed in the United Kingdom in 1953, nearly 75 per cent were actually *manufactured* in the UK.[13] Manufactured imports from the United States in that year, excluding defence equipment, were valued at £140 million,[14] while consumption from home production amounted to £475 million. This, however, makes no allowances for those products supplied by UK firms manufacturing under US licence, which in 1953 would probably have been another £200–£250 million.

Of the US-affiliated firms, those which were producing before the war employed about 90,000 people in 1939. Between that date and December 1953, forty-nine new manufacturing subsidiaries were set up, and ten British firms became wholly or partly US-owned.[15] Between them, these concerns employed 21,400. Thus, nearly 135,000 or 87 per cent of the post-war expansion in employment is accounted for by those firms already manufacturing in the UK in 1939. This, of course, makes no allowance for those US firms which have become Anglicized since 1939, for the labour force of all American firms before the war was probably nearer the 130,000 mark – the AEI group alone employing more than 30,000. On the other hand, it does show the tremendous post-war expansion of US firms which have retained their identity: for example, compared with an average increase in the labour force of UK manufacturing industry of 40 per cent,[16] the corresponding figure for US firms was 175 per cent (or a *net* increase, i.e. in respect of pre-1939-established US firms, of 150 per cent).

A detailed breakdown of these firms, by employment for 1953, is given in Table 2.2. Grouped on the basis of the Standard Industrial Classification, the percentage of the numbers employed in the leading industrial sectors is given, and compared with the distribution of British industrial output as a whole. In column 6, applying a technique first utilized by Professor P. Sargant Florence,[17] a US *concentration quotient* is derived, which indicates the importance of various industries from the viewpoint of US investors. From this, an overall *coefficient of concentration* may be calculated which measures the degree to which US affiliates are concentrated in certain sectors. The higher this latter figure, the less evenly is employment dispersed between industries, compared with that which is average for UK industry in general.

From Table 2.2, it can be seen that three main industrial groups producing chemicals and allied products, engineering and shipbuilding goods and vehicles respectively, attracted between them two-thirds of the total labour force in American firms in 1953. In terms of value of output produced, the percentage would probably be even greater. The US concentration quotient is greatest in the chemical, precision instrument and motor vehicle groups, and least in the textile

Table 2.2 Industrial distribution of US-financed and British manufacturing firms by employment

	US affiliates, December 1953			UK firms, December 1953		US concentration quotient	Rel. growth of employ. in US firms[1] (1939 = 100)
	No. of US firms	Employment	% of total employment	Employment	% of total employment	(col. 3)/(col. 5)	
Chemical and allied trades	48	31,300	12.7	498,800	5.7	2.23	334.5
Metal manufacturing	11	8,400	3.4	551,100	6.3	0.52	142.0
Engineering and shipbuilding	67	77,000	31.3	1,604,000	18.4	1.70	197.5
Electrical goods	10	13,600	5.5	329,200	3.8	1.45	213.2
Motor vehicles	6	56,000	22.7	1,121,900	12.8	1.77	402.1
Metal goods not otherwise specified	2	2,500	1.0	491,300	5.6	0.18	265.5
Industrial and scientific instruments	9	16,200	6.6	138,300	1.6	4.13	214.4
Textiles and clothing	7	3,900	1.6	1,640,000	18.8	0.06	159.1
Food, drink and tobacco	13	16,400	6.7	844,100	9.7	0.69	207.7
Wood, cork, paper and printing	7	4,400	1.8	300,400	3.4	0.53	155.0
Other manufacturing industries[2]	25	16,500	6.7	1,212,300	13.9	0.48	243.6
All manufacturing industry	205	246,200	100.0	8,731,400	100.0	–	256.6

Source of UK statistics: Ministry of Labour Gazette, February 1954.
Notes:
1 In respect of firms which were US-owned in both 1939 and 1953.
2 Including leather, leather goods and fur.
N.B. The US coefficient of concentration = total + or − deviations between the % of employment of US firms in various industries and that of the % of employment of all UK firms in the same industries + 100. The figure for December 1953 was 0.35.

and clothing sections, and the coefficient of concentration is shown to be 0.35, which implies a moderate degree of industrial specialization by US firms.[18]

Table 2.2 also sets out the relative growth in the labour force since 1939, of those firms which were American-owned in both that year and 1953. Here, little real change in the importance of the various industrial groups is evident, save that employment in the chemical and vehicle industries has expanded rather more than the average, while that in the metal manufacturing and food trades has risen less than the average. What the table fails to show, however, are the substantial changes which have taken place *within* these broad classifications. Since 1939, for example, employment in the producer good sectors has risen twice as fast as that in the consumer good sectors, while the labour force in export-oriented industries has expanded relatively to those which rely mainly on the UK market for their sales. It is only by analysing a subdivision of industrial groups that the true significance of the role of US subsidiaries and Anglo-American firms can be fully appreciated. This procedure we now adopt with reference to eight major sectors of British manufacturing industry.

Chemical and allied trades

This is a broad industrial sector which supplies products ranging from refined petroleum to cosmetics and perfumes. Its scope and importance has enormously increased since the Second World War with the discovery of many new materials, ever widening spheres of application for both these and existing materials, and more efficient methods of processing. For plastics, artificial fibres, chemical fertilizers, synthetic rubber, petrochemicals and the new drugs are all of comparatively recent origin and, by the markets which they serve and industrial development which they allow, affect economic and social welfare in far greater measure than the money value of their products suggests. In 1955 the chemical industry's gross output was valued at £1,846 million,[19] of which the contribution of US affiliates was £180–£200 million. Yet, of the forty-eight American firms included within our survey, forty produced a highly specialized range of products, and were all concentrated within five main sectors of the industry, viz.: basic chemicals, mineral oil refining, pharmaceutical preparations, cosmetics and toilet articles and soap products. How selective US investment has been is shown by the fact that these groups between them employ less than one-half of the total labour force in the chemical industry. To illustrate further, let us briefly examine these main sectors in turn.

First, basic chemicals. Of the six leading US companies in this field, viz. Union Carbide, Monsanto Chemical, American Cyanamid, Dow, Du Pont and Allied Chemical,[20] the first five operate branch units in the UK. Yet the range of products they supply is considerably less than that of their parent companies. There is virtually no US capital in the manufacture of coal-tar and ammonical liquors – in coal distillation, in dyes and dyestuffs (except for boot and shoe dyes), nor in the production of acids, alkalis, explosives and salts. Only one Anglo-American company – the Monsanto Chemical Co. Ltd (assets £14.4 million) – might be called an all-purpose chemical supplier, with its production of over 200 basic materials which serve a wide range of industries; and this is one of the three largest manufacturers of its kind in the UK. Otherwise, investment in this field is limited to the production of certain specialized materials. Cabot Carbon Ltd, for example, supplies over three-quarters of the carbon black manufactured in this country; Monsanto Chemical, with two other Anglo-American firms, Bakelite Ltd – a subsidiary of Union Carbide Ltd – and British Geon – a joint subsidiary of the Distillers Company and the B. F. Goodrich Chemical Company – produces a substantial share of the output of phenol-plastics; BB Chemical Company is an important manufacturer of shoe and leather dressings and industrial adhesives, while Forth Chemicals – a joint subsidiary of Monsanto and British Hydrocarbon Chemicals – processes styrene monomer. A recent new venture is that of Grange Chemicals Ltd, owned jointly by the Oronite Chemical Co. of California and British Petroleum Chemicals Ltd, set up to supply a synthetic detergent base.

Second, petroleum refining, is virtually a new industry in the United Kingdom. Up to 1939, three-quarters of the refined petroleum consumed in the UK was imported – the production of domestic refineries being only 2.3 millon tons in 1938. Yet, by 1954, Britain possessed eight major, and four other, oil refineries, which in that year supplied 24.5 million tons of petroleum products, worth £302 million[21] – 38 per cent more than was actually consumed in the UK. Since 1945, over £200 million has been invested in refining capacity, and with an employment roll of 16,700, the United Kingdom is now the fourth largest oil refiner in the world and is largely self-supporting in its production. The more important reasons for these trends are (i) the need to economize foreign currency (and particularly dollars), (ii) the importance of developing an additional source of fuel to meet growing domestic demands, (iii) the Anglo-Iranian oil crises, (iv) the desirability of developing a petroleum chemical industry (e.g. for the supply of such products as solvents, detergents, sulphur, synthetic rubber, etc.), (v) the growing differential in international transport costs between crude and refined petroleum, and (vi) the technical advances which have made home refining more feasible.[22]

Of the 1955 output, the two United States'subsidiaries – Esso Petroleum Co. Ltd (assets £65.6 million), and Vacuum Oil Co. Ltd (assets £21.0 million) – supplied about one-third, and between them employed 6,500 operators and staff. Both companies had been distributing their products in the United Kingdom before the war, but only the latter operated a manufacturing unit, for the production of lubricating oils. Their joint capital investment since 1943 has amounted to over £80 million, about one-third of which has been financed by direct capital flows from America. The Esso refinery at Fawley (on Southampton Water) alone cost £37½ million to construct, and is the biggest of its kind in this country, with a 1956 annual throughput of 7½ million tons. In its first two and a half years of operation, it is thought to have saved the UK more than $300 million in foreign currency. Besides operating refinery plants, both companies own blending plants for lubricating oils, grease units and research laboratories, and plans are now under way for refinery extensions of £13 million and the construction of a £9 million petrochemicals plant adjacent to the main site at Fawley.[23] The effects of these investments have been far reaching, particularly on the petroleum refinery equipment, shipbuilding and synthetic chemical industries, as is further described later in this book.[24]

Third, pharmaceutical products. The total output of this industry in 1955 was £143 million, compared with £19 million in 1935. Allowing for price changes, this represents a threefold increase in output, the contribution of US firms today being between one-fifth and one-quarter of the total. Almost all the important American drug houses are represented among the twenty-five subsidiaries now operating manufacturing units in this industry, which between them employ 8,500 workers. Though mostly pre-1939 in origin, it is only in the last five years that their American parentage has shown itself to be of real importance. Right up to the Second World War, for instance, over three-quarters of the world's drug output was produced outside America.[25]

In point of fact, the earliest US investment in the UK pharmaceutical industry dates back to 1860, though the company concerned is now wholly British. Since that time, the flow of capital to the UK has steadily increased. Characterized by its large expenditures on research and development – American firms are currently allocating over $80 million to this end[26] – this industry produces a large number of different products which help to meet a wide range of wants. Today, however, there is a tendency for pharmaceutical firms to be of two broad kinds: (i) those companies specializing in the production of ethical drugs, and (ii) those mainly supplying household remedies of which proprietary medicines are the main brand.

Ethical specialities are distinguished by the fact that they are supplied direct to the National Health Service, and can usually be purchased only with a doctor's prescription. Advertising is restricted to medical publications. For the most part, these are items which are either in their primary stages of production and are costly to produce, or are strictly limited in supply. Of the twenty-four UK companies *specializing* in this field, seven are British-owned, thirteen are US subsidiaries, three are Swiss-controlled and one is financed partially by French capital. Most of the major developments of recent years have emanated from the American firms, partly because of the tremendous technological lead gained by the United States during the Second World War – six years of a vital stage in the development of antibiotic drugs – and partly because that country is most able to bear the huge expenditures on research at present involved. These two facts largely account for America's pre-eminence in this field, and explain why she has supplanted Germany as the world's chief supplier of drugs. That the US contribution to British drug development is a very marked one is shown by the fact that a large proportion (probably nearly two-thirds) of the new ethical proprietaries prescribed by UK doctors in post-war years have been American-originated, and of late have been produced in the UK either by US subsidiaries, or by British firms under licence to an American company. At the same time, in 1956, the proportion of ethical products prescribed was less in the UK than in the US – 36 per cent compared with 83 per cent.

In particular, the output of antibiotic drugs – other than penicillin – has been largely monopolized by US-financed firms. (In 1952, it was estimated that such products accounted for one-third of all ethical drug output in the United States, and over \$20 million is being spent each year on antibiotic research alone.)[27] Parke Davis and Company, Merck-Sharp and Dohme Ltd, E. R. Squibb and Sons, Abbott Laboratories, Cyanamid Products Ltd, Eli Lilly and Co. Ltd, Bayer Products Ltd, Pfizer Ltd, G. D. Searle Ltd, are all producing various kinds of 'mycin' drugs (e.g. terramycin, aureomycin, chloromycetin, streptomycin, etc.) in British plants, and new firms are still coming. As a result of these developments, UK imports of antibiotics fell from £4.8 million in 1954 to £400,000 in 1955.[28] In other fields, e.g. anti-malarial and histaminic drugs, hormones, etc., the American contribution is rather less important.

Over a score of US subsidiaries supply proprietary medicines, i.e. those which are publicly advertised and sold direct to the public. Generally speaking, the firms producing these drugs do not supply ethical proprietaries as well, though some American subsidiaries are in both fields and, in particular, one might mention International Chemical Company (a subsidiary of American Home Products Corporation), Sterling Drug Co., and Vick International Ltd. As regards manufacturing chemists as such, the best known American names in this country are Wm. R. Warner and Co. Ltd, The Mentholatum Co. Ltd, Miles Laboratories Ltd, Evans Chemical Ltd, Bristol-Myers Co. Ltd, Johnson and Johnson Ltd, and Chesebrough-Ponds Ltd, which supply a variety of products such as ointments, suppositories, sedatives, deodorants, analgesics, tonics and antiseptics.

Fourth, toilet preparations and cosmetics. A number of firms in the previous category also produce toilet preparations and cosmetics, but the larger part of the output is supplied by such specialists as Elizabeth Arden, Max Factor, Dorothy Gray, Revlon and Helena Rubenstein, most of whom were established in the United Kingdom before the war. These US subsidiaries are thought to supply about half of all the cosmetics consumed in this country, and for the most part are concentrated in the high-quality products group. There is less American investment in the perfumery industry, where French interests tend to predominate.

Lastly, soap products – and, in particular, synthetic detergents. In 1938 Thomas Hedley Ltd (a wholly-owned subsidiary of Procter and Gamble Ltd) launched the first powdered soap detergent 'Dreft' on to the British market. Its success was limited, and not until after the war with the introduction of a technically superior product, coupled with intensive advertising, was full consumers' acceptance gained. In 1950, 'Tide' appeared, and in 1953 'Daz'. Unilever Ltd, the main UK competitor, retaliated with 'Surf' and 'Omo' – an earlier product 'Whisk' had failed – but today, the greater quantity of detergents is still produced by Hedley's – and another US concern, Colgate Palmolive Ltd (established in 1925). These firms employ some 4,500 people between them, and as well as detergents, supply household soap and various kinds of toilet preparations.

In addition to these five main product ranges, American-financed firms manufacture a number of chemical specialities. The foremost supplier of vitreous enamel frit in this country is a US subsidiary, while a similar influence is evident in the production of wax polishes, adhesives, surgical dressings, sealing compounds, paper-making chemicals, herbicides and disinfectants.

Engineering and electrical goods

Also comprising a very large number of heterogeneous trades, this industrial group employs nearly one-third of the total labour force of American firms in the manufacturing sector. Once again, however, investment tends to be confined to a relatively small number of selective fields. There is, for example, little or no US capital at present invested in the shipbuilding and ship-repairing, marine engineering, ordnance constructional engineering, electrical machinery and small arms, wireless valves and electric lamps and battery and accumulator sections of the industry, which, between them, account for 35 per cent of the total labour force of the group as a whole. Indirectly, though, since 1945 the development of the shipbuilding industry has been very much influenced by the expansion of the oil refining industry. Over 60 per cent of the British ships built in the last ten years have been oil tankers, and the Esso company alone purchased twenty-one vessels between 1951 and 1956.[29] Between 10 per cent and 12 per cent of the UK output of machine and engineering small tools are supplied by a score or so of US firms, though it is in the milling, broaching, drill chuck and pneumatic tool sections where the American impact is primarily felt. A large number of UK firms are, however, producing under US licence. Two US subsidiaries supply textile machinery and accessories.

There is, however, a sizeable American interest in the 'other engineering industries' group, and more specifically in three main subsections. First, the production of agricultural machinery has been strongly influenced in recent years by US and Canadian subsidiaries operating in the UK. Though this is not a new industry to the British economy,[30] until the outbreak of the Second World War, output had not exceeded £10 million a year. Yet, during the following decade, the British farming industry became the most mechanized in the world, and by 1954 the output of agricultural machinery and tractors had risen to £120 million. The two facts that (i) the British manufacturer was both technically and economically ill-prepared for the demands for mechanization consequent upon the shortage and rising cost of labour after the war, and (ii) imports from North America had to be drastically reduced, were sufficient to assure any prospective US or Canadian subsidiary in this field a ready-made market, not only in the UK but throughout the entire sterling area. Geared to, and with some fifteen years' experience of, a fully mechanized farming economy, and with the available equipment and machinery at hand, American companies supplying the home market were quick both to establish new factories in the United Kingdom and to extend their existing ones.

In 1954, between 60 per cent and 70 per cent of all UK agricultural implements were either American-produced – the main firms being International Harvester Co. Ltd, Allis Chalmers Ltd and the Anglo-Canadian venture Massey-Harris-Ferguson Ltd – or manufactured to American specifications. In particular, since 1945, many UK firms, including one of the largest British implement producers – Ransome Sims and Jefferies Ltd – have operated design and production agreements with the UK Ford Motor Company – a foremost producer of agricultural tractors – for such items as hydraulic lifts, mounted ploughs, winches and manure loaders.[31] This is because technical advances in this field have been allied to those in tractor design and engineering. As the tractor has developed, so with it has the ancillary equipment, and a good deal of help and advice has passed between tractor and implement manufacturers. For example, the new Fordson tractor introduced by the Ford Motor Company in 1951 necessitated a whole new range of implements, and these, though manufactured and marketed by established UK implement firms, were designed by the American subsidiary to operate specifically with its particular system of tractor and mounting.[32]

As illustrated in Chapter 1, progress in the UK tractor industry was entirely dominated by the Ford Motor Co. Ltd, up to the Second World War; in 1938, for example, that company accounted for 8,500 of the 10,000 wheel and tracklaying farm tractors produced in the UK. This monopoly was maintained during the war, when, in the face of acute labour shortage, the industry expanded rapidly; Ford in fact supplied 120,000 out of the 128,000 tractors manufactured in the United Kingdom between 1940 and 1944. Since 1945, with the intensification of mechanization, other companies have entered the field. Harry Ferguson, who had an agreement with the US Ford Company, contracted out at the end of the war, and in 1947 transferred his interests to the UK Standard Motor Company. Since that time, the output of Ferguson tractors has overtaken that of Ford, especially since the merging of Ferguson with the Canadian implements specialist Massey-Harris in 1954, which has considerably strengthened its world competitive position. The Ford subsidiary, however, has maintained an important position and in 1955 supplied one-third of a UK output of 170,000 tractors. Each of the other US subsidiaries mentioned above also supply a specialist range of tractors, though their combined output is under 10 per cent of the total. However, as a result of the efforts of these producers, some 400,000 tractors were in service on British farms in 1955 – eight times the number utilized in 1938.

Apart from tractors and accessories, US subsidiaries in the UK have tended to specialize in harvesting and grain handling equipment, e.g. pick-up balers, reapers and combine harvesters, which, before the war, were produced in very small numbers in the UK. In other fields, e.g. hedge-trimming, manure-handling, ditch-clearing, potato-planting and dairying, the major advances have been of British origin. In all, some 16,000 people are employed by American affiliates in the agricultural engineering industry today, and indirectly as a result of US licensing agreements, many thousands more. Substantially resulting from the growing use made of agricultural machinery, the volume of output produced by UK farmers in 1954 was 56 per cent[33] above the 1939 level, despite a slight fall in the labour force.

Second, the office machinery industry is well represented by American interests. Before 1939, well over four-fifths of the typewriters, calculating machines, cash registers, duplicators, etc. bought in the UK were imported from the United

States. Since that time, the annual turnover of the UK industry has risen from £2 million to £40 million in 1955.[34] The United Kingdom is now the second largest producer of office equipment in the world, and in 1955, 40 per cent of its output was exported – one-third to the dollar area. In 1957, there were twelve US subsidiaries in this industry, which between them employ 11,000 people and supply an annual output worth more than £25 million. Like the pharmaceutical industry, most of these firms were producing in Britain before the war but on a very limited scale. The best-known names in the field are Remington Rand Ltd, National Cash Register Ltd, Burroughs Adding Machine Ltd, Underwood Business Machines Ltd, International Business Machines Ltd and Felt and Tarrant, and these firms supply one-half to two-thirds of the calculating machines and cash registers and about half the typewriters produced in the UK. Dictating machines are produced by Dictaphone Ltd – which, in 1955, accounted for 90 per cent of the export, and about one-third of the UK home market – while Addressograph Multigraph Ltd is an important supplier of addressing and duplicating machines. Remington Rand Ltd and the Art Metal Co Ltd both manufacture a wide range of filing systems, and the latter office furniture as well.

Three particularly interesting features about the US subsidiaries in this industry deserve comment at this point:

1 Their management methods generally follow those practised by their parent concerns.
2 Of their total labour force, in the UK over three-quarters is concentrated in the Scottish Development Area.
3 More than in any other industry, they engage in international product specialization, by which the US and UK factories supply a limited range of items, which they exchange with each other.

Both Remington Rand Ltd and Burroughs Adding Machine Ltd, for example, produce in their Scottish factories equipment for world markets (including the USA). Over 50 per cent of the output of these and the other subsidiaries is, in fact, sent overseas, while their presence in the UK has enabled the most recent developments and refinements of existing products, e.g. electric and executive typewriters, special-purpose book-keeping and adding machines, etc., to be imported from the US more quickly than would otherwise have been possible. The International Business Machine Company, which at the time of writing is marketing three machines, is the only US subsidiary engaged in computer production, though an important UK firm – Elliott Brothers – has a close tie-up with a number of US companies.[35]

Third, brief mention should be made of the impact which US-affiliated firms have made on the development of the petroleum field and refinery equipment industry. In 1955 this industry produced some £123 million worth of instruments, oil-drilling equipment, pressure vessels, pumps, valves, control gear, constructional material, etc., and other oil refinery requirements.[36] Like the petroleum refining industry, to which its development has been complementary, the equipment industry is almost entirely post-1945 in origin, and while, except in specialized cases (e.g. welding machinery, instruments or oil-drilling equipment) US firms do not figure as important suppliers of refinery equipment, the American impact in other directions has been most obvious. For, as a recent OEEC Report has pointed out,[37] 70 per cent of all the equipment manufactured for European oil refineries since the war has been American-designed. In the United Kingdom, the design, engineering and construction of all the important refineries built since 1945 (and those which British contractors are now building overseas) has been in the hands of specialist consultant firms; rarely is it the case that the petroleum company concerned builds its own refinery as in pre-war days. And all but one of these refinery consultant firms are American subsidiaries, of which the most important are Kellogg Ltd, Foster-Wheeler Ltd, Lummus Ltd, Procon Ltd and Badger Ltd. Though possessing only limited manufacturing facilities of their own, these service companies have played an indispensable role in Britain's £200 million expansion programme. Sometimes, as in the construction of the Fawley refinery, only one main contractor – Foster-Wheeler Ltd – is employed; in others, more than one firm may be concerned.

It is but a reflection of the contrasting pattern of Anglo-American resources and technological capabilities that US influence in the refinery equipment industry is so strong. For obvious reasons, the American economy has been particularly suited to the use of petroleum as a source of energy from the earliest of days. Also, during the Second World War, when there was some specialization of industrial production among the Allies, the US was clearly in the best position to deal with any questions relating to the innovation or improvement of refining equipment. Hence, that country was able to forge still further ahead. Nevertheless, with the present shortage of alternative fuels, the expansion of the UK petroleum and petroleum refinery equipment industries is likely to be of long-term economic importance to the UK. In addition, the construction of overseas refineries offers many potentialities for the future.

These then, are the three main fields in which there is a significant concentration of US capital, though representation is equally evident in a number of the more specialized sectors of the engineering industry. For example, Waygood-Otis Ltd – an Anglo-American concern – is the largest manufacturer of lifts and escalators in the UK. The British United Shoe Machinery Co. Ltd (net assets £12.3 million), and the Singer Sewing Machine Co. Ltd (net assets £6.7 million) occupy leading – almost monopolistic – positions in the boot and shoe machinery and sewing machine industries respectively. The pre-eminence of American-originated companies in the printing and typesetting industries has already been mentioned, with Linotype, Intertype and Goss Printing Press Co. Ltd (combined net assets £10.5 million) as the major suppliers. Nash Kelvinator Ltd and Frigidaire Ltd are both well established in the domestic refrigerator market, while the latter company and York Shippley Ltd are the leading producers of industrial and commercial refrigeration machinery. Between them these firms turn out between a third and a half of the refrigerators manufactured in the UK. Materials handling equipment is produced by Ruston-Bucyrus Ltd, Yale and Towne Manufacturing Ltd and Blaw Knox Ltd,[38] while four important US subsidiaries, including Joy-Sullivan Ltd and British Jeffrey Diamond Ltd supply specialized mining equipment, e.g. loading, tunnelling and conveying machinery – particularly for longwall and open-cast mining purposes. Finally, US-financed or originated firms also manufacture a major proportion of the UK output of food production machinery, petrol pumps, air-conditioning equipment, laundry machinery, road-making equipment, bottle-washing machinery, catering and dairy equipment.

Finally, electrical equipment. As described in the previous chapter, most of the original US interests in this field have been repatriated. Only the Standard Telephones and Cables Ltd (net assets £14.6 million), with a labour force of many thousands, retains a substantial American shareholding: even here, however, the management is wholly British, and the subsidiary is largely autonomous in its decision-making. Licensing and patent agreements are still, of course, very common, and most of the large British electrical equipment companies maintain close touch with their counterparts in the US in one way or another. Three American-financed firms produce radio and television apparatus, and though US participation in this industry is at present (1958) relatively small, it may well become more important in the future. In July, 1954, the Sylvania-Thorn Colour Laboratories Ltd was jointly formed by the Sylvania Electric Products Inc. (New York) and Thorn Electrical Industries Ltd (UK) to make cathode ray tubes for television, while another Anglo-American venture, Semiconductors Ltd set up in 1957 by the Plessey Company of Ilford and the US Philco Corporation, is shortly to produce transistors and other semiconductors.

Two US subsidiaries supply over two-thirds of the electric switches produced in the UK and Erie Resistor Ltd is a leading producer of electrical components. In the manufacture of domestic electrical products, transatlantic influence is also important. The need to save labour in the home, coupled with the (comparatively) high income standards of the average American family, account for the large output of this type of equipment in the United States, but it has only been since 1945 that the British housewife has freely benefited. Substantial quantities of electric washing-machines, vacuum cleaners, steam irons, electric razors, etc. are produced by US-affiliated companies, the most important of which is Hoover Ltd (net assets £8.8 million) – a jointly operated Anglo-American enterprise set up in 1930 with a present-day labour force of 5,500. An important newcomer is Sunbeam Electric, which first started producing in its 200,000 sq. ft Scottish factory in 1954. Eventually this subsidiary plans to manufacture a wide range of household, garden and electrical appliances.[39]

To summarize, where there is any American representation in the engineering industry, it is an important one. Of the total UK output of those sectors specifically described, US subsidiaries and Anglo-American firms supply between them one-fifth and one-quarter, and the US concentration quotient is equal to 4.6.

Vehicles

American participation is solely confined to the manufacturing of motor vehicles and motor vehicle accessories and components. As far as we know, no firms of American origin are producing aircraft (though a number of subsidiaries are supplying specialized aircraft components): neither are there any in the bicycle or motor-cycle industries. In 1956, the Ford and General Motors companies, with a combined capital of £82.0 million, employed more than 70,000 people in their dozen or more factories, which not only assemble vehicles but manufacture a wide range of components and parts for the finished product. This latter trend has reflected the growing vertical integration of the auto industry in which the two firms have themselves participated. Vauxhall, for example, is one of the few car assemblers who make their own bodies. The Ford Company has gradually become more self-supporting over the years, with the purchase of Kelsey-Hayes Wheel Co. Ltd (manufacturers of wheels) in 1948, and Briggs Motor Bodies ltd (manufacturer of car bodies) in 1953. Both these latter concerns were of American origin. In 1955, with an output of 480,000 vehicles (of all descriptions) and a joint turnover of £226 million, Ford and Vauxhall supplied two in every five cars produced in the United Kingdom. As has already been noted, the former concern is the second largest supplier of agricultural tractors in the United Kingdom, while Vauxhall enjoys a prominent position in the production of commercial vehicles. In addition, the General Motors Organization operates two other vehicle subsidiaries in the UK, viz. A. C. Delco and Delco-Remy and Hyatt, which manufacture a wide range of car accessories. In addition to these two major concerns and their associate companies, seven other US component manufacturers supply sparking plugs, electrical goods, dashboard instruments, wipers, fuel pumps, brakes, tyre valves, ignition coils, etc. Among these is Borg Warner Ltd who is now manufacturing automatic transmissions and morse chains in its recently constructed Letchworth factory. At one time, US influence was even greater with the presence of Willys-Overland-Crossley, Hudson-Essex (motor vehicles), British Timken (roller bearings) and Raybestos (brake linings). Even now, the latter two concerns, while no longer US-controlled, still enjoy an exchange of technical know-how with their one-time American parents.

Finally, the Euclid Co. Ltd (also part of the General Motors group) is one of the foremost suppliers of earth-moving trucks and wagons (e.g. dumpers, etc.) while the Caterpillar Tractor Co. Ltd in its Scottish factory produces a range of crawler-tractors for excavating and open-cast mining.

Textiles and clothing

This is an important industrial group employing 1¼ million people, but one in which US representation is largely insignificant. For example, in the great staple trades of cotton and wool, which in 1914 produced over one-third of all UK exports, and which today (1958) still give employment to half a million people, there are only two firms of American origin, while in the expanding man-made fibres section (rayon, nylon, etc.), apart from one recently established subsidiary – Chemstrand Ltd – which is to supply acrilan from its £3.5 million plant in Northern Ireland, American influence is confined entirely to licensing and patent-sharing agreements.

The clothing industry has attracted rather more American capital, but even here it has been almost entirely concentrated in the foundation garment, swimwear and lingerie sections. Though no longer US-controlled, the important lingerie and hosiery firm, Kayser-Bondor Ltd, has long enjoyed a close technical association with the Julius Kayser Company of New York. Jantzen is a well-known name, and occupies a major position in the sportswear and swimsuit market. In the foundation garment industry, there are no less than eight American firms, which between them supply over two-thirds of the total British production of corsets, suspender belts and brassières. Spirella, Gossard, Twilfit, Warner, Barcley, Spencer and International Latex are all important producers, and most have been operating in the UK since pre-war days. Not only do these firms employ a labour force of over 5,000 in their factories, but they also operate a wide network (largely self-originated) of corsetières throughout the country, to whom they have given training. No US influence is apparent in the other branches of the tailoring industry (except for one very modern medium sized firm operated by an American national at Crewe), nor in the production of boots and shoes.

Industrial and scientific instruments

This industrial classification comprises four subsections of manufacturing, namely: (1) all kinds of instruments – scientific, photographic, industrial, medical, etc., (2) watches and clocks, (3) jewellery and refining of precious metals, (4) musical instruments.

In the first group, US representation is largely confined to the industrial instruments sector, which in 1954 produced between £40 and £50 million worth of equipment for measuring and controlling temperature, humidity, flow and pressure. This is an industry which dates back to the nineteenth century with the innovation and commercialization of water meters and level gauges, but the real importance of which has only become apparent in the last decade or so. Much the same might be said of the American instruments industry, though partly because of a more favourable industrial structure, and partly due to the quicker recognition and greater receptiveness of the US consumer of the advantages of instrumentation, that industry was expanding quite rapidly in the 1930s. While there were technical advances in the United Kingdom during these years, there did not seem to be the same avenues for exploitation. With the advent of the Second World War, which enabled the US economy to leap still further ahead, carrying instrumentation with it, that country was able to build up what was virtually a world monopoly in the output of instruments.

Meanwhile, the development of new industries and production techniques in the United Kingdom, and a growing appreciation by UK industrial consumers of the uses of the functions of instrumentation, have combined to raise the level of internal demand. Since 1939 the numbers employed in the UK instruments industry have trebled, while the value of output has increased eight times. Yet American influence has been so dominant during this period that it is likely that only a fraction of the progress which has been made would have been possible had it not been for the presence of US-affiliated firms, and the growth of Anglo-American licensing agreements.

Since, too, it is a feature of the firms in this industry to specialize according to the type of instrument supplied *or* the market served, the American contribution is naturally of particular significance where the consuming firms are also likely to be influenced by US techniques. In all, there are two large, two medium and four small American-financed firms producing in the UK, which between them employ 8,500: Foxborough-Yoxall (oil specialists), Short and Mason (rubber specialists) and Honeywell-Brown (electronic instruments) are the main firms, while Sperry Gyroscope is a foremost supplier of aircraft and navigational instruments. Since 1953 Bendix Aviation Ltd (US) has had a 30 per cent interest in the British firm of Elliott Bros. Ltd. Most of the other important UK producers, e.g. George Kent and Cambridge Instruments, manufacture, in part at least, under licence to American companies. US influence is less well evidenced in the production of electrical instruments, though Sangamo Weston is an important supplier of electricity meters.

Two important jointly financed Anglo-American concerns – British-American Optical Ltd and UK Optical Bausch and Lamb Ltd – supply ophthalmic products, while the Kodak Company still produces the larger part of the British output of photographic equipment. In addition, about 40 per cent of the talking picture apparatus used in British cinemas is supplied by an American firm.

Two post-war US firms – Westclox Ltd and UK Time – produce watches and clocks; both are situated in the Scottish Development Area, and have done much to introduce a completely new trade (that of light precision engineering) into the local economy. In addition, the International Business Machine Company has been supplying time-recording apparatus for some years now.

The Baker Platinum Company is an important refiner of precious metals; otherwise there is little direct US participation in the jewellery and precious metals trade. At one time, however, there was a good deal of American capital in the musical instruments industry. The Aeolian Company was a foremost supplier of pianos, while, as has already been recalled, gramophones and gramophone records were produced by US firms in the inter-war period. Today, American influence in the UK is limited to a 50 per cent equity stake in Oreole Records Ltd by the Mercury Record Corporation of Chicago.

Metal manufacturing and metal goods not otherwise specified

This is another traditional British field of manufacturing, and one well established long before US capital was invested in any quantity. There are no American firms in the blast furnace and wrought-iron sections, and while in steel manufacturing a number of important British companies, e.g. Head Wrightson, Davy and United

Engineering, enjoy an exchange of technical know-how with US firms, the influence of American capital is small. As regards cast-iron products, three US subsidiaries – Ideal Boilers, Crane and Florence Stoves – probably supply 60 per cent of all the domestic boilers used in the United Kingdom, while a fourth – Aladdin Ltd – is an important manufacturer of heating appliances. Apart from these firms, US influence is restricted to a number of specialist fields.

Specialized copper tubing is produced by British Bundy Tubing Ltd and nickel alloys by British Driver Harris Ltd; the International Mond Nickel Co., a subsidiary of a jointly owned US–Canadian enterprise, is the sole supplier of nickel, while the Northern Aluminium Co. – one of the largest manufacturers of fabricated aluminium products in the UK – is a branch of a Canadian company, the share capital of which, until recently, was US-owned. Finally, lead refining, though now wholly in the hands of British companies, is still influenced by Anglo-American licensing agreements.

A foremost supplier of kitchen cutlery-ware, and in particular the 'Prestige' and 'Skyline' range of equipment, is the jointly owned Anglo-American concern, the Prestige Group Ltd. This company owns five factories in the Midlands and Lancashire, and its subsidiary Colly Ltd is an important producer of scissors in this country. Over 90 per cent of the razor blades, and a substantial proportion of the safety razors bought by UK consumers, are manufactured by the Gillette and Ever-Ready Companies, while Black and Decker Ltd and Stanley Works (GB) Ltd hold leading positions in the portable electric appliances and high-quality carpenters' tools market. Yale and Towne Manufacturing Ltd (which bought out the UK firm of H. and T. Vaughan in 1929) is the largest lock producer in Europe. Until its original patents expired in 1946, Ronson Ltd enjoyed a virtual monopoly in the cigarette lighter field.

Food, drink and tobacco

Comprising a wide range of separate trades, this industry employed nearly one million people in 1955. US influence is once more restricted to a number of selected fields. First, practically all the UK output of starch is supplied by Brown and Polson Ltd – a subsidiary of the Corn Products Group USA Starch, or its derivatives, is used by almost every industry, and forms the basis of many hundreds of products such as glucose, preservatives, size, adhesives, ice cream and custards. The production of this latter item is still largely in the hands of three American concerns – Alfred Bird and Sons Ltd, a subsidiary of the General Foods Corporation, Brown and Polson Ltd and Standard Brands Ltd.

Libby, McNeill and Libby Ltd and Carnation Milk Ltd share with Nestlés – a British firm – the greater part of the evaporated milk market, while Kraft Foods Ltd and Swift and Co. Ltd supply over three-quarters of the processed cheese products consumed in the UK. The breakfast cereals market is to all intents and purposes monopolized by American firms – the Kellogg Co. of GB Ltd, Nabisco Foods Ltd, Quaker Oats Ltd and Bird's being the main manufacturers. In the sugar and chocolate confectionery trade, apart from Mars Ltd (a subsidiary of which is a major supplier of cat and dog food), there is no American influence, and much the same applies to the biscuits and bread and flour confectionery industries.

The name of Heinz – with its '57' varieties – has long been associated with canned and bottled food products, e.g. soups, baked beans, strained baby goods, sauces and pickles, etc., and since 1905, when manufacturing first started at Harlesden in North London, it has maintained its premier position in most of the markets it serves. There are also a number of American firms in the canned meat and fruit field but, as yet, they import the greater proportion of their output from the US.

One of the most recent US infiltrations has been in the supply of ready-made cake mixes. Two American, and one Canadian firm share the market with a number of British companies. In 1954 the turnover of this industry was over £5 million, though one American subsidiary recently estimated that this would double itself in the next four years. In the rapidly expanding soft drinks market, the Coca-Cola Ltd and Pepsi-Cola Ltd have both established important footholds and have bottling agencies throughout the country. Horlicks Ltd, at one time a US subsidiary, now has its headquarters in Britain. Shortly after the Second World War, the UK company bought out its American associate, which it now operates as a branch concern. For alcoholic beverages, an important development in 1956 was the investment, by Schenley Industries Inc., New York, of a $9 million controlling interest in Seager, Evans and Co. Ltd, the proprietors of the 'Long John' brand of whisky. Part of the American capital will be allocated to an enlargement of the Strathclyde grain distillery and it is expected that the output of whisky will be increased by 60 per cent within the next year or so. Finally, most of the chewing-gum bought by UK consumers is produced by an American firm – Wrigley Products Ltd – while J. Wix and Co. Ltd, manufacturers of 'Kensitas' cigarettes, is the sole remaining US representation in the tobacco industry.

Other manufacturing industries

Comprising a group of miscellaneous activities, US representation is most evident in the rubber products industry. Three of the four largest UK rubber-tyre companies, viz. Goodyear Tyre and Rubber Co. Ltd, Firestone Tyre and Rubber Ltd and North British Rubber Co. Ltd (combined capital £15 million), are US-controlled, and between them supplied over two-fifths of the vehicle tyres produced in 1955. As might be expected, their best customers are the American motor vehicle subsidiaries. Employing some 11,000 people, their output also includes rubber clothing and footwear, tubing, belting and sponge rubber products. Perhaps the most important recent development has been the formation of the International Synthetic Rubber Co. Ltd – comprising Dunlop Rubber, Goodyear Tyre and Rubber, Firestone Tyre and Rubber and Michelin Tyres – and a £5 million plant planned to produce 50,000 tons of synthetic rubber each year is now under construction adjacent to Esso's refinery at Fawley.[40] It is hoped that this will eventually lead to an annual saving of rubber imports of $30 million.

As far as is known, only one specialist producer of toys is US-owned. Spaldings Ltd, the important sports equipment firm, though once American, is now British. Though the per capita consumption of pens and pencils in the United States is double that in this country, it is perhaps a little surprising that the output of American-affiliated firms should account for 35–45 per cent of UK production. The Venus Pencil Co. Ltd, Eversharp Ltd, Eagle Pencil Company, Esterbrook-Hazell Ltd, the Waterman Pen Co. Ltd and the Parker Pen Co. Ltd are all US-owned. Inked typewriter ribbons and carbon papers are supplied by the Columbia Ribbon and Manufacturing Co. Ltd. The printing of films and the manufacture of photographic paper is very much in the hands of the Kodak Co. Ltd which today employs over 7,000 people in its North London and Liverpool factories. Ninety per cent of the UK production of cinematic films and about two-fifths of roll films are supplied by this affiliate. Four US film companies – Warner Brothers, Metro-Goldwyn Mayer, Twentieth-Century Fox and RKO – operate film studios; their contribution to British film output is between one-quarter and one-fifth of the total.

Finally, though separately classified by the Standard Industrial Classification, we have included in this section the production of (1) paper, wood and cork products and (2) abrasives and glassware. As regards the former, subsidiaries such as Armstrong Cork Ltd, Celotex Ltd and British Sisalkraft Ltd supply specialized industrial materials, while the recently established Anglo-American venture Bowater-Scott Ltd, and Cellucotton Products Ltd, with a number of smaller US concerns, produce such items as paper handkerchiefs, toilet tissue, crêpe paper, and paper patterns. Carborundum Ltd, Norton Grinding Wheel Ltd and Minnesota Mining Co. Ltd are three of the largest firms in the grinding wheels and abrasives industry; between them, they employ 4,000 people, and supply about 40 per cent of the market. Until recently, there was no US capital in the glass industry, but in 1954, Corning Glass Works (US) bought out a 40 per cent interest in James A. Jobling and Co. Ltd, manufacturers of 'Pyrex' glassware, and in the autumn of 1955, the Rockware Glass Co. (UK) concluded an arrangement with the Wheaton Glass Co. (US) to produce and sell in the UK certain American-designed small glass containers in the pharmaceutical and cosmetic fields.

So much for the general scope of US participation in British industry. Though widely spread, such investment is nevertheless highly selective, both as regards the character of the products supplied and the type of markets served.

First, it is clear that American representation is highly concentrated in the 'newer' – though not 'brand new' – British industries, the origin of which, for the most part, dates back to the inter-war period. Almost without exception, the rate of expansion of such industries is greater than that for UK industry as a whole. Yet, though new to the UK, most of the industries concerned had been previously well established in the United States. In the main, they embrace technologies, trades and skills which, if not discovered by, were first exploited on any scale in, the United States, and/or those which the comparative advantage of production in the past – if not at present – has favoured that country. In some cases, branch manufacturing units, and particularly those established since 1945, have been set up because trade barriers have prevented these comparative advantages asserting themselves. As a consequence one has a curious reversal of the classic dictum that the international mobility of goods compensates for the international immobility of factors of production.

There are, in fact, many well-known cases of new products or manufacturing processes which have originated from the UK but which the United States has either been the first to exploit or has subsequently built upon. The typewriter, the fire extinguisher, silicones, fluorescent lighting, the jet engine are all examples of products which have been later reintroduced into the United Kingdom by way of imports, licensing agreements or US branch plants. This would seem to be especially the case in those sectors which are faced with high overhead costs and are heavily reliant on research and development for their prosperity and growth, and those engaging in mass production; nearly one-half of all US-financed firms come within one or other of these two categories. At the same time, many US subsidiaries in the UK are able to manufacture more cheaply than can their parent concerns. Quite apart from any question of foreign exchange difficulties, it is often cost-efficient for British factories to supply at least some export markets. Before the war, for example, the UK branches of American oil refinery consultants accepted orders to design and produce equipment, but all manufacturing was carried out in the United States. Nowadays, this procedure would no longer be an economic proposition because of the differences in labour costs. Such differences have been an important factor in helping to improve British industry's share in the newer exports in relation to that of the United States in recent years.

Second, account must be taken of the markets served by US firms, and the changing pattern of demand which has evolved since 1939. For example, in the case of capital goods, the nature of production economics in the UK has undergone a marked change as a result of such factors as (a) full employment, coupled with labour shortages and rising wage levels, (b) the growth of many consumer good industries which has made possible highly capitalized production techniques to be more efficiently utilized, (c) the increased cost and productivity consciousness of many UK businesses, (d) the need to replenish capital assets depleted by war, and (e) rapid technological advances, particularly within the technology and capital-intensive industries (e.g. the engineering trade increased its labour force by 130 per cent between 1935 and 1955 compared with 51 per cent for that of industry in general).[41] Production techniques and processes hitherto considered uneconomic or impracticable have now become both profitable and competitiveness enhancing: hence the expansion in output of those industries supplying all types of labour-saving and cost-reducing machinery. It is helpful, however, to distinguish these industries from those newer trades the growth of which has depended upon the introduction of previously *unknown* production techniques (or materials) by US firms.

In like manner, consumer demand conditions in the United Kingdom have moved more in line with those in the United States. Not only has this been the result of rising living standards, and by a more equitable distribution of income, but also of the changing pattern of consumers' expenditure – itself partly a reflection of new price structures – which has particularly stimulated the demand for the semi-luxury class of goods. For example, the UK national real income per capita has risen by 35 per cent since before the war, but there has been a marked change in the way that income is spent. Not all prices have risen in the same proportion. Food prices have been artificially pegged by subsidies, and the Rent Restriction Acts have kept down the cost of housing accommodation; as a result more income has become available for such goods and services as clothes, motor-cars, durable household goods and so on.

Domestic vehicle sales have, for example, trebled since 1938, those of cosmetics and toilet preparations quadrupled, and those of refrigerators and washing machines have risen by eight to ten times. In addition, within these and other groups, there has been a movement towards the production of higher-quality goods. The extension of hire purchase and credit facilities has also encouraged more spending in this direction, which increases in UK expenditure taxes have only partially offset. In the main, however, the price elasticity of demand for such products is less than it was in pre-war days. Such would seem to account for the considerable success which American firms have had in their sales of cosmetic and toilet preparations, motor-cars, domestic electrical products, kitchen cutlery-ware, cigarette lighters, electric razors and packaged food products.

It is, however, important to view these trends in their right perspective. The fact that much of the recent influx of US capital has been induced by the circumstances of the time must not in itself be regarded as a direct criticism of British firms or British managers. For in the three vital fields of industrial progress since the war, viz. atomic power, electronics and aircraft, American participation has been comparatively unimportant,[42] while in the petrochemicals and man-made fibre industries, British firms, though more dependent on US technical expertise, are holding their own. To be sure, much of the research and development expenditure has been financed by the UK government, either directly or through its own co-operative research establishments, but this is no adverse reflection on the skill, enterprise and ingenuity of the British engineer, scientist or technician. Equally clear, however, is the fact that much of the research carried out has been fundamental or basic, and not applied, or, as yet, fully commercialized. For in each of these industries the methods of manufacturing so far evolved have been comparatively suited to the resources and capabilities of the UK. The building of an atomic power station, of an electricity generating plant, of a special-purpose aircraft or a complicated electronic computer all require essentially jobbing or idiosyncratic techniques of production and a substantial skilled labour content, in which the United Kingdom, with her long experience, enjoys a comparative advantage over the United States.

Each of these industries is still in its infancy: it may well be, as so often has been the case in the past, that as the commercial applications of atomic power and electronics widen, the United States will profit more than the United Kingdom.

As regards the former sector, the opposite is nearer the truth at the moment, with the greater urgency to provide nuclear energy in Britain being the main impetus to research; as regards the latter, the US is currently investing $1,000 million a year on electronic computer research.[43] It is true that, in many respects, this country is especially favourably placed to exploit these and other similar possibilities. On the other hand, there is no denying that many British firms have been slow to grasp opportunities and to adapt their production techniques to changing circumstances; too often has the solution of increased mechanization offered by US-affiliated firms been greeted with indifference or scepticism. It is also quite possible that insufficient attention has been paid to the opportunities offered by Anglo-American licensing agreements; in any event, US firms have been quick to gain a foothold in the British economy. Making due allowance for these factors, however, care should be taken when assessing the impact made by American direct investment on recent industrial developments not to exclude the many spontaneous innovations which have taken place in UK industry.

With the passing of years, the composition of British industrial output has been gradually moving closer to its American counterpart. This chapter has outlined the main spheres of influence in which, by their presence in this country, US subsidiaries and Anglo-American firms have helped this adjustment to take place more efficiently and speedily than might otherwise have been the case. Such, we must conclude, is the dominating feature of the present-day scope and character of American investment in British manufacturing industry.

3 The structure and organization of US affiliates in Britain

Geographical distribution, size and ownership patterns

In subsequent chapters we shall identify and evaluate some of the ways in which US manufacturing subsidiaries and jointly owned Anglo-American concerns operating in the UK have promoted, and are promoting, British industrial development and competitiveness. But first in this chapter we shall examine some aspects of the structure and organization of these companies, where possible, making comparisons with the situation as it exists in British industry as a whole.

THE LOCATIONAL PATTERN OF US AFFILIATES

Between them, in December 1953 the 205 firms covered in our survey operated 306 manufacturing units; 52 firms, with a labour force of 137,000, were *multi-plant* in character, a considerably higher proportion than the average for UK industry as a whole.[1] One firm operated 12 production units, eleven others 4 or more, and eight had at least 2 branches.[2] Included within our definition of *branch* factories are nearly thirty associate companies or subsidiaries of UK-based firms, which are themselves owned by US corporations. For example, Hughes Brushes Ltd and Ethicon Sutures Ltd are part and parcel of the Johnson and Johnson organization, and Chappie Ltd is a subsidiary of Mars Ltd.

For the most part, the development of branch factories, i.e. of already established US firms, has been post-war in origin. For example, twenty-six, i.e. half of those firms which are multi-plant today, operated only one production unit in 1939. And, of the thirty-five new factories established by such companies, twenty-one have been set up in the Development Areas[3] under Board of Trade approval. Moreover, at the time of writing, the branch plant movement is still growing. In December 1956, more than twenty-five firms were building – or contemplating building – new factories.[4] It appears usual for subsidiaries in the motor vehicle, office machinery, agricultural implement and heavy chemical trades to own the greatest number of establishments and for firms in the pharmaceutical, toilet preparation and industrial instrument industries to own the fewest. The size of firms and the degree of *vertical* or *horizontal* integration practised by them, the nature and variety of goods produced, the relative economies of dispersed and concentrated production units, and government regional policy make up the main determinants of the number of plants operated by any one enterprise.

Table 3.1 Geographical location of US-owned plants and UK plants in manufacturing industry[1]

Region	No. of US factories	Employment in US factories (Dec. 1953)	% of total employment	Employment in all UK factories (May 1953)	% of total employment	US location quotient:[2] (Col. 3 Col. 5)
London and South-East	129	115,700	47.0	5,274,000	25.2	1.87
Eastern	23	26,900	10.9	1,101,000	5.3	2.06
South and South-Western	28	15,900	6.5	2,057,000	9.8	0.66
Midland	17	14,600	5.9	2,011,000	9.7	0.61
North Midland	16	10,400	4.2	1,418,000	6.8	0.62
East and West Riding	11	8,700	3.5	1,785,000	8.5	0.41
North-Western	24	13,200	5.4	2,935,000	14.1	0.38
Northern	9	4,200	1.7	1,247,000	6.0	0.28
Scotland	32	29,700	12.1	2,116,000	10.1	1.21
Wales and Monmouthshire	17	6,900	2.8	926,000	4.4	0.64
Total	306	246,200	100.0	20,880,000	100.0	–

Source of UK statistics: Ministry of Labour Gazette, June 1954.
Notes:
1 Excluding those in Northern Ireland.
2 US coefficient of localization = total of + or − deviations of % of US factory employment in various areas from % of all UK factory employment in the same areas ÷ 100 = 0.29.

The geographical location of these factories and that of all British manufacturing firms is shown in Table 3.1. From these figures a US *location quotient*[5] may be derived, which relates the importance of American subsidiaries to the economies of individual regions, and also an overall *coefficient of localization,*[6] which identifies the extent to which US firms are localized as compared with the average for British industry.

In view of the nature of the products described in Chapter 2, the marked concentration of factories within London and the South-East, and the relatively high US location quotient for this area, is not surprising; in fact, an area within twenty miles radius of the capital accounts for 46.1 per cent of the total UK employment in American firms. Scotland – or more precisely, the mid-Scottish area around Glasgow and Dundee – is second in importance, with the Eastern and Southern regions following in that order. By contrast, the least attractive locations appear to be North England, the East and West Ridings of Yorkshire and Wales.

The reasons for this geographical distribution can best be appreciated if we examine the original date of investment by American companies, this either by (1) the purchase or part-purchase of an existing UK firm, (2) the establishment of a *de novo* manufacturing unit or (3) the setting up of a branch of an existing subsidiary. As in Chapter 2, only those firms which are both US-financed and still operating are taken into consideration.

Table 3.2 Geographical distribution of employment in US plants in the UK[1] by date of establishment

Region	Pre-1914		1915–39		1940–53	
	No. of est.	Nos. empl'd	No. of est.	Nos. empl'd	No. of est.	Nos. empl'd
London and South-East	15	22,700	92	88,719	22	4,288
Eastern			16	22,865	5	2,102
South and South-West	} 5	4,050	19	10,366	7	5,360
Midland			13	11,550		
					6	1,776
North Midland			8	5,300		
East and West Riding	} 6	4,425	4	7,808	6	840
North-Western	5	5,800	13	5,537	6	1,902
Northern	}	12,600	3	3,050	6	1,180
Scotland	2				26	15,100
			6	4,450		
Wales and Monmouthshire					15	4,432
Total	33	49,575	174	159,645	99	36,980

Note
1 Excluding Northern Ireland.

Table 3.2 shows that, up to 1914, London and the South-East and the North-West regions attracted between them the majority of US firms. The high employment figure for Scotland is made up almost entirely of the (contemporary) labour force of the Singer Sewing Machine Co. Ltd.[7] Investments at this time were mainly in the heavy-metal-using industries, and tended to follow the normal locational pattern, except that, for obvious reasons, proximity to an Atlantic port was of more than average importance. Undoubtedly, this was one of the main factors making for the attractiveness of the Trafford Park estate to American investors in the early 1900s, on or around which at least eight US subsidiaries (including the Ford and Westinghouse companies) built their plants. Even in these years, however, the pull of London as a market and distributing centre was strong, particularly to the newer and lighter industries then springing up, e.g. musical instruments, pharmaceutical preparations, foundation garments, canned foods, photographic equipment, etc.

Between 1919 and 1939, industrial growth in Britain was most pronounced in the southern regions, and in keeping with this trend, nearly two-thirds of all the new US factories established during these years were sited in London and South-East and the Southern Area. It was now the lighter engineering, motor-car, precision instrument and consumer goods industries which were proving attractive to American investors. At the same time, the movement towards planned industrial conurbations was getting under way, and between 1925 and 1938, nearly forty American branch manufacturing units were set up in three of these, viz. (1)

on or around the (a) Great West Road and (b) North Circular Road, (2) Welwyn Garden City and (3) Slough. It is worth noting that during the inter-war years, two-thirds of the new US affiliates were set up to supply consumer or consumer/ capital goods as compared with 40 per cent prior to 1914.

Since the end of the Second World War, UK government policy, as exercised through the Distribution of Industry Acts 1945 and 1950, has played a major role in influencing the geographical siting of new factories. Industrialists intending to erect buildings over 10,000 sq. ft in area have been required to obtain Board of Trade approval. Control has also been exercised through the selective granting of building licences and planning permission under the Town and Country Planning Acts. By such measures as these and the provision of incentives in the form of first-class modern factory accommodation at subsidized rents, cheaper service costs, investment allowances and favoured raw material allocations (the latter an important consideration in early post-war years), post-war-established factories have been persuaded to produce in the newly created Development Areas. These are the successors of the pre-war Special or Distressed Areas, such as South Wales, North-East England, South Lancashire, West Cumberland and Mid-Scotland, the economic prosperity of which was almost entirely dependent on the basic industries of coal, iron and steel, and shipbuilding, then suffering from unemployment well above the national average.[8] In addition to, and in some cases more important than, these government measures, the high costs and scarcity of labour and housing in the more traditional areas of manufacturing, especially London and the Midlands, has provided a direct economic inducement for firms to look elsewhere[9] for factory accommodation. Thus many of the newer and lighter industries have been drawn to the Development Areas, with the result that a certain measure of stability has been injected into the economies concerned.[10]

The above measures have affected both new American investors, and already-established US subsidiaries and Anglo-American firms desiring to expand their capacity. Of the 99 new US factories which have started manufacturing operations since 1940, 49 with a labour force of 18,000 are located in the Development Areas, and of the remainder, 26 are operating plants vacated by existing manufacturing concerns or already-established British firms, which have been taken over, or invested in, by US firms. Only the balance are supplying products from newly built factories outside the Development Areas. It should, perhaps, be noted that extensions of existing factories, which have been substantial, are not included in these calculations. In all, 58 US factories employing 36,800 (or 16.3 per cent of the total labour force) are at present situated in Development Areas in Britain. Sixty-one of the 99 post-war factories belong to those firms setting up in the UK for the first time, and of this number, the Development Areas claimed 29.

Among the Development Areas, the clustering of American-financed firms in Scotland has been especially marked – an area within a 15-mile radius of Glasgow and Dundee claiming nearly two-thirds of the increase in the total labour force of the scheduled regions since 1940. There would seem to be four main reasons for this. First, a high proportion (nearly 75 per cent) of the post-war employment expansion in US affiliates has been confined to the engineering industries, and the facilities offered by the Scottish Development Area – with its solid background of well-reputed skill in general engineering and shipbuilding – have been equal to, and generally more attractive than, those available in the other Development Areas. Second, the wooing of foreign investors by the Scottish Council has been in a class of its own, and the concentrated efforts made to attract US investment has far exceeded in quality and enthusiasm anything attempted either by the other Development Areas or the United Kingdom as a whole. By means of two special missions to America, and a regularly maintained organiza-tion in the United States, much has been done to further the diversification of the Scottish economy by the importation of new skills and manufacturing technolo-gies. Third, over a long period of time, a strong sense of kinship between Scotland and the United States has been built up. In particular the nineteenth-century export of goods, followed by the migration of labour and capital from Edinburgh and Glasgow to the US, helped further the early development of the New World and establish a sound commercial relationship between the two countries. Fourth, as an industrial location, Scotland, if somewhat distant from the main European markets, is well endowed with most industrial materials, has (or had) a reasonably plentiful labour supply, and is excellently placed in relation to world trade move-ments. Hence the attraction of this Development Area; of its recent American newcomers, seven out of ten are engineering firms, and many new trades and production techniques, e.g. electronic and precision engineering, watch and clock-making, etc., have been introduced.

The South Wales Development Area – largely because of its proximity to the main market centres and more traditional areas of manufacturing – has attracted more branches of existing US affiliates e.g. in the electrical appliances and chemical sectors, than first investors; of the fifteen factories set up in this region between 1940 and 1953, nine were branches of established firms. A few miscella-neous firms have also located their plants in the North-Eastern and North-Western Development Areas.[11]

For particular industries, the geographical location of American affiliates has tended to follow that of British firms. The twenty-three vehicle assembling and manufacturing and component factories are, without exception, concentrated in the Midlands and the South, and all within a radius of two hundred miles of each other. As for the balance of the engineering industry, the Mid-Scottish industrial region now produces the major part of the UK output of office machinery and sewing machines, the North Midlands is the traditional home of the boot and shoe industry, while the East and West Ridings of Yorkshire tend to attract the greatest number of the agricultural machinery factories. The earlier established electrical equipment firms were almost entirely confined to the Midlands and the North-West, but over the years the centre of this industry has tended to gravitate southwards. Apart from these cases, however, the spatial distribution of American-owned firms is fairly evenly spread. Firms within the food and drink, clothing, metal manufacturing and chemical industries are widely dispersed, though within this latter group, three-fifths of the pharmaceutical and cosmetic factories are sited in the London and South-Eastern Region. Similarly, the industrial and precision instrument subsidiaries, apart from a certain clustering around the Birmingham and London areas, are located in several parts of Britain. The two American-owned oil refineries are situated on Southampton Water and the Thames Estuary.

Within these broad geographical regions, there can be little doubt that US firms have often played an important role in the economy of their immediate vicinity. In quite a few cases it so happens that the US subsidiary is one of the largest employers in its particular area, drawing heavily on the local labour supply, and making available many thousands of pounds of spending money every week, e.g. Ford at Dagenham, Ideal Boilers at Kingston-upon-Hull, Vauxhall at Luton, Briggs Motor Bodies and Esso Petroleum at Southampton, British United Shoe Machinery Company at Leicester, Goodyear at Wolverhampton, and so on. For example, as the Ford and general Motor Companies have developed in the UK, so other US firms, who in America were supplying the parent organizations of these subsidiaries with components and parts, have found it profitable to set up their own branch units to perform a similar function: clearly, other things being equal, the location of such factories is largely predetermined from the start. Similarly, with the expansion of the UK oil refineries, many related industries have been established and in such cases the firms in question have tried to site themselves as near to their customers as possible, both to obtain technical economies and to avoid unnecessary transport costs. Accordingly, most of the main refinery equipment manufacturers today are located in the Midlands or the South of England.[12]

On the whole, then, the locational pattern of US firms in the UK is broadly comparable to that of British industry as a whole. Though there may have been a few isolated cases where the decision to locate a factory was taken hastily without full knowledge or appreciation of the facts, the siting of American plants largely accords with what one might suppose. The only exception is that where subsidiaries are likely to rely heavily on imports from their parent company, or have been established in the United Kingdom with the prime objective of serving the entire non-dollar market, in these cases there has been a tendency for them to value a location near a major port rather more highly than the average British firm. In support of this argument, it is interesting to note that, in 1953, 60 per cent of all the US manufacturing plants were sited within thirty miles of the five major ports of London, Liverpool, Southampton, Glasgow and Cardiff.

THE SIZE DISTRIBUTION OF US FIRMS AND PLANTS

In January 1954, the average number of people employed by a British manufacturing establishment employing over eleven people was 125.[13] The distribution, however, was unevenly dispersed; nearly 85 per cent of the 56,000 establishments employed less than 100 workers, and only 1,049 – less than 2 per cent of the total – had a labour force of more than 1,000. On the other hand, of the total numbers employed, 45 per cent was concentrated in firms employing more than 750 workers. While, then, there were a very large number of small establishments, in 1953 the medium- and larger-sized concerns accounted for much the larger

Table 3.3 Size distribution of US-owned plants and all UK plants[1]

Employees	US firms (Dec. 1953)			UK firms (Jan. 1954)		
	No. of establishments	No. of employees	% of total employees	No. of establishments	No. of employees	% of total employees
11–24 } 25–49 }	10	300	0.1	16,521	285,000	3.9
				25,225	1,258,000	16.9
50–99	16	1,100	0.5			
100–249	80	12,400	5.0			
250–499	82	25,200	10.2	11,902	2,487,000	33.5
500–999	56	37,900	15.4	1,510	1,034,000	13.9
1,000–1,999	31	45,100	18.3	685	941,000	12.7
2,000–4,999	20	50,700	20.6			
Over 5,000	8	73,500	29.9	364	1,422,000	19.1
Total	303	246,200[2]	100.0	56,207	7,427,000	100.0

Source of UK data: Annual Abstract of Statistics, 1955.
Notes:
1 As in other tables US subsidiaries located in Northern Ireland are excluded from our analysis.
2 Figures rounded to nearest 100. There are three US firms with less than eleven employees.

proportion of employment. In contrast, the average number employed by a US-financed plant was 799. One in every six factories had a labour force of 1,000 workers or more, and the 28 largest establishments – each employing more than 2,000 people – accounted for 50.5 per cent of the total labour force. Compared to UK manufacturing industry in general, fewer than one in ten production units gave employment to less than 100 workers. Table 3.3 sets out these details.

To be sure, this is not an entirely fair comparison as no allowance is made for the unique industrial structure of American investment. For, as must be apparent from the nature of the products already described, representation is most marked in those industries where, for one reason or another, the average size of the establishment tends to be large. Allowing for this, the differences in size composition become less significant. Yet, even so, it is the rule rather than the exception that the size of the American manufacturing unit is larger than the average UK plant, as Table 3.4 clearly shows.

Turning from the *establishment* to the *firm* – which is essentially the unit of coordination, control and decision-taking – we see that the average US subsidiary, or Anglo-American firm, employed 1,201 people, at the end of 1953. In terms of the proportion of industrial output supplied by the three largest firms, concentration is greatest in the motor-car, rubber-tyre, agricultural machinery, oil refining and printing machinery industries, and least in the pharmaceutical, toilet requisite and clothing trades. The range of dispersion between the largest and smallest US-financed firm is most pronounced in the chemical industry. Of the thirty-two US enterprises which employed over 2,000 people at the end of 1953, five were in the chemical industry, twelve in engineering, three in food, drink and tobacco, four in

Table 3.4 Comparative size of US-owned and all manufacturing plants in the UK, selected industries

Industry	US firms (Dec. 1953)			UK firms (Jan. 1954)
	No. of plants	Employ.	Size of average plant	Size of average plant
Abrasives	5	4,000	800	192*
Agricultural machinery	5	4,600	920	64
Chemicals and dyes	14	6,300	450	255*
Industrial, optical and scientific instruments	14	7,600	543	108
Motor vehicles (including the manufacture of components and parts)	23	56,000	2,345	390
Office machinery	18	10,700	594	250†
Petroleum refining	6	6,500	1,083	700
Pharmaceutical products and toilet requisites[1]	38	12,300	324	161
Refrigeration machinery	4	3,500	875	450†
Rubber products	5	11,000	2,200	337
Telephone and telegraph apparatus	7	14,000	2,000	960
All industries	139	136,500	982	235 (appx.)

Source of UK statistics: Ministry of Labour, except for figures marked * which are derived from Trade Association data, and † from Census of Production data (1953).
Note
1 Including cosmetics.

motor vehicles, three in metal manufacturing, three in rubber and two in the precision instruments and photographic equipment industry.

Again, in relation to their UK competitors, no less than twenty-nine US firms were the largest employers in their particular industry. Included in this number were firms in the motor vehicle, boot and shoe machinery, razor-blade, breakfast cereal, vacuum cleaner, synthetic detergent, kitchen cutlery-ware, starch, sewing-machine, typewriter, fire extinguisher, lock, foundation garment and photographic equipment industries. Each of another thirty enterprises, manufacturing agricultural tractors, rubber tyres, refrigerators, abrasives, motor vehicles, refined petroleum, electric switches, pneumatic tools, surgical products, agricultural implements, cosmetics and lifts, etc., was among the three largest employers in their sector.

As might be expected, those firms which have been established in the UK for the longest time also tend to be amongst the largest. For example, thirty-seven of the fifty-five firms employing over 1,000 people were set up before 1929, and as Table 3.5 shows the average size of branch subsidiaries and Anglo-American concerns gradually falls as the date of establishment becomes more recent. On

Table 3.5 Date of establishment of US manufacturing affiliates in Britain

Date of establishment	No. of firms	1953 employment	% of total	Average no. employed	No. of firms employing over 1,000
Up to 1900	8	34,800	14.1	4,350	8
1901–14	23	80,400	32.7	3,496	13
1915–29	46	56,800	23.1	1,245	17
1930–39	64	51,600	20.8	806	13
1940–53	59	21,300	8.7	361	4
Not specified	5	1,300	0.5	260	–
Total	205	246,200	100.0	1,201	55

the other hand, Table 3.6 shows that the rate of expansion of pre-war-originated factories has been no greater than that since 1945, as only twenty-three, or less than half the firms employing 1,000 people or more in 1953, employed that number in 1939. The average size of these companies in that latter year was about 602, compared with the then average size for all of UK industry of 135.

The economic implications of these structural developments will be examined in more detail in Chapter 6. Suffice it to note at this stage the four main reasons why US firms within the same industrial group are larger than their native competitors.

First, in many instances, American firms were themselves the first, or among the first, companies to manufacture a particular product, or group of products, in the United Kingdom. Such has been particularly the case in the sewing machine, telecommunication, cigarette-lighter, toilet preparations, pharmaceutical and

Table 3.6 Distribution of US manufacturing affiliates by size groups, 1939 and 1953

	1939			1953		
	No. of firms	Employ.	% of all employment	No. of firms	Employ.	% of all employment
1–49	10	250	0.3	10	300	0.1
50–99	16	950	1.1	14	1,100	0.4
100–249	32	5,200	5.9	43	6,300	2.6
250–499	14	5,200	5.9	44	13,400	5.5
500–999	13	9,800	11.2	39	25,300	10.3
1,000–1,999	13	18,500	21.0	23	34,000	13.8
2,000–2,999	3	6,500	7.4	16	34,900	14.2
3,000–4,999	3	10,500	12.0	7	25,000	10.2
5,000 and over	4	26,000	29.6	9	105,900	43.0
Not classified	38	5,000[1]	5.7	–	–	–
Total	146	87,900	100.0	205	246,200	100.0

Note:
1 Estimated.

food products industries. Consolidating an initial lead and often protected by patents or by technological and financial difficulties facing potential competitors, in only one instance, to our knowledge, have such firms been surpassed in size by UK firms, save where mergers have taken place.

Second, over the course of years, US branch manufacturing units and Anglo-American concerns have tended to enlarge the volume of their output more rapidly than have their competitors, and, in consequence, have increased their share of the total market. In answer to the question posed to our respondent firms: 'Has your share of the UK market for your type of product(s) (a) increased (b) decreased, or (c) remained constant since 1939?' of the US-financed firms producing in both 1939 and 1953, 55 per cent said it had increased, 33 per cent said it had remained constant and 12 per cent said it had decreased. In most industries in which there was any US representation before the Second World War, American affiliates would appear to have increased their market shares. In some instances, e.g. in the oil refining, carbon black and office machinery industries, this movement has been primarily at the expense of goods previously imported, as the actual amount of manufacturing carried out in 1939 was small, and, in the main, confined to purely finishing operations. But in others, e.g. in the motor-car, rubber-tyre, abrasive, cosmetics, foodstuffs, soft drink, soap and razor-blade industries – all well established in the UK before the war – there has been a definite expansion in the market share held by US affiliates of the total British output supplied.

In a wide range of other industries, including those supplying cinematic films, sewing machines, breakfast cereals, hardboard, foundation garments, pencils and pens and oil drilling equipment, US firms have maintained their relative position without increasing it, while fifteen firms, e.g. in the portable electric tool, agricultural tractor, refrigerator and metal manufacturing industries, said that their share of the market had fallen, but argued that this was mainly because they were the sole producers in 1939 of their particular products, the demand for which had expanded rapidly since that date.

Third, the great majority of the American subsidiaries operating in Britain are branches of very large United States' corporations. Of these, some were set up specifically to supply the British and export markets which had previously been satisfied by the parent company. In such cases the subsidiary had waiting for it a ready-made market of not inconsiderable size, e.g. in the radio, office equipment, refrigeration machinery, industrial instrument industries. The fact that the American associate is more likely than not to be one of the foremost producers in its particular industry (over one-quarter of the 200 largest US corporations had manufacturing affiliations in the United Kingdom at the end of 1954) means that managerial decision-taking will tend to be in terms of fairly large production and sales targets.

Fourth, there tends to be a certain minimum size below which the establishment of a branch manufacturing unit will not be considered worthwhile. This, for obvious reasons, is likely to be larger when looked at from the viewpoint of a potential overseas investor and tends to vary according to the size of the parent organization. Only three US subsidiaries, for example, in our sample, employed less than ten people, and all of these subcontracted the bulk of their output to British firms. Certainly, one of the big difficulties associated with the organization of US branch plant enterprises in the UK has been the scaling down of US managerial perceptions, and the adaptation of US-designed products to suit British economic and cultural needs.

Finally, it would be true to say that there is no marked contrast between the degree of product specialization practised by the average American firm and its UK counterpart. Just over 55 per cent of the subsidiaries might be described as being *multi-product* inasmuch as they are turning out products which either require substantially different manufacturing techniques or serve distinctly separate markets. This figure would not be greatly different from that for UK industry as a whole, making due allowances for the type of products supplied and size of firm. In specialized cases, however, e.g. in the ethical drug industry, there is a tendency for certain subsidiaries to be rather more specialized in their product range than their indigenous competitors.

PATTERNS OF OWNERSHIP IN US-FINANCED FIRMS

Table 3.7 shows how far American branches once established in this country retain their parentage or are absorbed by British capital. Once more, it should be noted that these figures represent not the actual number of firms established during this time, but only those which were still financed, wholly or partially, by US capital in December 1953. Hence, the figures do not necessarily correspond to those given in Chapter 1. For example, during the course of their development a large number of US-originated firms have either been liquidated or taken over by British interests. Over and above this long-term trend, however, particular periods, viz. 1929–33 and 1945–50, for reasons already described, have seen especially large capital repatriations.

Of those subsidiaries established before the First World War, only a comparatively small number – between 30 per cent and 40 per cent – are still American, or indeed exist at all. Yet those firms which have remained under US financial control now employ nearly half of the total labour force. A larger number of those firms which first set up British factories between 1915 and 1929 have retained their American interests, and over three-quarters of those established during the 1930s. Employment within this latter group has particularly expanded since the Second World War, and now accounts for something over one-fifth of all those employed in American firms. Of the post-1940 firms, almost all are still US-controlled today, though their average size is relatively small, and their contribution to the total labour force is less than 10 per cent. This latter figure does not take into account the newly established plants of those firms which were operating before the war, but only the employment of post-war-originated subsidiaries and Anglo-American firms or existing British firms, in which American capital has been invested since 1940.

Table 3.7 Numbers employed (December 1953) and US equity stake in UK firms, by date of establishment

% of US equity stake	No. of firms	Pre-1914	No. of firms	1915–29	No. of firms	1930–9	No. of firms	1940–53	No. of firms	Total employment
25–40	⎱7	⎱62,400	⎱5	⎱5,200	⎱4	⎱3,100	⎱6	⎱1,000	3	2,100
41–60									19	69,600
61–80	5	34,500	5	7,000	9	10,900	⎱5	⎱1,100	21	53,100
81–99	3	5,800	4	1,400	⎱51	⎱37,600			11	7,600
Fully owned[1]	16	12,500	32	43,200			48	19,200	146	112,500
Total	31	115,200	46	56,800	64	51,600	59	21,300	200	244,900
Approximate number of US subsidiaries etc., which actually set up manufacturing units during this period	80–90		80–90		75–80		60–65			

Notes:
1 Including nine branches employing 4,800 people.
N.B. Five firms did not give information of the kind requested.

The same trend is revealed when one relates the percentage of equity share-holding held by the US company to the date of establishment of the branch concern. Of the thirty-one US-financed firms operating in December 1953, which were established prior to 1914, only sixteen, employing one-sixth of the group's total labour force, were still completely American-owned. Yet, of the balance, twelve *originated* as 100 per cent US-financed subsidiaries. The proportion of fully-owned subsidiaries, however, is shown to increase as the establishment date becomes more recent. For example, we see that such firms account for 70 per cent of the branch units set up between 1919 and 1929 – while, for the most recently originated subsidiaries, the proportion rises to 81 per cent. In contrast, up to 1939, the number of Anglo-American holdings tends to fall, though since 1945 this trend has been reversed.

It seems then, that, as a general rule, US-affiliated firms in the UK start out as fully owned subsidiaries, but with the passing of years, as the subsidiaries become more experienced and embedded in the local economy, they gradually secure additional capital from British sources, and/or surrender their American paren-tage. Should the branch concern be incorporated as a British public company, it may obtain new capital – especially non-equity capital – from the new issues market; if it is a private company, then there may well be a transference of interests to British hands, accompanied by an increase in the number of UK directors.

In some cases, it may be the deliberate and predetermined policy of the parent firm to set its subsidiary on its feet and then leave it to develop independently. In others, detailed control is planned right the way through. Those subsidiaries which supply identical, or near identical, products to those of their parent con-cerns, engage upon similar manufacturing methods, rely heavily on American research and development expertise, and supply export markets previously served from the United States, usually tend to be 100 per cent American-owned, while those in which product or process adaptations are necessary because of different market or supply conditions in the UK often gain some financial independence from their US parents.

Whether in fact an American parent concern does decide to establish a *wholly-owned* manufacturing subsidiary, and if it does, the extent to which it retains full financial control as the years pass principally depends on its attitude and interpretation of the functions of ownership, and the various factors associated with the day-to-day organization and the operation of the branch plant. These are discussed in more detail in the following chapter.

4 The structure and organization of US affiliates in Britain

Financial and managerial supervision of branch units

We have now to answer two further questions: (1) What are the main forms which US financial participation in British industry take? and (2) what is the character and degree of managerial control exercised by American parent concerns over their UK subsidiaries?

Concerning the former, apart from the *agency* or *representative*, the principal purpose of which is to establish market or distribution outlets, and the *licensing agreement* which, in its purest form, is unaccompanied by any investment of capital, there are four main forms of organization which an American company may choose as its medium for a British investment:

1 The *branch house* of an American corporation which does not maintain a separate existence of its own, and is not incorporated in the United Kingdom. The main difference between this form of organization and the incorporated subsidiary, is that its earnings are treated as those of a foreign company and taxed accordingly.[1] With the high rate of marginal taxation now prevailing in Britain, this form of investment has lost many of its earlier attractions, and though one might suppose that the functional organization or managerial set-up is strongly US-controlled, this is not always the case. Only nine firms within our survey – among them Yale and Towne, Parke-Davis and Art Metal (established post-1945) – were identified as branch houses. With an unincorporated foreign subsidiary, no distinction is made in the balance sheet of the parent concern between its domestic and foreign operations.

2 The *wholly-owned US subsidiary* where the entire equity capital is held by a US corporation, and which is a formally incorporated British company. As such, it is subject to normal UK taxation, with the exception that – and this applies to all cases where the US interest is 51 per cent or more – the distributed profits tax payable on all profits over £12,000 is 3 per cent, and not 30 per cent as for a UK company. Earned profits transmitted back to the US are thus taxed at $42\frac{1}{2}$ per cent, plus a 3 per cent distribution charge.

A 100 per cent US subsidiary might be originated either by the establishment of a completely new company by its American parent – 121 firms in our sample were of this kind – or by the acquisition of an existing British firm. Eighteen US subsidiaries now operating were founded in this way: these include Thomas Hedley Ltd, purchased by Procter and Gamble, and more recently Alfred Bird and Sons Ltd, acquired by the General Food Corporation in 1947. In a number of cases, the acquisition has been accompanied by an exchange of share capital between the firms involved, e.g. in 1955, the Ever-Ready Razor Products Ltd purchased the share capital of Pal Personna Blades Ltd.

3 A *jointly owned Anglo-American-originated company*, of which there are two forms:

(a) An American corporation may join with a British firm – both of which are likely to be in the same line of business – to form a new subsidiary, each company supplying part of the equity capital: this form of joint enterprise has been quite common since the war, and fifteen firms in our sample fell into this category. Of these, British Geon Ltd is 55 per cent owned by the Distillers Co. Ltd (UK) and 45 per cent by B. F. Goodrich Chemical Co. (US); Marinite Ltd is a joint-subsidiary of Cape Asbestos Mining Co. (UK) and Johns Manville Co (US); Esterbrook Hazell Pens Ltd is owned by the Hazell Watson and Viney Ltd (UK) and Esterbrook Pen Co. (US).

(b) Alternatively, an American firm may invest, or buy a part shareholding in an existing British manufacturing concern. Twelve firms of this kind, including Jacobs Manufacturing Co. Ltd (49 per cent US-owned), were included in our survey. The impetus for either or both these kinds of investment may come from Britain or America. For example, it may be that a US company will only allow access to its research and manufacturing techniques, or give permission for its patents to be exploited, if it is given a part-financial interest in the British company. Thus, in the Willys-Overland Crossley deal of 1919, the Willys-Overland patents were exchanged for cash and a majority of common stock of the new company.[2] Sometimes a part-financial interest may become a fully-owned one later on – Monsanto's interest in the UK Monsanto Chemical Company is a case in point[3] – but more usually, unless the British company is purchased outright, the US shareholding is likely to remain a *minority* one. Particularly since the two world wars this form of organization has been favoured by US and UK firms.

4 A *partly-financed American subsidiary*. Though similar to (3) above, we have confined this classification to cover either those US firms which originated as fully-owned subsidiaries, but which have since become partly UK-owned – usually by raising additional finance on the new issues market – or those which are financed by direct investment from the US and from the UK capital market. Thirty firms in our enquiry were of this class, of which the Ford, North British Rubber, Bakelite and Singer companies were typical examples. In point of fact, it is usual for such companies to be wholly-owned from the start, and later to become partly UK-financed. Some countries, indeed (though not the United Kingdom), make it a legal requirement that no foreign firm should be allowed 100 per cent control.

The amount of capital invested and taxation policy are perhaps the two main determinants of the form of subsidiary organization adopted, and hence the degree of control exercised by the parent concern. The choice between acquiring a 100 per cent interest in a going concern, and that of establishing a completely new manufacturing unit, is partly a question of convenience and the availability of the right factory at the right time; partly one of finance – usually the outright purchase of an existing company involves less initial outlay, and in any case can be paid for in various ways; and partly one of time – it is often possible to get production under way more quickly in an existing factory than if a completely new one has to be built. Over and above these factors, however, a number of other considerations are also important. In particular – (a) the nature of the manufacturing process, the extent to which it is complete, and the type of products turned out, (b) the organizational philosophy of and the degree of decision-making influence exerted by the American parent concern, and its experience of, and attitude towards, foreign production, (c) the economic conditions prevailing in both the investing country and the country of investment, (d) the restrictions placed on the extent of US participation in industry by the UK government (e) the advantages associated with a smaller capital risk, plus the benefit of the experiences of local owners and (f) political circumstances – may each have an effect on the extent of financial control exerted by the investing company, and deserve especial mention.

Moreover, the majority of the US parent companies are loath to invest capital apart from the initial outlay, which has often to be raised internally. In some cases, even the original investment takes the form of plant and equipment, and as post-war capital movements show only too well, additional capital is mostly obtained from profits ploughed back by the UK subsidiaries. This attitude has often meant that additional sources of capital have had to be obtained from UK investors. Most of the larger US subsidiaries, e.g. Kodak, Hoover, Hedley, Ideal Boilers, etc., have grown almost entirely out of their own undistributed earnings. Official data as to the extent of capital repatriation are scant, and only reliable for post-war years. However, as Table 3.7 in Chapter 3 has illustrated, sizeable outflows of capital have occurred, and these primarily from firms of early origins who have either (1), for one reason or another, lost interest in their British subsidiary, e.g. as in the case of Florence Stoves, Worthington Simpson, Bristol Instruments, and, being attracted by an offer from the British directors, have sold their equity stakes, or (2) have unfavourably viewed the likely outlook for their investments, e.g. Lincoln Electric Co. Ltd, Martindale Electric Co. Ltd. More often than not, however, the absolute US shareholding is maintained, while control is gradually relinquished as new capital is raised within the United Kingdom.

For fiscal and administrative reasons, however, many American companies prefer to maintain a 100 per cent financial control over their subsidiaries. This situation is by no means unique to US investments in British manufacturing industry. In other countries and in other investment categories, joint participation is less common, and generally less desired by investing companies, than full ownership.

There are few reliable official statistics of the capital and corporate structure of US-financed firms in Britain. We have seen that the average investment by a US subsidiary in manufacturing industry has risen from $1¼ million in 1929 to $4 million in 1953.[4] As mentioned, however, no attempt has been made to obtain detailed financial statistics from individual companies since preference was given to other criteria in assessing the contribution of these firms to the British economy. However, some details of the asset structure of US companies in Britain were given in the 1950 Census of Overseas Assets.[5] In that year, the *total* net assets of US-controlled firms in UK manufacturing, i.e. fixed plus circulating assets minus current liabilities, totalled $1,137 million, of which the US share was $822.3 million. Comprising the (US) liabilities, common or equity stock accounted for $315.7 million, earned surplus $283.5 million, surplus reserves $117.4 million, and inter-company accounts, debentures and mortgages, the balance. Of the UK liabilities, the greater part was directed to interest-bearing securities or second preference shares, rather than voting stock. From the credit side of the picture, fixed assets in US direct investment enterprises amounted to $560 million, and circulating (or current) assets to $2,889 million.

In terms of net assets, the ten largest US-financed manufacturing units in 1954 were Esso Petroleum, Ford Motor, British United Shoe Machinery, Monsanto Chemical, Vacuum Oil, Vauxhall Motor, Kodak, Hoover, Standard Telephones and Cables and Goodyear Tyre and Rubber. Their combined net assets were then worth $500 million or 53 per cent of the US capital stake in UK manufacturing industry. Add to these investments the capital value of the next fifteen largest companies, and share of the leading twenty-five US investors rises to 70 per cent. Thus, with an average investment stake of $26 million, the top 10 per cent of American firms assume great weight in relationship to the remainder, the average net assets of which were $1¼ million in 1954.

There is no need for us to go into further detail about exactly how American investment originates.[6] Chapter 1 has already outlined some of the main forces leading to the establishment of US branch enterprises in the UK. The great majority of the more recently established manufacturing subsidiaries have evolved from existing sales and trading ventures, selling US products. In some cases, US patents have been exchanged for a shareholding in the UK concern – the Parsons Chain and Marinite companies started in this way – while in others, a financial stake has wholly or partly taken the form of specialized machinery and plant shipped over from the US associate, e.g. Jacobs Manufacturing Co. Ltd. When the Yale and Towne Manufacturing Co. (US) bought H. and T. Vaughan Ltd (UK) in 1929, it paid in terms of shares of its own common stock valued at $1.5 million.[7] In such cases as these – which are comparatively rare – there is no net increase in direct investment, though American participation in British industry has been extended. And as has been noted, as far as the American parent company is concerned, such investment is usually financed out of existing profits, though, where the sum involved is very large, new capital may be floated on the American market.

The comparative advantages of 100 per cent and joint participation vary according to individual circumstances, and it is difficult to give any general ruling. However, we may perhaps note in this respect the conclusions of Professor Barlow in his study of the operation of US manufacturing subsidiaries in Mexico. Substantially, these words can be generalized to apply to branch units in the UK:

> Those companies that have preferred to share ownership in foreign subsidiaries with others have typically done so because of (1) the smaller capital investment and the limitation of risk (2) the fear of discrimination against United States' companies and (3) the belief that local owners bring assets to the company (such as local experience, certain skills, physical facilities and a growing organization), that are difficult for the United States' parent to duplicate . . . Against this must be set the biggest advantage of 100 per cent ownership is that all profits go to the parent organization and it need share control with no one.[8]

Finally, as regards corporate structure, apart from *individual undertakings* and *partnerships* which are virtually non-existent in manufacturing industry, three basic types may be considered:

1 The *branch concern*. The features of this form of business unit have already been described. However, notwithstanding the fact that there is no incorporation in the UK, a branch concern must file with the Registrar of Companies, within a month of establishment, a certified copy of its Charter or Certificate of Incorporation and By-laws, a list of its directors and secretary, its balance sheet and profit and loss account, and the names of one or more persons in Great Britain authorized to accept service of process on its behalf. In addition, it must file annual financial statements thereafter, and particulars of any change in its Board of Directors or statutes.

2 The *private company*. This is one of the most important forms of business organization where its members have the advantage of limited liability, but where the shares are not quoted on the Stock Exchange and capital is raised privately. The number of shareholders is limited to fifty, and a corporate structure of this kind must not invite the public to subscribe for shares or debentures. Under the Companies Act, 1948, an English private company must file accounts if a body corporate is a director or holds any of its shares or controls its policy. Accordingly, unless exempted for special reasons, a subsidiary of an American corporation is bound to file its UK accounts. The great majority of US subsidiaries and Anglo-American concerns are of this nature – 178 out of our sample of 205.

3 The *public company*. Sometimes private companies are 'floated off' and converted into public companies, where there is no limitation on the number of members who may subscribe to the share and debenture capital (though the minimum number is seven) and there are no restrictions on advertising. Shares may, or may not, be quoted on the Stock Exchange. As in the case of most private companies, a public company has to file an annual balance sheet with the Registrar of Companies. In general, English law contains no restrictions

against aliens holding shares (apart from compliance with the exchange
Control Act, 1947), or against aliens forming the Board of Directors: in theory,
all the shareholders and all the directors of a British company may be American, though, in practice, it is usual to issue at least a single share to each of two
persons resident in Britain, and to appoint persons resident in Britain to the
Board of Directors in sufficient numbers to establish a local quorum, thus
enabling a shareholders' meeting and a directors' meeting to be held conveniently in Britain. As might be expected, it is usually the larger US-affiliated
firms which are public companies: of the eighteen covered in our survey, the
smallest employs over 500 people, and in all, such firms account for one-third
of the total US labour force.

It is not proposed to discuss in further detail the legal factors associated with the
operation of US firms in the UK: these are adequately dealt with elsewhere.[9] It is
also felt that any further analysis of the taxation of overseas subsidiaries would also
be outside the scope of this book. As has already been observed, there is no
discrimination in either respect on the grounds of nationality of ownership; a
foreign-owned company, once established in the UK, becomes a resident concern
and is treated in exactly the same way as British companies. In certain instances (e.g.
in respect of distributed profits), the treatment is more favourable. Against this, a
non-corporated branch of a US company is treated as a foreign firm and taxed as
such. In all other cases, 'double taxation', e.g. taxation by both the UK and US
governments is avoided by the Washington Convention of 1946.[10] Finally, no
attempt is made to examine the many and varied ways by which the parent company
may be able to derive financial benefits from its overseas assets e.g. by transfer price
manipulation, apart from the profits and dividends it earns, and the royalties
and fees it receives from the technical and administrative services provided.

FORMS OF MANAGERIAL CONTROL[11]

There is no common pattern to which the day-to-day organization of US-financed
firms conforms, nor the degree of supervision exercised by their parent. Overall
managerial and administrative control is sometimes exercised through a special
overseas or export division of supervising and co-ordinating branch plant activities
outside America, and ensuring a proper flow of information between the parent
and foreign units – e.g. as is the case in such organizations as Colgate-Palmolive
Ltd, Vauxhall Motors Ltd and the International Chemical Co. Ltd. More usually,
however, and especially where the opportunities and challenges faced by the
subsidiary are rather different from those faced by the parent company, the
Managing Director of the branch subsidiary is directly responsible to the President or to a specially appointed Regional Controller of the parent organization
– in practice usually the Vice-President. Where the foreign activities of the
American company are important, a sizeable staff is usually required. In large
subsidiaries it is also common to find departmental heads being directly responsible to their opposite numbers in America. Clearly, when a US company has

many overseas branches, each interrelated to the others in manufacturing or sales policy, some overall co-ordination and integration is necessary, if only to ensure an adequate and efficient communication between the individual subsidiaries. For example, some parent firms and overseas branches specialize according to product or stage of manufacturing, and each is reliant on the other, either for its supplies or for its markets. Centralization of policy is likely to be required in respect of research and development, to rule whether or not each subsidiary should confine its facilities either to a particular aspect of, or kind of research. Decisions relating to marketing and advertising procedures must also be co-ordinated at this level, and a uniformity of administrative and accounting procedure achieved. The parent concerns of one in six US-financed firms in the UK have other foreign plants, and there is no doubt that the latter are more closely controlled from America than those which are the sole overseas organizations.

The actual supervision of the foreign subsidiary and the degree of autonomy which it is allowed will depend upon the attitude of the parent company towards retaining decision-making control, and those questions already mentioned, e.g. the date of establishment, extent of financial interest, environmental factors in the country of operation, and so on. Almost without exception, both wholly-owned US subsidiaries and Anglo-American concerns had US citizens on their Board of Directors. In 30 per cent of the firms, half – or more than half – of the Board were American; in 45 per cent of cases more than a quarter, and only in 2 per cent of firms (where there was a very low US shareholding) was there no US representation at all. The extent to which day-to-day departmental, managerial and operational practices are a reproduction of their US counterparts will be further discussed in subsequent chapters. For the moment, however, we shall examine only the question of general policy and control exercised by the parent concern.

The firms included in our survey were asked the following question: 'Do you consider that the administration, operation and overall management techniques adopted by your British plant(s) are (a) strongly (b) partly, or (c) negligibly controlled by your American parent or associate company?' We defined a *type (a)* relationship as one in which both the organization and internal administration of the British affiliate follow very closely that of its US parent or associate, and in which, either the top-ranking managerial executives are American nationals, or the whole approach to decision-making was US-based. It also suggests that all decisions of any importance – apart from those associated with the day-to-day operation of the plant – and their means of implementation have to be referred back for approval to the American company, e.g. on matters such as finance and capital expenditure, changes in product range or design, prices and profit margins, production methods, sales estimates and sales budgets, advertising policy and recruitment of senior staff. In addition, copies of all Board Meeting minutes, regular statements – sometimes daily, but usually weekly – relating to production, finance and sales, have to be dispatched to the USA (one subsidiary in this category said it had to send copies of every letter written or received back to the US). As a matter of course, both American manufacturing techniques and managerial methods, such as those relating to production, purchasing, personnel, sales, advertising, etc., are (consciously) assimilated and rigidly adhered to wherever possible. Very frequent interchanges of personnel take place between the US and UK plants. In particular, management, production, costing, time and motion experts pay special visits wherever a change in departmental policy in America needs to be implemented in the branch plant. Export orders are often routed by the parent company and co-ordinated with its own and its other foreign subsidiaries, marketing strategies and production capacity.

In a *type (a)* relationship, the UK affiliate tends to be simply a replicate, or mouthpiece, of the parent company, having little autonomy or freedom of its own. Some American companies provide their subsidiaries with the most detailed operating manuals, which are regularly brought up to date and revised. More often than not, all fundamental research and development is centralized in the US, and only a limited amount of applied or developmental research is carried out by the subsidiary; sometimes, in fact, this is discouraged. A number of UK companies within this group commented that any new ideas or suggestions (e.g. in respect of product design, manufacturing techniques, etc.) which it might put forward to its US parent were squashed or treated with the greatest suspicion, and rarely – if ever – acted upon. Finally, it is, perhaps, worth noting that not all the firms within this category are subsidiaries of large US corporations. The degree of parental supervision is equally seen in a number of small subsidiaries in the pharmaceutical and toilet preparation industries. However, in these latter instances, the control of the branch plant is very much in the hands of a particular individual – usually the Managing Director – who is invariably on the Board of Directors of the parent concern.

A *type (b)* relationship covers a wide range of firms which are only partially controlled by their US associate in the ways outlined above. There is less direct interference with the day-to-day organization of the British subsidiary, though any major decisions, particularly those involving large capital expenditures, e.g. over £10,000, or the introduction of new product designs, still have to be referred to corporate headquarters for approval. The administration of such firms may, or may not, be a copy of US procedures, though normally the Managing Director is allowed more flexibility and operating freedom, within the broad policy framework decided upon by the American company. As with *type (a)* firms, such affiliated manufacturing units invariably have to submit regular reports on their activities, but less frequently, and with fewer details; on the other hand, information and advice from the US in the form of specifications, drawings, technical sales and advertising literature, appear to be no less voluminous. In eight out of ten cases, as a result of the deliberate strategy by the US investing company, these firms are entirely British-staffed. This, however, does not preclude annual visits from US departmental heads, with senior UK production and marketing personnel frequently being sent to the parent company for training. A more appreciative viewpoint of the specialized needs of UK suppliers and customers, and a greater faith in the capabilities and judgement of the subsidiary's management, are other features of this type of company. Finally, most *type (b)* firms recognize the dangers inherent in any wholesale duplication of their parent plant's administrative, manufacturing or managerial techniques. Responsibility for decision-taking is delegated, and advice and guidance rather than orders are given, with respect to personnel, management and sales policies. In summary, a less hierarchical organizational structure and a higher degree of delegated autonomy distinguish a *type (b)* from a *type (a)* relationship.

A *type (c)* relationship typifies those US companies which have little or no interest in the administration and organization of their UK subsidiaries. Communication channels are poor, and, in general, are confined to technological and production matters. Regular exchange visits of top-ranking executives – a feature of the preceding two classes of firms – are noticeably absent, and although reports of some description (e.g. quarterly financial and sales statements) are usually required by the US associates of this type of company, there is a minimum of detailed control, and even important capital expenditure and policy decisions are often taken independently of American consultation. As long as the branch unit continues to make reasonable profits, it operates free from any US intrusion. It may, but more usually does not, *consciously* assimilate American managerial practices. Most of the jointly owned Anglo-American firms come within this category, as do those US partially financed subsidiaries which have been operating in Britain for many years, and which, for one reason or another, have lost touch with their parent concern. An extreme example of this relationship is summed up in the words of one executive: 'We never hear whether the US parent is satisfied with conditions over here; they simply leave us alone' or another, who said: 'Nobody in authority in the US has ever visited the UK subsidiary, nor has anybody from this country ever visited the parent factory.'

Within these three broad types of relationship, there are, of course, many variations and degrees, and in the final analysis, the borderline between 'the bottom' of *type (a)* and 'the top' of *type (b)*, and 'the bottom' of *type (b)* and 'the top' of *type (c)* must be subjective and arbitrary. *Type (b)* especially covers a very wide range of inter-firm relationships. In all, however, 150 US subsidiaries gave us information of this kind, and although there are obvious difficulties, we have attempted to classify them into one or other of these types. The results are as follows:

Type (a) Forty-nine firms (or 32.7 per cent of the sample) said that they were strongly controlled by their US associates. Of these, forty-two were fully-owned subsidiaries (or branches) and the remainder partially-owned subsidiaries; none, however, was a jointly owned Anglo-American concern. Twenty-seven of the subsidiaries of this type have only been established since 1940 – sixteen were set up between 1930 and 1939, and the remainder before 1930. In the case of twenty-three affiliates, the Managing Director was an American, and in twelve affiliates, US nationals were employed in other executive posts. Eighteen of the subsidiaries were among a number of US companies' overseas manufacturing units. In twenty-one cases, the products supplied by the parent company and by the subsidiary were identical, or near identical (although the UK affiliate usually produced a truncated range of products); while some twenty-three firms either competed with their parent organization in the export market, or sold to those countries which were previously supplied from America. Four of the above subsidiaries were public companies, forty private companies and five were branches.

Type (b) Of the fifty-nine firms (or 39.3 per cent of the sample) that said that they were partly controlled, forty-one were fully-owned subsidiaries and the remainder jointly operated Anglo-American concerns. Thirty-six of the fifty-nine firms were rather nearer the *type (a)* end of the scale, and twenty-three were towards *type (c)*. Fifty-two per cent of these firms were set up between 1925 and 1939, with the balance being fairly evenly spread over the remaining periods. In eleven subsidiaries, the Managing Director was an American, but only in three instances were other US executives employed. In this category, only 21 per cent of the firms had other overseas associations. In the main, there were more differences in the goods produced by the US and UK plants than in *type (a)* firms, and usually different export markets served. Ten of the above subsidiaries were public companies, forty-six private companies and three branches.

Type (c) Forty-two firms said that the control exercised by their US associate over managerial policy and plant organization was negligible. Of these, twenty-two were Anglo-American concerns or partly-owned US subsidiaries. Twenty-two subsidiaries were set up before 1929 – nine before 1914. In no instance was the Managing Director an American national, and with few exceptions the products produced in the US and UK factories differed markedly from one another. Three of the US-financed firms within this group were public companies and the remainder private companies.

As examples of subsidiaries which – to the best of our judgement – may be conveniently classified within the first category, we might cite Gillette Ltd, National Cash Register Ltd, Thomas Hedley Ltd, Caterpillar Tractor Ltd, Dictaphone Ltd, Kraft Foods Ltd, Goodyear Tyre and Rubber Co. Ltd, Elizabeth Arden Ltd, Remington Rand Co. Ltd, and Borg-Warner Ltd.

The second group is typified by such companies as Esso Petroleum Co. Ltd, Ford Motor Co. Ltd, International Chemical Co. Ltd, Kodak Ltd, Monsanto Chemicals Ltd, Platers and Stampers Ltd, Jantzen Ltd, Alfred Bird and Sons Ltd, Hoover Ltd, and Black and Decker Ltd.

The third type of relationship is evident in such firms as Singer Ltd, British United Shoe Machinery Co. Ltd, Standard Telephones and Cables Ltd, Waygood-Otis Ltd, Stanley Works Ltd, Jacobs Manufacturing Co. Ltd and Wayne Tank and Pump Ltd.

Classifying parent–branch relationships by the type of the products manufactured, US control appears to be most strongly exercised in the pharmaceutical, office machinery, rubber-tyre, foundation garments, toilet preparations and cosmetic industries; partially exercised in the motor-car, refrigerator, refined petroleum, food and drink, abrasive, film and agricultural machinery industries; and negligibly exercised in the industrial instrument, printing, boot and shoe, sewing machinery, machine tool and domestic electrical appliance industries.

To offer any definitive judgement as to which of the above three types of relationship has proved by experience to be the most successful would require more intensive investigation than this study has been able to give. Indeed, one suspects that if any conclusion is possible, it is that no hard and fast rules relating to the 'best' organization of US-financed firms or the 'most efficient' degree of parental control exercised can be laid down: each case must be judged on its own particular merits. Some tentative conclusions are, however, put forward in Chapters 5 and 9.

On the other hand, we may perhaps say with some confidence that US managerial and financial control is likely to be fairly rigid for the first five years or so of the subsidiary's life, with the branch unit being under the supervision of an American managing director in six cases out of ten. This is especially the case where similar markets are being served to those previously supplied from the United States, and where similar production techniques need to be implemented. As, however, with the passing of time the subsidiary becomes integrated with its local environment, and it gradually assumes an autonomy and individuality of its own, detailed control is relaxed. As experience is gained by the British managerial and technical staff, and as products become adapted to the specialized needs of the British consumer, existing relationships between parent and subsidiary need to be reassessed. As the personalities behind the original establishment leave the parent company, and as new capital is raised by the branch enterprise in the country of operation, interest and contacts become more distant. The size of the subsidiary, its profitability and importance to the parent firm, and the general political and economic climate in the investing and recipient countries, also combine to determine the kind of organizational relationships which exist between US investing companies and their UK offshoots.

5 Comparative operating methods and productivity in US parent and UK branch plants

In the last ten years many comparisons have been made between the productivity of British industry and that of its American counterpart. In his book *We Too Can Prosper*,[1] Graham Hutton has summarized most of the results. He found that, in the early 1950s, the average US worker in manufacturing industry produced, on average, $2\frac{1}{2}$–4 times the (real) output per period of time as his British counterpart; that productivity in the United States over the last half-century has trebled, while it has doubled in the United Kingdom; and that the US, with only three times the population of Britain and a smaller proportion of her labour force engaged in manufacturing industry, supplied half the world's output of manufactured goods.

While such facts as these are beyond dispute, there is less unanimity of opinion as to their interpretation and implications for the British economy. At the one extreme there are those who appear to believe that, by a wholesale assimilation of US manufacturing and managerial methods, most, if not all, the UKs economic problems would be solved; at the other, there is the argument that the high American productivity is solely a reflection of the particular industrial and social environment of that country, which cannot be transmitted across the Atlantic.[2]

With such considerations as these in mind, this chapter seeks to answer two basic questions: (1) How far, and in what respects, do US-financed manufacturing units in the UK find it economic to reproduce the operating methods utilized by their US associates and (2) what is the comparative productivity of the American and British plants of the 205 firms in our sample, and where differences do exist, what are the explanations for such differences?

At the outset it is important to distinguish between two terms which we shall make frequent use of in the course of our argument – viz. productivity and efficiency. *Productivity* simply expresses a relationship between the physical input of factor resources and the physical output which such resources help to produce; the greater this ratio, the higher the productivity. Because of the inherent difficulties involved in apportioning output between the contributing factor inputs, productivity is usually expressed in terms of one factor only – and this, more often than not, is labour. It is then measured by the output produced per unit of labour per period of time – or, alternatively, the number of man-minutes, hours, etc. it takes to manufacture a particular product. The result may be expressed in physical or in value terms. The important point to notice about this measure of productivity, however, is its convenience. There is no necessary causal relationship between changes in the productivity ratio and the productivity of the factor in the terms of which it is being expressed.

The level of productivity is determined by many factors, of which efficiency is one. *Efficiency*, in the sense in which we use it, is a relative term; from the point of view of the individual firm it may be defined as the ratio between *actual* productivity and the optimum or best productivity which any particular firm believes it is within its power to produce profitably. Productivity is then essentially a technological concept; efficiency is purely economic in connotation. The actual productivity of any firm, industry or country may only imperfectly reflect the efficiency of its management and workers. For example, though almost without exception the physical output per man-year in US-financed plants in this country is lower than that in their parent companies, it is impossible to say, without further examination, how far this difference is due to deficiencies on the part of UK management or British labour, and how far to those other factors which affect productivity but which cannot, for one reason or another, be economically deployed in British factories. Questions such as the range of products made; the extent to which the manufacturing process in Britain is fully integrated; how far the American technical and managerial expertise is available to the branch unit; the size of the market and the prices of factor services and subcontracted items: all these may affect productivity in one way or another. Some of these differences are avoidable, or more correctly are within the power of a firm's management to avoid; others are caused by factors outside its control. Inter-plant comparisons of this kind are inherently difficult,[3] and our conclusions are bound to be qualitative rather than quantitative in character. At the same time, where possible, we have tried to illustrate our main argument by drawing on the experiences of individual firms. But, first, it is necessary to discuss briefly whether, in an analysis of American and British plant operating methods we are comparing like with like. More particularly, to what extent are (1) the end products and (2) the manufacturing processes comparable.

Comparability and range of products supplied by US parent and branch plants

Some 150 or 68 per cent of the 205 US subsidiaries and jointly owned Anglo-American concerns questioned on this point stated that those products which were manufactured in both their American and British factories were comparable in all major respects, and that on this count there was no reason for manufacturing methods to be different. At the same time, 115, or 74 per cent, of these firms, noted minor or marginal differences in respect of the materials composition, quality, style, design, size, packaging or finish of these products. This was the case both for US-designed and styled *consumer* goods, e.g. motor-cars, electrical appliances, cosmetics, foodstuffs and clothing, and for *producer* goods, e.g. roofing materials, agricultural implements, mining machinery and catering equipment, which for climatic, topographic, geological, technological and other reasons require adaptation.

It was the experience of other subsidiaries that many materials and component parts, e.g. maize, starch and dextrines, specialized steels and rubbers, alloys, chemical compounds, instrument and electrical components, all of which were readily available in the US, were difficult to obtain in the UK. As a consequence, substitutes had frequently to be found: not only were these often less satisfactory for the purpose in hand but their search usually involved a good deal of time and energy. Sometimes, too, such differences in the quality of materials necessitated modifications to the plant or to production methods.[4] A large number of US-affiliated firms also commented on the differences in British and American legal regulations and safety requirements; and asserted that, in general, British standards were more demanding than their US counterparts.

The product range of 150 firms, or 75 per cent of the total sample, was a truncated version of their US counterparts, though *within* any particular product group the models manufactured (in respect of size, styles, quality, etc.) were often more numerous. For example, to quote from an executive of a bottling engineering subsidiary:

> It is a fact that the range of bottling machines we make in this country is greater than that produced by our parent concern by virtue of the greater variety of bottle shapes and sizes used here. This is partly explained by the fact that US Federal Law forbids the re-use of bottles that have contained spirits, and partly because, by common agreement, such glass-ware as jam jars, pickle pots and many pharmaceutical preparations are never used more than once in that country. In the UK on the other hand, it is common practice to re-use every receptacle – even the bottles that have contained blood plasma for transfusions are washed and sterilized by automatic machines. In addition, there is far less standardization amongst British bottlers – one distilling company alone, to my knowledge, produced over 750 different shapes and sizes.

Another instance is that of the Dictaphone Corporation in America which, although it produces a wider range of dictating machinery than its British subsidiary, only has to cater for a voltage system of 110, while the British factory has to supply equipment to meet both the 110 (e.g. Canadian) and 200–250 (e.g. European) markets.

The parent concern's output is usually more diversified than that of its subsidiary in the chemical and foodstuffs industries. For example, the American Cyanamid Company, one of the biggest general-purpose chemical concerns in the US, limits its output in the UK to a range of ethical drugs. The American Kodak Company is an important supplier of inorganic chemicals, while its subsidiary's activities are entirely confined to films and photographic equipment. Libby, McNeill and Libby Ltd, of New York, produces an extensive range of canned fruit products; its UK branch factory only supplies evaporated milk and baked beans. The Philco Corporation in the US is a foremost producer of all kinds of domestic electrical products; the activities of its UK branch plant are taken up entirely with the production of radio and television sets. Many of the office and agricultural machinery subsidiaries also supply fewer products than their parent concerns.

On the other hand, because more than half the US affiliates export at least 40 per cent of their output,[5] and serve a wide variety of markets with a multiplicity of specialized tastes and needs, many adjustments – mostly minor but sometimes costly – have to be made to American product designs and materials specifications. Only where the parent and branch factories are in direct competition with each other, or where the British plant is supplying overseas markets previously served from the American factory, is there a complete identity between the products offered for sale. This, for example, was particularly noted by those subsidiaries exporting spares and replacement parts to countries which purchased their original machines and equipment from the US. The international standardization of many drug formulae, of industrial instrument designs and of oil refinery equipment specifications, has added to this trend. Even in these industries, however, export requirements are apt to vary from those of the home market; for example, one engineering subsidiary noted that the replacement parts for an American product differed from those currently being incorporated into equipment for the home consumer, and that this meant a duplicated range of parts had to be carried.

The technical nature of the products manufactured by the remaining fifty-five American and British plants differed markedly from each other. Some ten firms, producing such items as sewing machines, office equipment, electrical appliances, etc., practise a policy of product specialization with their parent companies, while in twenty-five others, products are made specifically to contract, e.g. enamelling equipment, laundry machinery, foundation garments, abrasives. Otherwise differences in customer needs and requirements explain product variations, with the motor-car industry being the classic case in point. For example, though the Ford Motor Company (UK) Ltd in its early days duplicated its famous American Model T in this country, since 1932, at which date the first 8 h.p. car appeared off the Dagenham production run, the type of vehicle produced in the United Kingdom has been quite different from those in the Detroit factory. At the present time, the British Ford cars have few common features with their American counterparts, except with respect to general design principles. Much the same holds true of the products of the Vauxhall Motor Company and, outside the motor-car industry, of firms producing agricultural machinery, food products, electric switches, refrigerators and chemicals. At the same time, it cannot be assumed that the techniques of manufacturing will necessarily be different because the end-product is. In the refrigerating equipment industry, for example, US production techniques are commonly utilized, in spite of the fact that the final products are far from being homogeneous.

The extent to which manufacturing is complete in the two countries

Of equal importance, is the extent to which the actual manufacturing process carried out in the US and UK factories is complete, and how far subcontracting is resorted to. In other words, what is the comparative degree of vertical integration in the two countries? Some 54 per cent of the firms in our sample, and nearly four-fifths of the post-war subsidiaries, said that they were more heavily dependent on outside contractors for their components and parts than their US associates. Many American branch plants, for example, in the engineering and metal goods industries, are purely *assembling* by nature, importing all their machined parts and materials from abroad or purchasing them from British suppliers. Some five subsidiaries in our sample said they contracted out practically their entire output on a royalty basis, and another ten only undertook assembling operations and a limited amount of tooling and after-sales servicing.

As one might suppose, those manufacturing units which are comparatively inexperienced in UK manufacturing conditions are those the most dependent on outside contractors. For example, the usual practice of a newly established subsidiary in the engineering industry is for it first to set up an assembly unit, purchasing most of its upstream parts and components either from its parent concern or from British manufacturers, and then, with the passing of years, gradually to become more self-sufficient. Altogether twenty-five US subsidiaries in our sample might be classified as coming within this heading, including one important producer of earth-moving equipment, who, while during the year 1951–2 it imported two-thirds of its parts and made (or bought) one-third in the UK, in 1953–4 it imported 25 per cent and manufactured for itself (or contracted out to UK suppliers) 75 per cent.

The relative profitability of subcontracting *vis-à-vis* internal manufacturing also varies in the two countries. Some materials such as cotton, wood, glass, iron castings and most chemical compounds are cheaper to buy in the UK than in the US, while specialized steels and alloys, copper, paper, cartons, fuel, etc. are dearer. Likewise with the cost of manufactured components; for example, one important engineering company which buys out over 200 major components for its products revealed that the UK prices it had to pay ranged from 30 per cent below those charged in America, to 200 per cent above, with the average price being 25 per cent higher in the UK. This same firm also suggested that, in its experience, the degree of competition between suppliers (or more accurately, the absence of same) was the most important single factor influencing prices in this connection.

In addition to the question of relative costs, the scale of production, the quality of subcontracted work, the reliability of suppliers in keeping to stipulated delivery dates and experience and plant characteristics of the subsidiary will all influence the nature and extent of manufacturing operations carried out. A typical instance of how the structure of subcontracting may differ in the two countries, was given by a large electrical appliances producer, who opined:

> Owing to the difference in relative costs conditions in the two countries and the nature of our plant capacity, we find it profitable to make switches and thermostats in our UK factory which are bought out in the United States;

on the other hand, it pays us to buy out our rubber parts and mouldings in this country, which our parent factory make themselves.

In general, however, these qualifications are of marginal importance, and once a branch unit is well established in the UK the nature and completeness of its manufacturing processes conform to those of its US counterpart in all major respects. Certainly such differences as there may be are insufficient to invalidate any general productivity comparisons which may be drawn.

FACTORS MAKING FOR SIMILAR OPERATING METHODS IN PARENT AND BRANCH PLANTS

We now turn to examine two factors which, in their wider context, have been frequently put forward by economists to explain differences in operating methods and productivity as between British and American *firms*, but which we have found to be common features in our inter-*plant* comparisons:

1 The British subsidiary is invariably allowed full and easy access to its parent concern's manufacturing methods, managerial capabilities, marketing expertise and organizational skills; and to its research and development and learning experiences.
2 Fundamentally, top management methods and business philosophy appear to be very much the same in both British and American plants.

(1) The many-sided benefits which US branch units in the UK derive as a result of their transatlantic associations and their implications to the British economy as a whole will be examined in more detail in the following chapter. Suffice it to mention here that the research, manufacturing and managerial competencies and experiences of the parent concern invariably extend back many years beyond that of its British subsidiary. In two-thirds of the firms in our sample, the American plant had been manufacturing for at least forty years prior to the establishment of a British factory, and in 35 per cent of cases, for seventy-five or more years. The advantages which age allow are self-evident, but, in addition, new products, processes and materials – unless they are intended solely for the British or non-American markets – are almost invariably tried out in the US, first in a pilot plant and then in full-scale production. This means that the branch plant is able to avoid many of the initial mistakes and teething problems which are associated with development, as well as profiting from new knowledge. Partly this latter takes the form of product and material specifications, blueprints, drawings, prototypes, formulae, etc.; partly know-how relating to machinery design and layout, waste utilization and materials handling; partly tacit knowledge, ideas and strategies; and partly of information of more general interest, e.g. literature about sales and advertising, the training and payment of labour, work procedures, methods of costing and budgetary control, inventory control, market opportunities and so on. Certainly, it is the rule rather than the exception for the design of most wholly-owned subsidiary factories to follow closely on US lines, and for specialized

equipment and skilled labour to be shipped over from the States to help production get started. Much the same applies to new branch factories and factory extensions, and even today specialized US equipment and tools are still imported by many old-established affiliates.

(2) The importance attached by the various Anglo-American Productivity Team Reports published in the late 1940s and early 1950s to the capabilities, attitude and entrepreneurship of management as factors influencing productivity and manufacturing methods, cannot be over-stressed. As the Management Accounting Team pointed out in 1951: 'The most significant factor in America, leading to high production at low cost, is efficient management.'[6] Moreover, it was generally believed that many of the differences which did exist between American and British industrial productivity were avoidable, for while it might not always be profitable to utilize American *production* processes, British firms could do much to raise their efficiency by assimilating best-practice US *managerial* strategies and techniques.

How far, in fact, are US subsidiaries managed on American principles, i.e. to what extent do their managerial techniques reflect those adopted by their parent concerns? Assuming the day-to-day management of the *subsidiaries* were to be in the hands of the executives of their *parent* companies, would policy be any different from that currently being practised?

We have already partly answered these questions in the previous chapter. There we saw that, in the great majority of cases, all important decisions, such as those relating to the future of the subsidiary, finance, and the introduction of new products, have to be referred back to the USA, where they are viewed in the light of the company's global policy and strategy. All senior executive (or decision-taking) appointments, and particularly that of the managing director, invariably need to be approved by the parent company.

We also saw that in their day-to-day management and operating methods, nearly four-fifths of US subsidiaries and Anglo-American concerns were either strongly or partially controlled by their parent companies. In a minority of branch units, American influence will be directly experienced by the employment of US nationals, in the capacity of either managing directors or senior executives. A US Treasury survey carried out in 1943[7] showed that, of 2,007 directors of US subsidiaries and jointly owned Anglo-American concerns operating in the UK, 69 were US nationals living abroad (i.e. 'working' directors), 723 US nationals living in America and 1,215 non-American (mainly UK 'working' directors). Of the 728 senior executives employed by US firms at that time, 52 were US nationals living abroad, 107 US nationals living in America and 569 non-American. Our own researches confirm this pattern, except that, as a result of an influx of new affiliates into Britain since 1945, the proportion of US nationals employed has increased. For example, of the 55 post-war US manufacturing subsidiaries operating in 1953, 24 were controlled by American managing directors and 8 had US senior executives (mainly departmental managers) and of their 256 directors, 153 or 60 per cent were US nationals. This latter figure compares with 38 per cent in respect of all US-financed firms.

On the other hand, where an American company has a part interest in an earlier-established British firm, management has remained largely unchanged, except in respect of specific techniques, e.g. budgetary control, cost accounting, job evaluation, advertising, etc. Nor have American managerial or marketing philosophies been found economically or psychologically suited to UK conditions. Cases of US-financed firms failing because of managerial inability to appreciate differences in the attitude of British and American labour towards incentives, and employment practices or of UK consumers to American marketing and advertising techniques, are far from being isolated.[8] More than one subsidiary has gone as far as to claim that it has only really prospered since the management had become British.

In all, however, there is sufficient evidence to suggest that the principles of management adopted by the great majority of US parent and branch plants are substantially the same. By this we imply first, that the top management of the UK manufacturing unit is of a sufficiently high calibre both to understand and appreciate American production and managerial techniques, and is willing to apply them where it is economic to do so; and second, that the managing director will do his best to ensure that his departmental managers operate their departments on the most efficient lines, both by sending them for training or periodic visits to the US associate, and by seeing that they are technically equipped to appreciate literature, ideas and guidance, made available from that source, while having the judicial competence to sort out the applicable from the inapplicable.

In view of the above facts, and for the rest of this chapter we shall make the assumption that any differences in productivity and efficiency between US parent and branch plants are not due to differences in managerial efficiency.

DIFFERENCES IN DEMAND AND SUPPLY CONDITIONS FACING US PARENT AND BRANCH PLANTS

Our next task is to examine how far any differences in the productivity of American parent firms and their subsidiaries in the United Kingdom are due not to differences of efficiency but to the fact that they operate in different economic environments and are governed by circumstances outside the control of the individual business unit.

Demand or market considerations

The size of the market clearly dictates production levels of both firms and industries, and also the productivity of each.[9] Lower costs and greater productivity in either parent or subsidiary plants could be due to a different scale of output and not to a difference in efficiency as such. If the optimum scale of output is small, i.e. if that output at which average (production) costs are at a minimum, and beyond which there are no more economies to be gained by increasing the scale of output,[10] is relatively small, then the size of the market is of little consequence. If, however, it is large, i.e. if, as output increases, superior techniques of production can be applied, productivity is likely to be correlated with size of plant. Such a relationship is also likely to depend on the flexibility of production methods. Sometimes, once a certain minimum output has been reached, it may be possible to produce that output only in one particular way, e.g. as in many chemical processes. In other cases, e.g. as in most light engineering and industrial instrument firms, production methods may be adjusted to suit the size of the output required of them.

Bearing these factors in mind, we can classify the type of production unit operated by the 114 firms in our sample which gave us the desired information (in respect of their main UK plant), as follows:

Type A. As operated by some thirty-one plants where production methods are more or less fixed and designed to serve a fairly large market. Technical economies of expansion are noticeable, and result from an increased utilization of expensive, single-purpose equipment and other specialized resources. As output grows, so these overheads are spread and average costs fall. Optimum output is comparatively large; in consequence the smaller the firm, the less the plant is utilized and the lower its productivity.

Type B. As operated by those sixty-one plants where it is possible to produce any given output in various ways, but where the optimum output is large. Hence a high level of demand enables such plant to benefit from the application of more productive techniques.

Type C. As operated by those twenty-two plants where the optimum output is fairly small, and where larger markets simply result in the replication of existing production methods, or bring with them cost diseconomies. In these plants, the degree of flexibility is likely to be comparatively insignificant.

In Tables 5.1 and 5.2 we attempt to show how these considerations apply to the firms of our sample. In Table 5.1 we compare the relative scales of output and employment of the UK subsidiaries and branch plants with those of their American parents where the products are identical or substantially the same. Where more factories in the US are manufacturing these product(s) than those in the UK, we have had to try and strike some sort of average ratio. More usually, however, the US parent operates a number of specialized factories, while in the UK one or two plants supply the complete range of products. This being so, we have tried to reduce the number of factories in the two countries to a common number. Thus, in the great majority of cases, the inter-factory output ratios expressed might also be expressed in terms of inter-firm ratios as well. In general, the ratios refer to the physical output of *main* products, but where a firm is highly multi-product, as are most of the manufacturing chemists, for example, aggregate production ratios have been taken. These ratios are presented for five industrial sectors: *inter alia*, these tell us that nearly half the employment of US subsidiaries in the chemical and allied trades is in firms whose output is a fifth or less that of their parent factories, while more than one-half of the employment in the engineering and allied trades is in firms which supply an output one-quarter or less than that of their US counterparts.

Table 5.1 Comparative outputs of main products supplied by US parent and UK subsidiary factories, 1953

Ratio UK: US output	Chemical and allied trades		Engineering and metal manufacturing		Precision and scientific instruments		Food, drink and tobacco		Other manufacturing industries		Total	
	No. of firms	Nos. employed	No. of firms	Nos. employed	No. of firms	Nos. employed	No. of firms	Nos. employed	No. of firms	Nos. employed	No. of firms	Nos. employed
Below 1:1	1 ⎱	⎱ 9,750	2 ⎱	⎱ 36,000					1	1,500	4	18,400
1:1 and below 1:2	4 ⎰	⎰	10 ⎰	⎰			2	2,500			14	28,850
1:2 and below 1:3			3	1,500	1 ⎱	⎱ 9,730	1 ⎱	⎱ 2,500	1 ⎱	⎱ 2,050	7	11,350
1:3 and below 1:4	3 ⎱	⎱ 1,770	3	5,500	1 ⎰	⎰	1 ⎰	⎰	2 ⎰	⎰	10	12,080
1:4 and below 1:5	1 ⎰	⎰	8	32,000	2	3,200			4	10,500	16	46,520
1:5 and below 1:8	3	4,000	8	6,500	3	2,300			2	1,750	13	12,250
1:8 and below 1:10	2	2,600	7	3,650	2	970	–	–	2	930	14	9,480
1:10 and below 1:20	5	700	14	7,250			2	550	2	1,070	25	10,540
1:20 and above	2	190	4	1,500			2	400	3	850	11	2,940
Not comparable	8	3,400	7	18,050			5	4,500	5	420	25	26,370
Total	29	22,410	66	111,950	9	16,200	13	10,000	22	18,220	139	178,780

Table 5.2 Differences of output in US and UK plants and their effect on productivity

Volume of output UK: US plant	Type A relationship[1] no. of firms	Type B relationship[1] no. of firms	Type C relationship[1] no. of firms
Below 1:2	5	8	5
1:2 and below 1:4	3	9	5
1:4 and below 1:8	8	14	7
1:8 and below 1:20	13	22	4
Over 1:20	2	8	1
Total	31	61	22

Note:
1 For definitions, see p. 88.

Basically the output of American-financed firms in this country is less than that of their parent companies because, in spite of a much larger market in the US than that in the UK (and, indeed, in Europe), there is not a corresponding difference in the number of important suppliers. The main reasons put forward to explain the higher demand of US consumers were:

1 The potential domestic market facing the US plant is both larger and more standardized than that facing the British plant. Only the first part of this argument loses force when the possible export markets open to the UK subsidiary are also considered.

2 The domestic consumer's *effective* demand is greater in the United States relative to that in the United Kingdom since:

(a) average disposable incomes are higher in that country.

(b) as a rule, the products spearheaded by US affiliates have a relatively high income-elasticity of demand.

(c) There are more extensive and generous credit facilities in the US.

(d) The price structure of the products supplied by US affiliates relative to that of other products is more favourable.

(e) An intensive advertising pressure and 'keeping up with the Joneses' attitude in the US which, together with (c), raises both the level of new demand at any given time and the rate of product obsolescence, which increases the frequency of demand.

(f) Various other factors more specific to individual firms (relative costs and management policies, differences in consumer tastes, etc.).

3 The effective demand for producer goods (capital equipment, machine tools, industrial instruments, etc.) is higher in the US relative to that in the UK because:

(a) Labour costs are proportionately higher, and this provides a greater inducement for capital and/or technology intensive methods of production.

(b) There is a larger finished-product demand (see (2) above), making such capital-intensive methods of production economic.

(c) Investment and depreciation allowances are generally more generous in the US.

(d) There is a much faster rate of obsolescence of producer goods in the US due to rapidly changing production technologies by firms in the US.

(e) There is a more dynamic attitude in respect of (d).

4 Lack of market exploitation by UK subsidiaries, either because it is:

(a) In its early stages of growth, or

(b) Producing to full capacity and cannot meet the demands of an increasing market as easily as can their parent concerns.

To assess the practical implications of these differences they must be related to the share of the market held by the individual firms comprising the industry in question. Professor Sargant Florence has shown in his *The Logic of British and American Industry* that, in general, the distribution of the sizes of plants and firms in the US corresponds broadly to that in this country. But from the viewpoint of the industries in our survey there appeared to be important structural differences. In answer to the question: 'Do you believe that your share of the total market in the UK is more, about the same, or less than that held by your parent concern in the United States?' 41 per cent of American subsidiaries replied *more*, 26 per cent *less* and 33 per cent *about the same*. Thus, with an aggregate market in the United States, anything from three to twenty times that in the United Kingdom, the *absolute* volume of output supplied by most American parent factories was con- siderably above that of their UK branch units. And, generally speaking, the greater the difference in output in the two countries, the higher the share of the market held in the United States and vice versa. In particular, competitive forces appeared to be rather more active in the United States in the petroleum refining, razor-blade, locks and keys, starch, carbon-black, kitchen utensil indus- tries, and rather less in the case of surgical dressings, bottling machinery, motor- cars, foundation garments, etc. Once more, our comparisons primarily relate to the total output of affiliates; for specific products, the answers may differ considerably.

The significance of these differences of output in influencing comparative operating methods and productivity may be seen from Table 5.2, which relates the output ratios in Table 5.3 to the three types of firms listed on page 88.

Thus, both the size and structure of the markets served will affect comparative operating methods in the US parent plants and those of the British subsidiaries. While there is often less product diversification in the United Kingdom, the variety of styles, sizes, etc., within any particular range, will make any given output less productive and more costly to produce. As a final illustration of this point, one Anglo-American firm, though equal in size to its US associate, supplies virtually the entire export market of both companies from its British factories. Its 'traffic' department employs fifty-five people, or 3.2 per cent of its total labour force, while in America the same department employs twelve people, or 1.2 per cent of the US labour force.

Supply or cost factors: differences in wage levels

The differences in this respect and their effect on comparative operating methods and productivity principally reflect the wage and salary levels prevailing in the two economies. In his recently published work *Dynamic Factors in Industrial Productivity*,[11] Professor Seymour Melman argues that the marked shift in the relative cost of labour and machine hours over recent years has been the main cause of the present manufacturing methods employed by US-based firms and their productivity. From the viewpoint of our enquiry, however, the differences in US and UK wage rates appears to be a less important determinant of relative production methods. It must, of course, be remembered that it is not the money cost which determines the relative profitability of employing a particular resource or capability but its efficiency in relationship to its price. Even so, American wages and incomes are currently, on an average, three times above their British counterparts (in spite of the disguised National Insurance contributions paid by all UK employers) and since there is no evidence to suggest that differences in labour efficiency are of that magnitude in the two countries, it may be assumed that the *real* cost of labour is rather less in the United Kingdom. For example, a toolmaker averages 5*s*. (25 new pence) in the UK and 16*s*. 6*d*. (82½ new pence) an hour in the US, an unskilled labourer earns 3*s*. 2*d*. (16 new pence) an hour in the UK and 9*s*. 6*d*. (47½ new pence per week in the US, and a clerk from £10 to £15 per week in the UK and £25–£40 per week in the US – the exact ratios varying quite considerably between occupations, industries and areas, and also the wages policies adopted by the employers.[12] While however, this latter distinction could make some difference, save in selected instances it would appear to have had little influence on the methods adopted by the US affiliates.

It by no means follows, however, that as a percentage of total costs, labour costs are higher in the US than in the UK. For:

(a) less labour and more machinery might be used in the US because it is relatively more expensive.
(b) the importance of labour costs varies with the level of output, usually falling as more is produced.
(c) in some cases, the efficiency of the US plant is higher than that of its UK subsidiary, which often means that, for any given output, less labour is used.

For illustrative purposes, we might cite three actual case studies:

Per cent of gross output value	Firm A Plants		Firm B Plants		Firm C Plants	
	UK	US	UK	US	UK	US
Materials or bought-out parts	60	35	45	50	40	60
Direct or factory labour	10	15	25	25	25	15
Indirect labour	30	50	30	25	35	25
Total	100	100	100	100	100	100

Firm A – which manufactures a range of medium engineering products – typifies a case where the labour cost content is relatively less in the UK than in the US. At the same time, output and direct labour efficiency are comparable in the two countries; and only marginally does the difference in labour costs affect production methods. Though above-average wage rates are paid by this firm in the United Kingdom, they are still only between one-half and one-third of those in the US. Overhead costs are proportionately higher in the US because it operates its world-wide research laboratory in that country. Material costs come out both relatively and absolutely cheaper in the US, mainly because less sub-contracting is done by the US plant.

The relative cost split-up in *Firm B* – a chemical subsidiary – is misleading. Here, output is very much greater in the US plant than in the British subsidiary. Once again, a comparatively high wage policy is pursued by the UK firm, but, as in the case of Firm A, wage differentials do not significantly influence its production methods, except at the packaging and handling stages. For example, whereas it pays to utilize fork-lift trucks and wooden pallets in the American plant, it is more economic to employ labour in the British factory, partly because the equipment costs 40 per cent more in the UK, and partly because the relative saving in labour costs is only one-third of that in the US. Otherwise production is continuous processing and inflexible by nature (save the 'speed' at which the machinery can be operated). This, coupled with the comparative lack of experience of the British work force accounts for relative wage costs being roughly equal in the two plants. Overhead costs are proportionately the same in the US and the UK. The fact that the parent company does most of its global research and development work in the US being balanced by the lower administrative overheads of the subsidiary. Much the same proportion of production is subcontracted in the two countries, with materials coming out slightly cheaper in the UK.

In *Firm C* – which supplies a range of packaged food products – current UK wage rates are paid, though a very generous bonus and pension scheme is provided. Productivity varies, but, in general is well below that of the parent factories in the United States. Methods of production differ noticeably; in many cases, it is just not economic to employ the specialized machinery operated by the parent company, output in the British factory being one-tenth of that in the US plant. More general-purpose equipment and indirect factory labour is employed in the UK. Most of the materials in both plants are imported and, in this respect, the British plant has the price advantage. Proportionately, indirect costs are more expensive in the UK where some basic research is carried out, and administrative overheads are comparatively high. Material costs are then rather less, and direct and indirect labour costs rather more, in the UK than in the US.

While, in themselves, these data prove nothing, they do emphasize the need to judge each case on its own merits, and to take account of all the relevant factors, and in particular the manufacturing techniques utilized, the price and transaction costs of the subcontracted items, and the degree to which the production unit is self-sufficient. For the most part, too, the larger the output and the more a firm can benefit from technical and managerial economies of scale, the less will labour cost differences affect production techniques. Of course, a difference in the labour/machine cost ratio may itself be a sufficient cause for productivity to be lower in the branch plant, even though a more extensive use of manpower is cost-effective. Machinery costs are largely comparable in the two countries, particularly as much of the basic equipment is produced in the United States or is manufactured in the UK to American design. As a whole, however, two out of every three firms visited judged that labour cost differences had very little effect on their basic production processes.[13] Certainly, as a percentage of total costs, direct labour costs were generally quite small, averaging between 10 and 15 per cent. *Marginal* adjustments, however, were shown to be more important, which frequently meant that the optimum size of the firm was reached at a later stage in the UK than in America. Since, then, *in terms of UK labour costs*, it is often only profitable for the subsidiary to install certain types of machinery and equipment, if a higher output is produced in the British subsidiary than the US parent plant, it follows that for any *given level* of output, productivity *must* be smaller in the UK than in the United States.

To illustrate further the significance of these unavoidable causes of productivity differences we have drawn upon a number of short case studies based on data supplied by firms in our survey.

Firm A, a medium engineering subsidiary, which produces a fairly standardized product, and has an output volume one-third to one-half of its parent concern, commented:

The nature of the differences between production methods in the US and in the UK as far as we know them in our own companies, lies mainly in our American company's ability to perform simultaneously several machining operations on a particular component which we normally have to carry out consecutively. Sometimes it is the performing of a number of exactly similar operations as, for example, the boring of several identical cylinders in a cylinder block, and in some instances it is the performing of several quite different operations, each of which may require specialized machine tools. Generally speaking, this procedure is only economical if output is so great as to enable the machines concerned to be operated continuously for very long periods.

In the first of the above two cases, simultaneous operations are usually achieved by the use of an entirely special-purpose machine designed solely for a particular job. In the second case, it is usual to employ a group of more conventional machines which, however, would be equipped with fully automatic controls rendering a skilled operator unnecessary and requiring only a semi-skilled minder to load and unload them. The former are, of course, useless for any purpose except for the particular job for which they have been designed, and the latter, while capable of handling a variety of jobs, usually require relatively long periods of 'setting', that is to say adapting them from one job to another, and this also requires highly skilled and expensive labour.

In the smaller scale operation which we have in this country, it would not be possible to keep such machines continuously occupied and one is, therefore, thrown back upon the use of non-automatic general-purpose machines which can handle a very wide variety of jobs which require less time and skill in setting, and can, therefore, be adapted more quickly and more cheaply from one job to another. They do, however, need handling by a skilled operator, who can, of course, tend only one machine at a time. It is quite common with fully automatic machines for one man to tend a group of three, and even if the individual machines do not of themselves have a higher output than would similar non-automatic machines, the operating labour cost is obviously reduced by more than two-thirds, having regard to the fact that cheaper labour can be employed.

Firm B, a supplier of refrigeration components, wrote:

Productivity is certainly higher in the US on certain items, entirely because their high volume justifies the tooling-up of special-purpose machines which is only practical for a very high volume. A case in point is a special component which, up to recently, we were making in low volume, and it was taking 23.6 minutes per hundred units to manufacture. The tooling cost for this low volume was of the order of £500 and presses to the value of £400 were used to manufacture the component. Our volume has now risen to such an extent that more expensive tooling is justified, and we are now producing exactly the same clip by methods similar to those used by our parent company and the time is now 1.5 minutes per hundred. To obtain this reduction, we have had to spend £1,800 on tooling, and buy a special-purpose press at a cost of approximately £2,000. Even allowing for the amortization of the press and tooling, we believe that we can now produce at approximately half the previous cost, and as our volume rises even further, we would actually produce it at something like one-tenth of our previous cost.

Another example is a phosphor bronze spring which we use in all our thermostats. Until recently, our volume was only 1,000 per day and we were making this spring using relatively simple conventional tooling and taking 8.75 minutes per hundred. We have now changed over to special-purpose tooling and special-purpose machines and can make the same spring in 1.5 minutes per hundred. The tooling, however, is three times as expensive, but again, we will recover this tooling cost quickly, now that our volume has risen to over 2,000 per day. The same sort of reasoning applies to many other components we are using here, but we find that, as our volume rises, we can justify the expenditure of special-purpose tooling and machinery and we are gradually bringing our methods completely into line with American methods. As soon as we do that, we find that the actual time to manufacture piece parts for assembly can be reduced to exactly the same time as the American time. In many cases, it is still not an economic proposition to change over to higher output tooling, bearing in mind that the cost of the special-purpose machine and tooling is approximately the same here as in the US, but labour costs here are still only one-third of those in America, so that the saving from special-purpose machines can be worthwhile in the US but not so here. Relatively short runs in the UK can also mean that the ratio of setting time to running time becomes too high to be economic, but to a certain extent, this is offset by the fact that setting-up time labour is only one-third in the UK to the US.

Firm C, a machine tool specialist, said:

Our UK factory has to serve a smaller market than its US counterpart and has to meet an overall demand comprising twenty-one standard models each consisting of five components, and we have to give customers satisfaction in line with demand, and have consequently to manufacture relatively smaller quantities of each model as compared with our US friends.

If we take as an example the production on six-spindle Gridley automatic machines, we find that on a group of four machines we have anything up to nine complete changeovers each month. Our US counterpart, in that period, would only change over the identical type of machine group once, and at a maximum, four times. We estimate that on this machine section alone we have a 14 per cent loss in production time against the US.

Most of the UK machines and methods of operations are identical with those used in the US but the above example of loss of production time for changeover applies throughout all other types of machines, such as drilling, milling, gear cutting and precision grinding, etc.

Due to the longer production runs, it is economical for the US to have sufficient machines to enable them to leave a number set up on one model. In the case of the UK, due to the smaller quantities being produced, it is not possible to lay down plant for completing any one operation on one model only, as this would result in a 50 per cent loss in productive time if a machine was left to await a further batch of the same size. We, therefore, have to change over our machines for other models, thereby losing approximately sixteen hours (14 per cent) of direct productive time.

It may be mentioned that, due to the wider market in the US, their policy is to maintain a large stock of all finished models in their warehouse, so that it is possible for their factory to have long productive runs on each particular model.

Firm D, a light engineering firm, argued:

In the UK, our output is approximately 1/16th part of the American output. This means that whereas in its machine shops our American company is able to use transfer machines where 90 per cent of the operations on a cylinder block are performed with a minimum of handling, and only two operatives are required, in the UK we use a few special-purpose machines and a number of general-purpose machines taking approximately twenty-one operators to do the same number of operations.

Firm E, which produces a well-known consumer goods product, in explaining why output per man-hour in its packaging processes is less than half that of its American parent, said:

This is a classic example of far greater productivity per man-hour being attained in America because the heavy investment in the automatic machinery used in our US factories would not pay off in England. For example, a packaging machine which would pay off in America in two years, would probably take from six to eight years to pay off in England, before which time the type of package may have become completely obsolete. In this connection, we estimate that it takes from three to four times as long for a machine to pay off in saving of labour in England as it does in America, and the trouble is that as likely as not, long before this, the type of package which it is intended to produce will have become obsolete.

Firm F, an important supplier of a range of domestic electrical appliances, noted a specific example of how productivity had been improved since new knowledge had been passed on by their US associate. It commented:

Until two years ago, the lacing of brushes (fixing bristles into the brush back) was carried out by a stapling machine. This was a slow and laborious practice. We recently obtained a machine from our American Company which enables brushes to be laced automatically, indexing each tuft on a predetermined position. The operator is thus able to glue, trim and inspect brushes, tasks which were formerly carried out by other operators. The net saving in time is roughly 50 per cent. We manufacture approximately two million brushes a year, and have been able to cue down the number of operators from twenty to nine.

Firm G, which manufactures a popular food product, wrote:

Our methods of manufacturing are basically the same in both factories, except for the packaging of the end-product. Here, output per man-hour in this country is approximately half that in the United States. First, because of the relative cheapness of labour in this country, it does not pay us to be so mechanized: second, whilst the UK factory packs in small bottles and cartons, and distributes to 40,000 retailers, the United States packs in large drums and sells direct to wholesalers.

Briefly summarizing the main points so far made in this part of the chapter we might say:

1 There is less special-purpose and fully-automatic machinery and more general-purpose and semi-automatic machinery in the UK subsidiaries than in their parent plants. Sometimes where machinery is identical, e.g. in toothpaste manufacturing and the packaging of toilet soap, the speed at which the machines are operated is often less in the UK than it is in America.

2 Because of the character and variety of markets served, and the comparatively smaller output produced in this country, the ratio of non-productive to productive times tends to be much greater in the UK plant than in its US counterpart.

3 There is considerably less specialization of labour tasks, particularly in the field of management, which, together with the reduced length of experience of the British plant, makes for lower productivity in the UK.

4 *Ceteris paribus,* market and labour cost differences are most important where production methods are flexible, and this is shown to be particularly so in

the case of overhead factory economies, e.g. materials handling, packaging, etc., and in the office, e.g. more use is made of dictating and electronic calculating machines in the US.

COMPARATIVE EFFICIENCY IN US PARENT AND BRANCH PLANTS

We now turn from the various factors affecting *productivity* to those specifically affecting *efficiency* and ask whether, at any given level of output, and assuming an identical factor price structure, that output could be produced at a lower money cost, i.e. more efficiently, in the US affiliate than in the parent plant. Here, largely human considerations will predominate, and leaving aside differences in managerial capabilities the question resolves itself into one of (a) labour, its quality and its will to work, (b) machine utilization and efficiency, and (c) quality of materials.

Efficiency of labour

The efficiency of labour as a productive factor will depend upon (1) its inherent qualities and capabilities, (2) the extent to which the firm sees that these are effectively utilized, (3) the way in which the labour is co-ordinated with the other factor inputs and (4) the will which it has to be productive, i.e. its attitude to work, skills upgrading incentives, etc.

The quality of US and UK labour

First, a general point. In answer to the question 'Do you consider the quality of labour (i.e. its "power" to be effective) in your subsidiary to be better, as good as, or not as good as that in the parent plant?' there was no general consensus: 28 per cent of the US-financed firms said *better*, 42 per cent *as good as* and 30 per cent *not as good*. There were, however, more criticisms respecting particular types of labour. First, many of the newer engineering and chemical firms noted the difficulty of obtaining certain types of scientific and technical workers, such as oil and chemical engineers, electronic physicists, instrument technicians, oil metallurgists, and the like. One large toilet preparation subsidiary went as far as to argue that its inability to obtain suitably qualified industrial engineers in the UK was the biggest single factor influencing the productivity differences between itself and its parent factory. Again, however, this is primarily a reflection of environmental conditions in the two economies. Second, the larger subsidiaries were quick to complain about the dearth of adequately trained foremen, whom they found to be both less well informed and trained than in the US. As one firm put it: 'Your foreman in the US is a better supervisor and enjoys a higher prestige and education; in addition, he commands more respect and his relative salary is much superior to his UK counterpart.'

Third, between one-third and one-half of consumer good subsidiaries noted the poorer quality of salesmanship material in the UK: sometimes this was sufficient to forestall the utilization of more economic and dynamic marketing methods.

Such complaints as these mainly refer to the labour raw material with which US affiliates have to deal. But sometimes difficulties arise because the American investors have been the first to create the demand for particular types of labour in the UK, and, in principle, are no different from those faced by British companies pioneering new fields. Nevertheless, the net result is that the branch unit often has to spend more time in training its workforce to conform to the standards laid down by its parent concern, and that in spite of wage differences, training costs – in relation to total costs – are usually higher in the UK than in the United States. Most of the larger subsidiaries either send their senior factory operatives and managerial staff (particularly on the sales side) to the US parent company for training, or arrange for them to have periodic refresher courses of from three to six months' duration. In a few cases, specialized schools – run on American lines – have been set up in the UK for foremen and senior operative grades of labour; these have met with some success by the Goodyear, Ford, Kraft and Hoover companies.

In contrast, the quality of unskilled and semi-skilled grades of labour was generally thought to be both more consistent and at least as satisfactory as that in the United States. Nevertheless, owing to the nature of the manufacturing processes involved, not always have firms – especially those setting up factories in the Development Areas – found it easy to get labour of the right kind and experience. This, most certainly, has been a most important factor leading to the differences in productivity as between post-war-originated firms and their parent companies, and was specifically mentioned by forty out of the fifty-five firms which have been manufacturing in the UK only since 1945. As one firm pointed out: 'In our Scottish factory we have no employees who have been with us more than 3 years. In our parent factory the average length of experience is 10 years.' When one also remembers that the parent plant is on an average 45–50 years older than its subsidiary, and invariably tries out new production methods and products before they are transferred to the branch plant, this cause of lower productivity might be extended to cover all subsidiaries.

The attitude to production and incentives

Concerning the *will* of the labour to work, and to the extent to which it makes the best use of its own capacities and those of the complementary productive resources, there was less unanimity of opinion expressed among subsidiaries. To the question: 'Do you consider the labour in your UK plant(s) works harder, as hard, or not as hard, as its counterpart in the US?' 12 per cent answered *harder*, 35 per cent *as hard* and 53 per cent *not as hard*. In effect, this question is a component of a wider issue – that of the attitude of labour as a whole. This shows itself in various ways, e.g. the degree of enthusiasm with which a particular job is tackled, the willingness (or lack of willingness) to find better ways of doing that task and of putting forward any suggestions of improvement to the management approach to team efforts, flexible work systems and industrial training, unionization and the response to incentives, monetary or otherwise. Some firms, for example, thought that British labour worked just as hard as American, but felt that it worked less effectively for those reasons. There was less appreciation of the function of time and motion study, less interest and enthusiasm shown in the actual job in hand, and less willingness of the worker to identify his interests with those of his company. The British operative, as one firm put it:

> just did what he was supposed to do, treating the whole thing as rather distasteful, certainly never giving any real thought as to whether he could do his job better with less mental or physical effort to himself. Your American, on the other hand, tends to think more, is more gadget-minded and really interested in what he is doing, and is all the time on the look-out to find some better way to do the job to his own benefit.

A more practical case in point was cited by another subsidiary in the medium engineering industry:

> In connection with one particular die-casting operation, the average worker in our US factory when he has removed the ejected casting from the die, holds it in one hand, and with the other operates the control to shoot the next casting. Whilst this is being done, he places in the work-container the previously shot casting. His opposite number in this country examines the ejected die, puts it down, and then picks up the next casting. The latter method is proving about 60 per cent as productive as the former, yet we have found it difficult to train the UK operative to do otherwise.

Again, these examples partly reflect the fact that there is more division of labour in American factories, by which an operative is allowed to concentrate his efforts on one particular task to the exclusion of others. He is thus enabled to gather a thorough knowledge and experience of his work, with the result that his proficiency is increased and he is competent to suggest improvements to it.

The percentage of effective to nominal work time also tends to be higher in the US than in the UK. The working week of most firms is forty hours in the US and forty-four in the UK, with the usual industry and regional variations. Since the war, overtime has been generally more widespread in US subsidiaries than in their parent factories, averaging between eight to ten hours a week: on the other hand, shift-working is considerably less. Yet, allowing for these differences, the *effective* working time is lower in the UK. One firm calculates that tea-breaks – which are nominally twenty minutes a day, but in reality amount to forty-five minutes – account for as much as 4 per cent of the differences in Anglo-American productivity. Three other subsidiaries observed that in their US factory meals are brought round to the man at the machine,[14] whereas in the UK since such a practice is not allowed under the Factories Act, a replacement is often needed.

Of the factors influencing worker motivation, none is more important than that of incentives, though not always are these within the plant manager or firm's control. The Anglo-American Productivity Teams have frequently suggested these to be an important factor influencing the higher labour productivity in the United States, including within their scope such variables as the availability of consumer goods, credit facilities, consumer attitudes towards a higher standard of living, the level of taxation and the general employment situation. The subject is an intangible one, about which we again found no general measure of agreement among US firms in the UK. Certainly the senior management of most subsidiaries seemed to believe that monetary rewards are valued relatively less highly in the UK than in the United States; once a certain point in the income scale has been reached, leisure becomes a more valued good than money income. Moreover, since the marginal rate of taxation is so much higher in the United Kingdom, that point is likely to be reached more quickly there than in the United States. The nature and effect of the various incentive schemes which have been tried out by subsidiaries in the UK will be further discussed in Chapter 9. Suffice to mention here that, in general, they are practised less extensively than in the US, and that where the same circumstances exist in both countries, the reaction is invariably more pronounced in that latter country.

So much for some of the factors which will affect the productivity of the individual worker. Their impact on operating methods is, however, of equal importance when collective considerations are taken into account.

The role of trade unions

A large number of US subsidiaries – 121 or 60 per cent of our sample – employ non-federated labour in as much as there is no one national union representing all workers in the factory and no shop stewards. More often than not there is direct bargaining, about wages and working conditions, between employer and labour representation appointed by the factory, as is common practice in the US. The question was asked: 'Do you have less trade union difficulties in the UK than in the US about the same, or more?' In response, only 14 per cent said they had more difficulty with trade unions, 35 per cent *about the same* and 51 per cent *less*. There appeared no doubt that time lost through strikes and labour disputes was considerably greater in the United States than in the United Kingdom, and in this connection, British unions were considered more mature and responsible. One personnel manager went as far as to say that 1 per cent of his time in this country was spent on labour disputes, whereas in America his counterpart spent nearly one-third of his time on such issues. Another firm put it in this way: 'UK conditions with national bargaining give far less scope for dispute, and conditions are much easier than in the US where individual bargaining in each firm prevails.' However, as one might expect, the extent of the difficulties in the UK varied from region to region. In the Midlands and the South of England there appeared to be much less trouble than in the North.

On the other hand, though there were fewer union problems on this count, and also on restricting the output per operative beyond a certain level, many firms noted a more conservative attitude of collective labour in the United Kingdom with respect to the introduction of new machinery and production methods, e.g. in the cotton textile, metal manufacturing and heavy engineering industries. The one-man one-machine outlook was more common and, in general, fewer operatives seemed to look after a given number of machines in the US than in the UK. One machine tool firm in our survey compared a ratio of 1: 2 in its UK factory with a ratio of 1: 4 in its US plant. The corresponding ratios provided by an engineering subsidiary were 1: 14 and 1: 30, while, in a British cotton mill, one operative minds eighteen machines, compared with a customary figure of forty in its US plant. In each of these cases, the machines were claimed to be identical in both countries. Both these difficulties are being gradually resolved, but tradition and the memory of the heavy unemployment experienced in the inter-war years, die hard.

Labour turnover and absenteeism

Labour turnover affects the magnitude of training costs and absenteeism the magnitude of total labour costs. Our findings suggest however, that there is insufficient evidence that either of these is uniformly greater in one country than in another. Much depends on individual circumstances: for example, those factories on UK trading estates tend to have a higher labour turnover than those more isolated. Otherwise there is no indication that, given the same circumstances, voluntary movements in labour would be any greater in the US than in the UK, nor that there is any marked difference in the volume of forced turnover. In general, however, the lower unemployment rate in the UK *vis-à-vis* the US has led to a greater mobility of labour between firms. One subsidiary noted that while its labour turnover was 10 per cent per month, its parent company had a substantial waiting list of would-be employees. There was a very slight bias towards more absenteeism in the UK. Special circumstances – holiday areas, poor public transport services, etc. – explain higher rates in certain regions, though a number of personnel managers argued that the presence of a National Health Service and a larger percentage of married women employed, was a chief cause of a higher rate of absenteeism in the UK. Several subsidiaries have implemented time-keeping bonuses, with encouraging results.

Machine efficiency and utilization

Although cost factors make for a more intensive utilization of machinery in American factories, in more cases than not one finds that identical or near-identical machinery is employed. At the same time, in a surprising number of instances a branch factory has to be content with its parent plant's old equipment when the latter purchases new equipment. In contrast, and especially in post-war subsidiaries, the latest factory design and most modern equipment are incorporated; this is naturally to the advantage of the branch plant's productivity. As regards machine and plant utilization, two factors are of considerable importance: (1) the extent to which shift-working is practised and (2) the nature of the market which influences the relationship between setting-up and running times:

Shift-working

Three-quarters of the firms in our survey claimed that shift-working was more pronounced in their American than in their British factories, and the balance said that it was about the same. This latter group was mainly made up of continuous processing firms, where for technical reasons, round-the-clock working is the norm, e.g. as in the petroleum refining, chemical manufacturing and certain food processing industries. As a general rule though, where any choice was involved, it seemed that overtime was preferred to shift-working in the UK. Of our sample, 25 per cent practised no shift-working in the United Kingdom compared with 10 per cent in the United States.

There are, of course, many different types and degrees of shift-working – 2-shift (8 or 12 hours), 3-shift (6 or 8 hours) and 2-shift plus a special half-shift, and so on. Where no shift-working was common in the UK, 2-shifts were usually practised in the United States. The married women's, or – as one firm calls it – 'grannies' shift, from 6 to 10 p. m. or thereabouts, appears most popular in British factories. Various explanations were given by firms for these differences. Of these, difficulties in arranging transport, full employment, the unpopularity of overnight shifts with the workers, the restrictive attitude of trade unions and the Factory Acts, and insufficient markets were most commonly cited (for example, as regards this latter factor though a particular technique might have to be employed, there is no point in working shifts if the level of demand is only sufficient for normal day working). Further to this, one Midlands firm said:

> Whilst our machines in the US are worked on a 3-shift system five days a week and exercised to 70 per cent of their maximum efficiency, in the UK, due to the unpopularity of shift-working with the trade unions, our machines are worked on a 2-shift basis, with the result that the effective utilization of these machines is 34 per cent.

The proportion of productive/non-productive mechanization

Of equal importance is the actual length of time during which machines and equipment are in productive service. This is largely a question of the ratio between changeover or setting-up and running time, which, in turn, will reflect the level and conditions of demand. As we have seen, one aspect of the larger volume of output produced by US parent firms is that such factories can avail themselves of special-purpose machines, which, related to a particular size, style or design of products, are often run continuously without change. With a smaller and less homogeneous market, such economies are not possible in the UK. Expensive single-purpose machines are generally uneconomic and, in their place, general-purpose machines with the appropriate adaptive jigs and fixtures are used. However, because of the shorter runs of such machines, the proportion of productive to running time is reduced. One firm commented:

> The fact that we, with an output of only one-twentieth of that of our US associate, have to produce exactly the same range of products, means that our setting-up to running costs in this country work out at 1:5, whilst in the US the corresponding ratio is 1:30.

Again, a number of pharmaceutical firms noted the fact that different language labels required for the export market often slowed down the overall production process considerably.

Besides this, the number of breakdowns, together with the speed at which the machine is operated, will be the main factors influencing the extent of machine utilization. A number of instances of slower speeds in the United Kingdom were recorded: for instance, one toothpaste manufacturer operated a machine at sixty-five tubes a minute in the US and thirty-five in the UK. Here, market conditions will, in effect, determine the effective utilization of the machinery in question.

The economic consequences of machine utilization show themselves primarily in the level of production costs rather than in physical productivity, save that if one includes indirect labour in one's calculations, the higher the ratio of changeover and setting-up time in this country, the lower labour productivity will be. One final point made by a number of subsidiaries is the fact that because machines are less fully utilized in the UK, it takes longer for them to cover their capital costs, and this, in its turn, tends to delay more up-to-date machinery being employed. Thus, not only are differences in labour costs and market sizes likely to hinder technological progress, but also insufficiency of machine utilization.

Procurement and quality of materials and parts contracted out

The quality of materials and components subcontracted, and the punctuality of the supplier in keeping to stipulated delivery dates, may influence productive efficiency in three main ways. First, the likelihood of shortage and delays will mean that more capital has to be earmarked for inventories so that the smooth fulfilment of any production plan may be achieved.[15] Three-quarters of the firms questioned on this point claimed that delivery dates were generally longer in the UK than in the US, and 60 per cent that UK suppliers were not so reliable in honouring delivery promises. This explains the larger quantities of incoming stock, e.g. metals, cartons, plastics, etc., which a large number of subsidiaries carry in the UK compared with the United States, notwithstanding the shorter distances between supplier and customers. In a few cases, materials which were easily available in the US were difficult to purchase in Britain, and had to be imported, e.g, specialized steel strip, non-ferrous metals, etc. In general, however, UK suppliers appeared to identify their own prosperity with that of their customers less than did their US counterparts: in addition such factors as an amateurish attitude to quality control by many British firms, the lack of inventory consciousness, the tightness of the post-war British economy and the government's lack of sensitivity in ensuring an adequate supply of materials to key industries have not eased the difficulties of recent years. Again, many subsidiaries commented that while in America it is usual for the supplier to hold a stock of materials, etc., ready for sale, in the UK it has been assumed that this was the customer's responsibility. For this reason alone, one affiliate said it had to order its materials far longer in advance than did its parent. At the time this firm was visited (January 1955), it had already ordered its bulk paper supplies for the following December.

Second, a number of subsidiaries claimed that because of differences in the quality of bought-out materials, changes in their own production methods were often necessitated. One large engineering firm commented:

> American raw materials are generally of a better and more consistent quality than those available in this country, with the consequent reduction in production delays due to tool modifications, added operations, inspection queries, etc. The department most affected by this question of material is probably the press shop.

Practical examples include the general hardness of UK cast-iron and strip steel, which makes for difficult precision die-casting and more machining, and the lower quality of steel-wool, which causes more breakdowns. Together with quality inconsistencies and the inexperience of many suppliers, this sometimes means that more labour has to be employed on testing and inspection work. One firm employed 2 per cent of its factory staff in this way in the UK compared with 0.5 per cent in the US.

Third, the quality and consistency of bought-out materials may affect the amount of scrap and wastage involved in production. A number of firms in the clothing and foodstuffs industries claimed that the characteristics of UK raw materials made a higher percentage of scrap inevitable. Another canning subsidiary said that in the US the fruit and vegetables bought were much cleaner and, in consequence, its own operating wastage was reduced. Here, too, and particularly where material costs are a large percentage of total costs, e.g. in the manufacture of foundation garments, the importance of efficient training is shown in its proper perspective. For obvious reasons, scant details were forthcoming on the comparative rate of scrap and wastage in America and in the UK: in fact, only a few firms made any precise calculations of such figures. Of these, ten said that the scrap percentage was *higher* in the US than in the UK, sixteen that it was *lower*, and six *about the same*. In explaining why the percentage figure was sometimes higher in the United Kingdom, one firm observed that since the proportion of running to setting-up time was lower, the scrap was greater because of the necessary adjustments which had to be made. Lack of experience was also instanced by post-war-established firms, and age of machinery by pre-war companies. A dozen or so subsidiaries, however, argued that more care was exercised in the UK factory – even at the expense of lower productivity – first because the ratio of material to labour costs was so much higher, second because a higher proportion of raw materials had to be bought out, third because of the better attitude and efficiency of UK operatives in reducing scrap and wastage, and lastly because British customers often demanded a higher quality finish of final goods than their US counterparts.

MISCELLANEOUS REASONS FOR DIFFERENCES IN PRODUCTIVITY

We have cited some of the main factors which firms have noted in explanation of the differences which exist in manufacturing methods and productivity between US parent and UK branch plants.

Numerous other causes may be added to these, most of which have, at one time or another, been cited in the Productivity Team Reports. The most frequently quoted might be briefly summarized as follows:

1 Excess demand has, in general, been much greater in UK factories than in US in recent years. In the words of one subsidiary: 'We have been expanding so fast in this country that we have not had time to concern ourselves with productivity.'

2 A common opinion of affiliates is that a higher product finish is required in the United Kingdom than in the United States. Again, as one firm said:

> In the US we design our cigarette lighters knowing full well that the average customer is constantly on the look-out for new products. In the UK, partly because a cigarette lighter is regarded more as a luxury good, and partly because of sentimental attachments, the customer expects his product to last very much longer. Thus, the UK lighter has had to be improved, both as regards durability and finish.

The same applies, but for rather different reasons to such products as kitchen utensils, roofing materials and electric tools.

3 In the main, safety regulations appear to be more demanding, and precautions of one kind or another more restrictive, in the United Kingdom, with the result, for example, that the rate at which machines are loaded and unloaded is considerably slowed down.

4 Both standardization and simplification of end products (and components) are generally more pronounced in the United States than in the United Kingdom, and the slower rate of obsolescence in the latter only aggravates the problem. Once more, with a fully-employed UK economy since 1945, there has not been the same inducement for the firms to follow the American pattern.

5 Except for the very modern branch plants, factory design and layout is usually better and more up to date in the United States than in the United Kingdom. Moreover, storage and handling problems are obviously increased where a diversified output has to be produced, while shortage of capital and materials, together with a rapidly increasing demand in recent years, has often brought with it exceptionally cramped factory conditions in UK plants.

6 Climatic considerations are generally (though not always) in favour of a US

location. One firm, for example, asserted that weather corrosion was a much greater problem in the UK; another, that materials shrinkage was higher; and a third, that the seasonal nature of the demands for its products in the UK made for unstable production.

SUMMARY OF PRODUCTIVITY DIFFERENCES

We have now to ask what is the combined effect of the factors studied on the relative productivity of the British and American factories. Unfortunately, it is not possible to disentangle the contributions each make to the productivity of the two kinds of plant. Some years ago, one firm tried to break down into its components an estimated difference of 57 per cent in the productivity of the branch and the parent unit. This was made up as follows:

8 per cent more efficient die-casting
8 per cent more productive plant
8 per cent more efficient operators
8 per cent more efficient supervision and organization
6 per cent longer experience of production
5 per cent longer and bigger runs, smaller range of models
3 per cent less safety precautions and guarding
3 per cent better raw materials and lower standards of finish
3 per cent more efficient tooling and equipment
3 per cent no tea breaks
2 per cent better materials handling and less congestion . . . in the US

In all, only twenty-five firms were able to give any reliable numerical estimate of their Anglo-American productivity differences. Each showed that physical output per man-hour was lower in the United Kingdom; 7 said productivity was less than 60 per cent of the US level; 8 between 60 and 75 per cent and 6 between 75 and 90 per cent, and 4 between 90 per cent and 100 per cent. In all these cases, there was direct correlation between the difference in productivity and the size of market served by the US factory compared with its UK counterpart. More firms, however, were able to express an opinion as to the general order of magnitude. In answer to the question: 'Do you consider that your average output per man-hour is (1) substantially less (2) slightly less (3) about the same or (4) more, in this country than in the US?' of the 128 firms, or 62 per cent of the sample, which replied, 32 said substantially lower, 63 slightly lower, 30 about the same and 3 higher. Table 5.3 sets out the opinions received. Within these groups, the biggest differences were recorded by the auto, refrigerator and agricultural equipment and pharmaceutical firms.

In our investigations, we came across only one real attempt to compare direct operative performance in the two countries. This took the form of relating actual performances to some identifiable standard performance – in terms of either cost or output. This measure specifically aims at isolating the factor of operative labour as a variable influencing productivity. The standard time is that time, judged by

Table 5.3 Comparative average physical productivity in British and US plants, 1953[1]

Industrial group	Productivity substantially lower in UK		Productivity slightly lower in UK		Productivity the same in UK		Productivity higher in UK	
	UK man-aged	US man-aged	UK man-aged	US man-aged	UK man-aged	US man-aged	UK man-aged	US man-aged
Chemical and allied trades	1	4	1	8	2	8	–	–
Engineering and metal products	12	3	18	16	6	2	1	1
Precision and scientific instruments	3	1	2	2	–	1	–	–
Food, drink and tobacco	1	1	1	2	–	3	–	–
Other manufacturing industries	3	3	8	5	3	5	–	1
Total	20	12	30	33	11	19	1	2
	32		63		30		3	

Note:
1 Estimate by sample of 128 firms.

time and motion study, production planning and budgetary control, which it can be reasonably expected that the operative will carry out a particular manufacturing operation or process. Related to this is the actual time which an operative (or group of operatives) takes to do the job. This figure is then expressed as a ratio of the standard time. The higher the result, the greater the operator's efficiency is presumed to be, and since the setting of the standard time has (or should have) taken into consideration the 'unavoidable' factors affecting such efficiencies, UK and US percentages are directly comparable. To obtain a figure of factory (or product) efficiency, a weighted average is usually taken of the various individual processes. A number of firms made comparisons in this way. In the eight cases (all engineering firms) about which information was given to us, the relative direct labour efficiency in the UK (US = 100) was 90, 93, 95, 95, 97, 96–102, 95–100 and 98–104 respectively. This would suggest that as far as the productivity of direct labour is concerned, there is not a great deal of difference in the two economies. However, these figures should be treated with caution as they presuppose that those responsible for setting the 'standard' are themselves behaving optimally and there is no guarantee that this is the case. Nevertheless, since these standards are usually set in relation to *US performance*, and in all cases are vetted periodically by the US parent, it would seem that the figures quoted give a good approximate guide to labour efficiency in the two countries. And from this, one

Table 5.4 Comparative plant operating methods in US and UK plants, 1953[1]

Industrial group	Markedly different methods in US and UK		Marginally different methods in US and UK		Identical, or near-identical methods in US and UK	
	UK managed	US managed	UK managed	US managed	UK managed	US managed
Chemical and allied trades	2	1	2	11	1	6
Engineering and metal products	7	1	21	24	4	4
Precision and scientific instruments	2	1	4	2	–	–
Food, drink and tobacco	1	1	1	4	–	1
Other manufacturing industries	3	1	9	12	1	1
Total	15	5	37	53	6	12
	20		90		18	

Note:
1 Estimate by sample of 128 firms.

might argue that, in general, *as far as US-financed firms* are concerned, this need not be an important variable.

In conclusion, in answer to the general question: 'Are you operating methods markedly different, marginally different, or the same in this country as in the US?' of the 128 firms answering, 20 said *markedly*, 90 *marginally* (mainly in connection with materials handling and packaging) and 18 *the same*. Once again, these firms may be further classified by industries and degree of US control in Table 5.4.

Finally, it is interesting to observe that a number of US subsidiaries thought they performed better than their parent plants. In twelve cases, the subsidiary maintained that its relative position in the UK economy was higher than the corresponding position of its parent concern in America. As one might perhaps expect, those firms which are American-managed are more likely to follow their associate plants' manufacturing techniques than those which are not.

RELATIVE PRODUCTION COSTS IN BRITISH AND AMERICAN FACTORIES

Finally, we turn from physical productivity to value productivity and firms were asked the following question: 'Are your overall costs of production (at the current rate of exchange) higher, about the same, or lower, in this country than in the US?' Of the 140 firms which replied, 21 said their costs were *higher* than in the United Kingdom, 36 *about the same*, and 83 *less*. Of these latter firms, 40 were able to be more precise in their estimate of the differences. Eight subsidiaries claimed that they were able to produce at below half the cost of their parents, 12 that they could produce at between one-half and three-quarters of the cost of their parents, and 20 between 80 per cent and 90 per cent of the cost of their parents. The relative cost situation most favoured the UK branch in the domestic electrical appliances, razor-blade, electric tool and metal products industries, and least in the mass-production, or largely capitalized industries, where costs were usually higher. As might be expected, the UK subsidiary came out the best where (a) value added by labour (in relation to gross output) was the highest and (b) the relative efficiency (as defined above) was the most favourable. One multi-product firm expressed the feeling of many subsidiaries by saying:

> Where labour is the prime factor, our UK costs run well below US costs, in fact down to as little as 60 per cent of US. Where volume makes tooling the prime factor, UK production costs are at least equal to, and in some cases up to, 40 per cent greater than US costs.

On the other hand, it must be remembered that, since the UK branch often bears only a small amount of the research, development and many overhead expenses of its parent company, its costs are lower by that amount. As one subsidiary put it:

> Our factory costs work out at 10 per cent above those of our parent company, but overall production costs are 5 per cent less; primarily this is because we do little research and development ourselves and get all that we can from America gratis.

It is, however, not possible to generalize on the importance of this factor. Thus, irrespective of any question of transatlantic transport costs, the UK plant is often able to sell in export markets more cheaply than can its parent concern. As a result, the parent company has sometimes allocated all its overseas markets to the branch plant, and in some cases, e.g. where customer needs differ across national boundaries, this has adversely affected productivity. At the same time, one firm calculated that it could sell each of its thirty products more cheaply to Canada than could its parent concern.

CONCLUSIONS

Is it possible, then, to generalize? Only very tentatively may the following conclusions be put forward.

First, we can perhaps say that in many, if not in the majority of cases, US manufacturing subsidiaries in the UK utilize very similar production techniques to those of their parent companies. But over and above this, there are many marginal differences which may be expected to grow in importance as the core production processes become more standardized. When looked at in terms of their significance to total costs, the differences in administrative procedures, mechanical handling and packaging techniques, purchasing and marketing arrangements, the handling of industrial relations, the choice between semi- and fully automatic mechanization, the degree of shift-working and the efficiency of machine utilization, etc., are all significant cost-related variables, and it is here that future economies would appear to be most promising. In many instances, it would appear that the smaller and more diverse market conditions facing the UK subsidiary limits it from taking advantage of these considerations. Thus, the productivity of both direct and indirect labour is reduced as there is not the same chance of specialization in the United Kingdom, with the consequent improvements in efficiency.

At the same time, as far as one can judge, the direct labour efficiency of branch plants approaches closely that of their parent concerns. This being so, assuming the order of our productivity estimates to be substantially correct, they would suggest that it is possible for British firms in like industries to reach a plant productivity at least within three-quarters of that of their American counterparts. A discussion of the relative efficiency of US-affiliated firms and their native competitors follows in the next chapter, which also analyses the extent to which American subsidiaries and Anglo-American companies have affected the structural development of the industries of their choice and the rate of technical innovation.

6 The influence of US firms on UK industrial development and on the efficiency of their UK competitors

In Chapters 1 and 2 we were concerned with the role which US-financed firms have played in the past, and are playing today, in influencing the course and direction of British industrial development. The present chapter tries to assess the more important aspects of the impact made by such firms – in whatever industry they may be producing – on those industries' structure and efficiency, and on how their British competitors have been affected in consequence. What, for example, has been the influence of the pricing policy adopted by US subsidiaries and Anglo-American concerns? How far does the research, manufacturing and managerial expertise which such firms derive from their US associates affect their market positions? To what extent has the structure of UK industry been made more or less conducive to economic change and development by their presence?

THE IMPLICATIONS OF THE INDUSTRIAL STRUCTURE WITHIN WHICH US FIRMS PRODUCE

The influence which the price and other competitive policies of a firm can have on an industry will obviously depend upon the importance of that firm in relationship to its competitors. If it is one of a small number of important firms which together supply most of the total output, i.e. it is competing under conditions of oligopoly, then it is unlikely to increase its share of the market without making serious inroads into at least one of its rivals' production. If, on the other hand, it is either one of a substantial number of firms each of which has only a modest share of the market, or one which is in a monopolistic or near-monopolistic, position, then it need not take into consideration the reaction of competitors; in the first case (assuming the impact to be evenly dispersed) because there are so many, and in the second because there are none. Technically, the degree of market interdependence may be measured by making use of the concept 'cross-elasticity of demand', which for any firm may be defined as the proportionate extension or contraction in the demand for that firm's product as a result of a change in the price of another firm's product. The higher this ratio, and assuming the reverse relationship also to apply, the greater the interdependence between competitors' output and sales policy.

At the same time, the influence of an important firm, which is one of a few supplying its particular product, is not confined to price policy; an enlarged advertising budget, the introduction of a better-designed or technically superior product, improved after-sales service or – more indirectly – an intensification of research and development, and greater managerial efficiency, by any one firm may equally induce some response from its competitors. The fact that three-quarters of the employment in US-affiliated firms is concentrated in industries where the five largest competitors supply 80 per cent or more of the total output shows that any policy change adopted by such a firm is unlikely to be isolated in its effect. Regard must also be paid to whether, whatever the strength of the position of an important foreign-owned firm in relation to indigenous producers, there is competition from imports. Table 6.1 attempts to show the possible influences of the 205 US-affiliated firms on price and other strategies of firms in their industries by classifying the latter according to the type of competitive structure associated with their produce:, viz. Group A – where the US firm is the dominant supplier and is faced with little or no competition; Group B – where it is one of a small number of important producers; Group C – where it is one of a large number of producers of modest size.

Apart from the fact that this classification of firms is approximate, it has one or two other limitations. First, about one-third of the multi-product firms in the sample supply both specialized products in which they are the only or dominant producer, and others where their share of the UK output is very small. For example, Thomas Hedley's relative position in the synthetic detergent market is very much stronger than its position in the dentrifice market; Libby, McNeill and Libby is one of two largest suppliers of tinned evaporated milk in this country, but its share of the output of baked beans is negligible. Second, many US affiliates, e.g. in the electrical equipment, motor-car, cinematic film, sewing machine industries, etc., though among a small number of producers, nevertheless face competition from foreign suppliers. Third, the relative position of the leading firms often fluctuates in the normal course of industrial development, and this sometimes within the context of an increasing *total* market for the goods in question; in consequence, it cannot be automatically assumed that any *potential* oligopolistic influence will, in fact, prove to be as effective as it seems at first sight.

Notwithstanding these limitations, the general picture is strikingly clear. In nearly three cases out of four, if an American-affiliated firm should introduce a new product, reduce its price or make any other important change in its innovating, production or sales strategy, this is likely to have some repercussions on the development of the industry of which it is part. In addition, in 136 instances, or two-thirds of the sample, the demand for the products of one or more rival firms is likely to be seriously affected.

The chief reasons for the size structure of American-affiliated firms have already been outlined. The fact that it is usually the larger and more prosperous American companies which invest in Great Britain; that the UK subsidiary has often been set up for the specific purpose of supplying established export markets previously satisfied by the US plant; that the American firm is often itself a

Table 6.1 Market shares of US-owned affiliates in British industry

Group A US firm the dominant producer	Group B US firm one of a small number of strong producers	Group C US firm one of a number of producers of modest size
12 firms employing 32,000 people	136 firms employing 200,000 people	57 firms employing 14,000 people
Products supplied include:	Within such an industrial structure US-financed firms are the *largest producers* of e.g.:	*Products supplied* include:
Sewing machines[1]	Domestic boilers	Proprietary medicines
Boot and shoe machinery	Breakfast cereals	Beauty and toilet
Starch	Synthetic detergents	preparations
Carbon black	Foundation garments	Industrial instruments
Cinematic films[1]	Printing and typesetting	Petroleum refinery
Motor vehicle tyre valves	machinery	equipment
	Oil drilling equipment	Machine and hand tools
	Road-making machinery	Cigarettes
	Sparking plugs	Foundation garments
	Roll films	Cotton textiles
	Lifts and escalators	
	Safety razors and blades	
	Typewriters	
	Cash registers	
	Calculating machines	
	Computers	
	Refined platinum	
	Commercial refrigerators	
	Vacuum cleaners	
	Computers	
	the second largest producers of e.g.:	
	Motor-cars	
	Agricultural tractors and implements	
	Rubber tyres	
	Abrasives and grinding wheels	
	Canned milk	
	Canned foodstuffs	
	Soft drinks	
	Home refrigerators	
	Electronic industrial instruments	
	Alarm clocks	
	Portable electric tools	
	Excavating equipment	

Table 6.1 Continued

Group A US firm the dominant producer	Group B US firm one of a small number of strong producers	Group C US firm one of a number of producers of modest size
	and the third largest producers of e.g.: All-purpose chemicals Other rubber products Refined petroleum Hardboard[2]	

Notes:
1 Subject to foreign competition.
2 Also included in Group B are firms supplying ethical specialities, telephone equipment, pneumatic tools, petrol pumps, bottle-washing machinery, cat and dog food, motion picture sound projection equipment and electric washing machines.

pioneer, of a particular product, material or manufacturing technique; and that the share of the market held by such firms in recent years has been increasing – all tend to make for the type of interdependence which will ensure that the price and other policies of American affiliates will have a significant impact on those of their indigenous competitors.

At the same time, in some cases US subsidiaries and Anglo-American manufacturing units have themselves played an important part in moulding the type of competitive structure just described. The manner of achievement has been varied, but three ways deserve especial mention: (1) through the normal course of economic growth and technical development, (2) by the deliberate process of *vertical* or *horizontal* integration, this either as a result of (1), or the prompting of competitors to pool resources against the growing strength of American-dominated companies, and (3) by injecting more competition into a market which otherwise might have been a near-monopoly.

First, then, we have structural changes following the introduction of new production techniques. Chapter 1 has already described how, from its inception, the UK electrical equipment industry was built on the foundations of a few highly capitalized firms. It is difficult to say how far such a market structure would not have occurred in any case, though viewed in the light of the pattern of growth of other British industries, it might be fair to suggest that the large initial investments undertaken by US-financed concerns – backed by American patents and expertise – helped to establish the industry on a sound competitive basis from the start. Likewise the new and capital-intensive printing techniques pioneered by the Hoe and Linotype enterprises, were largely responsible for the decline of the small hand printer, while the superior managerial and marketing methods of the American meat subsidiaries in the early 1900s led to the concentration of chilled beef distribution within the hands of four or five major companies. In the motor vehicles industry, the Ford Company – in adopting the mass-production techniques of its parent company from the time of its original establishment at Trafford

Park – set the pace for its competitors, while between the wars the same company, in pioneering technological advances in agricultural tractor production, did much to change the composition of that industry from a complexity of small firms of village blacksmith size into a handful of large producers. Finally, since 1945, the output of razor-blades has been increasingly concentrated in the hands of the Gillette and Ever-Ready companies. Largely as a result of improved, but highly capitalized, production techniques, the number of important suppliers of blades and razors in this country has steadily fallen, and is now effectively reduced to two US subsidiaries. American influence in the canned food, soft drink, refrigerator and refractory products industries has been similarly marked.

Second, sometimes the establishment or expansion of an American-financed unit has had the effect of stimulating a number of competing British firms to take joint action to protect their interests. The result has been an increased concentration of industrial output in the hands of a few strong producers. The classic example of the formation of the Imperial Tobacco Company in 1902 by the amalgamation of thirteen independent UK companies to combat the actions of the American Tobacco Company has its modern counterpart in the merger between the Austin and Morris Motor companies in 1953, which, among other things, was an attempt to offset the growing competitive strength of the Ford and Vauxhall organizations. And only a year later, the largest British agricultural tractor firm of Ferguson Ltd joined forces with the important Canadian farm implement specialist, Massey-Harris Corporation, to help it improve its marketing position *vis-à-vis* Ford Motor Company and the International Harvester Company. In other cases, there is evidence of British firms resisting acquisition by strong American established interests: not infrequently, and notably in the photographic equipment industry, this would appear to have prevented a potential monopoly from becoming effective.

Third, and in contrast to the second trend, American-financed firms have sometimes injected a new element of competition into a market which would otherwise have been dominated by an existing British firm. For example, the Diamond Match Company, established in 1896, was directly responsible for breaking up a monopolistic position previously held by the British company Bryant and May Ltd.[1] During the 1920s, the establishment of the Goodyear Tyre Company and the Firestone Tyre Company did much to prevent the Dunlop Rubber Company from strengthening its already dominant position in the rubber tyre market. Had not Procter and Gamble bought out and rejuvenated the old-established British firm of Thomas Hedley, which at the time of purchase was a small company trying to compete in an industry increasingly influenced by the powerful Unilever combine, the latter's control of the market would, almost certainly, have become more pronounced. In as much as it induced its major competitor – Ideal Boilers and Radiators Ltd – to be more alert to technical progress, the entry of the American subsidiary – Crane Ltd – into the domestic boilers field in 1930 had a similar impact. Since the Second World War, the UK balance of payments disequilibrium has led many US firms who were selling in the UK before 1939 to set up manufacturing units and, by prices and their presence, stimulate competition and thwart potential monopolies, as for example in the oil, watch and clock, office appliance, refrigeration machinery and excavating equipment industries. Looking to the future, it also seems likely that any monopolistic element in the pricing of television tubes[2] will be substantially curtailed by the formation of the joint Anglo-American venture Sylvania-Thorn Ltd. In its plant, with an initial capacity of 500,000 21-inch picture tubes each year, American know-how plus US-designed fully-automatic production equipment are scheduled to cut a third off the present price of UK tubes.

Other instances of where major American and British interests compete with one another in oligopolistic markets and which have evolved for one or other of the three reasons mentioned above, include Intertype Ltd v. Linotype and Machinery Ltd (two US firms), H. J. Heinz Co. Ltd v. Crosse and Blackwell Ltd, Libby McNeill and Libby Ltd v. Nestlés Ltd, and Black and Decker v. Wolfe Electric Tools Ltd.

The above examples suffice to show the influences exerted by US foreign direct investment on UK market structure. Yet, while deliberate attempts to gain complete control of the market have largely failed,[3] in a number of instances US firms have maintained an *initially* established monopolistic or near-monopolistic position by means of patent or trade-mark protection, e.g. cigarette lighters, fire-fighting equipment, or by erecting economic and financial barriers to prospective new entrants, e.g. in the boot and shoe and sewing machinery industries. For the most part, however, these have been in selected fields where markets are limited and any exploitation of the monopolistic position is curtailed by foreign competition. Often, in the course of years, these concerns have widened their activities *vertically* or *laterally*, either through internal growth or by integrating with other firms. For example, the British United Shoe Machinery Company now owns seven subsidiary companies manufacturing respectively shoe eyelets, leather dressings, stains, adhesive compounds, wooden heels and shoe-repairing machinery which it has purchased at one time or another during the last sixty-five years. The Johnson and Johnson organization controls five separate business units which supply respectively surgical dressings, toothbrushes, sutures, toilet preparations and personal products. Likewise with the Corn Products Group which first set up in Manchester in 1921 to manufacture glucose and starch products, amalgamated with Brown and Polson Ltd in 1935, and now grinds its own starch in its Scottish factories. The motor-car companies have evolved in a similar way, while other subsidiaries have integrated *forwards* by setting up their own distribution outlets, e.g. Singer Ltd, Black and Decker Ltd, Remington Rand Ltd, and Esso Petroleum Ltd.

How far can such trends as these be said to have beneficially affected British industrial competitiveness and progress? Is an oligopolistic structure most conducive to economic efficiency? These are questions which forbid any clear-cut answer, and concerning which it is exceedingly difficult to generalize either way. There are many arguments both in favour of and against large-scale business units. Balanced against the technical advantages of size must be set the possible abuse of economic power by monopolies or oligopolies, which, assuming the absence of state intervention, cannot easily be curbed without losing the advantages as well.[4]

The problem arises because, in the majority of the industries to which we have been referring, technological factors do not allow the optimum scale of plant or best practice manufacturing methods to be utilized until a fairly large output is produced. Yet, at the same time, because of market limitations, it may very well be that if each firm is to supply at minimum or near-minimum costs, then the industry will only be able to support a small number of producers. If in such circumstances it could be assumed that there was no anti-competitive collusion between sellers, and that the final price agreed upon was no more than sufficient to cover the opportunity costs of production of the efficient producer, and to enable adequate innovatory activities to be pursued, then a competitive structure of this kind might well be considered as ideal.[5] But the point is that a situation in which only a few firms compete itself militates against these advantages. For on the one hand there is a constant possibility of anti-competitive behaviour among the oligopolists, and on the other, since the gains of driving one's rival out of business are great, the associated dangers of price instability, cut-throat competition and sharp business practices. Because, too, as we have seen, an oligopolistic structure often means that the industry in question can support only a small number of important producers, the likelihood is that each competitor can earn above average profits without fear of new entrants being induced: should it then happen that the decision takers of the relevant firms were not solely interested in maximizing profits, a possibility arises of slackness and inefficiency being tolerated, or insufficient attention being paid to research and development. Lastly, where the oligopolists are selling heterogeneous products, competition may be sub-optimally directed, e.g. to excessive advertising or product differentiation. Especially is this likely to be the case where manufacturers' profit margins are delicately adjusted so as not to permit any price downward adjustment without a corresponding reduction in costs.

On the other hand, what of the alternatives? A monopoly *may*, it is true, give price stability at the cost of yet higher prices, and even less spur towards research and technological progress, while the fostering of a more competitive structure (e.g. by making entry conditions easier) may raise the level of operating costs and prevent full technical efficiency being reached. Only if such measures resulted in the reduction of surplus profits, the stabilization of prices and the upgrading of productivity might it be argued that net economic welfare had been increased.

To what extent, in fact, do US-affiliated firms in the UK engage in restrictive practices in the sense defined above? Here, there is insufficient evidence to permit of any definite conclusions. One has a most marked impression in visiting American branch factories that there are no signs of technical progress or managerial efficiency being sacrificed once a comfortable profit is earned. The maxim 'Business is business all the way' as applied to the United States Beef Trust in 1909,[6] remains the dominant attitude today. If anything, the prestige value of a large and thriving business is likely to drive American firms to produce beyond their most efficient output. Their enthusiasm for technical advances, plant efficiency, and product development may well result in their production planning and research departments being overloaded. Certainly in most of the industries in which there is strong US representation, e.g. motor-car, refrigerator, office equipment, washing machine, American-affiliated firms are among the leaders in new ideas and innovations, while in many of the more recently established subsidiaries there is an eagerness to finance expansion as quickly as possible. And though it is often the parent companies which decide policy matters of this kind, this does not prevent a very real competitive spirit from existing between many branch plants and their US parents; indeed, in a number of instances, the former go out of their way to impress the latter with their efficiency and technological ability.

In marketing and selling procedures, the general tendency is for American-financed firms to conform closely to the pattern prevailing in British industry, except where they themselves have pioneered new techniques. Only a very small minority of subsidiaries, for example, do not belong to the appropriate trade associations and abide by their regulations, and with one or two notable exceptions, such widely discussed practices as exclusive selling, dealers' rebates, resale price maintenance, fixed service charges, etc., are as much a feature of these firms as they are of their native competitors.[7]

THE COMPETITIVE ADVANTAGES OF AMERICAN TECHNICAL EXPERTISE AND MANAGEMENT PHILOSOPHY

What next of the *specific* contributions to British industrial development which American-affiliated firms have been able to make as a direct result of their transatlantic associations? These might conveniently be classified under three main headings:

1 *Technical know-how or expertise*
     in the form of (a) research and technological developments.
     (b) manufacturing experience.
2 *Non-technical know-how or expertise*
     in the form of (a) managerial, organizational advertising, sales methods, etc.
     (b) financial backing (which sometimes allows branch plants, etc., an additional source of capital).
3 *The American philosophy or attitude towards production and management*
     in (a) the practical application of 1 (a) and (b).
     (b) the application of 2 (a) and the 'will' to be efficient.

Chapters 4 and 5 have already partly described, and Chapters 7 and 9 will have more to say about, the nature and significance of these two latter benefits. This being so, with the exception of certain aspects of managerial procedure, which we find particularly convenient to discuss in this present context, the following observations will be confined mainly to matters relating to the nature and value of the *technical* expertise which US-financed firms are able to draw upon, over and above that which is normally available to their British competitors.

Research and development

The expenditure of large sums of money on organized research is of comparatively recent origin. At the turn of the present century, for example, when the gross
national product of the UK was rising more rapidly than it is today, the amount
expended on systematic research and development was probably not more than
£1 million per annum,[8] and the ratio of non-operative (including research and
development staff) to operative workers engaged in manufacturing industry then
stood at 1: 12.[9] At the same time, the 'time-lag' between the discovery of a new
process or product and its commercial exploitation was comparatively short and,
for the most part, inexpensive. Few firms had specialized departments or laboratories for organized invention; in the United States, for example, the first industrial concern to organize research as a separate and continuing activity founded its
research laboratory in 1900.[10]

By 1950, however, as a result of changing economic circumstances, and the
tremendous strides made by industrial science and technology, the attitude
towards the role of research and development had undergone a profound change.
So too, with the rapid mechanization of the factory, the growing importance of
pre-production planning and the vast expansion of all kinds of paperwork, the
burden of the administrative overheads has increased, the above ratio falling to 1:
5 by 1951. With every successive improvement in living standards demanding a
proportionately greater technological input, the function of research and development is becoming more and more recognized by government and industry alike
as being the life-blood of the UK – and any other – industrial country's progress.
It is no accident that the United States spends more each year than any other
country in the world on research, *and* has the highest productivity and income per
head. At the same time, the trend has been for post-fundamental research to
increase in both time and cost. In 1951, for example, Professor R. L. Meier
estimated that for every dollar expended on basic research in the United States,
about $10 of new capital had to be invested before any benefits could accrue,[11]
while in a report 'Applied Research in the United States' published by the
National Academy of Science in 1952, it was stated that the average amount
spent on laboratory facilities and equipment per graduate scientist varied between
$10,000[12] and $30,000 per annum. The commercialization of nylon is thought to
have cost the Du Pont organization over $270 million[13] and that of the various
'mycin' antibiotics more than $100 million spread over six companies. It took, the
US Bristol Myers Company five years to market successfully the analgesic bufferin
from the time of its original inception, while the vast General Motors organization
is currently employing more than 4,000 research, design and machine specialists
in its new $140 million research headquarters at Detroit.

The chief consequence of all these developments is that research – unless co-
operatively organized – is becoming increasingly the province of the large firms,
which, with their ability to derive scale-economies, gives them an important
advantage over their smaller competitors.[14] Not only does this apply to the
research laboratory itself, it is equally evident throughout the firm's organization.

Some years ago, for example, it was calculated that one-half of the research and development ideas of one American chemical company emanated from outside its research department.[15] Large firms, too, by reason of their ability to effect various other economies, e.g. in finance and marketing, are able to devote more resources to research and, in doing so, reap the added advantages which it is possible to obtain from specialization in this field. They are also in a much better position to shepherd new ideas through each of the three main stages of the production process, viz. research, manufacturing and marketing. Industrial research is both circular and cumulative in character: if successful, it makes for higher profits and these, in turn, empower the firm to apply more capital for the support of further research. According, again to Professor Meier, for every dollar currently put into research, three dollars in profit are being earned from the results of past research.[16] In the newer, dynamic and research-conscious industries, closely interdependent in market structure, the possible rewards are especially attractive. The main limiting factor is, however, that a large initial investment is often required to start the operation of the cycle, and to cover the risks of likely mistakes and failures.

The research function, in its search for, and application of, new knowledge, covers 'a spectrum of activities with continuous gradations of utility from the most abstract to the most practical'.[17] Not always is it possible to demarcate where the responsibilities of the research and development department ends and where that of actual production begins. Research may be further classified according to the purpose for which it is undertaken, by the pre-production stage at which it takes place, or by the type of problem it tries to solve.

Fundamental research seeks to advance knowledge. Sometimes personal curiosity and scientific considerations may be the only end in view, though most industrial research programmes are undertaken for the ultimate benefit of the firm in question. *Applied* research is the exploitation of new knowledge with a specific object in mind, or as the National Academy of Sciences and National Research Council would have it defined – 'the solving of problems of practical significance'. Such research may be of various kinds, and designed to meet a multiplicity of ends: it may be short- or long-term in objective; it may be related to process improvement, product innovation, the discovery of new kinds of raw materials, waste utilization, accounting procedures, marketing and distribution to the general management of the company as a whole.[18] The term *development* – or *development research* – is usually restricted to covering the stages of the value-added process between the inception of any idea and its full commercialization on the factory floor, though it may sometimes refer to the actual adaptations or developments which are necessitated as a result of the earlier research as defined above.

So much for broad definitions. What then of the research relationships which exist between US parent firms and their British subsidiaries, and their implications for the UK economy? The fact that, with one or two minor exceptions, all subsidiaries and Anglo-American concerns are able to draw upon the research and development output and facilities of their US associates, and that this gives them an important advantage over most of their native competitors is axiomatic from what has already been said. The extent of the value of these benefits may best be illustrated by the fact that, of the $1,600 million which American industry spends on (private) research and development each year, 25 per cent to 30 per cent is made directly available to the UK economy in this way; this is more than British industry (including the co-operative research associations) annually spends on research.[19] To the extent that an American subsidiary can freely draw upon such knowledge and, in most cases, adapt it to the specialized needs of the markets it serves, it is afforded a vital competitive advantage – an advantage which is further underlined by the fact that it is also able to send back to the parent company any ideas for experimentation, development or commercialization.

The value of this gain to the British economy will naturally depend on such considerations as the relative sizes of the parent and branch plants of the US investors, the competitive structure in the two countries, and the nature of research in question. The actual organization of company research may also be important. In most cases, each operating division or subsidiary company has its own research department, though usually its functions are co-ordinated by a Central Research Laboratory of the parent concern. In one or two larger firms, the Central Laboratory is even organized as a separate company; for example, the Standard Oil Development Company serves as the research department for all companies – home and overseas – which are under the control of the Standard Oil Company of New Jersey. Such research and development companies carry out research, install pilot plants, develop products and processes and sometimes manufacture equipment or products on a limited scale: they also make available the results of research and development to their operating companies throughout the world. A research structure of this kind proved itself of particular value at the time when the Esso Refinery at Southampton was being built.

Concerning the actual amount and type of research carried out by US-affiliated companies in this country, the general picture is as follows:

1 Twenty-five per cent of the affiliates in our sample said that they maintained no separate research and development department and, apart from a small amount of product or material adaptation and the development of specialized products and processes, operated solely as manufacturing units. In the main, these firms (a) tended to produce identical products in their US and UK plants, (b) were small, (c) were of recent origin and (d) were strongly dominated in policy and thought by their American parent companies.

2 Fifty-six per cent of the subsidiaries and Anglo-American firms said that they did some applied and development research, while relying on their US parent companies to provide them with all fundamental and basic know-how. In some cases independent research, specific to the needs at hand, might be undertaken, but, by and large, laboratory activities were confined to adaptations of American product designs, manufacturing techniques and material formulae. Most of the pharmaceutical, cosmetic and rubber tyre companies came within this category. As one firm put it: 'The engineering department of the British company limits its designing function to the modification of ranges, or of

individual tools, to suit conditions peculiar to the UK market.' Another commented that: 'By far the largest proportion of our time is spent in finding out
new materials to substitute for those asked for in American formulae.'

3 Nineteen per cent of subsidiaries said they engaged in some basic research of
their own. As in the preceding two cases, however, strong reliance was placed
on the Central Research Laboratory in the US. A handful of these branch units
limited the scope of their research to those activities for which their resources
were comparatively the best suited, and made available such information to the
group as a whole. For example, one light precision engineering firm concen-
trates its manufacturing design research in the UK while depending on its
parent concern to supply it with product and process development know-how.
Another chemical subsidiary specializes in cast-iron enamelling research in this
country, while its American and Dutch laboratories concentrate on the technology of sheet steel and glazed enamelling. The larger and well-established
subsidiaries and Anglo-American firms which mainly make up this category
include most of the companies supplying motor-cars, cosmetics, boot and shoe
machinery, basic chemicals, petroleum products and industrial instruments.

The number and variety of subsidiaries engaging in fundamental research is
growing. Thomas Hedley has just opened a £500,000 laboratory in Newcastle,
and in the last ten years has quadrupled its expenditure on research. Monsanto
Chemicals has greatly enlarged its research facilities at Newport (South Wales)
since the war, while a non-ferrous metal firm's new laboratory cost £100,000 and
is larger and more up to date than that of its parent. A fourth subsidiary supplying
light engineering products spends more on research and development each year
than its American counterpart. Work recently started on a five-year expansion
plan for the Abingdon research headquarters of the Esso Petroleum Company
which at present employs over 200 qualified scientists and technicians. Much
pioneering work has emanated from these laboratories, including the discovery
of a new synthetic lubricant for high speed jet aircraft. Other US-financed firms
which operate sizeable research and development departments in the UK include
Kodak, Sperry Gyroscope, Standard Telephones, Hoover, British United Shoe
Machinery, Johnson and Johnson, and the motor vehicle subsidiaries.

The technological character of the expertise transferred from parent to affiliates
varies a good deal. Some 20 per cent of the US subsidiaries said that it mainly
took the form of chemical formulae and processes, 15 per cent materials and
product composition, 20 per cent product and machinery design, 10 per cent
manufacturing techniques and the balance, all-round information. Over one-third
of companies noted specifically that they derived important benefits from sending
new discoveries and ideas to their parent concerns to be tested, developed or
exploited.

We were unable to obtain any precise figures on the comparative research
expenditure of all parent and branch plants either because the American-affiliated
firms did not have such information, or because they were not prepared to divulge
it. Some data were, however, provided by thirty-five affiliates, which between

them employed over 60,000 people, or 25 per cent of the labour force of the total sample studied. Expenditure by the parent companies of these firms totalled $78 million in 1954, compared with less than $10 million spent by their UK associates. Two firms allocated over $10 million to research, five between $5 and $9 million, fourteen between $1 and $4 million and fourteen under $1 million. In eight cases, more people were employed in the research and development departments of the American parent than in all departments of the UK affiliate. The position of twenty of these firms is summarized in Table 6.2.

In general, then, there is no doubt that the parent companies of the 100 most important US-financed firms manufacturing in the UK devote more of their resources to research and development each year than does the whole of British industry combined. The *direction* of this expertise is such that in the abrasive, motor-car, pharmaceutical, industrial instrument, photographic, cosmetic, food and drink, and office machinery industries, US-affiliated companies have direct access to more research and development expertise than do their UK competitors. Unless international in scope, as in the case of some oil, motor vehicle and soap companies, and apart from any Anglo-American licensing agreements or co-operative research in industry, a British competitor is clearly shown to be at a potential handicap.

It is not proposed to examine in any detail the kind of product or process development which has been directly assisted by the presence of US-controlled manufacturing units in the UK. Examples have been given in Chapter 1 of how, in the past, progress in the printing, electrical equipment, match, photographic, gramophone and shoe machinery industries was strongly influenced by American capital, and the following chapter discussed the nature of the products supplied by US firms today. In addition, Table 6.2 on pp. 126–8 lists a sample of the main commodity and processing innovations of American origin pioneered or jointly pioneered by US firms in the UK. In particular, the benefits have been especially notable in the pharmaceutical industry where the larger American companies are currently spending between 5 per cent and 9 per cent of their sales turnover on research and development, and where the average size of the British subsidiary is less than one-tenth that of its parent. From an initial British discovery of penicillin, all subsequent major antibiotic advances have emanated from US laboratories.[20] Recent technological advances in industrial and scientific instrumentation have also been particularly subject to American influence. The range and use made of electronic and pneumatically controlled type apparatus has enormously increased over the last few years, and one very large UK company has estimated that 80 per cent of the measuring and recording instruments now being bought by British industry was innovated in the US. Much the same is true of the post-war history of the petroleum refinery equipment industry, as the following chapter will describe in more detail.[21] Again, the research output of the American chemical industry has placed at the disposal of the British industrialist a whole new range of materials, in the detergent, plastics and petrochemicals fields, while in the food and drink, toilet preparations and electrical products industries the consumer has been offered a much larger variety of products from which to choose.

Table 6.2 Research and development activities of US parent and UK branch plants[1]

Products	(1) Nos. employed or (2) amount expended on research and development (a) in the US and (b) in the UK	1a or 2a as a % of total UK labour force or factory turnover	Nature of research carried out in UK	Nature of research information received from US	Type of payment made for US know-how	Whether information of value returned to US
Precision instruments	2(a) $4m² (b) $480,000 1(b) 200	16	20% basic research 80% product Development	General information and advice	None	Yes
Food products	1(a) 50 (b) None	20	–	Manufacturing and materials processing know-how	Fee related to turnover	No
Vehicles	1(a) Over 500² (b) 150	Over 25	All kinds	General information and advice³	Lump sum payment for designs, etc.	Yes
Instruments	1(a) 375 (b) Minor	330	Materials and machinery design adaptations	Product design and manufacturing techniques	Patent royalties and service fee	No
Medium engineering	1(a) 200 (b) None	95	–	Machinery design	General engineering fee	No
Food and drink	2(a) $2.5 m² (b) $150,000	30	Materials and product adaptations (differences in UK tastes)	Plant layout-and-process technique	Overall fee	Yes
Light chemicals	2(a) $1.9 m (b) Minor	25	Materials adaptation	Machinery design and materials formulae	None	No
Precision engineering	1(a) 70–80 (b) 30	3.5	Basic and applied research on machinery design and process development	Product and process development³	Service fee related to turnover	Yes

Table 6.2 Continued

Products	(1) Nos. employed or amount expended on research and development (a) in the US and (b) in the UK	1a or 2a as a % of total UK labour force or factory turnover	Nature of research carried out in UK	Nature of research information received from US	Type of payment made for US know-how	Whether information of value returned to US
Wood and cork	1(a) 325 (b) Minor	30–35	Product design and materials adaptation	General information and advice	General engineering fee	No
Office machinery	2(a) $1m (b) Virtually none	10	–	Mainly relating to product development: limited machinery design	Service fee related to turnover	No
Heavy machinery	1(a) 29 (b) 5	17	Development research and machine adaptation only	'A mass of material information'	Limited royalties	No
Vehicle components	(a) 300[2] (b) Virtually none	100	–	General information and advice	None	No
Wood and cork	1(a) 500[2] (b) Minor	110	Materials adaptation	Process techniques and materials formulae[3]	Nominal payment only	No
Medium engineering	1(a) 600 (b) 200	10	Machinery design adaptation	General information and advice	None	Yes
Pharmaceuticals	1(a) 250–300[2] (b) 25	25–30	Materials adaptation	Materials formulae[3]	None	Yes
Light electrical engineering	1(a) 30 (b) 10[4]	10	A little basic research where products specialized to UK; otherwise product design	General information and advice	None	No

Table 6.2 Continued

Products	(1) Nos. employed or (2) amount exp ended on research and development (a) in the US and (b) in the UK	1a or 2a as a % of total UK labour force or factory turnover	Nature of research carried out in UK	Nature of research information received from US	Type of payment made for US know-how	Whether information of value returned to US
Precision instruments	2(a) $400,000[2] (b) $10,000	55	Development research and materials adaptation	Design and engineering	None	No
Chemical and allied trades	1(a) 70[2] (b)5	65	Materials adaptation	Materials formulae and machinery design[3]	None	No
Light and medium engineering	1(a) 64[2] (b) 37	4	Design modification for export markets	Product and machinery design	None	Yes
Paint and varnish	1(a) 100[2] (b) 10–15[4]	75	Some basic research specialized to needs at hand: otherwise materials adaptation	Manufacturing methods and materials formulae[3]	Fixed engineering fee	Yes

Notes:
1 20 case studies. All figures relate to 1954.
2 Central Research Laboratory-operated.
3 Including that which first originated from the parent company's other overseas subsidiaries.
4 Part-time.

What was the cost to the branch firms of these benefits? Some 57 per cent of US-affiliated firms in our sample made some sort of payment for technology received, while 43 per cent did not. As regards the former, the nature and amount of the sum involved varied according to the type of knowledge made available, the extent of the US financial interest, parent company policy, the size of the dividends remitted, and the attitude of the Bank of England. Of those firms which did make a payment, 10 per cent allocated a specific fee for the research facilities and/or patents and trade-marks provided by their parent concerns, and 30 per cent paid a percentage of their sales turnover in the form of a technical service or engineering charge. The remaining firms either made a nominal payment, or remitted a lump sum for specific and identifiable know-how such as new designs, chemical formulae, special drawings and so on. Such a payment in 1954 averaged 2–3 per cent of the turnover of the subsidiary – though in selected instances it was very much higher: this, however, in relation to the information passed on, and compared with the research outlay which a British company would be required to make to produce such a benefit is comparatively minor.

Manufacturing experience

The manufacturing expertise of the parent plant available to US-affiliated concerns is, in most cases, the result of many years' accumulated learning and experience. Coupled with the fact that the economic environment in America is frequently more favourable to the development of those industries in which there is strong American representation in the UK, the gains which low and direct investment might bring are substantial. The more marked the differences between current British and American production methods, the greater the potential benefits likely to result from associations of this kind.

Such knowledge is far from being confined in form to drawings, specifications, blueprints, formulae, prototypes and the like; personal visits can be, and are, paid between subsidiary and parent plants and other American companies, and the 'ins and outs' of manufacturing – especially those techniques which can only be gained by learning from the operator at the job – mastered. Seven out of ten firms in our sample arranged yearly exchanges to be paid by selected departmental heads and/or senior operatives and, should a revolutionary new manufacturing process or product innovation be taken up by the American company, then an immediate visit is made to that concern by the subsidiary. One or two of the larger affiliated firms periodically send out research teams to make detailed studies of various aspects of production and management control, such as factory layout, machine design, inspection, time and motion study and so on.

To the extent that the British economy has been able to profit by this knowledge, development has been advanced more speedily and smoothly than would otherwise have been the case. With the setting up of US financed firms in the newer British industries, many teething problems which arise at the experimental and initial stages of production have been overcome by drawing upon the earlier manufacturing experiences of the parent company. For in nine cases out of ten where a new product is supplied and marketed by the British plant, its early production will be undertaken in the United States' factory, and will there bear the brunt of any rough edges, mistakes or failures. A recent example of Anglo-American co-operation in this field is afforded by the Vauxhall Motor Company who in February 1957 launched their new 'Victor' saloon car on to the UK market. Its prototype, though designed and built at Luton, was sent to Detroit, where replicas were constructed by American production experts for testing and developing by US engineers at the General Motor's proving grounds. The fact, too, that most subsidiary factories are constructed to US design also facilitates comparable developments in the UK.

How quickly are US-originated manufacturing techniques or processes introduced into the British factory? On average, minor changes, such as modifications to product design and materials mix, are adopted in a matter of weeks. A major change, however, may take anything from six months to two years to introduce, depending upon such factors as (1) the effectiveness of liaison between the American and British plants[22] (2) the relative cost and availability of materials, (3) the rate of machine utilization and obsolescence, (4) the extent to which modifications need to be made to existing machinery and plant (and possibly to the product itself), (5) marketing considerations and the estimated time of consumers' acceptance,[23] (6) the amount of capital investment, and the ease with which the required finance may be raised and (7) managerial readiness. For the most part, like their parent concerns, the subsidiaries adopt a ruthless attitude towards the replacement of old machinery, though where the rate of technical obsolescence is particularly fast, the British company may find it uneconomic to scrap equipment at the same rate.[24] Concerning the time-lag of marketing a new product, and depending upon the factors listed above, opinion among executives of US firms was fairly evenly divided as to whether the British consumer was getting a new or improved product more quickly through the medium of branch plant activity than he would have done had it been possible to import direct from the US parent company.

Management methods and attitude

The extent to which, and the speed by which, the technical benefits described above are utilized by US subsidiaries, is essentially a question of management competence and attitude. Basically, what has been said about technical capability applies to non-technical or human capability as well. All the management techniques utilized by the parent concern are freely available to the subsidiary. By nature, however, they are less easily definable or set down in black and white. Partly, at least, that there are such benefits to be derived is yet another aspect of the different environmental conditions facing parent and branch plant. Because the US factory is almost invariably larger, more specialized management can be economically employed, and greater efficiency attained in the operation of the various departments. Sometimes it happens that certain economies are discovered which are perhaps as, if not more, applicable to the smaller firm, yet because of the latter's lack of capital or the specialized resources which made such an economy possible, they were simply not discovered.

This question of decision-taking itself reflects the *will* to embark upon a particular course of action as well as the *power*. While the latter is a fairly objective consideration, the former is very much a question of the decision-taker's personality, i.e. his *attitude* towards risk, uncertainty-bearing and entrepreneurship, which, coupled with his *interpretation*, or assessment of the economic costs and benefits likely to follow from various strategies, will determine the final decision taken. This holds true for both the Board of Directors and departmental managerial heads.

Even where the same amount of risk is involved, there is nothing certain as to which course of action will be finally decided upon. If the decision itself is not at variance, then the *speed* of decision-taking may be. This is because the valuation of the variables in question, including that of the appropriate timing, may differ in the two countries. The explanatory reasons are complex – non-economic as well as economic – but the fact remains that, given identical, or near-identical, circumstances, the nature of the final decision may well depend on whether a British or American businessman is making it. That many policy judgements have to be referred back to the parent company and examined, if not in the light of US circumstances, then certainly from the American attitude towards business risks suggests that the pace and direction of development and innovation in the subsidiary will be at least partially determined by the investing company. And, as we have seen, in nearly three-quarters of the subsidiaries in our sample, overall management is 'partially' or 'strongly' influenced by American thinking. Finally, the continual contact of the branch unit with its US associate and the latter's economic environment also tends to make for a greater receptivity to new ideas.

Financial backing

Also affecting the managerial attitude towards a particular course of events is the fact that the American subsidiary – implicitly or explicitly – can be assured of the financial backing of its parent company and, should speedy expansion seem desirable, is able, if need be, to obtain additional capital from this source. Again, to a greater or lesser extent, this is an advantage which is enjoyed by all branch plants, irrespective of their nationality; the important difference is, however, that a US associate company is likely to be more independent, as regards both its economic prosperity and its ability to raise capital, than a parent concern which has to operate within the same market and tax structure as its branch. For example, during the inter-war years, a number of promising but then financially struggling subsidiaries in the UK were kept going solely by additional capital being supplied by their parent concern – a unique advantage which was not available to their competitors at the time. Even in todays' more growth-oriented environment, some US affiliates are circumventing the UK credit constraints by drawing on short-term loans from their parent concerns. Psychologically, too, the presence of a financially sound parent company considerably greater in size than its subsidiary must inevitably have a bearing on the latter's financial decisions; the assurance that there is a capital reserve available in the last resort may well allow favourable situations to be exploited more quickly than might otherwise have been possible.

On the other hand, the significance of this factor should not be overrated. It would seem, for example, that most US companies are reluctant to invest more money in their UK affiliates beyond the initial capital stake, except where it is used to purchase an additional, yet already established, company or where the loan takes the form of machinery, tools or equipment shipped over by the parent concern. In a number of instances, this has been the direct cause of a private subsidiary converting itself into a public company, and in one recent case, of an American-financed firm selling its interests to a British concern. Generally speaking, however, capital expansion is financed through the undistributed profits earned by the subsidiary, and only to the extent that the US parent concern is willing to accept a lower rate of return from its branch unit in its early period of growth than an independent company, might this be considered as an added source of capital. Owing to the fact that the British subsidiary is usually only a comparatively small part of its parent firm's activities, the shareholders (or directors) are able to obtain their capital returns elsewhere. For example, over the period 1950–6 repatriated dividends amounted to 9.1 per cent of the average US capital stake in UK manufacturing industry, a figure which compares favourably with that earned by the rest of UK manufacturing industry in the same period.

By such means as these, then, which reflect the advantages offered by the kind of Anglo-American partnership described, the British economy is put directly in touch with the competitiveness and dynamism of the American industrial system, and the efficiency and entrepreneurship of its corporate structure. By virtue of their American associations, British concerns are able to call upon resources of knowledge and experience much greater than those available to their competitors. It should, too, be remembered that the technical and managerial contributions to which we have been referring represent not only the achievements of one particular US firm, but the industry of which that firm is part. It also mirrors the tastes and attitudes of its (the US's) consumers and, in turn, the character of the American economic system as a whole.

RESULTING IMPACT OF THESE ADVANTAGES ON UK COMPETITORS AND INDUSTRIAL DEVELOPMENT

It is one thing to list the various advantages which American-affiliated firms enjoy over their competitors; it is quite another to assess the resulting impact of these advantages. For example, even if it could be proved that there was a difference in productivity between US affiliates and their indigenous competitors, how far is it possible to say this is due to technical (but non-transferable) advantages enjoyed by these affiliates, e.g. in respect of patents, trade-marks, etc., and how far to the managerial shortcomings of UK industry. Or alternatively, if British firms were shown to be as productive as their US-owned rivals, to what extent would it be correct to infer that the latter's impact had been negligible? To reason so would presuppose that, had that competition not been present, British firms would have been just as efficient. There is a constant danger of *non sequitur* in such cases – a danger which is enhanced when one remembers that it is the young and dynamic industries with which one is dealing, and at a time when the sales for their products is expanding. That is to say, though it is the case that American-affiliated firms have increased their share of the UK market over the last ten years or so, it cannot be implied that their competitors have been adversely affected or that their absolute output has fallen. This makes it almost impossible to draw any accurate conclusions. There are few, if any, clear-cut cases in recent years to compare with the impact made before the First World War by such companies as the Diamond Match Company and the United States Beef Trust on their UK competitors, or by Cherry-Burrell Ltd (dairy and ice-cream machinery suppliers),[25] and Lincoln Electric Co. Ltd (electrodes and welding equipment), during the inter-war period. Impressions there are many, e.g. Kraft Foods Ltd cannot but have had a tremendous impact on Aplin and Barrett Ltd which, before the former's establishment in this country, enjoyed a virtual (UK) monopoly in processed cheeses. Likewise, intense competition, largely from American subsidiaries, coupled with a fall in the real price of razor-blades and dry shavers, has markedly affected the fortunes of those companies supplying the more traditional implements of shaving, e.g. Rolls Razor Ltd.[26] While, *other things being equal*, a larger share of the market captured by a firm over a period of years is a reasonable indication of its superior productivity, the reverse argument does not necessarily hold. Though a constant (or falling) market share may mean that the US firm has had no impact on its UK competitors, it might equally mean that the latter have themselves stepped up their efficiency as a direct result of more intense competition. Particularly where one is dealing with an industry subject to rapid technological change, comparisons are made very difficult, as one company is constantly forging ahead of its competitors with new products, manufacturing techniques, etc.

Nevertheless, with these reservations in mind, and in an attempt to make some assessment of the efficiency of US-financed firms *vis-à-vis* their native competitors, we have examined three possible indices of efficiency. No one of these indices is sufficient in itself to permit of any definite conclusion, as in each case efficiency is only one of the important variables influencing the result. Only when these individual measures are taken as a group may it be possible to come to any assessment of efficiency which approaches reliability.

First measure – comparative productivity

Table 6.3 compares the *gross output per employee* of US firms with that of the Standard Industrial Group in which they are producing, for selected industries in the years 1950 and 1954. By 'gross output per head' is meant the establishment's net selling value divided by its total number of employees. Data in respect

Table 6.3 Comparative value productivity of US manufacturing affiliates and the industries in which they produce, 1950-4

Standard industrial classification	1950			1954					
	US firms o.p.m.y.[1]	For all firms in industrial group o.p.m.y.[2]	Comp. US–UK productivity Col. 1 / Col. 2 × 100	US firms o.p.m.y.	For all firms in industrial group o.p.m.y.[2]	Comp. US–UK productivity Col. 4 / Col. 5 × 100	Rate of US productivity growth Col. 4 / Col. 1 × 100	Rate of UK productivity growth Col. 5 / Col. 2 × 100	Rel. rate of US productivity growth Col. 7 / Col. 8 × 100
Abrasives	2,247	1,884	119.5	2,698	2,367	114.0	120.0	125.5	95.7
Chemicals (general)	3,125	2,204	142.0	5,246	3,394	154.1	168.0	154.3	108.9
Pharmaceutical preparations	2,456	2,184	112.5	3,421	2,495	137.1	131.1	114.7	114.1
Mineral oil refining	11,030	9,628	114.5	21,717	18,415	117.5	197.4	191.2	103.3
Printing and book-binding machinery	1,106	1,053	105.0	1,950	1,753	111.2	176.3	166.5	105.4
Mechanical engineering (general)	2,320	1,486	155.7	2,758	1,846	148.6	118.8	124.3	95.8
Motor vehicles	2,532	1,890	134.0	3,668	2,607	140.8	145.0	137.9	105.1
Scientific, surgical and photographic instruments	1,080	964	112.0	1,380	1,267	108.9	127.8	131.3	97.3
Tools and cutlery	2,246	999	224.6	2,936	1,713	171.4	130.7	171.3	76.3
Rubber products	2,624	1,767	148.5	3,073	2,113	146.1	117.1	119.6	97.9
Average of above industrial groups[2]	2,654	1,980	134.0	3,825	2,880	132.8	144.1	145.5	98.9

Notes:
1 Gross per man-year.
2 Weighted according to number of US firms in each group.

of US-financed firms were provided by a sample of subsidiaries, and for the industrial group as a whole,[27] obtained from the (UK) by Census of Production.

The industries represented in the table have been chosen on the basis of the relative homogeneity of their products. Others, by their nature, comprise establishments which manufacture such a wide range of heterogeneous products that comparisons of the productivity of one firm with that of the group as a whole is precluded. Such, for example, would substantially apply to the food, drink and tobacco industries. As an exception to this rule, we include the 'mechanical engineering (general)' group, which, though comprising many diverse trades, contains mainly those in which there is strong American representation.[28]

The figures presented show the American-financed firms to have a higher gross output per head than their competitors in both 1950 and 1954, the comparative superiority being particularly marked in the tools and cutlery, mechanical engineering, chemical and pharmaceutical trades. At best, the figures are a poor indication of relative efficiency as they take no account of differences in cost structures, nor the proportion of work contracted out by US firms. For example, in 1955 one precision engineering subsidiary recorded an output of £6,500 per employee in one of its factories mainly engaged in assembly work, while in another, which bought out only basic raw materials, the figure was £1,665 per employee. To this extent, it would have been preferable to have computed net output figures, i.e. the firm's contribution to the total product, or the value added to the outside purchases by its manufacturing processes. Too few subsidiaries, however, were able or willing to give this information to permit any general conclusions. Perhaps one advantage – albeit a disguised advantage – of our present measure is that it includes any impact which US firms might have made on their suppliers' efficiency. In actual fact, however, such firms do not contract out any more than their native competitors. Indeed, studying the relative cost structures of the firms in our sample, we find that 65 per cent buy out fewer components and parts than the average for their industrial group as a whole, and of the 42 firms on which Table 6.3 is based, 31 were less dependent on outside suppliers than were the average of their competitors. None of the subsidiaries in our sample was purely assembling in character, and with the exception of two office machinery subsidiaries, all had been established before the war. The only bias within the chosen sample of US firms would appear to be in respect of size, there being a tendency for US subsidiaries – particularly in the abrasives, petroleum refining, scientific instruments and motor vehicles group – to be concentrated within those employment ranges the productivity of which is among the highest.

While, then, accepting that the absolute figures have little meaning in themselves, the general picture clearly shows a tendency for US-financed establishments to have a higher output per head than their UK competitors. Individually, of the forty-two such firms represented, only five had a productivity less than the average for their industrial group in both 1950 and 1954. For reasons already given, no account has been taken of firms in the food and drink industry, though, in fact, from all indications, it is likely that the differences would have appeared even more marked (in favour of US subsidiaries).

From this same table, one might also derive comparative productivity trends between 1950 and 1954. The main difficulty here is that any conclusions one may draw may be belied by price movements and changes in the amount of subcontracting. For example, a lower value output per head growth does not necessarily mean a lower growth in physical output, as product prices of American-financed firms have tended to rise less steeply than those of their British competitors. In any case, the picture is inconclusive, with productivity trends most favouring American firms in the chemical and pharmaceutical industries and least favouring them in the tools and cutlery, mechanical engineering and abrasive trades.

Second measure – market shares

Rather more US-financed firms provided information about their share of UK output over the period 1939–54. Table 6.4 shows that over half of the American firms claim that their share of UK production has risen since before the war: another quarter, that it has remained constant, and only 15, or 13 per cent of the total sample, that it has actually fallen. This tends to confirm the point made in Chapter 2, that the post-war growth of employment in US-financed firms has been four times that of UK manufacturing industry in general. Such would also seem to apply to their immediate competitors. In terms of individual industries, the most notable advances would appear to have occurred in food and drink,

Table 6.4 Estimated changes in share of UK production of US affiliates, 1939–54[1]

	No. of US firms who claim their market share to have increased since 1939	*No. of US firms who claim their market share to have remained constant since 1939*	*No. of US firms who claim their market share to have decreased since 1939*	*Total no. of firms*
Chemical and allied trades	10	7	1	18
Metal manufacturing	4	1	1	6
Engineering and shipbuilding goods	18	11	8	37
Electrical goods	3	1	0	4
Motor vehicles	2	2	2	6
Precision instruments, etc.	4	3	0	7
Textiles and clothing	3	2	1	6
Food, drink and tobacco	9	3	1	13
Other manufacturing industries	10	7	1	18
Total	63	37	15	115

Notes:
1 Data relate to 115 firms or 78% of total sample.

industrial instruments, pharmaceuticals and tools and cutlery. At the same time, the determinants of market share trends are many, of which the efficiency and growth orientation of competing firms are only two. It may be, for example, that competitors shift their production emphasis away from the products being supplied by American firms to others perceived to be more profitable; alternatively, the limits placed on factory expansion may hinder the rate at which firms are able to develop. The rate of output growth might also reflect the purchase by the American firm in question of competitive interests; and finally, it must be borne in mind that the share of output trends will vary from year to year, and that, according to the reference point taken, the picture emerging may be somewhat different.

Third measure – profits

From the published financial data of a company various accounting ratios may be computed to assess its efficiency in whole or in part. For our particular purposes, we have adopted a similar measure to that used by the National Institute of Economic and Social Research in its publication *A Classified List of Large Companies Engaged in British Industry*, viz.: the return on capital employed or the ratio of net profit to net operating assets.[29] This purports to assess the efficiency of capital utilization, a low ratio indicating that either capital is under-employed or fully, but inefficiently, employed.

Table 6.5 classifies these income/asset ratios according to five main industrial groups. Within these groups we have taken a number of US-financed firms, 'paired' each of them with its nearest British competitor, and averaged the appropriate income/asset ratios for both over the three-year period 1952–5. Column 5 also gives an estimate for the industrial group as a whole for the period 1951–3. While, by necessity, the British firms in the sample are all quoted public companies, there is a sufficient similarity both as regards *type of products supplied* and *size of firm* to permit rough conclusions to be drawn. In all, thirty-five US firms were 'paired' – and the results compared. Since in this case individual comparisons are largely meaningless, we classified the appropriate figures into six broad industrial groups.

The results are perhaps slightly less conclusive than those of the preceding two measures. Though a *weighted* average of income/asset ratios of all US-financed firms works out at 35.3 per cent compared with 28.5 per cent for their 'paired' competitors and 23.2 per cent for the average of all firms in the industries identified, within two of the groups the US ratio is lower. Inflationary trends, the threat of takeover bids and historical cost valuation of assets all tend to make for under-valuation, and distort the true picture. Also, the efficiency ratio of private companies may contain an upward bias, to the extent that the composition of their assets does not require to be as well publicized, nor are short-term loans always included in the valuation. Further, for these ratios to have any real meaning, they should be supplemented by secondary ratios, e.g. as between the constituent elements of capital employed and other balance sheet items; the ratio between the constituent elements in the calculation of profit, and that between the

Table 6.5 Income–assets ratios and profits for selected US affiliates and their UK competitors, 1952–5

	US firms		UK firms		
	Average income/ assets ratio 1952–5	Relative income growth 1952–5	Average income/ assets ratio 1952–5	Relative income growth 1952–5	Average for UK industrial group as a whole
Chemical and allied trades	25.4	125.3	27.5	130.3	18.0
Engineering and metal[2] products	39.5	105.3	29.9	117.6	24.8
Vehicles and vehicle components	41.1	110.9	33.7	146.7	29.7
Food and drink	36.5	151.2	22.0	98.1	16.9
Scientific, photographic instruments, etc.	18.7	146.3	28.5	100.3	n.s.c.[3]
Miscellaneous[4]	38.9	128.3	29.3	122.9	22.5
Weighted average for all firms	35.3	125.3	28.5	111.1	23.2

Notes:
1 From information kindly provided by the National Institute of Economic and Social Research.
2 Including printing and bookbinding machinery, machine tools, office equipment, agricultural machinery, telecommunications equipment, domestic electrical appliances and household boilers.
3 Not separately classified.
4 Including rubber products, tools and cutlery, paper and hardboard, clothing, heating appliances, abrasives and roofing materials

constituent elements in relation to the capital employed and those of profits, e.g. the ratio between sales income and capital.[30]

The position is equally indefinite when one examines the comparative income trends for US affiliates and their competitors for the three-year period 1952–5. In the food and drink, scientific instruments and miscellaneous industrial groups, the rate of profit growth of American-affiliated companies is well above that of their competitors, while for the remaining groups they would appear to have lost some ground.

Consolidating the information contained in the three previous tables, Table 6.6 summarizes the position as a whole. Here, the evidence, such as it is, would strongly suggest that the US affiliates are more efficient than their competitors – and particularly so in the foodstuffs, tools and cutlery and pharmaceutical industries. In only six cases out of fifty-five are there indications to the contrary. While the results of any one measure of efficiency may be open to question, it is most unlikely that in *each* of the five measures in *each* of the main industrial groups, the efficiency variable would be so much out of character as to give a false result.

In the final analysis, of course, any improvement in industrial efficiency must be reflected in the quality of the product, its price and the speed of technical development. What of the influence of American-affiliated firms in these fields? We have already noted the willingness of subsidiaries to adopt new production methods and managerial practices and market new products as quickly as possible.

Table 6.6 Comparative efficiency of US affiliates and the average for all firms in selected UK industries[1]

Industrial group	Indications that US firms are more efficient	Indications that US firms are of average efficiency	Indications that US firms are of below average efficiency
Abrasives	A B	C D E	
Chemicals and oil refining	B C	D E	A
Pharmaceutical preparations	A B C D E		
Printing and bookbinding machinery	A D	B C E	
Mechanical engineering (general)[2]	A B C	E	D
Motor vehicles	A B C	E	D
Scientific, photographic, etc., instruments	C D	B E	A
Tools and cutlery	(A) B C D		E
Food, drink and tobacco	A (B) C D (E)		
Rubber products	A B C	E	D
Other manufacturing[3] industries	A (B) C D E		

Notes:
1 Data derived from Tables 6.3–6.5
  Key to symbols of tests
  A = Net income–assets ratio (average 1953–5)
  B = Comparative productivity (average 1950 and 1954)
  C = Output shares (1939–54)
  D = Income trends (1952–5)
  E = Productivity trends (1950–4)
  A bracketed sign indicates 'estimated' degree of efficiency – not included in previous Tables 6.3–6.5.
2 Covering those industries as listed in n. 28 on p. 322, excluding printing and bookbinding machinery.
3 Covering those industries as listed in n. 4 of Table 6.5, excluding rubber products and tools and cutlery.

This has, undoubtedly, made its impact on competitors and, in consequence, has reduced the time-lag between the initial discovery of a new method or process and its application. Thoughts are turned into deeds more quickly than heretofore; there is less idling with ideas and resting on earlier-won laurels or easily come-by profits which now, through the impetus of increased competition, are under threat. This has shown itself in a variety of ways, viz. improved manufacturing techniques, better merchandising methods, after-sales servicing and so on. To the consumer, the resulting benefits have taken the form of an increased range of goods, better-quality products and price reductions. In this latter respect a somewhat startling claim was made by one UK-originated firm which was purchased outright by an American corporation shortly after the last World War. To quote from a senior executive of the company (who was British):

> but for the association with an American parent concern and the exchange of technical and marketing expertise, the firm's chief product would, without

doubt, be retailing at a price somewhere around 60 per cent higher than the current selling price.

Concerning price policy as such, here, too, the picture is inconclusive. While there is insufficient evidence to suggest that US-financed firms, as a whole, are more price-conscious or more scientific in their price-fixing methods than their UK competitors, in individual instances this is very much the case. A study of trends over the past five years shows that the Ford, Bakelite, Hoover, Hedley, Heinz, Bird's, Blaw-Knox and Evans Chemical companies have been among the leaders in their respective industries in the drive to keep prices down and cut profit margins. The Hoover Company, for example, has helped to stabilize the prices of domestic electrical appliances by marketing its own products at a cost between 25–30 per cent above the pre-1939 level, while in its 1955 annual report, the Heinz Company stated that its prices between 1947 and 1954 had been raised by 47 per cent compared with an average increase in all manufactured foods of 81 per cent. Between 1953 and 1954, this same company's prices actually fell, when those of other manufactured foods rose by $2\frac{1}{2}$ per cent. Another subsidiary's main product is retailed at 25 per cent above pre-war cost compared with an 85 per cent increase of that of its main competitors, while until recently, the price of razor-blades was actually below that charged before the war.

On the other hand, many affiliates supplying such consumer goods as refrigerators, cosmetics, cigarette lighters, kitchen cutlery-ware, cooking stoves, steam irons and electric razors deliberately cater for high-quality markets, and supply at prices above the average; in all these instances attention tends to be focused on the other variables influencing sales. It is, in any case, difficult to assert whether any particular price charged is the result of deliberate policy, an indication of the efficiency of the company concerned, or the structure of competition. Likewise, and especially in times of rapid technological development, there is nothing automatic about an increase in efficiency or reduction in costs being passed on to the consumer in the form of lower prices. When an improvement in product function or design is foremost among the determinants affecting sales, it may well be appropriate that any discretionary profits would be better allocated to more intensive research and development.

Lastly, technical innovation. What of the major advances in product, process or materials development which have originated from US subsidiaries and Anglo-American manufacturing concerns? We have seen the impact made by such firms on the competitive structure in which they produce and sell; what of their pioneering contributions to industrial advancement? In many cases, of course, it is not possible to say which firm has the prior claim to the discovery of a new technique or product, and, once again, it would be outside the scope of this book to give a full list of the innovations of these companies; as it is, some repetition between Chapters 2 and 8 is inevitable. For our immediate purposes, however, it may be sufficient to tabulate some of the major technical advances which *to the best of our knowledge* have been pioneered or jointly pioneered by American firms. These are set out in Table 6.7 without comment.

Table 6.7 New production methods, materials and products pioneered or jointly pioneered by US firms in the UK as a result of their transatlantic associations[1]

New production methods introduced into the subsidiary's plant	New materials or materials formulae made available to UK producers
All-continuous soap-making process	Liquid industrial adhesives
Watch-making techniques on a mass production basis	Resin-based adhesives
Continuous ovens for biscuit manufacturing	Metallizing process for worn parts
Ink-drying process in manufacture of sparking-plugs	Asphalt shingles for roofing
Specialized injection moulding of toothbrushes	Incombustible marine board
A continuous process for digesting and bleaching of cotton linters	Colloidal graphite
Sulphuric acid process for steeping of starch	Sealing compounds for can-making industry
Production of high octane gasoline by hydroforming	'Bundy' copper-plated tubing
Conveyor belt radio production	Graded paraffin
Continuous smelting process for production of enamels	Toxyphine – a chlorinate camphine, used as an agricultural insecticide
Automatic high-speed processes for manufacture of razor-blades	Tri-acetate (a cellulose acetate)
Hollow-grinding of kitchen cutlery ware	Additives for lubricants and synthetic lubricants
Flow production techniques in motor vehicle assembly	Pliofilm and laminated cellophane wrapping
Continuous ribbon process for manufacture of cheese	Titanium and zirconium enamels
Moulding of photographic lens from glass	Various plastic powders (polystyrene), detergent bases (docecyl-benzene) and preservatives (pentachlorophenol)
Electric process for baking of abrasive materials	Carbon black
'Lindberg' system for brazing copper components	Photographic emulsions
Thermofor continuous percolation process for oil filtering	Freon refrigerants

New products or product designs made available to UK consumer

Cylindrical windscreen wipers and washers	VHF radio equipment
Bottom dump wagons and scrapers	Decorative wrapping papers
Various antibiotic drugs	New-styled kitchen implements
The 'Strowger' system of telephone communication	Pneumatic road drills
Electric typewriters	Combine harvesters and rotor balers
Locker refrigeration plants	Hormone beauty preparations
New types of locks	Automatic submerged arc welding equipment
Rotary electric switches	Wickless paraffin cooking stoves
Solid extruded (electrode) rods	Oil hose and plastic footwear

Table 6.7 Continued

New production methods introduced into the subsidiary's plant	New materials or materials formulae made available to UK producers
Automatic defroster component for refrigerators	Powdered glucose
Electric time recorders	Various sulphonamides
Oil well drilling equipment	Electric dry shavers
Arcair process for cutting and gouging metal	Electric space heating controls
The diesel tractor	Automatic cigarette lighters
Flatwork ironing machinery	Synthetic resin-bonded wheels
Silicon carbide refractory products	Cellophane ('scotch') tape
Lifeguard tyre tubes	Broaching machines
Polythene bag-making machines	The analgesic, 'bufferin'
Steel and alloy steel chain (for haulage purposes)	Continuous mining machinery
'Microfilming' apparatus	Stereophonic sound equipment
Coloured refrigerators	Various applications of starch for industrial uses
Automatic transmissions for motor vehicles	The 'Pyrene'-type fire-extinguisher

Note:
1 Selected sample. See also data given in Chapters 7 and 8.

REACTIONS OF UK COMPETITORS TO THE US PRESENCE IN THE UK

From the above conclusions, how far is it possible to judge how UK competitors have responded to the presence of US manufacturing units in the UK? Once again, we must confine ourselves to some general observations.

First, following from the technical impacts described above, it would appear that there has developed a wider appreciation by British industry of the importance of the research and development function, and the rewards of efficient management. Concerning this latter factor, US firms have also shown that it is not only technical efficiency which is an important determinant of the prosperity of a company, but that of the wider sphere of managerial and organizational competence as well. It cannot be entirely coincidental that the industries in which American representation is most evidenced are also those which are both the most dynamic in character and which rely for their success on those variables which the US economy is best suited to supply. To be sure, they are also the newer industries, and are, therefore, less hampered by the tradition of inherited ideas and practices restrictive to progress. Because, too, they compete within an oligopolistic market structure, the tendency is for them to be less individualistic in approach and more amenable to technical change than firms in the older trades. At the same time, even within their fields of enterprise, US firms have encouraged a freer interchange of knowledge. As we have seen, many subsidiaries welcome visits to their factories and they are well to the fore both in organizing technical competitions and in giving support to local or national schemes to further productivity. By giving lectures on scientific and business subjects to various interested bodies, and contributing articles to a wide selection of journals and magazines, they advertise their manufacturing and managerial methods in the UK. Two particular examples in this latter connection are the British Productivity Council's monthly publication *Target*, which gives details of ways and means by which productivity may be advanced in the factory and office, and its *Productivity Reviews*, which is geared to the needs of particular industries. In both publications, case studies of US-financed firms are particularly well represented. In like manner, information and advice passed on by subsidiaries to their UK suppliers are frequently used to the benefit of the latter's other customers.

Second, the fact that US-controlled enterprises have helped publicize both the importance of research and development as a competitive enhancing tool, and the rewards of efficient managerial methods, has indirectly increased the attraction of co-operative research, trade and professional associations to British firms – not least as a means of counteracting the advantages of the larger US affiliates. The smaller producers, which cannot afford to devote the same resources to research and specialized management, have had to look elsewhere to protect themselves from extinction. In doing so they had paid increasing attention to the various technical and business publications and to the services offered by such bodies as the British Institute of Management, Institute of Industrial Administration, Institute of Production Engineers, Federation of British Industries. Day-to-day competition against firms with US connections cannot but increase the awareness of their production and managerial methods, and this has undoubtedly stimulated the efficiency consciousness of firms which previously gave little thought to, or failed to do anything about, modern work study techniques, capital budgeting, inventory control, scientific purchasing and so on, partly because competition was less keen, and partly for sheer lack of appreciation that such knowledge was, in fact, available somewhere.

Third, many competitors have been given an added incentive to visit the United States and study the latest production methods and technical advances for themselves. The presence of US-financed firms in the UK has increased the realization that it is possible to emulate many American production methods with success, and especially so in those industries where American participation is of recent origin, but which previously had been shielded from overseas competition by tariff protection.

Finally, and most particularly, in the newer industries, British companies have reacted to inward direct investment by US firms by concluding licensing agreements with their competitors. Apart from the innovations in the electrical equipment industry at the beginning of this century, a classic case is that which occurred in 1930, when, in retaliation to the American Can Company setting up a subsidiary factory in Liverpool to manufacture tin cans on US lines, the Metal Box Company made a licensing agreement with the Continental Can Company – a chief competitor of the former firm in the United States. Since the war, many hundreds of such contracts have been concluded: as recalled in Chapter 2, there is hardly an important industrial instrument firm in this country which has not some technical association with an American concern, while a similar growth in Anglo-American licensing agreements in the petroleum refinery equipment industry has followed that of an influx of US capital into the UK. In the domestic electrical appliances, cosmetic, earth-moving equipment and machine tool industries, non-equity alliances with US companies are also numerous. Once again, the *awareness* that such benefits are there to be taken advantage of has been spurred on by the directness of American competition.

There, of course, remain those industries, the development of which has been affected little or negligibly by the presence of US-affiliated firms in the UK or in which the results described above have been brought about by other means. This would particularly apply to those UK companies which themselves engage in international production. For example, it might be fairly argued that the impact made by the Esso Petroleum Company on Royal Dutch Shell is minor in relation to that arising from the latter's presence in the US and other world markets. Again, the Dunlop Company is much larger than its three American competitors in the UK – Goodyear, Firestone and North British Rubber. It is also in a position to benefit from research and development of its many overseas subsidiaries including its US interests, and in so far as it is forced to keep abreast in American production techniques to protect those interests, it is likely to be as advanced in its technological and managerial competence as are its main transatlantic rivals in the UK. Similarly, the main competitor to those subsidiaries supplying refrigerating equipment has Swedish associations; Italian interests are well represented in the typewriter industry; there are three Swiss-controlled firms in the pharmaceutical trade, while an important French influence remains in the toilet preparations industry. This internationalization of production and knowledge is an interesting feature of many of Britain's newer trades.

Summarizing, then, though the impact made by US-financed firms on the market structure in which they compete and on their rivals' efficiency has been positive and in some cases marked, without further and detailed research it is not possible to assess with any accuracy how significant this impact has been. Any figures which one is able to supply to support impressions must be regarded as little more than intelligent guesses. Yet, while in no way claiming that American firms in the UK have been solely responsible for the developments described in this chapter, there is sufficient evidence to suggest that their role has been important and very largely to the good. There is, for example, no doubt that the transatlantic associations enjoyed by such firms have brought very considerable advantages in the form of technical and managerial knowledge. As far as can be judged, these benefits show themselves in terms of rising shares of the total market, favourable comparative productivity figures and higher income/asset ratios. We know, too, that such industries are among the most dynamic and productive within the UK economy; that their rate of productivity and capital growth is well above average; that they are among the most prominent exporters; and that they are the first to recognize the need for continual product and/or process improvement if they are to sustain their share of world markets.

7 The influence of US firms on their UK suppliers

The ramifications of modern-day industry are both widespread and complex. Few firms are self-contained isolated units; the majority, in one way or another, are economically related to each other and their fortunes closely intertwined. The previous chapter examined one aspect of this interdependence, viz. that associated with the influence exerted by US-affiliated firms on their British competitors. As it is only between those firms within the same industry, and at a similar stage of the production chain, that such a relationship might occur, it is best described as *horizontal* interdependence. We now turn to examine a further possible way in which US business investment in the UK has affected the pattern of British industrial development and efficiency – namely, through impact which it has made, and is making, on British component and raw material suppliers.

In 1954, between one-half and two-thirds of the £750–£800 million gross output produced by such American manufacturing affiliates consisted of parts and materials bought-out from other manufacturers. Of those US-controlled companies in our sample, 61 per cent might be classified as being within the *assembling* or *fabricating* industries which, by their nature, subcontract a fair proportion of their components and parts to outside specialists, and the balance within the *continuous processing* industries which largely confine their external purchases to raw or semi-processed materials.[1] To the extent that American research and development has significantly affected the progress of both these industrial groups in recent years, there is a *prima facie* likelihood that the various US purchasers and their suppliers may be *vertically* interdependent on each other – at least in technical matters. At the same time, within any particular group, the degree of subcontracting will vary considerably according to such factors as the age and size of the firm concerned, the price and quality of subcontracted work *vis-à-vis* the cost of internal manufacturing and available plant capacity, the reliability of suppliers and the extent to which the relevant know-how is made freely available from the US. Chapter 5 has already dealt with these points at some length and it is not proposed to enlarge upon them here. Chapter 1 also discussed the impact made by the earlier US firms on their subcontractors, particularly in the printing, electrical, match and boot and shoe machinery industries. The analysis which follows is essentially that of the present-day position.

It is, in fact, only since the end of the Second World War that such an impact has been an important one. Partly, this is a reflection of the marked growth of US investment and technological progress since 1945, partly of the increased attention paid to quality control procedures, but, most especially, to the reduced dependence of US subsidiaries on imports. For while before the war nearly one-third of the sales turnover of such companies took the form of imported raw materials and parts, by 1954 this figure had fallen to less than 10 per cent.

On the basis of information received both from the 205 US-financed firms in our sample, and also from forty-five of their UK raw material and component suppliers, we seek to answer three main questions in this chapter:

1 Have the purchasing methods and attitudes adopted by US subsidiaries and jointly owned Anglo-American concerns enforced their suppliers to produce to a higher level of efficiency than that which would otherwise have been the case?
2 To what extent has new knowledge, either in the form of production methods and techniques or materials processing, permeated into British industry in this way?
3 How far has the demand created by US affiliates helped to speed up the exploitation and commercial development of materials and processes already known to British manufacturers, but, as yet, not applied?

THE PURCHASING TECHNIQUES OF US AFFILIATES

Though in no instance to our knowledge is the purchasing department of a US-financed firm managed by an American national, in the great majority of cases its operation is partly, if not strongly, based on current US procurement procedures. Three-quarters of the subsidiaries visited expressed the thought that some gain had followed from their transatlantic associations in this respect. The majority of firms, including all subsidiaries employing more than 1,000 people, operate a central purchasing department assisted by inspection and engineering sections. Since being bought out by US corporations, eight of the twelve UK firms in our sample said that they had centralized their buying activities.

The feature, however, what one immediately observes in making contact with such firms is the attitude which they adopt towards their suppliers and purchasing responsibilities. The average fully-owned subsidiary does not just order a particular part or material from a British firm and wait for it to be delivered, but tends rather to treat its supplier as an integral part of its organization, recognizing the importance of bought-out costs to total costs, and of the quality and consistency of the purchased items to its own efficiency and, indirectly, to its share of the market. This interest shows itself in the form of various practices, some of which are widely adopted in the UK, but the thoroughness with which they are executed is unusual. Almost without exception, the American firm supplies its subcontractor with the most detailed material or part specifications, drawings, blueprints, formulae, etc., and, in some cases, prototypes of the part itself, sent over for the purpose by the parent company or its supplier. In the event of a change in techniques or processes in the US, these are made freely and, in most cases, speedily available to the British supplier, who is also kept informed of current technological advances. Where the product is a new one or production methods are unfamiliar to the subcontractor, specialists and work study experts – including some from the US – are often provided to supervise production in the initial period. Such was the case, for example, in the construction of the Fawley oil refinery, where thirty Americans were employed by the Foster-Wheeler Corporation and Standard Oil Development Company, including technical experts in some of the items subcontracted, e.g. structural steel, industrial instruments, welding equipment, etc., while a British supplier in the packaging industry commented:

> In order to assist us in meeting their demands, our main US customer is more than ready and willing to pass on the most detailed information relating to American techniques and developments, and to visit us regularly to give us advice on these subjects. Yet, though it is generally thought that our US counterparts in this industry are well ahead of similar concerns in this country, it should be understood that US manufacturing methods are not always applicable in Great Britain.

Again, US design and constructional assistance is being received by the Heinz, Goodyear, Kraft and Caterpillar Tractor companies in their current factory expansions.

On the other hand, nearly half the US subsidiaries and three-quarters of the Anglo American companies said that assistance is only given as a direct request from their suppliers. Even so, if a subsidiary remains unsatisfied with quality, price, delivery times, etc., it is usual for the supplier in question to be asked to accept more detailed technical help from the subsidiary or from its American suppliers, or, indeed, for it to visit these suppliers in the United States. This will naturally depend on the size of the subsidiary in relationship to its supplier, the kind of arrangement each has with the other, and the type of work contracted out. Many of the larger subsidiaries noted specifically that they had made available to their suppliers testing apparatus and measuring instruments, one electrical products firm recording a reduction in the price of one of its component parts of 30 per cent since more efficient testing methods had been applied and a design improvement had been made. A smaller number of subsidiaries also made it their practice to provide their subcontractors with specialized tools and machinery. In giving his reasons, one executive commented:

> We did this originally, partly because our subcontractors' tool rooms were then fully loaded with other work, but mainly because of the vast amount of know-how which our parent company had accumulated over the years, particularly in regard to welding fixtures and press tools for the blanking, piercing and forming of heavier section components. This experiment was so successful that it has now become standard company procedure. The great advantage in our experience has been the fact that one is guaranteed that the limits of accuracy asked for in components are met with by the subcontractor.

Of course, in many cases, components, parts and materials can be produced by more or less standardized methods, and the expertise involved is simply a question of design or materials specifications. This, in itself, however, may be quite important, one engineering subsidiary recalling that as a result of information passed on to its supplier, the number of operations involved in the manufacturing of a particular component had been reduced from twelve to three. If anything, it would seem that more attention is paid to the plant and product design than is common in British industry. Further, there is little doubt that the average tolerances allowed by a subsidiary, particularly in the precision engineering field, are smaller than that which is normally demanded, and frequent visits may be paid to a supplier to ensure that these are kept. Only a small minority of suppliers said that their other UK customers were as demanding. As one subcontractor of a light chemical subsidiary put it:

> They are the only concern amongst a very large number of our customers who do insist that we make to their specifications and meet their necessary standards in all supplies to them. We find that if we are able to satisfy this firm then we can meet all the requirements of our other customers with considerable ease, and in this way we feel our industrial development has been furthered, and our efficiency raised.

This, of course, does not necessarily mean that the firms in question are inefficient; it may be that the demands of its other customers have been, or are, less exacting. As another supplier put it:

> It is our experience that the American specifications are generally stricter than those usually demanded by British customers. Obviously these call for more care in production. Should other consumers finally emerge with similar specifications, they are naturally the first to benefit from the work done on the original requisition.

On the other hand, it may be that the subcontractor's testing or inspection instrumentation is at fault; rejections do tend to be very numerous, both due to inconsistencies in product quality and to the lack of knowledge on the part of the supplier, as well as the insufficient appreciation of the subsidiary of the materials availability position in the UK. This latter view was strongly voiced by suppliers selling to post-war US affiliates who claimed that the management of such firms, often recruited from ex-sales staff of the parent concern, was unnecessarily inflexible in its purchasing demands.

Another common criticism levelled against British suppliers by American firms relates to their failure to adhere to delivery dates, thus dislocating production timetables and the need to keep inventories to the minimum. Visits are sometimes paid to suppliers in order to find out the reasons why there is a hold-up in delivery and to hasten the order. One of the reasons for the high efficiency with which the Fawley refinery project was executed was the careful synchronization of the various processes and the ready accessibility of materials when they were required. Special expeditors were employed to keep a constant check on the progress of orders and to make sure that delivery dates were honoured. Where rail schedules were slow, trucks were sent from Fawley to all parts of the country to collect materials, and no effort was spared in tracing the most efficient and reliable sources of supply. From the purchasing department, personnel travelled all over the country, while a system of coding orders enabled the supply situation at any stage in the construction to be gauged immediately.[2] As a direct result of their contact with the main American contractor responsible for this particular project, two large building concerns adopted similar expediting procedures, and, in connection with the building of its synthetic petroleum catalyst in 1949, another chemical manufacturer wrote:

> Comparing the purchasing and expediting techniques employed by the US consultants with our own, we found that they detailed their orders more completely and employed staff of qualified men to follow up the orders at the contractors' and at any subcontractors' works, inspecting at all stages of manufacture. If hold-ups occurred, these expeditors assisted the contracting firm in overcoming their difficulties. By these means, delivery schedules were achieved which would have been otherwise impossible.
>
> In our experience, we believe that, whilst British equipment manufacturers at first resented the method of approach employed by the US consultants, in due course they have come to appreciate the mutual advantages to be gained and, in consequence, have introduced some of the ideas into their own manufacturing procedures.

Another specific consequence of the presence of US subsidiaries in the UK is that where the know-how is of a specialized character, the UK supplier is able to visit its counterpart in the US. Many American-affiliated firms, and particularly those of post-war origin, make a point of putting their suppliers into contact with their opposite numbers in the States, and, if necessary, arranging for them to produce under licence.

Such assistance has proved especially valuable to smaller firms, for while the larger suppliers are likely to have already visited the US, or learnt the latest techniques by other means, the smaller firms – either through inability to apply these techniques or appreciation of what in fact is available – are not as well situated. In particular, where the purchase of a subsidiary is an important one, a real effort is made to study the methods which are required at first hand. If the order by a US firm involves specialized machinery not easily obtainable, the necessary design information will be passed on or, in certain cases, the actual equipment will be procured by the subsidiary or parent concerns; and where the bargaining power of the supplier is weak, the US firm may even purchase some of its parts for it at a cheaper price.

Finally in the case of a selected group of larger American firms, where the manufacturing techniques demanded do not involve specialized knowledge unavailable to the subsidiary, bought-out items are costed in detail and priced. To quote again from the Ford Motor Company: 'We are interested not in what price is, but in what it should be, based on the concept of an efficient producer using modern facilities, and earning a reasonable profit commensurate with other companies in the industry.'[3] Such firms as these, then, tend to treat the supplier as being an integral part of their value-added responsibilities, or, as one subsidiary has put it – 'one of our family'. Not always, however, is the advice given of practical use, and again there is evidence of a lack of appreciation, by US purchasers, of the tooling costs and/or the availability of the parts or materials required; in some cases, improvisation is the only answer. Sometimes, where the US firm is noticeably larger than its supplier, it may carry out research on the latter's behalf, or send its own work study experts to the supplier's factory. Not only are the subcontracted items costed initially, but should there be a change, for example, in the size or regularity of order, or in labour and raw material costs, then the product is re-priced. On the whole, this practice has proved extremely popular with suppliers. As one medium-sized engineering firm put it:

> We do not carry the risks of changes in costs. The American subsidiary always pays us our profits on a percentage basis. On the other hand, this does not mean that we can afford to be inefficient, as from time to time work study experts visit our factory to re-cost. However, we find the profits reasonable and thus are willing to put up with these inconveniences. In any case, it enables us to give better service to our other customers.

By such methods as these, and by a constant rejection of products which do not come up to the standards demanded, the US firm usually gains what it wants, and in the course of so doing, often makes an impact of some importance on its subcontractor's efficiency. Sometimes the result is a reduction of prices. One agricultural machinery specialist said that over the past four years it had reduced its average bought-out costs by up to 15 per cent. Another light engineering subsidiary noted the lowering of the price of a particular component by 25 per cent since sending its own work study experts to reorganize the production control system of its supplier. Two further examples from the motor vehicles industry are given later in this chapter. From the start of a particular project, it is usual for the supplier to be taken into the subsidiary's confidence and be given advice. An interesting feature noted by a number of firms in the chemical, motor-car and light engineering industries was the policy of US firms to hold joint conferences with their suppliers at which information is exchanged. As one supplier put it:

> One of our main customers makes a habit of calling us and our competitors together at regular intervals to compare production methods and techniques. I think I can say that all have benefited from such conferences; I know we have gained quite a bit of information from our competitors, and vice versa in this way, and it is undoubtedly true to say that the subsidiary has got a better product as a result of these meetings.

The general picture, then, might be summed up as follows:

1 Compared to their indigenous competitors, US-affiliated firms tend to be stricter in their demands for close tolerances and for adherence to rigid specifications, together with an insistence on very high quality.

2 US subsidiaries as a whole are keener bargainers over price and more thorough in their methods of costing components than are UK firms. An exception was, however, made by one engineering firm who referred to one of its US customers as 'God's gift to a supplier'.

3 They are uniformly more willing than the average UK firm to supply detailed information concerning techniques, formulae, specifications, etc., though it was pointed out that the right way of doing a particular job can sometimes only be gained after several months, or even years, of experience.

4 They show more interest in their subcontractors' production methods, though sometimes business etiquette prevents undue criticism being made. This is not a universal tendency; there is, for example, a noticeable difference in the methods adopted in this connection by the two main motor-car subsidiaries in the UK. However, where such interest is displayed, it is very marked, and there is a definite tendency for US firms to treat their suppliers as 'part of the family'.

In contrast to these generally beneficial features, a number of criticisms were levelled against US firms:

1 Insufficient allowance is made for differences in and availability of materials, and too often there is a failure to appreciate the nature of manufacturing conditions in the UK. The US affiliate often has some difficulty in scaling down its requirements to meet the UK economic environment. Tolerances are often unnecessarily strict. One component supplier went as far as to point out that, whereas in the States such tolerances were made to break, in the UK they were made to keep!

2 The latest blueprint specifications and formulae were, in fact, not always available, and thus not always could US demands be met. Moreover, information of real value is sometimes deliberately held back by the US parent concern for fear it might be made available to competitors of component suppliers. This latter problem is sometimes overcome by licensing or patent agreements.

3 Orders tend to be inconsistent, frequently changed, and sometimes broken off altogether at very short notice. Too often the supplier was considered as a stop-gap until the US firm had built up sufficient capacity to manufacture for itself. In general, American-financed customers expected the supplier to carry much larger inventory stocks than was accustomed practice, thus increasing their storage costs.

4 In certain instances, there was too much interference by US firms with the day-to-day operations of suppliers.

While, then, it might be true to say that US-financed firms and especially those which adopt American manufacturing practices are more generous in the help which they are ready to offer their suppliers, they are at the same time more stringent in their demands. By the means described, in more than one instance, this has led to an improvement of the efficiency of suppliers which, as a result, has benefited UK industry as a whole. In other cases, the impact has been of more general interest. As one engineering supplier explained:

> In order to meet the demands made by one important firm, we were forced to adopt more efficient and up-to-date work study techniques, which led eventually to a reorganization of our whole production planning and budgetary control system. This of course has benefited us all round. Whilst we had such improvements in mind anyway, there is little doubt that the immediate cause of their adoption followed from our contact with this US firm.

Lastly, it may be noted that as part of a deliberate strategy, a number of US firms have chosen not to procure their parts and materials from larger companies who – so it was claimed – were charging monopolistic, or near-monopolistic, prices, but instead have themselves built up smaller companies. Examples of this were quoted by firms in the motor-car, agricultural tractor, industrial instrument, petroleum equipment and chemical industries.

KNOWLEDGE CONCERNING TECHNIQUES, NEW PROCESSES AND MATERIALS PASSED ON BY US FIRMS TO THEIR SUPPLIERS

It is only to be expected that US-affiliated firms, through their various contacts in British industry, and the implementation of those purchasing techniques described, should have aided the technical development of their suppliers, both by making available new knowledge and by enabling existing knowledge to be used more effectively.

The nature of this information has taken various forms, and has been spread over a wide – albeit a selected – range of industries. The potential benefits arise partly because what is subcontracted in the UK is often produced by the US parent firm itself, and partly by the growing attention now being given by American manufacturers to all aspects of the purchasing function. Such knowledge is made available to the subsidiary, who, in turn, may pass it on to its supplier. In other cases, American and British suppliers may be put in direct touch with each other: this, of course, will naturally depend on whether any patent or trade-mark isssue is involved. Other expertise made available may be the result of the accumulation of many years' manufacturing experience of the affiliated firms, and sometimes it is not easy to separate this from their close association with American industry. As some of the earlier developments have already been outlined, the present analysis will confine itself to more recent examples of the ways in which US subsidiaries have influenced their UK raw material and component suppliers.

We have selected three *assembling* industries – supplying respectively office machinery, petroleum refinery equipment and motor vehicles – for especial mention. The value of these industries' output in 1953 was about £800 million, of which the share of US-financed firms would have been between 40 per cent and 50 per cent. Of this amount, however, probably up to 70 per cent would have represented items contracted out to specialist firms, and it is the impact made on these companies by the US subsidiaries and Anglo-American concerns in which we are particularly interested. It is also a feature of these industries that the assembling firm is usually larger than the component supplier. For example, there are only six major motor-car assemblers, but over 300 component suppliers. There are only five major petroleum refining companies and six petroleum refinery engineering consultants, but more than 350 firms producing refinery equipment. There are a score or so of important office equipment manufacturers, though many times that number of specialists supplying components and parts, and so on.

It is, of course, virtually impossible either to measure with any accuracy the real significance of the knowledge passed on by American subsidiaries, etc., in these industries, or to identify how far this originated from the United States. All that we can hope to do is to direct attention to some of the main ways in which US firms have aided their suppliers' development, and give a number of actual examples cited to us. In this respect, it seems convenient to discuss the main benefits derived under four main headings: (a) more efficient methods and processes, (b) plant design and construction, (c) materials formulae, (d) information resulting from visits to the US. In some cases, of course, it is not so much a question of new knowledge being made available, as techniques and methods already known but not yet put into practice, being hastened or made economical by the demands of US firms.

New methods and processes

Technical data emanating from US affiliates in this field may either take the form of machinery and design expertise or information concerning the actual manufacturing process. It is most significant in the firms supplying the assembling industries, and has resulted in both a reduction of costs and a speeding up of industrial development.

Our first case study is taken from the *office machinery* industry. This provides a good example of the kind of relationship which may exist between a US-financed firm and its subcontractor. For first, its main products have many hundreds of parts which demand a variety of production techniques, which in America are produced by the office machinery manufacturers themselves but in the UK because of the smaller size of the market and limited experience of the subsidiaries, are subcontracted to a greater extent. Second, as the industry is predominantly of post-war origin (those firms which were producing in the UK before 1939 were primarily assemblers relying on imports from America), it affords one of the most recent examples of some of the teething problems associated with the building up of a market for materials and subcontracted items. Third, eight of the twelve US firms in the UK are strongly controlled by their parent concerns, and the fact that they export a large percentage of their output, which was previously supplied from US factories, means that their products (and their components) have to be interchangeable with their American counterparts. For these reasons, it might reasonably be expected that some specific US impact might have been exerted on component suppliers and their technical development advanced.

On average, 60 per cent of the ex-factory value of most types of office machinery is bought out. The larger proportion of this amount represents raw materials such as flat strip steel and rods, rubber, and iron and aluminium castings; miscellaneous finished components such as wooden cash drawers, printing type castings, springs, nuts, powdered metal parts, etc., only account for 5–10 per cent of total value, save in the case of the more recently established subsidiaries. The relative costs of these items vary. Certain materials, e.g. iron and aluminium castings, plastic mouldings, are cheaper to buy in the UK: others, e.g. specialized steels and individual components, are more expensive. It would seem, however, that these differences largely cancel themselves out: the raw material cost of one particular typewriter worked out to be identical in the US and the UK in 1955. Rigid adherence to specifications is a feature of these subsidiaries' purchasing techniques (1/1000–5/1000th of an inch is the usual tolerance allowed) because of the interchangeability of US and UK products. Criticism both of, and by, suppliers has been more pronounced in this industry than in others, but at the same time it is readily admitted that US firms are more liberal than British firms with their help, e.g. in providing machinery and specialized tools, castings, etc. (or in the know-how for same) – and, in some cases, have much aided their suppliers' growth by enabling them to become more specialized in their output. In the course of years, a good deal of technical data has been passed on, which have since been applied for the benefit of other customers, both within and outside the office machinery field.

The main raw material purchased from outside sources is steel, but apart from specialized technical data in respect of the chemical and physical properties of the type of steel required, and exacting requirements as to straightness, size and gauge, no new knowledge seems to have been passed on. Complaints in respect of quality, delivery dates and the attitude of suppliers have, however, been very numerous. Partly has this been due to the specialized demands made of some suppliers, and the (relatively) small size of orders. Moreover, at a time when attention has mainly been directed to supplying 'quantity' rather than 'quality', and the prices of special-grade steels have been controlled, it is not perhaps surprising that the more exacting demands have been unpopular. Specialized chemical formulae, such as, for example, are necessary for the production of synthetic rubber typewriter platens, have also been made available by two subsidiaries, while a number of suppliers recalled how they had visited their counterparts in America and gained information in respect of die-casting techniques, gear design and methods of electric motor manufacturing. Suppliers have also benefited from new techniques of tumbling, stud-welding, sintering, the manufacture of plastic key-tops, magnesium die-casting and copper brazing. Four such instances might be enlarged upon.

First, four US subsidiaries noted that information has been made available to their plastic key-top suppliers in respect of the double injection moulding process, which has been confirmed by the suppliers in question. The latest US method is to make one part (the body of the key) by the special casting of heated plastic crystals in a steel mould, and then to inject the letter or number separately moulded into the first mould. This replaces the old system which involved the sticking of the second part on the top of the first, with inevitable abrasion and displacement through time.

A second American manufacturer of dictating machines has, in conjunction with a British company, developed a system of manufacturing multi-wave connectors by soldering the terminals of the cable on to each other, and then moulding, by cellulose acetate butyrate, terminal housings directly over the cable. This prevents damage or deterioration to the terminal. Such techniques have since become so popular with other office equipment and electrical producers that this supplier has become a specialized producer of plastic and metal components, and is now selling 80 per cent of its output to US subsidiaries in the UK.

The parent concern of the third office machinery subsidiary is the largest supplier of powdered metal parts in the world which, in the UK, are contracted out to a specialist concern. By means of materials specifications, joint consultation, visits by the UK supplier to the US, and with the aid of machinery either imported from America or made in this country to US specifications, sintered metal production has become possible. Though the supplier in question would not ascribe its initial foray into this field solely to the influence exerted by this or other US subsidiaries, there is little doubt that the information made available by them has aided development. In addition, the increased demands by such firms have directly made economical the sintering of parts previously milled by hand or automatic machinery. As a result, unit costs have been lowered.

The popularization of a new production technique was cited by a fourth manufacturer, who commented:

> We were the first firm to order a Lindberg-type gas hardening and carburizing furnace in this country, which, because of its oxygen-free atmosphere for the complete work cycle, gives both a brighter (scale-free) and less distorted product than was previously possible. On its completion we allowed the furnace manufacturers to demonstrate with our equipment. To my certain knowledge this has resulted in the company concerned selling an additional 25 units in England and Scotland.

More pronounced has been the impact following from the growth of *petroleum refining* capacity since the war. Whilst any initial American influence must be put down to the construction of the Fawley or Coryton refineries – owned respectively by the Standard Oil Company of New Jersey and Socony-Vacuum Oil Company of New York – the actual construction, design and engineering of all the major UK post-war refineries has been entrusted to specialist consultants – which, as noted previously, are mainly subsidiaries of US corporations. Up to 1939, the oil refining companies in the UK carried out this function themselves, but with the growing complexity of refinery designs and manufacturing techniques, these have become more and more the province of specialist firms. The fact too that most new developments had originally been pioneered in the US, while during the Second World War that country had been charged with the responsibility of supplying the allies with all their petroleum equipment, meant that in 1945 the US was completely dominant in the field.

Thus, while most of the actual manufacturing of refinery equipment (which amounted to £125 million in 1955 compared with £15 million in 1937) is now subcontracted to British firms, the design consultants with over fifty years' experience of refinery requirements made available by their US associates, have enabled technical knowledge to be passed on more quickly and more easily than would otherwise have been the case. This development, of course, has not been confined to the UK; since 1945, for example, over £500 million has been invested in European oil refineries, and the output of petroleum products there has expanded at the rate of 11 per cent per year, compared with 5 per cent in the US. Nowhere, however, has the growth been as marked, or perhaps of such far-reaching economic significance, as in the UK.

In all, about 350 UK firms supply oil refinery equipment, ranging from the building contractors who are responsible for the actual construction of the plant to the manufacturers of pumps and compressors, filters and precipitators, pressure vessels, structural heat exchanges and condensers, steels, instruments, piping, electrical and insulating materials and so on. Of these, the first three items represent equipment specifically customized, in whole or in part, for the oil industry; the other categories require no specialized production techniques and, for the most part, are manufactured to standard designs. About a score of the producers are US subsidiaries, and at least as many supply under US licence. Since 1945, this new industry has been strongly American-dominated, particularly in the field of process development. In the last five years, however, British refinery equipment manufacturers have evolved products and techniques to their own specification. To quote from a recent OEEC Report: 'In many processes, European engineers are now as capable as the Americans. In some smaller refineries Europeans are now sometimes in charge of the engineering and process design.' The Report goes on to say:

> It will, however, take European consultants a long time to establish the large-scale research laboratories and pilot plants (involving large capital investment) and to train the necessary staff of competent engineers and chemists specializing in petroleum work necessary for them to develop research on new processes comparable to that done by US firms.[4]

To illustrate further, all work associated with the construction of the £37½ million Esso refinery project was placed in the hands of the American petroleum engineering consultant, Foster-Wheeler, Ltd. Jointly with the Standard Oil Development Company of New Jersey, this company was entirely responsible for the design, engineering and erection of that refinery. They prepared over 10,000 drawings. For each item it was necessary to decide whether to purchase or produce internally, the decision being influenced by time of delivery, price and quality: over 3,500 purchase requisitions for materials, parts and components and services were issued, together with specifications and drawings. During the initial stages, most of the process equipment was imported from the USA but after 1951 the fullest participation of British firms (some of which operated under licence to American companies) or US manufacturing subsidiaries was employed. Partly because of the size of the refinery operation, and partly because the managerial and manufacturing methods utilized were strongly American, these developments attracted particular attention at the time. For example, all orders purchased by Foster-Wheeler had to have at least three bids before a contract was placed. Many of the British firms involved visited the United States to study production methods and quality control procedures at first hand. Typical examples of the impact made by Foster-Wheeler, Ltd, on their UK subcontractors were, to quote from the firm's own words:

> Established British manufacturers had for years made pressure vessels for the chemical industry and the resources of these companies were fully utilized in the production of pressure vessel equipment required for refineries. However, several special techniques concerning the fabrication of alloy-lines vessels was made available to British manufacturers, thus assisting them in the rapid production of this specialized type of equipment.

or again:

> Our demands for oil process pipe work involved the production of specially welded fittings which were not produced in the United Kingdom. British firms undertook the manufacture, and we were able to place before them information regarding inspection jigs and equipment as used in the USA. After a short time, the final products reached a high quality, and, indeed, British fittings have since been exported to the USA.

and third:

> In our heavy demand for instruments, we were fortunate enough to obtain many of these from US subsidiaries operating in this country. However, they could not satisfy our wants fully, and we had to go to British firms to obtain the balance. While it would not be true to say we ourselves have passed on any information to these firms, we did help them to obtain licences to produce ranges of equipment which were not previously manufactured in this country, thus enabling the complete instrumentation requirements to be undertaken more quickly than would otherwise have been the case.

Similar examples might be cited from the construction of the other UK refineries; technical expertise has been passed on in respect of pump, valve and control gear design, techniques of piping and methods of erection, special steel and bi-metals.

In connection with constructional techniques, one US firm commented:

> It is true that we have gained some knowledge concerning methods of American construction, though it is in the field of welding techniques where there

has been the most specific gain, which we have since been able to apply in our contracts for other refinery buildings. Though this could have been acquired by visits to the United States, we feel that but for the direct contact with American firms in this country, it would have been thought of being of academic interest only.

However, a UK supplier said: 'Too often do US companies underestimate the constructional ability which is available in the United Kingdom, and, as a consequence, have brought over an unnecessarily large number of specialists.'

A general point on field construction work was made by one American refinery consultant:

We have found that whilst there are many British firms well grounded in the *civil* aspects of construction work (the erection of foundations, buildings, structural steel, piling, grading and roads), they have not the unique experience of the American in the mechanical aspects, e.g. the erection of pressure vessels, tanks, pumps and compressors, electrical materials, instruments and particular piping. Piping work, especially, represents more than 30 per cent of the labour on most refinery installations. The procedure in the last few years has been to subcontract most refinery construction work to British firms under the direction of American superintendents. However, this has not made for good progress due to the division of responsibility. Notable exceptions, however, were the Fawley and Coryton Refineries. Because of their US origin – at that time the saving of dollars was not a paramount consideration – they gave the erection work to the same US-financed firms who had done the engineering work. Both jobs benefited from the close liaison between procurement and construction which resulted, as well as from the experience which the American supervisors were able to bring to bear.

In all, fifteen petroleum refinery equipment firms were approached in our survey. Eight thought they had benefited from technical knowledge and quality control procedures made available by the US, and the balance said they had in no way been affected. All fifteen, however, admitted American influence in the design and manufacturing of their products, and eight had visited the US. The granting of licences by US companies has been a reciprocal benefit. As one writer put it, they:

have not only saved the newcomers to the industry much laborious trial and error, but have also compensated American industry for some of its work over many years. Above all, it has given the necessary confidence to the oil companies themselves.

At the same time, care must be exercised in attributing any new knowledge specifically to the presence of US-financed firms in the UK. The oil refining industry is essentially international in scope and character, and it may very well have been that knowledge of this kind would have been developed anyway, or been obtained from other sources. On the other hand, it is undoubtedly true that

the direct US contact made possible by such firms as the Standard Oil Development and Foster-Wheeler, Ltd has meant that US techniques and processes have
been applied more quickly than would otherwise have been the case, to the
construction of both home and overseas oil refineries. Summarizing in the
words of one UK supplier of oil pressure vessels:

> It is difficult to see just how much of the progress made since the war can be
> strictly accredited to American influence. Much of it is, no doubt, due to
> natural development which has been accelerated over the post-war years by
> new and revolutionary ideas which originated during the war and have since
> developed at a rapid pace. However, it would be true to say that the more
> intimate contact which we have had with American firms, which itself has been
> the natural outcome of our association with US branch subsidiaries, has
> stimulated the competitive spirit and this, being of a friendly nature, has
> been a help to both parties.

And in those of another firm in the same industry:

> Whilst we have in certain cases copied American techniques and processes, the
> traffic has by no means been all one way, and, in general, they have not much
> to teach us in the world of heavy plate and vessel fabrication. Their general
> liveliness and enterprise is, however, a stimulus, and it undoubtedly has
> accounted for some of the lively things we ourselves have done.

The *motor vehicle assembling* industry relies heavily on subcontractors, and the two
main US-financed firms are no exception to this rule. The Ford Company has
over 8,000 production items listed on its specification register, in spite of the fact
that it controls subsidiaries producing wheels and car bodies. The Vauxhall Motor
Company is hardly less dependent on outside suppliers, and buys from over 400
British firms. At the same time, the strategy of the two firms towards their
subcontracting responsibilities is rather different; while one subsidiary stipulates
its demands, but does not give technical assistance unless specifically requested,
the other, with a view to keeping its raw material and component costs as low as
possible, takes the responsibility of ensuring that, wherever possible, the technical
methods utilized by its suppliers are the most efficient available. Such detailed cost
analyses have, however, only been practised since 1945, as indeed has the close
attention paid by the same company to inventory and stock control. Both companies order on the basis of three to six months' delivery schedules, though the
degree of flexibility allowed in scheduling these orders differs.

In the course of our researches we visited fifteen motor vehicle component
suppliers, apart from the two US rubber tyre subsidiaries. Their labour force
varied between 100 and 4,000, and the items produced included fuel injection,
lighting and ignition equipment, shock absorbers decorative items, machine tools,
and hardboard for door interiors. Most of the firms in question also sold to British
assemblers as well.

While there was some unanimity of opinion that the purchasing techniques of
the two US firms were more thorough, and their specification demands more rigid

than those of their British competitors, there was less agreement about the extent to which new knowledge had been made available by these firms, as a result of their transatlantic associations. Seven of the fifteen suppliers thought that they had benefited from technical advice passed on; four of these were now largely dependent on their American customers, with the major result that more productive methods of manufacturing are now being undertaken than previously, and in factories more specialized in their output. One supplier pointed out that, whereas at one time its main component had been assembled by hand, now, as a result of its contact with an American subsidiary, manufacturing operations had been fully mechanized, and unit costs had been substantially reduced. The same firm recalled that it had gained a good deal of information in respect of manufacturing technique and product design as a result of its visits to the US. In another case, improved heat treatment, tooling and materials handling technqiues suggested by one US customer enabled such economies in materials and time to be achieved that the price of a formed steel part was reduced by one quarter; in like manner, another component supplier, in adopting advice given in respect of improved mechanization, was able to effect a 10 per cent saving in costs – the initial capital outlay being amortized over a two-year period. A machine tool contractor said that as a result of an increased volume of orders placed by US motor vehicle firms, broaching machines could now be economically installed, thus making possible an all-round reduction of costs. A fourth firm derived some technical assistance in the form of a materials treatment process which had since achieved cost-savings in the production of bumpers, while a fifth was particularly impressed by new manufacturing techniques which it had derived for the production of lighting equipment. Suppliers have also benefited in respect of heat treatment for steering gears, shell moulding techniques and various machining operations. In another case, a new type of insulating board was jointly designed by a US subsidiary and its UK subcontractor, while two other suppliers commented on help received in the form of machinery design and factory layout.

On the other hand, eight of the fifteen component firms visited said that they had received virtually no technical assistance from US-controlled companies. A majority of these suppliers – including some who admitted help – said that the specifications demanded by American companies were often impracticable and unrealistic in the light of UK conditions, and that the help offered was inappropriate for the volume of output normally produced by the firm. Three suppliers in this category mentioned specifically that their unit costs had been reduced by the enlarged volume of output supplied to US subsidiaries, but it was difficult to say how far other customers would not have made similar demands in any case. Eight of the fifteen subcontractors we contacted had visited their counterparts in America, and six said they had benefited as a result.

We found it rather difficult to get any accurate assessment of the importance of the information gained by motor vehicle component and raw material suppliers. While it would seem that this has been positive in particular fields, a completely objective picture is hampered by the fact that we found some suppliers very unwilling to admit help given to them by their customers, especially those with parent concerns in other countries. There was a readier admission that the demands made by the American subsidiaries had sometimes been the cause of more efficient production techniques being put into place, and that, since visiting the US, their research and development departments had been strengthened. A general point made by a number of suppliers was that their contacts with US firms had been stimulating to the extent that they had been afforded a closer view of American manufacturing methods, organizational structures and managerial strategies.

In a variety of other spheres, too, both subsidiaries and suppliers have quoted examples of how American manufacturing techniques have been successfully applied in the UK. The experiences of a large steel works are perhaps worth quoting in this connection:

> We were approached by an important American supplier of small kitchen equipment. They stated that their parent concern was manufacturing a line of products from a type of alloy steel which was proving very satisfactory, and wished us to emulate it. The analysis of the material which we were given was a 'mongrel' from our viewpoint, lying between two fairly standard types of steel. We were also furnished both with samples of the finished job and details of the physical tests that were expected of us. The know-how in question was primarily related to the finish of strip produced by hot and cold rolling, etc. To start with, our efforts were not 100 per cent successful. However, one of our Technical Directors was in the States at that time investigating other matters, and was permitted to visit the American main branch, and, as a result of information gained, we were eventually able to satisfy the subsidiary in this country. Following from this, the subsidiary in question was able to put on the market a line of kitchen tools which is now selling very satisfactorily.

The same firm goes on to say:

> In due course, various other small cutlery manufacturers in Sheffield approached us asking if we could supply similar material so that they could try and compete with the American subsidiary. As a result, several British firms are now offering a similar line of goods to the American firm and apparently all are selling the finished articles satisfactorily. We estimate that we are probably supplying three to four times as much of this special type of strip to other users in this country as we are doing to the original US firm.

An industrial instruments subsidiary told us:

> We required varying types of fractional horse-power motors which were available on the open market in America, but were not manufactured in this country due to lack of demand. This firm approached one manufacturer but they were not prepared to produce unless given the necessary technical information. This was obtained from the parent company and gradually a market was made available for this type of motor.

Examples are numerous in the metal goods industry. One pre-war firm commented:

> Information concerning hot-dip tinning, since having been passed on to our component suppliers, has enabled the quality of our components to be improved. The US practice is to double-tip, first in a very hot liquid and then in a temperature-cooled liquid so that the second application does not damage the first.

And a subsidiary supplying cast-iron products said:

> The technical liaison enjoyed by one of our suppliers on the production of steel castings, which included visits of British steel foundrymen to USA steel foundries has resulted in minimizing the time required to produce satisfactory steel castings for our purpose in this country. Also the technical information provided by the USA on special heat treatment for steel forgings has had similar beneficial effects.

A British component firm referring to its relationships with an American chemical subsidiary noted:

> There is not the slightest doubt that we have gained both in respect of new techniques of manufacturing packaging materials, and as regards the chemical composition of the materials themselves. In the past, this country has lagged well behind America in packaging standards, but more recently, due to our supplying an American-controlled organization, we have noticed a marked improvement, and with it, the quality we have been able to offer our other customers.

Another British supplier selling to the same subsidiary commented: 'This firm visits us regularly, notes our production methods and gives us advice as to the actual manufacture of our products, their chemical composition and the methods of finishing.'

A somewhat unusual case was recalled by a light precision engineering subsidiary:

> One particular subcontractor who was supplied with the plastic parts used in the assembly of an article he was making for us, at one time experienced considerable difficulty as a result of the fragile nature of the parts concerned which were subjected to a good deal of pressure in use. Our American parent company, who had been using identical parts for some years, had originally experienced the same trouble, but had overcome the breaking tendency by annealing the plastic articles in a hot-water bath before assembly. We passed on the technical details of the annealing process to our subcontractor with completely satisfactory results, and the breaking tendency has now been virtually eliminated.

An example of knowledge being passed on to UK suppliers as a result of a visit paid by the Chairman of the UK's subsidiary to the US was cited by an important producer of electrical appliances:

> Shortly after the war, the UK Chairman, when visiting our US associate, found that that factory was using plastic-covered wire for armatures. Samples were brought home and passed to our wire manufacturers. This resulted in the commencement of synthetic coverings in this country with improved insulation and abrasion resistance. To be sure, this technique would eventually have been picked up by normal channels, but, with the large quantity of wire which we use, our suppliers were able to go ahead with their experiments with the technical help given by ourselves, with the firm knowledge that if they were successful they would automatically have a guaranteed market.

Finally, an abrasive producer commented:

> There have been many examples with component suppliers where we have been able to increase their technical and general ability to serve this industry. In one instance, where we had a highly technical calendering operation, we brought a specialist in this type of operation over from the United States to work with a supplier. With his help, they have been eminently successful in producing a first-class material comparable to any which we have had made in the United States. In another case, where a supplier was manufacturing a rather involved engineering product, we were able, with our own industrial engineering group, to provide him with sufficient know-how to increase his profit margin considerably, and reduce the total cost to us.

Other instances, too numerous to mention in detail, include information being passed on to UK subcontractors with respect of the making of sprockets for film projection equipment, heat-resisting glass for lanterns and rotors and field coils for refrigerating machinery, the chemical treatment for silk fabric of mantels, the production of stainless steel capillary tubing, the heat treatment of iron and steel forgings and tractor transmission, the moulding of non-porous castings, pressure and magnesium die-casting, the chemical composition of colour printing and specialized inks for cartons, spot-welding, chromium-plating, the bleaching and digesting of cotton linters and the chemical formulae for specialized steels. Such knowledge has resulted in new and better designed products being supplied, e.g. control valves, cartons, light pressed steel axles, electric motors for office equipment, improved inks, fuel injection and pump equipment, and various components for the motor-car, electrical equipment and agricultural implements industries.

In conclusion, it may sometimes be the case that adaptations need to be made to existing UK products to meet the specialized requirements of US firms. For example, one chemical subsidiary found that the pumping equipment supplied in the UK was unsatisfactory for its particular requirements, since in the process of production it became corroded by fatty acid. Special techniques then had to be sent over from America to surmount this difficulty. Indirect help and advice has also been acquired through visits paid either by the US firm to its supplier's factory, or vice versa. Particularly has the smaller British firm been helped in this direction. Materials-handling methods, work study, factory layout and quality control production techniques have been instanced by supplier and purchaser alike as having been made available by the larger chemical and engineering firms in the UK.

Yet, at the same time, it is worth noting that knowledge and information is not a one-way flow only. Improvements to American-originated designs and manufacturing techniques have frequently been suggested by UK suppliers and returned to the United States. Among these, one might mention product and production expertise in respect of eyeless needles, cast-iron and steel strip, gears and photographic components.

New plant created

Sometimes the demands made by US-affiliated firms have been sufficiently large or specialized to necessitate the construction of new factories or plants. Though, in a few instances, knowledge has been passed on about the processes of plant design and construction (e.g. one British supplier was given help by its US customer in the building of a new production unit for the manufacture of insecticides), the impact of American firms has been mainly to create a sufficient demand for such plant to justify its initial installation. Frequently this has meant that such capacity has been made available to other firms. The impact made by the synthetic detergent subsidiaries is well known, while one seller of the basic material for this product also erected a new plant especially to supply another US firm with an ingredient for its new household toilet preparation. No transfer of design or constructional information was involved, but the demand created enabled the plant to be economically installed and, at the same time, to satisfy the demands of the other customers in the chemical and pharmaceutical industries which were not previously sufficient to justify the plant's installation. Likewise, partly to satisfy another subsidiary's orders for hydraulic tubing, steel strip and copper, a well-known UK concern was encouraged to put up the first Zenzimir mill and copper plant in the UK. To use the firm's own words:

> Although we originally built our plant to supply an initial demand of five tons of steel strip per week, its capacity was very much greater. This led to our pushing sales in other directions and we are now selling over 50 tons a week.

An important motor-car component manufacturer has, as a result of standardizing the design of its main product to meet the requirements of one US firm, increased its orders to other customers to such an extent that an enlarged, more specialized, and technically superior plant has become an economic proposition. The presence of the Esso and Mobil Oil subsidiaries in the UK has been responsible for more than thirty oil tankers being built at the cost of £25 million since 1950. A catalyst plant has also been installed to meet the needs of these same oil companies, and is now producing under licence to the American firm which supplies their parent organizations. Several suppliers of office machinery components have been induced to build new and more efficient plastic moulding plants, while a steel foundry firm, which some years ago set up a specialist unit specifically to produce castings for an American subsidiary, is now exporting these back to the US. Finally, while one pharmaceutical subsidiary has directly created a demand for a plant which is enabling new techniques of penicillin manufacture to be deployed, the production of chloromycetin in the UK has led to three firms setting up plants to produce the basic material.

In other cases, increased utilization of existing plant capacity has meant lower production costs. One precision engineering firm, since supplying more than twenty US subsidiaries, has increased its output of a specialized type of spring a thousand-fold, with an appreciable reduction in its unit costs. Another manufacturer of electrical components estimates that its average productivity has been raised by 20 per cent as a result of large-scale orders given to it by two US subsidiaries.

New materials

Though many US-financed firms in the continuous processing industries, and particularly those supplying chemical and pharmaceutical products, are virtually self-sufficient in respect of bought-out components and parts, they rely quite heavily on British suppliers for their basic materials, either in raw or partly processed form. Because of the tremendous progress which has taken place in materials innovation and development in the US over the past few years, branch units have been able both to pass on information relating to new materials formulae and processes to their UK suppliers and to create an initial demand for others which have since been put to widespread use. The most commonly cited case was that of specialized steels, to which we have already referred, and a number of firms argued the need for rationalization in this field. In commenting on the growing impact exerted by American purchasers, one supplier wrote:

> In part, this is due to the operation of branch manufacturing units in this country, but perhaps the greatest influence of recent years has been the offshore purchases by America which have naturally been made to US specifications. Particularly as regards stainless steels, American specifications are more widely known and used than their British counterparts, so much so that the bulk of our export business in this commodity is made to the former's demands. Gradually, British specifications are coming into line, and both by their demands and the technical assistance readily made available, US-financed firms are helping this transition.

Once again, it is not easy to cite examples which are representative of the whole, though the following selected instances indicate the type of influence which American-financed firms have exerted in these ways:

A small post-war subsidiary producing pharmaceutical products said:

We required the material Sulphonamide (N'Benzoyl Sulphanilamide), but found it to be unavailable in this country, and several companies were not prepared to co-operate with special production, as they lacked information on the chemical composition concerned. However, following from technical data received from our parent company being passed on to one company, a satisfactory material is now being produced, and is in free supply to pharmaceutical firms. Likewise, we wanted a revolutionary rubber appliance. No British company was, at that time, producing a product of the required standard though several UK companies tried but failed. Once more, we sent over to the States to get full specification and production data, and successful production in England is now in sight.

While a medium-sized engineering concern commented:

Through our American associations, we were able to pass on information about the processing of ny-clad wire, a product which costs one-third as much as cotton wire, and allows faster armature winding, and which is now being widely used by UK industry.

American influence has also been noticeable in the packaging materials field. Some years ago a well-known producer of packaged food products helped its supplier to develop a chemical formula for a new type of laminated cellophane. Many suppliers of cartons, too, have noted technical assistance given by US-financed firms in the pharmaceutical, cosmetic and soap industries. Knowledge about a new paper-backing for resins has since been put to general use by a UK firm supplying an abrasive subsidiary. Lastly, information originally provided by a US producer of photographic equipment on the manufacture of gelatin and base paper has been used to supply UK firms in other product sectors.

Perhaps of more general importance, however, has been the speeding up of the exploitation and application of materials already known, but not yet demanded. For example, one UK producer of packaging materials wrote:

Though, in general, our American customers in this country have not made any new knowledge available to us, they have been largely responsible for popularizing the use made of polyvinyl and polystyrene for moulding purposes, in place of the less efficient acetates.

And a supplier of basic chemicals said:

We are supplying an important US subsidiary with a well-known 'builder' for its household product. There can be little doubt that as a result of this contact, the material concerned has been made available to the UK economy quicker than would otherwise have been the case, and this, to the mutual benefit of both us and our other (UK) customers.

A London subsidiary supplying electrical components commented:

I can well remember when the brass we asked for to American specifications was really unobtainable in this country, and this applied very generally to steel and other metals. The introduction of phosphor bronze, beryllium copper and such other alloys gave further opportunities to English suppliers to produce materials that they had not done heretofore.

A specialist metal-producing firm said:

> As far as new materials are concerned, we were amongst the first people to exploit the advantage of butyral resins in this country (as a result of American expertise), and in the same way have also created demands for special alloys, as, for example, an alloy for manufacturing moulds for the plastic industry with very special characteristics, a very special aluminium bronze having physical properties making it particularly desirable for the metallizing industry, a high molybdenum material for bonding sprayed metal coatings, and a wire consisting of a plastic embedded with hard metals which opens a wide field on hard-facing not previously possible.

In addition, the commercialization and application of special alloys – such as beryldur, everdur and beryllium – high-grade steel strip, freon (a refrigerating gas first developed by General Motors and Du Pont, and now produced by ICI), specialized chemicals, e.g. aluminium acetyl salicylate, calcium saccharin and methyl alpha hydroxy isobutyrate, and plastic materials have also been speeded up by the presence of US-financed firms in the UK.

Knowledge gained through visits to the US

Of the forty-five suppliers contacted, twenty-six had paid visits to the US as a direct result of their associations with American-financed firms in the UK. Likewise, a similar percentage of US subsidiaries said that they had arranged introductions for one or more of their suppliers to their associate companies. One post-war engineering subsidiary noted that 'Since doing business with us, about 20 of our suppliers have visited the United States, and five have taken out licensing agreements in order to meet our demands.' In like manner, between one-third and one-half of the main subcontractors for the Fawley Refinery visited their counterparts in the US. Once more, it is not easy to assess the significance of the knowledge derived from visits either to the US parent or to the counterpart component supplier: selected examples made available by individual firms must suffice for our purpose.

For instance, one important steel producer supplying a light engineering subsidiary went to the US some years ago on the latter's instigation to learn about the electro-zinc method of coating steel. In due course, this was successfully emulated and the production process in question is now being applied to meet other customers' requirements.

In another case, an important office machinery manufacturer observed that one of its components was costing substantially more to make in the UK than in America. On approaching its supplier, its techniques of manufacturing were found to be outdated, and a visit to the subsidiary's parent factory (which produced the part in question for itself) was recommended. This took place and, as a direct result, new machinery was ordered and is now being installed; in its turn this necessitated improvements in plant layout. Ultimately, it is hoped that unit costs will be reduced by up to 25 per cent.

A third manufacturer of paints gained valuable information about the composition of oils, while a fourth producer of motor-car wheels, after visiting its opposite number in the US, was led to install a new kind of pressing machine and line operation. Knowledge has been likewise advanced about heating and air-conditioning techniques, electric motor and gear production, packaging materials and paints, resins and adhesives, wire contact relays, the manufacture of lighting equipment and the casting of steel valves.

Not only has the information gained been confined to technical matters. One businessman writes of his visit to the US:

> The experience which I acquired when visiting a number of American foundries was invaluable, particularly with regard to their materials handling, and there is no question that I would not have visited the States at that stage had I not been in close contact with an American firm in this country.

Benefits have also accrued from visits in the reverse direction. One electrical component firm wrote:

> Insofar as the metal beryllium copper is concerned, we are probably the most stringent customer in the world, and whilst we have, as yet, not obtained supplies in this country as reliable and consistent as those of USA origin, our American supplier has visited our British suppliers on at least two occasions and there have been distinct improvements made as a result of this co-operation.

CONCLUSIONS

To summarize: of the forty-five component and raw material suppliers which gave us information, fourteen thought that there was no reason to distinguish American-affiliated firms from their other British customers. The majority, however, as can be seen in Table 7.1, noted such a difference. Sixteen felt that the former's purchasing thoroughness had been to their ultimate benefit in some way or another, though ten argued that too many unnecessarily rigid and impractical demands were made. Twenty-nine considered that some specific gain in the form of materials formulae, manufacturing or processing methods and machinery design, etc. had been acquired, and one-half of these asserted that the knowledge in question had since been applied to supply other products and/or customers. Twenty-eight thought that the demands of US firms had stimulated the application of new knowledge, from which other companies were now benefiting: twenty-six suppliers had visited their counterparts, or the parent company of their US customers, in America; of these, seven had subsequently concluded licensing agreements.

Table 7.1 The influence of US affiliates on their UK component and material suppliers
Information given by a sample of 45 suppliers

Key to table
A = Marked impact   B = Some impact   C = Negligible impact   * = indicates that the benefit in question has since been applied to meet the demands of other customers.   † indicates that supplier in question has complained about unnecessary rigidity in specifications and tolerances demanded by US firms.

Firm no.	Products supplied	General influence made by US firms in relation to that made by other UK customers	If supplier has noticeably benefited from information passed on by US firms	If supplier has benefited from purchasing techniques of US firms	If US firms have created demand for new (a) plant (b) production methods (c) materials	If supplier has visited US resulting from its contact with American firms in the UK	Any other impact made by US firms
1	Specialized metals	B	Yes	No	Yes (a) (c)*	Yes	Increased exports
2	Plastic components	A	Yes*	Yes*†	Yes (a)	Yes	Increased exports. Reduced unit costs – more specialized production
3	Pumping equipment	B	Yes	No†	No	No	Interchangeability of parts encouraged
4	Packaging materials	B	Yes	No†	Yes (c)	Yes	
5	Precision engineering components	A	No	No†	Yes (a) (b)	Yes	Considerable reduction in unit costs. More specialized production
6	Metal parts	B	Yes	No	Yes (b)	Yes	

Table 7.1 Continued

Firm no.	Products supplied	General influence made by US firms in relation to that made by other UK customers	If supplier has noticeably benefited from information passed on by US firms	If supplier has benefited from purchasing techniques of US firms	If US firms have created demand for new (a) plant (b) production methods (c) materials	If supplier has visited US resulting from its contact with American firms in the UK	Any other impact made by US firms
7	Plastic components	A	Yes*	Yes	Yes (a) (b) (c)	Yes	Reduced unit costs and more specialized production
8	Specialized woodwork	C	No	No†	Yes (a)	No	
9	Steel castings, etc.	A	Yes	No	Yes (c)	Yes	Increased exports
10	Motor and electrical components	B	No	Yes	Yes (b)	Yes	Machine tools and testing equipment supplied to subcontractors
11	Constructional services	B	Yes*	Yes†	No	No	
12	Basic chemicals	B	Yes	No	Yes (a) (c)*	No	
13	Packaging materials	B	Yes*	Yes	Yes (b)	No	
14	Specialized steels	B	Yes*	No	No	No	

Table 7.1 Continued

Firm no.	Products supplied	General influence made by US firms in relation to that made by other UK customers	If supplier has noticeably benefited from information passed on by US firms	If supplier has benefited from purchasing techniques of US firms	If US firms have created demand for new (a) plant (b) production methods (c) materials	If supplier has visited US resulting from its contact with American firms in the UK	Any other impact made by US firms
15	Motor vehicle components	A	Yes*	Yes	Yes (a) (b)*	Yes	Reduced unit costs – more specialized production. Certain materials and parts purchased by US firm on supplier's behalf
16	Cast iron products	C	No	No	Yes (c)*	Yes	
17	Constructional services	B	Yes*	Yes*	No	Yes	
18	Motor vehicle components	B	No	Yes*†	Yes (b)	No	Reduced unit costs. Work study. Assistance regularly provided
19	Ground minerals	B	Yes*	Yes*	Yes (c)*	No	
20	Packaging materials	B	Yes	Yes*	No	Yes	
21	Machine tools	C	No	No*	No	No	
22	Plastic components	B	Yes	No	Yes (b)	No	New line of business started
23	Motor vehicle components	C	No	No*	No	Yes	Reduced unit costs

Table 7.1 Continued

Firm no.	Products supplied	General influence made by US firms in relation to that made by other UK customers	If supplier has noticeably benefited from information passed on by US firms	If supplier has benefited from purchasing techniques of US firms	If US firms have created demand for new (a) plant (b) production methods (c) materials	If supplier has visited US resulting from its contact with American firms in the UK	Any other impact made by US firms
24	Pumping equipment	B	Yes	No	No	Yes	
25	Motor vehicle components	A	Yes	Yes	Yes (a) (b)	Yes	Reduced unit costs and output specialization
26	Packaging materials	C	No	Yes	Yes (b)	No	
27	Motor vehicle components	A	Yes*	No†	Yes (b)	Yes	Reduced costs through increased efficiency
28	Specialized steels	A	Yes*	Yes	Yes (a)	Yes	Increased exports
29	Various machinery and motor vehicle components	B	No	No	Yes (a) (b)*	Yes	Reduced unit costs
30	Motor vehicle components	C	No	No†	No	No	Reduced unit costs
31	Electrical components	B	Yes	No	Yes (a) (b)	Yes	Reduced unit costs
32	Packaging materials	C	No	No	No	Yes	
33	Motor vehicle components	C	No	No	No	No	

Table 7.1 Continued

Firm no.	Products supplied	General influence made by US firms in relation to that made by other UK customers	If supplier has noticeably benefited from information passed on by US firms	If supplier has benefited from purchasing techniques of US firms	If US firms have created demand for new (a) plant (b) production methods (c) materials	If supplier has visited US resulting from its contact with American firms in the UK	Any other impact made by US firms
34	Pressure vessels for oil refineries	B	Yes*	No	Yes (a) (c)*	Yes	Trend towards standardization of parts and formulae extended
35	Pressure tools, jigs and gauges	B	Yes	No	Yes (b)	Yes	Increased exports
36	Electrical components	B	Yes	No	Yes (b)	No	Increased exports
37	Motor vehicle components	C	No	No	No	No	
38	Engineering components	C	No	No†	No	No	
39	Motor vehicle components	B	Yes*	Yes	No	Yes	Reduced unit costs
40	Packaging materials	C	Yes	No	No	No	
41	Steel strip and wire	B	Yes*	No	Yes (a) (b) (c)*	Yes	New line of business started
42	Electrical components	B	No	No	No	Yes	Increased exports

Table 7.1 Continued

Firm no.	Products supplied	General influence made by US firms in relation to that made by other UK customers	If supplier has noticeably benefited from information passed on by US firms	If supplier has benefited from purchasing techniques of US firms	If US firms have created demand for new (a) plant (b) production methods (c) materials	If supplier has visited US resulting from its contact with American firms in the UK	Any other impact made by US firms
43	Aluminium castings	C	No	No	No	No	Reduced unit costs
44	Engineering services	A	Yes*	Yes*	Yes (b)	No	Increased exports
45	Motor vehicle components	B	Yes*	Yes	Yes (b)	Yes	Testing equipment provided. Reduced unit costs. 75% of output now supplied to one US firm

Finally, one point of reservation. Our choice of suppliers has been biased inasmuch as we only contacted those firms who, *potentially* at least, were thought to have derived some benefit from their associations with American-affiliated firms. It may well be, then, that the general impact made by such concerns in this direction is less significant than that just portrayed. Undoubtedly, however, the transatlantic contact has been important in that it has both directed and advanced thinking along certain desired lines, and has speeded up the adoption of more efficient manufacturing methods and materials processing techniques. It has been responsible both for new capacity being created and for existing plant being utilized more fully. Most of the evidence points to the fact that the purchasing techniques have been beneficial to both supplier and purchaser alike, and small firms, in particular, have profited directly by the size of the orders given, and indirectly through the insistence by their customers of efficient production methods, closer tolerances and with stricter adherence to delivery dates.

8 The products supplied by US firms and their contribution to industrial productivity and consumer welfare

We now give further attention to the nature of the products manufactured by American-affiliated firms in the UK and the role which they have played, both in helping to improve the level of industrial efficiency, and in raising the living standards of the domestic consumer. Chapter 2 has already shown that in 1954, of the 205 US subsidiaries and Anglo-American firms comprising our sample, 129 – with a labour force of 160,000 – manufactured in whole, or in part, *capital* goods bought by other firms.[1] Moreover, a further examination of these items shows that the specific purpose of most of them is the implementation of new production techniques or processes, which, in turn, help to raise efficiency, improve quality, reduce waste and lower costs. Significantly, the resulting impact has not only been confined to the manufacturing sector: the economic prosperity and technical expertise of the farmer, office manager, building contractor and mining engineer has been no less affected. The seventy-six remaining firms, employing 86,000 people, have helped add to the material well-being of the domestic purchaser by making available an increased range and variety of *consumer* goods – sometimes at lower prices.

At the same time, it is important that one should evaluate the significance of American-designed and styled products made available by US-controlled companies in the UK in the light of the next best alternative – that of their import direct from America. That is to say, assuming the absence of currency restrictions, but given the existing structure of tariffs, what are the net advantages of supplying a US-designed product from an American-financed firm manufacturing in the UK, as compared with importing the same item direct from its parent concern in America, or one of its other foreign subsidiaries?[2]

THE NET ADVANTAGES OVER IMPORTATION

To the prospective buyer, the presence of American-affiliated manufacturing units in the UK offers four main advantages over any alternative policy of importation.

First, by manufacturing in the UK, an American subsidiary is both able and willing to give closer attention to its prospective market and adapt its products to meet any special customer requirements more easily than it could if it were producing 4,000 miles away. The benefits of this kind of Anglo-American co-operation have already been stressed. The parent concern supplies the basic research and development expertise, together with the appropriate manufacturing and design principles, while the branch factory, with its appreciation of the particular needs of the market at hand, applies these principles in the way required. In many instances, this had undoubtedly led to productivity improvements and the British consumer being supplied with a product which suits his needs more satisfactorily, e.g. in the motor-car, mining machinery, agricultural implements, building materials and several consumer goods industries. It is unlikely, however, that such adaptations *would* have been made by the parent concern if it were simply exporting to the UK, because only very rarely is the domestic market sufficiently important to the American firm to justify the trouble and time which specialized requirements demand.

Second, with the growing scientific and technical complexity of end products and their need for specialized and expert attention, the quality of marketing technical advice to customers and after-sales servicing as a determinant of sales has assumed increasing significance. Only a firm which is manufacturing in or near the country of marketing is able to offer these facilities adequately.

Third, a company manufacturing in the country of marketing is likely to pay more attention to informative advertising. That is to say, it is quite possible that those products supplied by the American-affiliated concern would not have been imported due to a lack of awareness by the British consumer that such products did, in fact, exist. The geographical separation of buyer and seller makes it improbable that consumers will buy from abroad as long as domestic producers can supply, if not identical commodities, at least broad substitutes. At the same time, for obvious reasons, an American company is unlikely to pay as much attention to publicizing its product in a foreign market as might its subsidiary which is more dependent on that particular outlet for its sales.

Fourth – and perhaps of greatest economic significance – there is the question of price. There are three main reasons why an American-affiliated company might supply its products at a cheaper price than if they were imported direct from America. First, some 40 per cent of the firms within our sample estimated that the average transport costs between America and the UK of their product would increase their current (UK) production costs by less than 10 per cent; 25 per cent thought that the difference would be between 10 per cent and 19 per cent; 22 per cent between 20 per cent and 29 per cent; and in 13 per cent of cases 30 per cent or over. Second, tariffs and other import barriers. The significance of tariffs is difficult to assess in view of the multiplicity of products (scheduled at different tariff rates) supplied by the majority of US-affiliated concerns. As far as one can judge, however, in respect of nearly two-thirds of the goods produced by American companies in the UK, the tariff charged would be between 10 per cent and 20 per cent, in 15 per cent of cases below this (only 10 per cent of goods are free from tariffs altogether) and 12 per cent above it. No less important, however, are a variety of non-tariff barriers, e.g. technical standards, a 'buy British' preference among some consumers, which only an American presence in the UK can overcome. Third, quite apart from these first two considerations, and as Chapter 5 has already shown, three out of every five American-affiliated firms believe they can produce more cheaply in the UK than their associate companies in the US. This, in itself, is not sufficient proof that consumers are able to buy a product more cheaply than they could if it were imported. For had the extra amount of output sold in the UK been produced in the existing US plant, the marginal costs might well have been less than the total costs of setting up a new plant and supplying the same output from the UK. Further, it would have been assumed that manufacturing, wholesale and retail and profit mark-ups, etc. were the same in both countries; in fact – as is the experience of a number of firms – this is not necessarily the case.

Nevertheless, in probably *nine cases out of ten* British consumers are able to buy a product at a lower price than if it were imported. In about 25 per cent of these, given the present UK price at 100, the price of the American product – inclusive of tariffs and transport costs – works out at 150 or more; in 60 per cent of cases, between 120 and 149, and 12 per cent of cases between 100 and 119, and in the balance less than 100. The most pronounced gains are recorded by firms supplying building materials, domestic electrical products, mining machinery, clothing and abrasives.

IN WHAT SECTORS, BY WHAT MEANS AND BY HOW MUCH HAS PRODUCTIVITY BEEN INCREASED?

There is no one answer to these questions. Indeed, the striking fact is the very width and diversity of industries served, inasmuch as the latest production techniques have been extended from the confines of factory productivity to commercial, agricultural, mining, road-making and domestic efficiency as well. Even where the industrialist has been the most affected, this has not so much taken the form of revolutionary changes in the production process *as a whole* – though in selected instances there have been such changes – but rather of the introduction or upgrading of machinery and equipment, machine tools and instruments, for specific *parts* of the process, and in what we have already referred to as the auxiliary spheres of manufacturing, e.g. materials handling techniques, packaging, inspection and testing methods, waste utilization, etc.

Following the approach adopted in Chapter 2, we now propose to outline briefly some of the main ways by which productivity has been affected, and the industries where US techniques have been most implemented.

Industrial or manufacturing productivity[3]

Within our sample, fifty-four firms, employing between them 35,000 workers, have pioneered the introduction of new products or materials, the main purpose of which is to help to raise manufacturing productivity or improve product quality. Of these, twelve subsidiaries, employing 11,000 workers, produce equipment or machinery the installation of which is meant radically to change the whole structure of existing production methods, either by the replacement of labour or less efficient equipment, or by effecting a more efficient factory lay-out, or by a combination of these. In the main, however, such products are specialized in character, and their impact is now largely of historical interest only. For example, at the turn of the century, the introduction of a complete range of boot and shoe machinery made possible the production of cheaper mass-produced shoes of uniform quality,[4] while the discovery of new types of typesetting and composing equipment was directly responsible for the development of modern newspapers and book production.[5] During the 1920s, the innovation of new kinds of machinery revolutionized existing techniques in the laundry industry and, more recently, improved types of canning and packaging machinery have had the same effect on food processing and canning methods. In each of these cases, the resulting improvements in productivity have been self-evident, and in all instances American-associated firms have played a prominent role. For example, in 1935, the American Chamber of Commerce in London, commenting on the growth of an American subsidiary producing laundry equipment, said that:

> it had been largely responsible for the extraordinary progress made by the laundry industry in the last ten years, as a result of the introduction of American machinery and methods. Laundering, formerly a trade catering for the well-to-do, now serves the masses, and is an industry of considerable consequence.[6]

Later, the same company pioneered the mechanization of flatwork ironing in this country.[7]

On the other hand, twelve firms, employing 7,000 workers, supply producer goods which either markedly affect individual manufacturing operations, or marginally affect the production process as a whole. For example, specialized machine and hand tools, e.g. pneumatic, broaching, milling, drilling, marking machines, have speeded up the production processes, improved the quality and reduced the likelihood of a wide range of metal-based products. To illustrate from an actual case study:

> In one instance a Double Ram Surface Broaching Machine, supplied by a US subsidiary, with three interchangeable fixtures, eliminated the milling operations requiring eight machines; in consequence, not only was the production time reduced, but a considerable saving in labour also effected, and a greater utilization of floor space achieved. In another instance, one Surface Broaching Machine in conjunction with a small Vertical Broaching Press replaced five Milling Machines, with a greater rate of output and improved finish or quality, also a reduction in labour costs and consequent floor space.

In like manner, American-designed automatic welding equipment has made possible welding speeds of up to 40 in. per minute compared with 9–10 in. per minute achieved by manual welding, and in doing so has particularly aided productivity in the shipbuilding industry, where it is now possible to prefabricate deck-plates, end sections, stiffeners and movable corrugated-type bulkheads at reduced costs. Such equipment also directly enabled the manufacture of the first

40 ft lengths of 36 in. oil piping in this country. The pipe is for use in oilfields throughout the world, and large orders from the dollar area are now being executed. Mechanical handling apparatus, as its name implies, is directly labour-saving in character, with fork-lift trucks and conveyors being demanded by a wide range of industries, while bottle-filling, bottle-washing and glass-forming machines are aiding the trend towards automation in the brewery, soft-drink and dairying industries. In this latter connection, one US-affiliated firm commented:

> Bottle-washing machines have increased productivity in a variety of ways. First, they do a dirty job in a simple and efficient manner – and much more economically. To take one example – a bottle which has contained tomato juice and has lain on a refuse heap for some time would normally take one person three minutes to wash properly by hand, and even then it would not be sterile. By the latest mechanical methods, it is possible for up to 200 bottles to be washed and sterilized every minute. Assuming that a firm needs to wash 5,000 bottles a day, then by mechanical methods the costs (allowing for capital depreciation) would be 40 per cent of those by hand. Moreover, in these days of full employment, it is extremely difficult to get labour to do such a dirty job, whereas by this kind of machine, it is not even necessary for an operator to touch the bottle, the whole operation being fully automatic.

In the food machinery industry, steam peelers are replacing the less efficient abrasive methods of fruit skin removal, while a whole range of dairy food processing and air-conditioning plant is extending the mechanization of dairies.

Finally, thirty firms, employing 17,000 workers, produce equipment which directly enables the quality of the products of the user firms to be improved, or aids waste reduction testing and other auxiliary improvements to factory efficiency. Included within this are the wide range of pneumatically and electronically operated industrial instruments, the functions of which are to measure and regulate temperature, flow, pressure, humidity and level gauging. Such instruments not only greatly decrease the likelihood of product defects, and lead to more precise tolerances – without which the modern oil, chemical, rubber and nuclear-power industries could not function efficiently – but allow a better-finished and more uniform product to be supplied. For example, instrumentation costs now account for up to 5 per cent of the total value of a modern chemical or oil-refining plant, and the giant Imperial Chemical Industries combine alone buys over £1 million worth of such equipment each year. To instance further the advantages of instruments supplied by US subsidiaries to modern industry:

1 In petroleum refining, the ability to centralize instrumentation and transmit temperature recordings over distances with a high degree of accuracy has made it possible to operate one control room for a large refinery staff. Temperature control is particularly essential in all stages of modern fractional distillation.
2 In steel manufacturing, the roof temperature of an open-hearth furnace when

controlled by an electronic potentiometer increases the roof life by four to five times, and, at the same time, allows substantial fuel economies to be achieved.

Similarly, new counting and computing machines are enabling production speeds and times to be more accurately recorded and controlled, and leading to dramatic improvements in labour productivity in a wide range of service industries. The use of specialized abrasives and silicon carbide refractories in the production of a variety of glass, plastic and metal products has upgraded quality and allowed more consistent surface finishes to be achieved more quickly and with less operator fatigue. For example, by the use of American-supplied abrasives, a mild steel bar stock can be cut through in about as many seconds as a power hack-saw takes minutes, while surface-coated abrasive belts, when applied to car bumpers, allow a lighter weight of nickel plating coating with consequent material savings. Substantial fuel economies in muffle furnaces used in enamelling have also followed from the use of silicon carbide superrefractories with their high conductivity. An emulsion and fast-setting adhesive (based on polyvinyl acetate), discovered by a US company during the Second World War, has since been made available to British consumers by its branch subsidiary, and is enabling a better-quality product in the bookbinding trade; an important new technique of palladium and rhodium plating introduced into the UK some years ago is helping to eliminate silver tarnishing, while an American metallizing process for the preservation and reclamation of worn metal parts is indirectly responsible for the economizing of many thousands of tons of material each year – one pound of metal deposited on worn parts salvaging seventy times its own weight.[8] The introduction of a new kind of American-designed insulating board has helped to reduce costs by making possible greater heat conservation, while 'marinite' incombustible wall-board is virtually eliminating the risk of fire on board ship. All American ships are now being fitted with such board, which helps replace the need for fire extinguishers. The name of 'Pyrene' is virtually synonymous with fire-fighting apparatus, and the same firm (now entirely British-owned) is producing an anti-corrosive process for application to iron and steel products. Refrigerating locker plants are directly increasing storage efficiency in the poultry and food processing industries, and are of especial value in rural areas. By the application of 'invisible' marking identification machines, garments for laundering and dry-cleaning can now be tagged at the speed of 200–230 an hour, compared with 30–100 an hour with hand-tagging, and 140–160 with 'visible' tagging equipment. In addition, such machines largely dispense with the need for identification labels.

Other American-supplied products which are directly or indirectly helping to raise the level of industrial productivity include 'Bundy' tubing (steel-based copper-coated), bituminous building materials, colloidal graphite (preservative), sealing compounds, gunite (lining of chimneys, tunnels and reservoirs, steel work, etc.), refractory linings for boilers and furnaces (protection and strengthening from corrosion and abrasion), mine safety equipment, and plastic alloy castings which allow switches to be more easily thrown in a power emergency.

Finally, within this section mention should be made of the many and varied new materials and materials processes supplied by the chemical and oil industries, which have generated productivity improvement throughout UK manufacturing industry. In the expanding petrochemicals field, the Esso Company at Fawley will soon be producing the gases – ethylene, propylene, butylene and butadiene – which are the basis for a wide range of industrial chemicals, including synthetic rubber, paints and plastics, while one step along the chain, styrene monamer, polyethylene and detergent bases are also being processed by US firms. Other industrial materials include silicone dyes, titanium and zirconium enamels, various plastic materials, colloidal graphite, rubber-like resins, carbon black, paper-making chemicals and starch.

Commercial productivity

Twelve US firms, employing 11,000 workers, supply equipment which is playing an important role in furthering efficiency in the offices of manufacturing business and the wider sphere of commerce. In the UK, until quite recently, the field of paperwork and administration had not been thought either suitable for, or worth, mechanization. There has been a marked absence of any scientific study of the application of business aids and computers and electronic machine tools in the office in contrast to the factory, yet the numbers employed in banks, insurance companies and the offices of factories and workshops have increased more rapidly than those employed in the factory. Rising labour costs, full employment, the growing amount of paperwork, the increasing attention paid to market research and statistics by government and industry alike, and the trend towards more scientific management have all led to this growth, and one authority has estimated that $2\frac{1}{2}$–3 million people are employed in British offices today – an increase of 750,000 over the past twenty years. At the same time, the factory has become increasingly mechanized, with the result that clerical labour costs have become proportionately more important. This, in turn, has directed attention to the need for more efficient office machinery. The change in thought since 1945 has been accomplished comparatively quickly, and in this respect US manufacturing subsidiaries have played an important role.

The most notable developments have been in the field of non-electronic accounting and computing machinery, the production of which has increased twenty-five times in the last two decades. Machines of growing versatility and flexibility – both key-driven and key-set – perform an important labour-replacing and time-saving function, while enabling hotels, banks, insurance offices, self-service stores, etc. to modernize their bookkeeping methods, e.g. in the field of job-costing, wage calculations, hire purchase accounting, storage control and so on. For example, the Thorn Electrical Industries Group recently mechanized its job cost accounts. Under previous hand methods, the work occupied the time of three to four ledger clerks; now, mechanically, one clerk is able to complete the work in three days.[9] Such equipment as this, at present, accounts for about one-quarter of the total output supplied by American-affiliated subsidiaries, and, as a result of expanding demand and improved techniques, the prices charged (in real terms) are little more than half those of pre-war. Most of the firms supplying such equipment are thus helping to improve productivity in many directions. The office executive, the industrial accountant, the works manager and clerical staff have equally benefited, and business forecasting, materials procurement, inventory valuation, market research, all made more efficient. The application of system techniques to machine and labour utilization has made possible visual production control and improved plant maintenance. The use of microfilms for records and statements is achieving large savings in storage space. One department store estimated that, whereas account records for six months would normally occupy six shelves each 12 ft in length, microfilm records for the same period could be contained in ten boxes, each only 4 in. square by less than 1 in. thick.

The output of typewriters has expanded from 29,000 in 1935 to 270,000 in 1955, while new types of machines, e.g. the noiseless, electric and executive models – all American innovations – are both speeding up typing and allowing a better-quality job to be done. Dictaphone machines are helping to counteract the acute shortage of shorthand-typists, and according to a survey carried out by the Organizing and Methods Division of Imperial Chemical Industries, are enabling typing output to be increased by one-third at the same cost. The initial outlay of such equipment is often covered in less than a year. Addressing and duplicating machines are also saving labour in a wide variety of spheres – one building society recently estimated that its annual cost of printing had decreased by 60 per cent since purchasing such apparatus, and a marked improvement in both the quality and functions of cash registers is not only affecting economies in commercial offices, but in retail stores and banks. While, as yet, only three types of electronic computers are being produced by US firms in the UK – IBM is the leading manufacturer and its main plant is in Scotland – the prospects for growth are considerable (the US is currently investing $1,000 million a year in computer research), with its possible widening repercussions on the saving of clerical labour and relief of repetitive drudgery in pay offices and banks, and in aiding pre-production planning. Finally, one should mention the impact made by streamlining various filing and indexing systems, e.g. Remflex, Kardex, Flexoprint, on standardizing office procedure, and the introduction of an inter-factory communication system, e.g. 'The Secretary', by which hand-written messages can be transmitted by facsimile for distances of up to several miles.

Farming productivity

Output in British agriculture rose by 56 per cent between 1938 and 1956, while the numbers employed fell by some 30,000 to 825,000. Productivity per man-year has thus increased by nearly two-thirds. Although this in part reflects a changing composition of output in favour of more highly productive crop varieties – itself a reflection of more efficient fertilization and new farming techniques – there is little doubt that the widespread implementation of farm mechanization has been the most important single contributory factor towards expansion. Today, British farming is the most highly capitalized in the world, and there can be little doubt that the quick transition in thought and technique which has taken place since 1939 owes much to the presence of US and Canadian affiliates in the UK.

Capital investment in farm machinery before the war was about £6 million per year, an amount then equivalent to one-quarter of the total wage bill. Between 1948 and 1953 an average of over £50 million a year was invested – or over one-half of the annual labour costs. The number of tractors increased from 50,000 in 1939 to 400,000 in 1954, while the number of farm horses fell from 940,000 to 360,000 during the same period. The yearly output of combine harvesters and pick-up balers rose from 150 in 1938 to nearly 17,000 in 1955,[10] and similar, if less spectacular, expansions took place in the production of milking machines, ploughs, corn drills, motor mowers, disc harrows and the like.

Chapter 2 has already indicated that American-affiliated firms, if somewhat conservative in the variety of products they supply, at present account for over half the British output of agricultural implements and tractors. In its move towards farm mechanization, the UK is now in the same position as the US was during the 1930s, but the transition period between 'old' and 'new' has been shorter, and has involved less frictional disturbance. In the last ten years, the attitude of the farming community towards mechanization has undergone a profound change and the repercussions have been widespread. Many traditional farm practices have had to be discarded. Perhaps the three most significant hallmarks of progress have been:

1   The invention of the hydraulic implement lift which has enabled farm implements to be coupled on to a tractor, and the tools to be raised out of the ground as the tractor turned at the end of the field.
2   The innovation of pneumatic tyres for tractors.
3   The evolution of the diesel tractor.

The Ford Company pioneered the third development, and was the first company to take advantage of the second. The operating costs of the diesel tractor are now little more than half those of a paraffin tractor, with an initial outlay of only £56 more.

Most of the improvements in farming productivity have been animal- or labour-saving in character, and while both arable and dairy farming methods have been affected, US-affiliated firms have been mainly concerned with providing equipment for the former. As, too, the output of machinery has expanded, so prices have fallen, with new adaptations being made on American principles. Thus, while before the war a combine harvester was three times as expensive as a binder, it is now only half as much again. At the same time, as a Leeds University enquiry recently revealed, the cost of reaping an acre of barley with a combine harvester is £5 15s. (£5.75 np) compared with £7 9s. 6d. (£7.48 np) with binder and thresher.[11] A sugar-beet harvester, which directly replaces labour, is farming an acre of root crops at £7 1s. 6d. (£7.08 np), compared with £8 3s. 7d. (£8.18 np) by hand.[12]

Thus, though it is difficult to compare the efficiency of American machines with their German or British counterparts which have developed concurrently, one can say with some confidence that the part played by US and Canadian manufacturing subsidiaries in the furtherance of UK mechanization since 1940 has been an important one; that the American research, development and manufacturing experience these companies have been able to draw upon has proved invaluable; and that in their absence, fewer – and, most likely more highly priced – machines would have been available to the UK farmer.

Mining, excavating, road-making and road-repairing productivity

Ten American-affiliated firms, employing 8,000 people, are supplying machines and equipment which are making possible new techniques in the mining, building and road-making industries.

As has been noted earlier in this chapter, British mining conditions differ markedly from those in America. Only in about 10 per cent of British mines is it economic to assimilate the room and pillar method as utilized in the US, and, as one might perhaps expect, it is in this field where the impact of US firms has been most felt.

While the United Kingdom is fairly well mechanized in the cutting of coal – in 1953, 83 per cent of the coal mined was cut by mechanical methods; in the same year only $8\frac{1}{2}$ per cent of coal was power-loaded. Of the 2.1 million tons power-loaded in room and pillar workings, 178,000 came from Joy-Sullivan continuous miners, 1.5 million tons from loaders of the gathering-arm type – also produced by US-affiliated firms – and 124,000 tons from duckbill loaders.[13] The continuous miner in particular has an exceptionally high productivity, the output per man-shift of mines using this machine being 34 tons compared with an average of 9.4 tons for normal mechanized pillar and stall work, and 5.6 tons for power-loading long-wall working. The National Coal Board is gradually increasing the number of these machines, mainly in replacement of the gathering-arm type of loader.

The Gloster-getter, originally designed and developed in the UK, is also manufactured by the Joy-Sullivan Company, and is now being used for coal-cutting purposes in long-wall mining. A range of rock-loading equipment, as manufactured by the Eimco Company – and applied, for example, in hydro-electric building schemes – is a great advance on previous tunnelling methods; the National Coal Board has already purchased over 500 of these machines. The production of rocker-shovels is such that output per man-shift in tunnelling operations has increased by half as much again. Then, one building contractor estimates that US-designed machinery (e.g. earth-moving and roof-bolting machinery) has directly raised productivity by up to 75 per cent over the past four years. Apart from these instances, and a range of drilling machines supplied by the British Jeffrey-Diamond Company, American influence has been confined to opencast mining. One Canadian firm is supplying a machine adapted from an American principle for long-wall mining, which has considerably increased output per man-shift, but the main technical advances continue to emanate from British and German firms.

Many new types of excavating equipment which help upgrade competitiveness in the construction and earth-moving industries have also been made available by American-financed concerns. In particular, the growing output of bulldozers, rear and bottom dump wagons, scrapers and crawler tractors, together with new kinds of materials, mixing plant and road finishers are enabling more UK roads to be repaired and maintained for the Ministry of Transport than was possible before the war with a larger road budget. For example, the operating costs of a finisher (for the laying of 250 tons of materials per day), including the wages for four men, averages out at £2 an hour, compared with £5 7s. (£5.35 np) an hour for hand-laying with twenty-five to thirty men. Since 1945, over £5 million of equipment has been supplied by this subsidiary and the innovation of its road finisher in the UK has meant that bituminous materials cost no more to surface mechanically today than they did when laid by hand before the war.

Other fields

Mention has already been made of the role played by American oil engineering consultant firms in the development of the petroleum refinery equipment industry. It is, however, important to note that such affiliates have also influenced technical progress in other fields, e.g. steam generation, chemical processes, industrial plant, etc., pioneering, for example, the development of a variety of water-cooled furnaces, superheaters, cooling towers, high-pressure cracking furnaces, etc. Immediately after the last war, the American Foster-Wheeler Corporation led the way in the evolution of land boilers and large power stations. The techniques adopted have since been taken up by the Central Electricity Authority in the UK and large orders for this type of work have been placed with the British subsidiary. The same company was also largely responsible for ship-owners replacing shell-type marine boilers with the more efficient and economical water-tube boilers, and for the introduction of new types of controlled heating systems.[14] Similar contributions might be cited from the experiences of Kellogg International Co. Ltd, Procon Ltd and Badger Ltd.

Then there are a wide variety of specialized fields where equipment supplied by American firms is leading to higher productivity. Canteens, restaurants and shipping companies are utilizing catering equipment and dishwashers, as produced by a subsidiary which manufactured the first mechanical potato peelers and bread cutters in the UK. The domestic handyman's lot has been made easier by the use of portable electric tools, the chief purpose of which is the saving of time and energy in carpentry, home decorating and gardening, while electric washing machines, steam irons, vacuum cleaners and refrigerators perform equally important functions in their respective fields. Pneumatic drilling equipment, which was originally developed in the UK by an American subsidiary in the 1920s, has helped to lessen the time of surfacing and resurfacing of roads by up to three-quarters. Many US-affiliated companies are also supplying products to government contract, e.g. telecommunication installations, automatic and precision instruments, electronic gear, parachutes, naval stores, high temperature coatings for the aircraft industry, specialized chemicals and plastics, etc., while the technique of broaching has directly aided the production of jet engine blades. For many years past, Royal Naval ships have been standardized on Sperry gyroscopic compasses, which, free from the vagaries of the traditional magnetic type, are in widespread use as aids to air and sea navigation. Another US-financed firm supplies thirty-two airlines and twenty-five national air forces with radio equipment and recently produced and installed the backbone of the present television transmission system in Britain.[15] A post-war American subsidiary has a virtual monopoly in the UK production of fully- and semi-automatic overdrive transmissions, the principle of which is eventually likely to replace the gear-box and clutch in a motor vehicle. In the rubber products industry, American-affiliated firms have pioneered, or helped pioneer, aero-wheels, rubber dock-fenders, giant pneumatic and tubeless tyres, lifeguard tubes, rotary drill hose, driving belts and PVC conveyor belting.

These, then, are some of the main ways in which the products supplied by American-financed companies operating manufacturing units in the UK have helped to raise the level of industrial efficiency and to further the prosperity of their customers. Because of foreign exchange constraints, and the lack of technological expertise in the UK, it is most unlikely that these gains could have been achieved through alternative means, e.g. imports or licensing arrangements. As will be appreciated, it is much easier to cite the products which one knows to have had an effect on productivity than to give any accurate assessment of the actual impact made. That a wide range of industries have been affected is very clear, and, in the main, the new techniques have not required large sums of capital expenditure. It is particularly noticeable that small as well as large firms have benefited from the trends. Recent developments in office and agricultural machinery, for example, have probably been of more significance to the smaller and medium-sized firm than to the larger firm, which, even before the war, had embraced many of these technological advances. Likewise, the average British company employing only a handful of workers has perhaps benefited most from improved auxiliary production techniques, while recent advances in industrial instrumentation have exerted an impact on factories of all sizes.

It will be recognized that developments of the kind described have been very largely post-war in origin. An examination of the kind of capital goods supplied by US-affiliated firms prior to 1939 reveals that these were mainly directed to the improvement of factory productivity and more often than not related to basic industrial processes: it has been only since the end of the Second World War that attention has been directed to the other fields which we have described, and to the extent that US firms have enabled their mechanization to be carried out quickly and smoothly this has been an undoubted benefit.

CONSUMER GOODS

To the domestic consumer, the presence of American firms has shown itself in the increased quantity and variety of goods made available. In many cases, one-time luxuries have been popularized to such an extent that they are now regarded as conventional necessities. From the viewpoint of US investment in British industry, this has taken a variety of forms. First, a pioneering attention has been given to the design and range of products offered to the housewife. In the mechanical kitchen, for example, the scarcity and increased cost of domestic labour, the greatly expanded number of working women, and the rising level of incomes, have meant that more attention has been given to labour-saving devices. One well-known Anglo-American company estimates that three-quarters of the culinary implements being used in the ordinary kitchen in the mid-1950s were not available prior to its establishment in this country in 1938. Items such as pressure cookers, electric mixers, egg-beaters and stainless steel gadgets have helped to make the housewife's task more pleasant, as have equally, if not more so, the increased range of better-designed and more efficient washing machines and refrigerators made available. Yet, even today, only eight out of every hundred wired homes in Britain possess a refrigerator, and only eighteen in every hundred a washing machine. There is obviously a huge potential for expansion here: US figures are ninety-four and eighty-four respectively.[16]

Second, American firms have also played an important role in popularizing canned and bottled foods, and have introduced an increased variety of products such as breakfast cereals, starch foods, cake mixes, beverages and cheeses. The improved packaging of processed food by pliofilm, polyvinyl film wrapping and laminated paper covering has also furthered the trend towards improved hygiene and food preservation. Another American concern operates a confidential processing and packaging service for pharmaceutical, cosmetic, toilet preparation and food firms.[17]

Finally, the availability of an increased range of ethical specialities such as aureomycin, terramycin, streptomycin, the penidural drugs (including an oral preparation of penicillin) and various medicinal proprietaries are improving health and reducing industrial sickness and absenteeism, while X-ray apparatus, surgical dressings and sutures have eased the work of hospitals and clinics.

Many other new products – some of which have already been referred to in Chapter 2 – owe their genesis in this country to US-affiliated firms. One well-known subsidiary pioneered the individual fitting of foundation garments in 1913, and the development of trained corsetières is now standard practice throughout the trade. Then, as regards cosmetics and toilet preparations, e.g. dentifrices, hand lotions, face creams, lipsticks and rouges, baby powders, shaving soaps, etc., the increased range of products using the high quality and packaging standards available have been strongly influenced by firms of US origin, and most of these tend to be purchased by middle or upper income consumers. A wide variety of other consumer goods – synthetic detergents, silicone polishes, abrasives and chemical cleaners, safety razors, electric shavers, oil lamps and cookers, floor-polishers, alarm clocks, thermoplastic tiles, new-fashioned sports and swimwear – have been either pioneered or popularized by US-originated companies. Many of these products are now available to the UK consumer at a lower price than either of their earlier substitutes or imports from the US.

CONCLUSIONS

In a variety of ways, then, American subsidiaries and Anglo-American concerns have had a direct impact on the British consumer. The progress and efficiency of the industrial consumer have been variously advanced, while the domestic consumer has been offered a wider range of, and better-quality, products. The fact, too, that such products generally cost less than their imported price, and the advantages accruing from more efficient after-sales servicing and informative advertising, adds to any inherent value which they themselves may possess.

These, of course, are the direct benefits made by the firms themselves. But industrial productivity and living standards have also been enhanced indirectly through the normal course of competition, and the 'spill-over' effect on the material and component suppliers of the industrial customers of US affiliates.

9 Managerial techniques adopted by US firms and their influence on UK ideas and policies

Apart from any question of the provision of finance, perhaps the feature which most discriminates between American-affiliated companies and British firms producing under US licence is that while both derive benefit from an exchange of technical and research information, only the former are directly affected, if not determined, by American entrepreneurial and managerial procedures. Already, in previous chapters, we have touched upon certain aspects of the managerial techniques adopted by US subsidiaries and Anglo-American concerns, and the impact which they have made on different sections of the British economy. Chapter 1, for example, briefly commented on the early influence exerted by such affiliates as the Westinghouse Company, British Thomson-Houston Ltd and United Beef Trust Ltd on current UK managerial techniques. Chapter 4 further outlined the various kinds of administrative and organizational relationships which might exist between parent and branch. Chapter 5 described the extent to which US managerial techniques dictated the operating methods of the UK subsidiary, and Chapter 6 examined these in the light of the competitive advantage which such techniques afforded. Chapter 7 analysed the purchasing techniques adopted by US branch plants, and the ways in which these had affected the efficiency and development of their component and raw material suppliers.

The present chapter has two main purposes. First, to draw together some of the earlier points made, and supplement these with a review of certain other managerial practices and a discussion of the extent to which US-affiliated companies assimilate the policies and methods of their parent companies. Second, to examine briefly, from the experience of those British firms concerned, the impact made on existing managerial policies and attitudes, as a direct result of their purchase, or part-purchase, by an American concern. In what ways, for example, did the change from British to US ownership of such companies as Vauxhall Motors, Thomas Hedley, Alfred Bird, by US corporations affect their organization structures, their sales and advertising strategies, their wages policies and so on? Three representative case studies enlarge upon these points in more detail.

It is perhaps worth noting that this latter question is not one solely of academic interest. In recent years the assertion that the superiority of American managerial techniques is the biggest single factor responsible for that country's high productive efficiency has been made time and time again; and, for the most part, the implication has been that there is no reason why such techniques should not be profitably assimilated by British industry. Various Anglo-American Productivity Teams have examined specialized aspects of the problem in some detail – for example, there have been separate reports on Education for Management, Management Accounting, Production Control, Training of Supervisors, and so on.[1]

In the final analysis, however, the problem resolves itself into the ability and the motivation to manage efficiently. The former not only presupposes sufficient knowledge and an appreciation of the various aspects of management, but also that it is economic for such techniques to be put into practice. For the fact that the economies of large-scale production can apply equally to the utilization of managerial as to factory manpower also means that, just as it is uneconomic to install certain types of machinery and processes in UK factories because of market limitations, a detailed division of labour and functional specialization of management may also not always be desirable. And although, as we have already seen, many American managerial practices in part, or in whole, can be, and are profitably transferred to the UK, it is equally true that some of these techniques are themselves the product of a more specialized management structure which only large-scale units can afford. Because new knowledge which one particular organizational structure makes available may sometimes be applied with equal success to other organizational structures it does not necessarily mean that the firms from which such knowledge emanates are the more efficient. One cannot compare *parts* of the system without examining the *whole*. It may well be that the cost of a particular managerial technique in itself is not prohibitive to the small firm, but the *structure which allowed the development of that technique may well be so*. In such cases it cannot necessarily be presumed that there is any relationship between America's superior knowledge and the shortcomings of UK management.

The function of management has already been defined as being inclusive of both organization and decision-taking. The task of the former is essentially that of the co-ordination of the various activities of the firm in conformity with the goals and policies as decided by the Board of Directors – or more particularly by the Managing Director of the Company; and of the setting up, and monitoring, of an organizational structure to further these goals and policies. Decision-taking – the ability to relate and appraise present decisions affecting the future with those taken in the past – is, as we have seen, a variable of (i) the power of decision-takers to assimilate facts and judge them effectively and (ii) their attitude towards risk and uncertainty bearing. In general, it would seem that the American economy offers more pronounced incentives to efficient management than does that of the UK. The pecuniary rewards both before and after tax are higher, and the businessman commands more social respect than in the United Kingdom, where, over the years, such status has been directed to the professions, which still tend to attract a large part of the cream of the country's intellect. Furthermore, the American educational system is better geared to providing specialized technical and commercial training, and several universities offer graduate courses in management and business administration. At the same time, for good or ill, that country's whole approach to education and training differs from the British, with more emphasis being placed on the vocational, and less on the purely academic aspect of learning.

Because of these factors – educational, cultural and economic – it is not surprising that the United States should lead the world in the development of management techniques, and for it to have a larger measure of ability both to take decisions and to administer them more effectively. But there is also the question of the attitude towards entrepreneurship and management, the dynamism and inventiveness of which, in America, so much impressed the Anglo-American Productivity Teams, who strongly argued that it should be emulated by British management. Even here, however, it is difficult to argue that this should always be the case, for to benefit from a particular managerial technique it may be that a whole set of conditions have to be brought about which are not in themselves economically justifiable.

To what extent have American managerial techniques been found economic to assimilate in branch manufacturing units? Following the lines adopted in Chapter 5, we shall examine each of the main sectors of management in turn.

Overall policy and thinking

This, we have seen, is largely in the hands of the Board of Directors – and implemented by the Managing Director. In 35, or 15 per cent, of subsidiaries, the Managing Director is an American. In fifty other US subsidiaries, though British, he is fairly closely controlled in decision-taking by the Board of Directors, the majority of whom are American. And in at least two cases out of three, all major decisions on new products, finance and the like have to be submitted to the US parent company for approval. Only in the case of thirty US-financed firms is overall policy and strategic thinking independently determined, though even in a proportion of these, the present Managing Director worked previously under an American Managing Director, and during that time became familiar with US policy and methods. As a British Chairman of one subsidiary put it: 'My constant contact with, and visits to, our US parent company makes me more receptive to new ideas than would otherwise have been the case.' This is important, for it means that the philosophy and approach towards such factors as finance, mechanizaiton, advertising, etc., is usually looked at through American eyes – albeit that the subsidiary is operating within an alien economic environment. This, in its turn, will reflect itself right the way down the pyramid of decision-taking.

One other factor is, however, important, and that is the qualifications and background experience of the Managing Director himself. Of the American holders of this office in our sample, the larger number were ex-sales executives rather than ex-production experts, and, in consequence, their approach to problems often takes a different slant. Management meetings in the US at which the appropriate departmental heads attend will put forward to the Managing Director a rather different picture than that presented by their counterparts in the UK. Thus, to keep abreast with the latest managerial and production procedures and strategies of the US parent company the Managing Director of the subsidiary must ensure a constant flow of information from America for his departmental managers. He must also see that his senior plant executives visit their US counterparts frequently to study at first hand the latest methods being practised. Nevertheless, his remains the ultimate responsibility for setting the right climate for production, and for strategic decision-taking. That is why some American firms prefer to staff themselves in the early years with American nationals – particularly where the attitude towards the problem in hand will be a decisive factor, and needs to be approached from an American viewpoint. It also explains why there is a tendency for American personnel to be employed in the sales and marketing departments. In the case of most manufacturing techniques, directives can be easily given from the parent plant; this obviously is not the case for post-productive activities where the human element is more important. In contrast, it is almost universally preferred to have a British personnel manager for his specialized understanding of the local employment situation and handling of labour.

Administration

The organizational structure of a US-affiliated firm is primarily a function of its size, both absolutely and relatively to that of its parent or associate company. The great majority of the larger subsidiaries follow American principles, in as much as they practise functional specialization wherever possible, and operate separate departments for each of the main products manufactured. There is more separation of managerial tasks than is usual in British firms, and lines of responsibilities and channels of communication are more clearly demarcated, in many cases, in writing. Few of the smaller firms try to assimilate the methods of their parent plants in this way, as their size does not permit such a division of labour. The main exceptions are in connection with the American policy of frequent production meetings, and in office and public relations procedure which tend to be adopted by subsidiaries irrespective of size.

Production control, budgetary planning, costing

Many of the Anglo-American Productivity Team Reports attached particular importance to the role of production planning and control in American company organization. In the words of the Production Control Specialist Team: 'British industry might well follow the lead given by the American industry in this respect, and the Team feels that it cannot over-emphasize the importance of this approach to what is the key to efficient production.'[2]

That it is clearly possible for most production planning techniques to be economically utilized in the UK, is shown by the fact that, more than in any other managerial field, and practically without exception, US affiliates embrace their parent plant's methods. In fact, 70 per cent of the firms in our sample said that they were strongly, and 20 per cent partly, influenced in their methods of financial control and pre-production planning by their American associates, and used the same formula to price their products and processes.

There is no necessity to describe these techniques in detail as they are adequately covered by the *Production Control* and *Management Accounting* Productivity Team Reports. Centralized pre-production planning and sales forecasting, detailed scheduling of output, the application of work study, standard costing and budgetary and process control, the proper integration of the various production processes, effective inter-departmental communications, efficient stock control, and the detailed presentation of balance sheets – all management practices commonly adopted in the US – are widely and successfully assimilated in the UK by both large and small subsidiaries, and, as such, reflect their American parentage.

As is amply brought to notice by the expanding literature published by such bodies as the British Institute of Management, the Institute of Industrial Administration and the Institute of Production Engineers, British firms are gradually recognizing the importance of an efficient system of production planning and measurement control and in the light of this are re-examining the organization of their value chains from the programming of raw materials and components to the sale of the finished product. But, up to now, it would seem that the scope has been more or less limited to those larger firms which were already renowned for their dynamic managements. Within our survey, however, we visited 125 firms which employed 750 or fewer workers, and over three-quarters of these stated that it was quite economic to practise most of their American associates' production control techniques. In their opinion, the main deciding factor was neither one of capital costs, nor an expensive use of manpower, but rather that of the competences of managers, and their readiness to adopt new methods. Notwithstanding the fact that the initial costs of implementation were generally greater in the UK than in America, the majority of subsidiaries agreed that properly organized pre-production planning was an indispensable prerequisite for efficient and profitable manufacturing,

Neither need much be said concerning the comparative accounting and costing procedures adopted; suffice to point out that in most cases, and universally where the UK subsidiary is one of a group of overseas companies, the method of accounting is standardized on American lines. While double-entry bookkeeping is used both by subsidiaries and parent concerns, differential costing and the voucher system are more widespread in America, and in two cases where a British firm has been taken over by a US company, this latter method has replaced the double-entry accounting: the differences, however, are of minor importance, compared with current British procedure. The feature which most marks out the larger subsidiaries from their UK counterparts is their first-class presentation of very detailed accounts and the volume of information contained in their balance sheets and related information – which in most cases includes sales turnover. Especial attention is paid to showing all the relevant facts clearly – these often being presented in diagrammatic form. In 1954, the Ford Company's accounts were judged by the *Accountant* magazine to be the best of all submitted by British public companies, and those of such affiliates as Vauxhall Motors, Esso Petroleum, Monsanto and Hoover are often held to the fore as examples of first-class balance sheet presentation. In addition, the trend towards the drawing up of three-monthly and half-yearly balance sheets has been popularized by subsidiaries, who have undoubtedly influenced the reporting procedures of a number of British firms in this way.

Wages and incentives

This is a large and complicated field, and one to which we can do only brief justice in a study of this kind. Though, as far as we know, in all instances, the personnel department of US-financed firms is entirely British-manned, the American influence is far from negligible.

Basic wage rates paid by subsidiaries, whether they are calculated on a *time* or *piece-rate* basis, vary from one-third to one-half of those paid by their parent concerns in the United States, notwithstanding the fact that a number of firms have deliberately assimilated the high wages policies of their American plants. Of course, the difficulty in these latter years of full employment is to say how far this has been due also to the scarcity of labour and how far to the efficiency and prosperity of the company in question. But US-financed firms have been renowned for their generous wages policies for several years. Even in 1896, the Diamond Match Company was paying considerably above the minimum rate for female labourers in this 'sweated' industry, and six years later, at the Annual General Meeting of the Linotype Company, it was stated that the American policy of paying a bonus above the minimum wage to good workers should be adopted in the UK.[3] In 1929, when the Federation of Engineering Trades was prescribing a weekly wage of 57s.8d. (£2.86n.p.) for skilled workers, the Ford Motor Company, then not a member of the Federation, was paying a wage varying from a minimum of £4 to a maximum of £8 a week. At the same date the Shredded Wheat Co. Ltd was offering a minimum wage of 75s. (£3.75n.p.) a week plus an average bonus of 10 per cent – more than half as much again as the average for the food and drink industry as a whole. In more recent times the Ford subsidiary has continued its high wage policy and, with the Vauxhall Company, is currently paying its operatives a basic rate between 10 and 20 per cent above the average for the motor industry as a whole. Other American subsidiaries to offer generous wages from the start of their operations in the UK include the Dennison Manufacturing Company Ltd, Kodak Ltd, and Colgate-Palmolive Ltd. The actual *method* of payment naturally varies between firms and areas: Thomas Hedley Ltd, for example, offers the average of the wage rates of the six highest paying firms in its particular area,[4] while other concerns, such as Johnson & Johnson Ltd, Armstrong Cork Ltd, Hoover and Thomas Edison Ltd, all deliberately pay above the competitive rates, in order to attract labour of the best possible quality.

The actual mechanism of wage determination differs in the two countries in one major respect: while in the US it is common practice for agreements to be made between individual plant managements and either officials of the local trade union or an elected advisory panel of the plant employees, in the UK wages are usually fixed on a national basis. The former system is proving increasingly popular with those US-affiliated companies in the UK who neither belong to employers' federations, nor recognize national agreements. For while it is accepted that such methods may give rise to more industrial disputes, it is believed that this is more than compensated by the fact that the firm does not have to suffer from national differences when it has no grievances with its own workers.

Almost without exception, the wages system operated by a US parent firm is less complex than that of its UK associate or branch. One subsidiary stated that there were fifty possible additions which could be made to a particular basic wage as agreed upon by the unions and employers' federations in the UK. The British Hoover Company has recently simplified its wages structure, yet still calculates its payments on a more complicated formula than that used by its US associate. Many factors – some avoidable, others unavoidable – explain these differences. Often a number of the extra payments have accumulated over a period of years and are not easy to dispense with. More important, the fixing of wage rates and the incentive systems operated are a reflection of the production methods employed, and the type of markets served. If these differ, then the system of wage payments is likely to differ too. In general, UK manufacturing techniques and processes allow for less specialization of machines but require more operative tasks: this makes it difficult for any straightforward time or piece-rate to be paid. A recent example of changing wage techniques, following the adoption of new production methods, is provided by the Vauxhall Company who, in April 1956, switched over from a system of paying its factory employees a group bonus to one of straight time rates.[5]

There is no common system of wage payments practised by subsidiaries in the UK. That there are obvious differences between the American and British methods in this respect is illustrated by the fact that, since being taken over by an American concern, one old-established British company has adopted the latter's wages system because it offered better incentives and promoted greater plant flexibility and productivity. At the time when another post-war American branch company set up its factory, US experts were sent over to organize its wages structure entirely on the lines of its parent company. In both the above instances, the new wage methods introduced were well accepted by the British workforce, but in a third case the introduction of a variant of the target system (by which each man was provided with a chart of his performance and, though allowed to fall below his set target twice, was dismissed the third time) caused such resistance from organized labour that it had to be withdrawn.

In all, 38 per cent of the US subsidiaries and Anglo-American firms covered in our sample stated that they replicated their parent plant's wages policy and methods in all major respects, while 22 per cent argued that, while it was not always desirable or feasible to copy the American sytem lock, stock and barrel, its main principles were adopted and modified to suit the particular needs at hand. It is interesting to observe that all the firms within these two groups aim at paying above the minimum trade union rates. The remaining two-fifths of the firms comprised those which practised a 'when in Rome do as Rome does' wages policy, and also those who were not fully aware of the system adopted by their US associates, but carried out their rate fixing and bonus schemes independently.

The following were the main types of factory operative wage systems practised by American-affiliated firms in this country in 1954–5: [6]

1 17 per cent of subsidiaries pay on a piece-rate basis plus a *group* or *individual* bonus once a minimum production target has been achieved, this latter being usually determined by standard costing.
2 23 per cent operate a time rate plus a *group* or *individual* bonus, usually based on saving of time to complete a certain job – but sometimes related to additional output produced.
3 16 per cent pay a basic rate (time or piece) without bonus, though usually the rate is above the average prevailing in their particular industry or region.
4 15 per cent pay a basic rate with various additions as determined by job evaluation and merit rating. (Job evaluation is a means of assessing the money value of a particular task or occupation with due regard to skill, responsibility, effort, training, job conditions, etc. involved. Each factor of each job is assessed and awarded a certain number of points, the sum of which places each job in a particular labour group, which might either be the basis for a merit rating payment, i.e. in addition to the basic wage rate otherwise determined, or the whole payment.)
5 7 per cent of firms pay on the basis of (1) and (2) above, plus merit evaluation.
6 10 per cent of firms pay a basic time rate (sometimes with bonus) and also operate a profit-sharing scheme – the sum involved usually being assessed on a half-yearly or annual basis. Some of these firms may only pay profits to their staff, but at least twelve firms in our sample offer a profit-sharing scheme to all operative workers.
7 The balance of firms operate a variety of wage-fixing methods, e.g. time rate plus time-keeping bonus, etc., etc.

The method of payment also differs between industries, size of firms and areas. For instance, it seems that those incentive systems introduced in South Wales, the North East and in certain areas of the Midlands, have been less favourably received than those in the London or Mid-Scottish areas. As one might expect, it is the larger subsidiaries which tend to pay on a merit-rating basis, though the number practising such schemes compares favourably with that of UK firms, and is still growing. Because of the 'anomalies and difficulties of managerial control' caused by their standard incentive bonus system, Black and Decker substituted one based on job evaluation and merit rating in 1951: the result was that productivity increased, and a greater flexibility of factory working was achieved.[7] Other companies to practise like schemes include Thomas Hedley, Monsanto, Thomas Edison, Vauxhall and Mars. An interesting plan was introduced by Thomas Hedley in 1947 by which every hourly rated employee who had been with the company for two years or more was given a *permanent* guarantee of forty-eight weeks' work a year: personnel could only be dismissed for disciplinary reasons and not as a result of changing techniques which might cause redundancy.

The resulting advantages, so the company argued, include security to the employees, a reduced labour turnover and a better structured production system. In the plan's first year of operation, absenteeism was reduced by 32 per cent and factory productivity raised by 7 per cent. An allied scheme is operated by H. J. Heinz, which purports to guarantee its 4,000 fully-paid hourly rated and piece-workers a minimum weekly wage for a year in advance.[8] Such guaranteed employment and wages systems as these are more widely practised in America than in the UK.[9]

A number of US firms are well known for their pioneering profit-sharing incentive schemes. In 1913, for example, the Kodak Company allotted shares to each employee of one-tenth par value, while six years later Bryant & May introduced a plan by which the balance of profit after a certain dividend had been paid was shared equally between shareholders and workers. The Dennison Manufacturing Company originated its profit-sharing plan in 1925 in the form of a non-contributory pension scheme by which employees were automatically granted shares in the company after a minimum period of employment.[10] The same subsidiary's first Managing Director was also one of the pioneers of budget-ary control in the UK; the present holder of this office, who was then an employee of the company, admitted that he had originally thought of it as 'a waste of time', but now regarded it as an indispensable aid to management. More recently, a small post-1945 pharmaceutical subsidiary, producing in North London, issued each of its employees with compensation certificates similar in kind to shadow shares, which are purchased back by the firm, if an employee has to leave, at prices reflecting the profits earned by the company at the time. Other companies to operate profit-sharing schemes of one kind or another include Vauxhall Ltd, Ferro Enamels Ltd and Hoover Ltd.

Several subsidiaries have gradually introduced new wages techniques as imple-mented by their parent companies in the course of their development. One machine tool company in the Home Counties introduced an adaptation of its American parent's bonus system in 1951 – and attributes the doubling of its output per man-hour in the last four years largely to this scheme. Another US corporation which has had a controlling interest in a British company since 1947 claimed that, by changing the wages system to that practised in the American plant, labour efficiency was immediately raised by 25 per cent. A third ex-subsidiary – quite small by British standards – was responsible for pioneering a new system of incentive management in the UK, the principles of which are so well recognized that it might be worth while describing it in a little more detail. To begin with, all workers receive the normal basic wage or salary for the job, and share in a group production bonus scheme operated on orthodox lines and determined by standard time-study methods. In addition, each receives a lump sum annual payment based on the criterion of 'Worker Assessment' which itself comprises six components – value, co-operation, quantity, quality, absenteeism and lateness. Value is purely an assessment of the importance of the job a man is doing, irrespective of the way in which he is doing it: it simply recognizes that the works manager contributes more to the prosperity of the organization than an operative or shorthand typist. The remaining components are self-explanatory. In these, the worker is put into one of four sections, representing respectively four degrees of quality. A series of marks is then given in relation to the rating, ranging, for example, from 10 to 50 for value, 3 to 11 or 12 for co-operation, quantity and quality, and 2 to 8 for absenteeism and lateness; when aggregated, these give the worker a maximum of 100. The total bonus received by any worker is then calculated as a percentage of his basic wage or salary, the actual percentage being determined by the number of marks he has received in his annual assessment.[11]

Apart from straightforward bonuses and profit-sharing schemes, there are a number of interesting examples of monetary and non-monetary incentives offered by US-affiliated firms. One post-war subsidiary gives its factory operatives barrels of beer on reaching their production targets, and its salesmen canteens of cutlery when their order books are full. Two other pre-war branch plants present each worker with a turkey at Christmas! Several companies operate a system of termination allowances by which operatives and staff receive lump-sum payments if they leave the firm before retirement – the amount varying according to their length and status of employment. A recent compensation scheme to cover redundancy adopted by the Ethicon Sutures Laboratories in Edinburgh has been described as a unique departure in the pharmaceutical industry.[12] A higher proportion of firms than the average for British industry as a whole operate social security or non-contributory pension schemes, and while these are mainly confined to the larger companies, post-1945 labour shortages, coupled with a growing awareness by American parent companies of their responsibilities in this area, have led to their implementation by a number of smaller firms.

With respect to industrial relations, only 15 per cent of subsidiaries and Anglo-American firms said that their labour was fully unionized and federated. There is little doubt that the high wages offered by many branch plants has enabled an open-shop policy to be successfully maintained, and for work relationships to be exceptionally congenial. There are, of course, exceptions where the labour techniques adopted by the parent company have not been applicable in the UK or have been resisted by the workers. Chapter 1 outlined some of the early difficulties encountered by the Westinghouse Company, and more recent examples include those experienced in the cork products and small power tool industries. High-pressure incentive schemes are not always as well received in the UK. Once again, attitudes vary according to the location of the US subsidiary.

Several American-financed firms, e.g. Kodak Ltd, Spirella Ltd, Johnson & Johnson Ltd, Sperry Gyroscope Ltd, Addressograph-Multigraph Ltd, Gillette Ltd, Ortho Pharmaceutical Ltd, etc., are renowned in their particular vicinities for the excellent working conditions they provide – in the office as well as the factory – and for their canteen facilities and social amenities. An electrical subsidiary operating in North-West London was the first to grant paid holidays in its particular area and a pre-war engineering subsidiary was congratulated by *The Times* in 1950 for pioneering shorter hours of work. Altogether there is a marked paternalistic attitude about the way in which many US-affiliated firms view their personnel responsibilities, which sometimes extends well beyond the confines of the factory itself. One company even has hotel rooms permanently booked at two seaside resorts so that those of its workers who may wish to do so should be able to convalesce there after illness free of charge. Another operates a rehabilitation scheme for injured or sick employees. In one or two cases this sense of responsibility had been of wider import. For example, at the time of food rationing in the UK, every employee of one light engineering subsidiary received a three-monthly $10 food parcel from its parent concern, which, in the words of an executive of the company concerned, 'did more to cement Anglo-American relationships than any political conference!'

Especial attention has also been directed to the design and appearance of factories. In the late 1920s the new Firestone factory attracted 'tremendous comment' for its bold frontispiece,[13] and, more recently, the National Cash Register plant at Dundee has been referred to as 'the industrial showpiece unrivalled in the North'. This same company has even gone as far as to make a grant to the Corporation of Dundee so that the brickwork of forty-six council houses, due to be erected opposite its factory, matched the latter in colour and style.

The informal relationships between management and labour, and the tendency for American executives to keep their employees well informed about company policies and developments was noted by many subsidiaries. In this respect the use of visual aids has proved very popular.[14] More than one Managing Director has mentioned how, at the end of each financial year, he calls his staff together and explains in detail the company's economic position. A large number of subsidiaries either publish their own house journals or make available those of their parent companies, in the case of one firm for the 'inculcation of solidarity amongst its employees'.

Concerning promotion policy, there are few unusual features to note, save that the majority of US-affiliated firms deliberately aim to recruit senior personnel from within their own ranks. One well-known company in a recent survey found that 85 per cent of its supervisory appointments of the previous year have been secured by its own employees. Though, in general, it is less usual for British industry to demand that university graduates should start work on the factory floor, many subsidiaries said that they are trying to assimilate their US associates' practices in this direction. Labour suggestion schemes are a very common feature in branch plants, and usually well-organized. Companies like Vauxhall Motors, for example, circulate an operational handbook to each of their employees, giving full instructions on how to make a suggestion, what will happen to it, the scale of rewards and so on. For the most part, such schemes have been very successful. The Ford plan, which was introduced into the UK in 1955 following its success in America, is believed to have cut costs by between £50,000 and £100,000 in its first year of operation. In a survey carried out by *Business* in 1950, Hoover Ltd was found to have received fifty suggestions per hundred workers in that year – 'the most exceptional result'. Payments are often high. One Anglo-American firm has been known to pay over £2,000 for top-ranking ideas, while another offers up to

50 per cent of the actual net saving in costs. That US companies are again well among the leaders in this field is confirmed by the fact that, of a sample of twelve suggestion schemes received in 1953 by the monthly journal *Target*, six came from US branch plants in the UK, and in a recent daily newspaper 'factory jackpot' competition,[15] a quarter of the first fifty firms to join were American affiliates.

Labour selection and training methods tend to follow along the lines of the parent company, but different economic conditions in the UK – more particularly the acute labour shortage of recent years, and lack of technical expertise or experience – has tended to raise average production costs in the UK plant. Very great care, however, is generally exercised in trying to obtain the best quality of labour. A number of large subsidiaries operate special training schools; but the key advantage which most branch plants enjoy over their UK competitors is that they are able to send their senior operatives and staff to America for instruction. For instance, the sales representatives of both Burroughs Adding Machine Co. Ltd and Minnesota Mining Co. Ltd regularly receive part of their training from the US parent company, while the policy of other subsidiaries, e.g. Thomas Hedley, Frigidaire Co. Ltd, is to encourage all promising personnel – technical and administrative – to visit their respective parent plants for several months. In addition, an impressive list of firms operate permanent training schools for their salesmen in the UK – such as one post-war industrial instruments company which currently runs three-monthly initial and regular refresher courses. Most noticeable, too, was the attention paid to the question of foreman status, responsibility and training, and the inclination of most subsidiaries to treat this class of worker as being part of management. In this respect one Midlands subsidiary operates periodic training courses for its 200 foremen on such subjects as piece-rate application, work study, waste utilization and accident prevention; another runs a TWI (Training within Industry) course, and outside speakers come to give regular lectures. Many companies stressed the importance of frequent meetings between management and workers. One firm argued that since these had been introduced several years ago, labour relationships and productivity had improved 'out of all recognition'. Another observed that they were considerably more successful in the UK, as too much time was spent on bickering in the US.

Summarizing, then, while the personnel and wages procedures of US subsidiaries and Anglo-American firms are not particularly unique, most of the larger fully-owned subsidiaries try to assimilate US procedures where possible. To assess, however, in any detail, the impact which such policies have had either on competitors or other firms within the same geographical region, is beyond our brief. Suffice it to note that many American-financed firms are recognized as being amongst the most progressive and enlightened of employers, both for their willingness to adopt the latest wage and incentive systems, and for their belief that a workforce well paid, properly trained and regularly consulted pays dividends in the long run through improved personnel efficiency and reduced labour turnover. This is well summarized in the words of a former Managing Director of the Ford Motor Company (UK), who, when asked in 1930 why his company was so successful, said: 'It is due first and foremost to the selection, training and maintenance of personnel.'[16] Once again, a scientific approach to personnel management has tended to be more widely accepted by individual firms in the US, and by the selective application of these principles in the UK and the general publicizing of ideas the presence of US manufacturing units has had an important stimulating effect.

Sales and marketing

Perhaps no other branch of managerial practice has been so obviously influenced by American techniques and thought in recent years as that of sales and marketing policy. In this article on the early history of the North British Rubber Co. Ltd in the UK, Mr W. Woodruff tells how that company by its salesmanship and distribution[17] techniques made serious inroads into its competitors' markets, while at the turn of the century, US merchandising methods were being increasingly popularized by such firms as the Singer, Pittsburgh, Deering Harvester and National Cash Register companies. Similarly, the early development of mail order business, direct customer selling and hire purchase trading in the UK was strongly American-dominated. New methods of advertising were also introduced. In this book *The Fabulous Phonograph*, Roland Gelatt tells how in 1898 William Owen, in an attempt to market the gramophone into the UK 'was one of the first advertisers to take full pages in London newspapers, observing none of the customary British reticence in his layout and copy'.[18] And today, too, it is in these fields where criticism by subsidiaries of current British techniques are the most numerous. As one subsidiary put it: 'The average British firm treats the function of selling as did America thirty years ago.'

Over the last quarter of a century, the status of the American sales-person and the increasing attention paid to product branding, advertising and market research have led to the role of merchandising being given equal status to that of manufacturing as a determinant of competitiveness. Many features are indicative of this trend, viz. the tremendous growth of all kinds of advertising (especially associated with products with a high income elasticity of demand), the attention paid to the training and remuneration of salesmen, and the number of sales representatives promoted to senior executive positions; and they are equally apparent in consumer and capital goods industries. The more technical nature of products has increased the need for expert knowledge by the sales departments of firms and by retailers; and with this, for attractive and informative advertising – features which have been far more readily accepted in America than in the UK.

The development of many of these techniques in the UK has been directly hastened by the presence of US branch units, and, for some years now, a quiet revolution has been going on in this respect. Yet, so far as issues to do with the psychology and tastes of the final goods consumer and the readiness of the industrialist to accept new items of capital equipment are concerned, US merchanting methods have not always been well received in the UK. Before the war, for example, one consumer goods subsidiary tried to apply the psychology and mass-production methods of US marketing, in the UK and almost bankrupted itself as a result. Another old-established concern, when taken over by an American company in the 1930s, slashed the price of its product by over half, thereby aiming to capture the market with its particular product; this policy completely failed to appeal to the UK consumer, who, as the subsequent experiences of the company were to prove, tends to be less *price* and more *quality* conscious than his American counterpart. The class of market served must also be considered. It may be that in America a particular product is bought by all income groups, whereas in the UK it can only be afforded by the relatively wealthy, who are wont to pay more attention to the novelty quality and reliability than price.

The British industrial consumer, too, is generally more cautious in accepting newly marketed products. In this connection, one precision instruments concern noted that it was invariably the American-affiliated firms in the UK who were the first customers of any newly introduced products. As an executive of this company put it:

> There is no doubt that prior to 1939, US-affiliated companies in this country were more receptive to instrumentation than their UK competitors. For example, H. J. Heinz Ltd established automatic controls in their Harlesden plant in 1929, when British food canners were still using no control. AGWI Ltd (later Esso Petroleum), at their refinery on Southampton Water, were certainly using automatic controls on the American pattern in 1927, and in the air-conditioning field, the Carrier Corporation were employing the latest instrumentation techniques to a much greater extent than their British rivals.

Another firm supplying marking equipment for the laundry industry said:

> Some years ago, we exhibited a particular product in an American trade show, and within six months most laundries had introduced it as a standard equipment. A year later, when it was exhibited in the United Kingdom, it took eighteen months to sell the first machine.

It was widely agreed by US subsidiaries that more selling effort was needed to sell a particular product in this country than in the US. As one firm put it:

> In our experience, the average American consumer is both ready and willing to try out anything which is new, and in fact it often has considerable sales appeal because it is new. Here, it is frequently necessary to convince people that others are also buying the product before you will get them to buy it themselves. In other words, they prefer to let someone else try it out, and it is quite rare to meet someone who has sufficient imagination to appreciate the possibilities of new ideas while they are still quite novel. Indeed, it would be quite safe to say that what would be put over in a matter of a few weeks in the United States, would take several months of intensive campaigning in the United Kingdom. It is essentially a difference of attitude of mind to new ideas.

A number of branch units, however, asserted that, in recent years, conditions had improved. In the words of one supplier of abrasive products: 'In the past, we have found UK industry very lethargic in accepting new products, but this attitude is changing rapidly. Indeed, in our opinion there is a "revolution" in thinking taking place.'

The importance attached by US subsidiaries to all aspects of merchandising is also shown by the fact that more American nationals are employed in the sales department than in any other department of the organization; and by the particular attention paid to the training, remuneration and status of sales personnel. No fewer than 87 per cent of the firms producing consumer goods, and 43 per cent of those supplying capital equipment, said that they assimilated the basic marketing techniques adopted by their parent companies, though some adaptation was often required to meet the particular needs of UK consumers. While for example, the parent company appeared to cater mainly, if not exclusively, for the domestic market, the subsidiary was frequently faced with a variety of export markets, each demanding its own particular brand of marketing. On the other hand, where such markets were allocated by the American associate, the sales forecasts for the individual subsidiaries were unified and integrated by the parent concern and production allocated accordingly. In some cases, the US parent company has set up a chain of foreign marketing outlets to which the manufacturing subsidiaries sell their output. Examples include the leading packaged food and pharmaceutical companies.

Because of their small size and their relative inexperience of the British market, newly established US subsidiaries often employ specialized marketing agencies to market and distribute their products and sometimes to conduct market research; of these Bristol Myers, Euclid, Honeywell-Brown are typical examples. In this respect they are well served by their own kind – A. G. Nielsen (market research) and W. Thompson (advertising) are both US-controlled enterprises. In a limited number of instances, particularly where the availability and quality of after-sales facilities is a vital element of their competitive advantage, subsidiaries may operate their own retail or wholesale outlets, e.g. such as do the Singer Company, Black & Decker Ltd, the Ford Motor Company, and Addressograph-Multigraph Ltd. Likewise, some branch plants maintain separate production and sales units; this is particularly likely to be the case where the American firm originated as a sales organization, and, in the course of its development, formed a separate manufacturing company.

In general, however, there is little substantive difference between the methods of distribution or marketing practised by subsidiaries and comparable British companies. These also tend to follow the American pattern, save in the consumer goods field, where there is more direct dealing with retailers in the UK. The practice of resale price maintenance, by which the selling price of a product is fixed by the manufacturer within agreed limits, is less common in the USA; there, it is more usual for a deal to be concluded by customers directly with the wholesalers. Subsidiaries in the UK, however, normally conform to current practice, and fix prices by the usual methods. There are exceptions, however. A number of food subsidiaries argued that they only suggested the price at which the retailer ought to sell their products, but no attempt was made to enforce this price in any way. No particular views were expressed by subsidiaries as to the advantages or disadvantages offered by resale price maintenance, other than that it made for better service before and after sales, and stability in production. Indeed, a number of American-affiliated firms have gone beyond the fixing of prices for their products and operate a scale of charges for after-sales services as well.

In general, it would seem that US-financed firms have directly encouraged the practice of exclusive dealing. For example, in petroleum distribution, the Esso Company imported from America the idea of the 'tied garage' by which garage proprietors, in return for a rebate on sales, agreed to sell only Esso brands of petrol. Since this scheme (which is now widespread practice) was first initiated, the number of UK petrol stations served by the company has been reduced by 40 per cent, and economies in distribution have been considerable. In addition, the refining company is assured a guaranteed market, while the garage proprietor benefits from help given in the modernization of his petrol station layout and in the training of his staff.[19] The criticism that all this has been at the expense of price reductions is probably untrue: both the rebate – usually given in kind – and the margin of gross profit received by the petrol company work out at less than $1d.$ ($\frac{1}{2}$ new penny) per gallon. Likewise, the Kodak Company was the first in its industry to promote exclusive dealerships in order to achieve a high standard of printing and developing of films. Other American subsidiaries following this practice include those in the motor vehicles, electrical products and toilet preparations industries.

Retailers' profit margins again also vary in the two countries. In certain industries, e.g. kitchen implements, razor-blades, toilet preparations, petroleum, etc., the margin mark-ups are lower in the UK; in others, e.g. abrasives, refrigerators, they are higher. These differences depend *inter alia* on the degree of competition, volume of output and the size of retailing establishments. Six subsidiaries claimed that they had been instrumental in lowering the average profit margin within the industry.

More particularly, US-financed firms would appear to have influenced current UK marketing procedures in three major respects. First, with the increasingly technological and scientific nature of many products supplied, the significance of expert sales advice and efficient servicing as factors influencing demand has also grown. In many cases, where plant and equipment involving new techniques and processes is being installed, the customer will either require it to be specifically tailored to his individual needs or need advice as to how such equipment is likely to affect his existing production methods. Sometimes, the installation of a machine or piece of equipment may demand a complete overhaul of the existing production system. Often, American-affiliated concerns have been the first to offer a comprehensive consultancy service in their particular industry. For example, the British United Shoe Machinery Company established a shoe factory organization department in 1920, the function of which is to advise on the layout of machinery, on the introduction of production control systems and on numerous general matters such as cost estimating and power installations. Similarly, the Singer Sewing Machine Company increased the scope of its planning production department in 1946 both for the footwear and the clothing industries. It maintains a consultancy service on layout, materials handling and work study, apart from the technical usage of its machines. A third subsidiary, which supplies vitreous enamel frit, also constructs enamelling plants for firms which wish to manufacture for themselves. In its experience, the installation of equipment has often entailed a complete redesign of plant and rationalization. Much of this reorganization has so far been carried out under the supervision of the American concern, which is reputed to be one of the first enamelling firms to have provided such a service in the UK.

Second, an impressive number of US firms offer training programmes for their customers' staff. Most of the larger office machinery subsidiaries operate their own schools free of charge. Felt and Tarrant run twenty schools and train 3,000 operators a year; Remington Rand operate a fourteen-day course and then send a demonstrator to the operator's firm until the installation is running smoothly; National Cash Register instruct 10,000 operatives a year at their customers' premises.[20] Training of this kind is usually backed up with instruction booklets. The Frigidaire Company was the first firm to introduce a training school for servicemen in the refrigeration equipment industry. The Westrex subsidiary pioneered technical service and training outlets for cinema service engineers in this country, and regularly gives advice on the latest sound and inspection equipment. The Foster-Wheeler Company operates welding schools for the benefit of chemical and engineering contractors, and the Elizabeth Arden Company was among the earliest cosmetic manufacturers in the UK to popularize specialized beauty salons along American lines. IBM is currently setting up a range of workshops and advisory centres for its computer customers. Firms in the accounting machinery, time recording, sewing machine, gyroscopic compass, motor-car and photographic equipment industries are other examples in this respect.

Third, mention must be made of the attention paid by some US subsidiaries to the efficiency of their distributive outlets. Here the motor vehicle industry provides a good example, as the cost and quality of the after-sales servicing of cars and commercial vehicles is a critical determinant of their sales. In this respect, the Ford Motor Company has an unrivalled reputation, with its influence being exerted in two main ways. First, since 1950, with every new car sold, the customer has been given a booklet which lists over 500 possible repair or replacement jobs, with their labour cost stipulated. In fixing a price for each repair or servicing operation carried out on a Ford vehicle, the subsidiary allows a profit margin which it considers reasonable for an efficient garage outlet, and, in addition, sometimes supplies specialized equipment. Second, to ensure a high level of service efficiency, some twenty training courses of between a week and a month's duration are operated for employees of Ford dealers. These cater for subjects such as transmission, electrical system, front axle, steering and braking, radio, body-work and diesel engines on the technical side, and instruction in business management and sales promotion as well. On an average, 2,500 students pass through the service school each year, and of these, 90 to 95 per cent pass and obtain a certificate. Advice is also given to Ford main dealers on costing and accounting techniques.

Regular visits are also paid by the company to its dealers to ensure that the proper method of time and motion study is being practised with job and stock cards, etc. A dealer's relation department concerns itself with staff and business management. No other auto company in the UK offers such a comprehensive range of training and advisory facilities, though more attention is gradually being paid to consumer needs in this way. For example, since 1955, the Vauxhall Company has offered regular courses in the reconditioning of used cars and commercial vehicles for its main dealers. These are the first of their kind in the UK and include instruction on a wide range of mechanical and electrical issues and the reconditioning of cars and commercial vehicles of all makes.

In the consumer goods field, the value of knowledgeable demonstrators, attractive and informative display techniques and dynamic selling methods is well recognized by subsidiaries. One food products firm noted:

> Our salesmen check shop-keepers' stocks and advise them according to the type of district and market surveys carried out by our market research department what their future requirements are likely to be. Such methods have proved successful, and our trained salesmen are in wide demand.

And a clothing subsidiary:

> Special girls tour the main stores in the country to display the products, and to give advice to consumers on the most suitable styles related to their figure, etc. Our competitors are usually too small and too weak to copy these methods. Our representatives are supplied with a comprehensive sales manual printed in the United States, and we have a special Public Relations Department which deals direct with customers.

A third branch plant, supplying electrical equipment, commented: 'We employ a special Service Manager to give technical advice and to tour our service and repair plants throughout the country, which are directly responsible for distribution and after-sales service.' In many other instances, e.g. in the cosmetics, cinema equipment, electrical products, cigarette lighters, films, food products sectors, more than average attention appears to be paid to marketing and distribution techniques and the recognition of their importance in the companies' organizational structure and strategic goals.

Like their parent concerns, American-affiliated firms also pay especial attention to all aspects of advertising and market research. The high income and price elasticity of demand for the great majority of consumer good products supplied by them is partly the reason for this. Whether the expenditure of such large sums of money is always to the consumers' benefit there is some cause to doubt. The economic disadvantages of *combative* or *persuasive* advertising are as well known as the advantages of *informative* advertising. It is not for us, however, to argue the point here, but rather to observe that as a proportion of their sales turnover US-financed firms in the motor-car, soap, foodstuffs, rubber tyre, office equipment, cosmetic, oil refining, cinematic film and domestic electrical appliances industries all spend considerably more on advertising than their indigenous competitors.

Practically all the subsidiaries are large enough to supply the national markets, and the amount spent by them on press advertising (per £000 of sales) is three times the average of their UK competitors. Fifteen US-affiliated firms spent over £200,000 on press advertising in 1954; and between them they accounted for 41 per cent of the £12.5 million devoted to the thirty-eight leading products in that year.[21] The largest advertiser on Independent Television in 1955 was also an American subsidiary.

Once again, it should be observed that such firms are selling products which are largely new and unfamiliar to the UK consumer. In this, however, they can benefit fully from literature sent over by their parent companies in some cases, e.g. in the office equipment, foodstuffs and chemical industry, there can be no doubt that the attractiveness and informative value of such advertising is first-class.[22] New methods to attract the consumers' interest have been pioneered, such as coupons – as introduced by the Kensitas Company in 1950; free samples – as first popularized by the Shredded Wheat Co. Ltd in the 1920s. More recently, the use of 'test' markets has been promoted by such companies as Thomas Hedley Ltd, though most subsidiaries admit that British consumers are not as responsive or gullible as their American counterparts to high-pressure advertising. The modality of advertising would appear to be much the same in the two countries, though, as might be expected, rather more use is made of the cinema and television by US subsidiaries than is usual for UK industry.

That a more virile and scientific approach to salesmanship and marketing has been injected into many UK industries by the presence of US-financed firms in this country is not open to question. The attention paid to the status and training of sales representatives has, through the normal competitive impact, helped to raise standards of quality throughout the country and, in this way, industry and the consumer have benefited. On the other hand, it is equally clear that any wholesale assimilation of American techniques and an insufficient appreciation of the different psychological, economic and cultural needs of US and UK consumers can lead, and has led, to inappropriate marketing techniques. As in wages policy and labour-management relationships, each case requires to be treated on its own merits and any sales and marketing methods which have worked well in the US need to be applied with caution and discrimination in the UK.

Purchasing techniques

Chapter 7 has already sufficiently discussed this branch of management and it is not proposed to deal further with the matter here.

While, in the main then, all available evidence supports the view that US subsidiaries have been successful in transplanting American managerial practices to the UK, in some cases this has only been achieved by the process of trial and error. It is naturally less easy to cite the unsuccessful cases as they do not receive the same publicity. A number of companies have, however, made frequent changes in their management structures since the time of their initial establishment. Sometimes, a British Managing Director is preferred, and particularly where the product has to be adapted and different manufacturing conditions are required in the two countries. Then again, one subsidiary argued that: 'Not always does US management fully appreciate UK patent and legal systems, and this company has been involved in some expensive settlements to avoid court proceedings', while another assumed that: 'In a number of cases, we have lost important orders because of the refusal of our parent concern to allow us to modify their standards to meet British customers' special requirements.'

Many firms believe that their actions are cramped or stifled by excessive parental control. Lack of flexibility and insufficient appreciation of specialized conditions are the most common complaints. The fact that many managing directors who are American nationals have insufficient experience of operating foreign branch plants means that difficulties and misunderstandings may arise. For example, it is usual for subsidiaries which have been manufacturing in the UK for a short while, and which are run by American expatriates, to be more critical of the efficiency of their UK suppliers than those which have been operating for several years, and who are in a better position to appreciate the differences in the two countries' economic and cultural environments.

US MANAGERIAL INFLUENCE ON UK-ORIGINATED FIRMS SINCE TAKEN OVER OR INVESTED IN

The significance of the managerial practices we have been examining is brought into relief if we look at the ways in which US corporations have affected those of the thirty UK-originated concerns in our sample which, at one time or another, they have acquired or in which they have made minority investments.

We shall primarily concern ourselves with three case studies, but first a few general remarks.

Broadly speaking, the permeation of American capital has affected British managerial and production methods in these firms in one of three main ways:

1 The infusion of technical and research knowledge only, and with no direct effect on overall or departmental managerial strategies.
2 The infusion of technical knowledge and in addition a partial influence on certain aspects of general or departmental managerial procedures and strategies, e.g. on sales, costing, purchasing methods, organizational structures, etc.
3 A thorough reorganization of the whole technical and managerial set-up of the subsidiary.

Eleven of the thirty firms in the sample come within the first category: Case Study no. 3 below is fairly representative of those. In twelve instances there has been a limited impact, viz. Case study no. 2. More details concerning the ways in which the second group of firms have been affected may be summarized in the form of a table given below.

Table 9.1 Influence on managerial techniques of existing UK firms since being invested in by US companies[1]

Managerial technique	Negligibly affected by US thought	Partially affected by US thought	Markedly affected by US thought
Administration	5	5	2
Production planning	0	5	7
Budgetary control	3	5	4
Labour selection and training	6	3	3
Wages system	5	4	3
Purchasing techniques	5	6	1

Note:
1 Selection of 12 firms in Group B above.

The remaining firms fall within the third group, of which Case Study no. 1 is an illustration.

Relating the distribution of the thirty firms by type of product supplied, it is interesting to observe that while the industrial instrument companies have been most influenced by the injection of technical know-how, the US influence on the food processing firms has been much wider. In general, more changes in line with current American practice have taken place in the consumer goods than the producer goods sectors. As one might expect, existing organizational structures and managerial practices have been most reconfigured in UK companies which have been bought out lock, stock and barrel. There were ten of these in our sample, seven of which have been strongly influenced and two partially influenced by US thought. Of the twenty firms in which there is less than a 100 per cent US equity stake, nine have been affected solely from the technical viewpoint and in only two instances has there been a thorough managerial reorganization. Eight of the seventeen firms taken over before 1939 have been markedly influenced, and five of the thirteen invested in since 1945.

1 ILLUSTRATION OF FIRMS MARKEDLY INFLUENCED THROUGHOUT BY US THOUGHT

CASE STUDY NO. 1[23]

This firm, prior to its acquisition by a US company some years ago, was an old-established family concern. The changes resulting from the new association were, however, substantial, and the way in which they were implemented presents an interesting case-history in the transition from the strongly personal control traditionally employed in a family business to the more hierarchical organization normally associated with managerial capitalism.

Under the previous regime, the structure of administration was simple. At the head was the Chairman and Managing Director. Under him were two general managers, responsible for production and sales respectively, and an accountant, who had charge of the office. And under each of these were a number of supervisors, salesmen and clerks. There was little middle-management, and no personnel department.

With a limited range of products and a comparatively stable output, this structure worked satisfactorily, but the advent of a range of new products introduced by the American firm brought an increase in activity and in the labour force. This, in turn, increased the burden on top management, both in scale and in complexity of decision-making. The span of control, for instance, was enlarged to such an extent that one executive had as many as thirty-five subordinates reporting to him.

This state of affairs obviously could not continue. A major structural change was made. Five separate divisions were created, viz. buying, works, sales, accounts and personnel, each of which was in charge of an executive answerable only to the Managing Director. The major innovation was the setting up of a personnel department, the first task of which was to sort out the detailed changes involved in the revision.

The initial step in this process was the construction of a detailed organizational chart (see Figure 9.1), showing the position held by each major decision-taker in the subsidiary, his function and to whom he was answerable. The preparation of this chart was a lengthy affair involving many months of discussion between the personnel manager and departmental heads. During this time, various anomalies and ambiguities were revealed, and, by futher discussion, resolved. Finally, the chart was completed to the satisfaction of all concerned. Today, copies are permanently exhibited in all departments. Any member of the firm knows, or can rapidly discover, what exactly is his position in the organization as well as that of any other individual.

The next step was the restructuring of administrative practices. First, a statement of 'the principles of employee relations and personnel administration' was prepared by the personnel manager, in consultation with top management. This was printed as a pamphlet and distributed to all workers and staff. Second, another booklet, 'Working Together', was issued, setting out for each employee just what he might expect from his employment, and giving full particulars of labour amenities, safety regulations and the like. Third, a more detailed supervisors manual was printed which laid down the recognized rules of procedure for various eventualities, along with such matters as holiday provisions, overtime payments and job rates.

Once the foundation of the new organization had been laid, the personnel

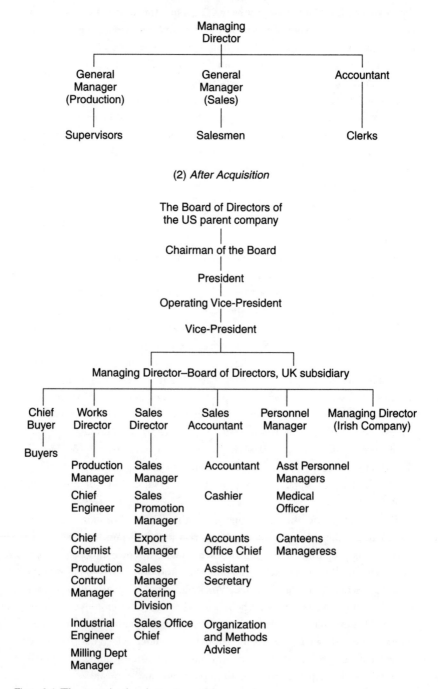

(1) *Before Acquisition*

Managing
Director

General	General	Accountant
Manager	Manager	
(Production)	(Sales)	

| Supervisors | Salesmen | Clerks |

(2) *After Acquisition*

The Board of Directors of
the US parent company

Chairman of the Board

President

Operating Vice-President

Vice-President

Managing Director–Board of Directors, UK subsidiary

| Chief | Works | Sales | Sales | Personnel | Managing Director |
| Buyer | Director | Director | Accountant | Manager | (Irish Company) |

Buyers

| Production | Sales | Accountant | Asst Personnel |
| Manager | Manager | | Managers |

Chief	Sales	Cashier	Medical
Engineer	Promotion		Officer
	Manager		

| Chief | Export | Accounts | Canteens |
| Chemist | Manager | Office Chief | Manageress |

Production	Sales	Assistant
Control	Manager	Secretary
Manager	Catering	
	Division	

Industrial	Sales Office	Organization
Engineer	Chief	and Methods
		Adviser

Milling Dept
Manager

Figure 9.1 The organizational structure of firm no. 1

department turned to the improvement and expansion of welfare facilities. Pension and life insurance schemes, sickness benefits, termination allowances and thrift schemes were introduced or expanded. Recreation rooms, a library, and facilities for a sports and social club run by a workers' committee followed.

Various new training programmes were introduced. The training of operatives encountered certain difficulties, due to the fact that, in this firm, the skill required of an average worker was minimal, and no vocational training could, or can, ensure any serious prospect of improvement. The policy finally adopted was to make available generous facilities to any operative wishing to undertake further education outside the plant, but not to intensify internal training. At the same time every effort was made to interest supervisors in training in human resource management. Every supervisor now has to go through at least one TWI (Training Within Industry) course and is encouraged to take an active part in conferences and other outside activities that will broaden his outlook. Special weekend conferences have been organized by this firm at local hotels. The trainee system has also been introduced on a limited scale. Young men have been drawn from both secondary schools and the universities to undergo a comprehensive course taking them through all sections of the organization for a period of between eighteen months and three years. The course is specially tailored for each individual trainee. Upon completion of their training, these men, if satisfactory, are appointed to junior supervisory vacancies. This scheme, however, is essentially of a long-term character, and has not yet been in operation long enough for its value to be assessed.

Thus, on the personnel side, this subsidiary has successfully adapted its structure and policies to meet its parent firm's requirements. Simultaneously other new divisions have been adopting new measures to meet the change of structure.

In the works division, for instance, considerable progress has been made in increasing output and efficiency. A complete new factory was acquired and equipped, to produce the American range of products, while at the original plant, where production is still confined to the traditional product lines, increased output has been obtained by more intensive mechanization, and by the introduction of work study and work simplification techniques. A full-time industrial engineer was appointed by the works director, with a time-study engineer and three assistants. As the result of a stage-by-stage analysis of the value chain, a considerable change was made in the factory layout to streamline production and increase productivity. Time studies were also carried out and production schedules checked against standard times to secure a better balance of output. Then, when sufficient time studies were available, the issue of employee compensation was tackled.

This firm's average rates of wages have always been at least equal to the national level, and for many years, they have also paid a bonus on output. Before their American association, this bonus was calculated on a group basis, with a target set for a whole department or category of workers. The introduction of time study has made it possible to fix targets more closely and more accurately and to offer bonuses either to individuals, or to a small team of workers. The first stage in the revision of payments was the introduction of a simplified form of job evaluation for hourly-rated jobs, on a points basis. Every job was discussed with the operatives affected, their supervisors, the chief industrial engineer and the organization and methods adviser. These discussions revealed, as was expected, that certain anomalies had grown up over the years. These were removed – in most cases by increasing the rate of payment for certain jobs, while holding other rates unchanged.

Where possible, individual targets were set from standard times obtained from time study, and bonuses paid in proportion to saved time. This was possible for about 10 per cent of all workers. Of the remainder, a considerable number worked in teams of two or three, and a team bonus was introduced in place of the overall departmental bonus.

With the administrative reorganization, the task of top management became highly complex. However, by a deliberate policy of decentralization of responsibility, the accompanying difficulties were largely overcome, and a drastic reorganization and extension of budgetary and cost control took place.

Budgetary control had been practised for some years by this firm, but the budget had been a single one for the entire business. Now each division, and each department within a division, prepares a series of budgets of its own for the coming four quarters of the year. The budget for the first quarter is a final budget, those for the following three quarters progressively provisional. Departmental budgets are consolidated into divisional budgets, which are then consolidated into a single budget for the company as a whole. Since the budgets include those of sales forecast by the marketing department, the final document is, in essence, a predicted profit and loss account for the twelve months to come.

Such a control system would be impossible without adequate costing. Hence the costing system used has been reorganized and made more accurate, so that the accounts department can now identify the true cost at any time of any single product item or item of equipment, and discern rapidly any changes in such costs.

Of the success of the revised personnel programme of Firm no. 1 there can be little doubt. *Inter alia* this is well illustrated by the drop in labour turnover – from 75 per cent in 1950 to 46 per cent in 1951 and 32 per cent in 1952.

2 ILLUSTRATION OF FIRMS INFLUENCED IN PARTICULAR FIELDS OF MANAGERIAL PROCEDURE ONLY

CASE STUDY NO. 2

Shortly after the Second World War, this important British company surrendered a 50 per cent interest in its equity capital to an American corporation. Since that date, the US company has acquired full financial control. In effect, the American managerial impact first began in 1950, since which date the total labour force has decreased from 4,136 to 3,550 in 1955, while net sales have increased from £4,938,093 to £7,186,756. During the same period prices have risen less than the average for the industry. Such developments are ascribed entirely to the introduction of US technical and managerial techniques within the main product division of this firm.

To begin with, thirty-five Americans – ten administrative and twenty-five factory personnel – were brought over from the associate company. Over the years, most of these have returned, it being a deliberate policy of the American associate to assign US nationals on a temporary basis only. Most of those who came over in 1950 had an expert knowledge of one or more production phases, and their main task was to train British personnel on technologies applied successfully in the USA. At the present time there are seven American executives, including the Managing Director, the general works manager, one factory manager and the head of the finance office. Of the nine directors, four are American and five British. Personnel are regularly sent each year to America for training; the majority of these are of superintendent level or above.

While there have been no revolutionary changes in manufacturing methods since the initial US investment, notable improvements in productivity have been brought about by the installation of more up-to-date plant manufactured in the UK under American licence. Likewise, neither production control nor administrative techniques have been markedly affected. At the time when the US company first gained a financial interest, however, there was a major change in company structure between board and executive level with the formation of a management committee to implement overall policy. The main US influence on production planning methods has been the increasingly specialized and scientific way in which they have been approached. There are, for example, fewer stoppages and late deliveries on the production line than previously. While control was at one time vested in the factory manager, it is now centralized under the production control superintendent in each division: the result has been a better supervised manufacturing programme and more systematic and integrated planning procedures. In 1950, the American system of standard costing, incorporating the better features of cost control, was introduced, the outcome of which is a more accurate historical cost ascertainment.

Careful comparison showed that few advantages were likely to follow the adoption of the American wages system instead of that previously operated. The quality of labour amenities, e.g. canteen services, sports activities and other welfare benefits, were already good by normal UK standards, though a number of specific improvements, e.g. new showers, have been introduced in the last five years.

The organization of the sales and distribution department was completely overhauled. Instead of district sales managers handling all products, regional sales managers were appointed to specialize in each of the firm's three lines of products. Commodity sales managers now have complete control in their division through the regional sales managers in each division to the salesmen. At one time, too, district sales managers were responsible for the detailed operation of their branches, which is now handled by a branch operating department. Sales targets are given to each salesman, and closely monitored. Finally, while there was previously no fixed programme of sales training, salesmen now have regular training sessions with their regional sales managers.

As regards distribution policy, whereas contact in one of the main divisions was almost exclusively with wholesalers and multiple concerns, the firm has now developed retail sales promotion and direct contact with retailers. Following, too, the link-up with another American associate, closer attention has been given to market research in guiding sales and advertising policies. Advertising budgets have been stepped up substantially. There have not been any appreciable changes in profit margins, except in one product line where the retail margin has been increased. As regards this firm's main products, however, margins are controlled by competition.

In the main, purchasing methods have fallen into line with current American procedures, and more attention has been given to inventory control. There is a more rigid insistence on standards and tolerances and a prompt timing of deliveries than previously. To the best of this firm's knowledge none of its raw material suppliers has visited the USA on its own behalf; however, a number of them have American connections and they have visited their counterparts in the normal course of business.

This company is now kept regularly advised of any raw material developments, and twice monthly receives an 'Export Purchasing Letter' from its US parent giving price trends as affecting its various markets – rubber, chemicals, fabrics, paper, etc., etc. In the main, it is the technical divisions which are notified of raw material changes, though these are normally passed on via the purchasing department to its leading suppliers.

The rate of product innovation since this firm first became US-financed has been less than one might have expected, partly because of the costliness of plant involved, partly because of the difficulty in procuring the right kind of raw materials and partly because of saturation of its main markets. Nevertheless, the existing range of products has been extended and new consumer goods marketed with American co-operation.

In concluding, to quote from a senior executive of Firm no. 2:

> It is certainly true that the presence of American nationals on the Board of Directors has led to a more dynamic attitude towards new manufacturing methods, product innovation, research, etc. There is constant pressure from these directors to new methods and forward-looking products. Whilst it would not be true to say that our American associate has the last word in everything, it is constantly striving to sell to all company directors the need for action, aggressive management techniques, financial policies and product designs. Such an attitude is undoubtedly even infiltrating into the most conservative of British minds.

3 ILLUSTRATION OF FIRMS NEGLIGIBLY AFFECTED IN THEIR MANAGERIAL PROCEDURE BUT THAT HAVE BENEFITED TECHNICALLY

CASE STUDY NO. 3

In September 1947 due to the curtailment of import licences granted by the UK government for American goods, negotiations were commenced for the production of a range of US machine small tools by a well-established UK concern. Part-production was started in 1949 by assembling components imported from the US. During 1949 and 1950, extensions of 24,000 sq. ft were made to the existing factory and seventy more people employed. A capital investment of £100,000 was approved, and backed by the Economic Co-operation Administration (ECA). This gave the US company a substantial – but minority – equity interest in the UK concern.

Of the total capital invested, three-quarters was allocated to a replica of the US plant and tooling purchased from the American company; other equipment was manufactured in the UK to American specifications. No US labour was initially brought over, but visits were paid to America by both the senior executives and technical managers of the British firm. An identical product is now made in both plants, and the manufacturing processes are closely comparable. Designs, jigs, tools, equipment, specifications and chemical formulae for bought-out parts and materials are all US-made. Some of these, however, have been modified in recent years to conform with the British market conditions; for example, domestic steels are now being used in lieu of the US specifications since testing proved them to be slightly superior to the US specifications.

Whereas, however, an exchange of technical know-how has been virtually complete, there would appear to have been few changes in managerial procedures since the initial US investment. However, information about US production costs and standard times are made available by the parent company, and frequent visits from American executives have enabled UK quality control and inspection methods to be improved. Nowadays, for example, a final inspection of finished components is made at the assembly point, but accurate sample inspections are made by a skilled machine shop floor inspector who covers every stage of manufacture several times per day. These inspection checks are recorded on a special card fixed to each machine. At the same time each machine operator is held responsible for the quality of his own work; the breakdown of machines, together with gauges designed for each operation, only makes it possible for the operator to check the accuracy of his own production. Any failure to pass the gauge is immediately reported to the section machine setter, who adjusts the machine and checks a number of components before passing the work back to the operator.

Productivity in British and American factories is regularly compared and the reasons for differences analysed. By 1954, given equal conditions in all processes, the UK times were as good as, or better than, comparative US times. Reduced output times are, however, inevitable on a few operations which, due to the smaller volume of output, do not warrant the capital expenditure on special-purpose machines or the complete use of magazine feeds.

Only to a slight extent has that part of the factory supplying the traditional range of products been affected by recent developments. In fact, the 'American' and 'British' sections of the business have been kept fairly self-contained. The only technical gain derived by the latter has been in respect of the heat processing of steel. At the same time, however, extensions to the factory consequent upon reorganization have enabled new plant layouts to be introduced, thereby increasing productivity, while all sections of the business have benefited by the bulk buying of certain commodities such as cutting oils, lubricants, washing compounds, packing materials, etc.

Toolroom and maintenance departments have also gained by the wider exchange of information on the handling of special machine tools, gauges, jigs and fixtures. British ideas on improved methods and designs of tooling have also been frequently discussed between the British and American companies and, in many instances, put into effect in the US plant. There is no market-sharing between the two organizations, which compete freely in export markets.

Since its US associations first started, the productivity per man of this firm has risen appreciably as a result of improved production control, materials handling techniques and scheduling of orders. In all major respects, however, the company has retained the character of its native origins. Its executives do, however, feel that their contact with an American company has had many indirect advantages, and that in particular it has given a more entrepreneurial stimulus to efficiency – or, in the words of the Managing Director: 'We are perhaps rather less conservative in our approach towards new manufacturing and managerial techniques, and quicker to apply them, than heretofore.'

10 Overall economic effects and future prospects of US direct investment in the United Kingdom

TRENDS IN INTERNATIONAL INVESTMENT

One of the most significant developments of world economic relationships over the past fifty years has been the gradual assumption by the US of the role previously occupied by the UK as the main source of supply of international capital. Changing economic circumstances and two world wars have been principally responsible for this. In 1914, British overseas investments were worth more than $18 billion, nearly five times the corresponding figure for the US.[1] At that time the United Kingdom was the centre of the international capital market, and was herself investing at the rate of nearly 7 per cent of her national income overseas each year, or nearly half her net capital growth.[2]

During the war years which followed, nearly one-quarter of these assets were liquidated, while the US increased her private foreign holdings to $6.5 billion to become a net exporter of capital. In addition, by July 1921, that country had granted inter-governmental credits of more than $10 billion. Throughout the comparative stability of the 1920s, both the UK and the US were able to build up substantial foreign investments, the latter alone exporting capital at the rate of more than $800 million each year. The Wall Street crash of 1929 ended the prosperity of that decade: US capital holdings fell by 67 per cent in three years, and the 1930s saw the United States a net importer of long-term capital to the tune of $2.6 billion. By 1939, the value of that country's total overseas assets had fallen to $11.4 million – compared with $13.6 million then held by the UK.

The future pattern of international lending was affected by the Second World War in three major ways. Allied countries sold dollar assets to pay for war commitments (the UK alone liquidated over one-third of her pre-1939 foreign investments), refugee capital flowed into the United States for security, and American government obligations held by foreigners enormously increased. In the decade since 1945, the US has almost monopolized private foreign investment. Yet, even so, the total net exports of that country's private capital between 1947 and 1955 – which averaged around $1,000 million per annum – were lower in real terms than those of the years 1920–9, and, is a percentage of her gross national product, fell from 0.95 to 0.47. Over the same period, there was a net decrease in UK overseas investments: the fact that considerable sums of money were exported to the non-dollar world by the UK was largely due to the substantial re-export trade in loans and grants received from the US and Canada. Only since 1950 has there been a small positive outflow of new capital; even so, valued at £60 million in 1953, the sum in question is equivalent to less than one-twelfth of the UK's pre-1914 rate of lending.[3] Most Continental European countries have been similarly placed: in fact only Switzerland has retained her pre-war position as a net exporter of private capital.

During these years, a number of changes have taken place in the direction, form and character of international investment. First, whereas, in her peak period of overseas lending, the UK invested substantial amounts of portfolio capital in the virgin territories or regions of recent settlement' such as South America and the Dominions. US firms have preferred to engage in direct investment both to gain access to raw materials for the American industrial machine, and (more recently) to secure outlets for the export of US manufacturing products. Both policies have been largely successful: by 1953, one-sixth of all the raw materials imported into the USA originated from that country's foreign subsidiaries, while one-fifth of American exports were financed by earnings from her overseas manufacturing outlets.

Over the years, the geographical orientation of US investments has also shifted slightly. Whereas in 1929 27 per cent of the total sum invested was located in Canada, 47 per cent in the rest of the Western Hemisphere, 18 per cent in Europe and 8 per cent in other countries, the corresponding figures for 1955 were 34 per cent, 35 per cent, 16 per cent and 15 per cent. By industry, some 48 per cent of the post-war investment growth has been directed to the petroleum industry, and 18 per cent to the other primary producing trades including agriculture.[4] Only Canada and Western Europe have attracted sizeable capital flows into manufacturing industry.

Second, unlike the movement of European international capital in the nineteenth and early twentieth centuries, American overseas investment, and particularly that of the post-1945 period, has been unaccompanied by any parallel migration of labour.[5] No longer do external capital and labour movements complement each other: rather they tend to substitute for each other. Except in specialized instances, e.g. petroleum and manufacturing investments in the underdeveloped areas, the American investor has found the supply of labour in the investing country adequate in quantity and quality for his immediate needs.

Third, the structure of financing overseas capital movements has changed – and this in three main ways:

(a) The relative importance of direct to other types of foreign investments has steadily increased. While during the 1920s more than two-thirds of the private long-term capital exported from the US was absorbed by *portfolio* investments, since 1945 – with the fear of defaults still fresh in the mind of investors – the corresponding figure has been less than one-fifth; since 1946, the increase in the value of *direct* investment has been more than seven times greater than that of portfolio capital movements.[6]

(b) The proportion of direct investments, financed by way of *reinvested earnings* of US-owned or US-controlled companies, has risen steeply. In OEEC countries alone, between 1948 and 1951, 68 per cent of the growth of US long-term direct investment was made up of ploughed-back profits and only the balance of *net capital flows* from America.

(c) The role of inter-governmental grants-in-aid and loans, and that of public bodies such as the Export–Import Bank has become more important in recent years. Of the total US overseas investment between 1945 and 1955, nearly 65 per cent was officially financed.

Fourth, recent developments have had their repercussions on the motives and attitudes towards overseas lending. Prior to 1939, private capital flowed abroad, simply attracted by the prospect of favourable earnings. Since the war, the imposition of tariff barriers and import quotas, in restricting the free movement of international trade in goods, has deliberately fostered movements of capital to protect existing markets, while the high risks associated with European investment have discouraged new capital flows to that region to capture new markets.[7] At the same time, a combination of current circumstances and estimated future requirements has led the American businessman to develop a more international outlook, the realization of which has shown itself particularly through the setting-up of overseas manufacturing outlets.

Before we discuss the overall practical implications of the recent trends of US investment in the UK, from the aspect of both the investing and recipient countries, it might be helpful to summarize briefly some of the main theoretical issues involved.

Externally, if Country A increases the value of its investments in Country B, this means that an equivalent amount of claims against the latter country's foreign currency has been created. The extent to which this allows Country B to finance an additional quantity of imports from Country A will depend on the form which the claim takes and the way in which the investment is deployed. If it so happened that the entire investment was conditional on there being an equivalent amount of machinery and capital imported from the investing country, there would be no net increase in the recipient country's supply of foreign currency; usually, however, the greater part of any inflow of foreign capital will be spent internally by Country A and, as a result, a net gain in foreign currency will accrue. Furthermore, it is equally important to distinguish between investment financed by a direct capital flow from Country B and that made up of reinvested earnings of companies already operating in Country A. In the former case, there is a net gain in foreign currency to Country A; in the latter, there is not, except in as much as a certain amount of profits which would otherwise have flowed back to Country B are now retained by Country A. The fact, then, that more than two-thirds of the post-war expansion of US investment in the UK has been financed by ploughed-back profits of existing US companies has meant that, whereas no additional dollar currency has been made available, dollar claims of that amount against the

United Kingdom have been created, on the basis of which future dividends will be paid. It is therefore quite possible then, for a once and for all capital inflow of dollars to be more than nullified by a recurrent outflow of dividends at a future date.

Internally, a direct investment will usually help to stimulate the demand for real resources of the recipient country, and thus help to raise its level of economic activity. Investment is both income- and employment-creating, except in times of full employment, when it could be inflationary. In practice, this has shown itself to be one of the principal differences between the effects following from an increase in US *portfolio* and that of *direct* investment in the UK. Though the former may create demand for real resources, e.g. where the investment is floated in the form of a new issue, in most cases (as for example was so in the 1920s and with the more recent purchases of British securities by US investors) it is more likely to be a transfer of assets away from the domestic shareholder to the foreigner; in such cases foreign currency is made available without there being any new claims on internal resources. Not always, however, will an increase in American direct investment affect the internal workings of the host economy; this would not be the case for example where an American simply purchased the interests of an existing British concern without investing any new capital in it. Alternatively, a company's surplus earnings may be retained in liquid form *in anticipation* of future expansion. We have, for instance, already noted the £100 million capital expansion programmes of the Ford and Vauxhall motor companies. These investments are being financed largely out of reinvested profits of the British subsidiaries which have been accumulating over a period of time.

It is difficult, then, to give any *a priori* assessment of the effects which might be expected to follow from an increase or decrease in the volume of foreign investment to the economy of the receiving country. Though there is a strong possibility that the total supply of capital available for internal development will be increased, this is not always the case. Neither does it necessarily follow that an additional supply of foreign currency will be made available. Where, for example, an increase in investment is financed by ploughed-back profits, and is used to import machinery and equipment from the investing country, the consequences might be the opposite of those intended. These points, and others, in relation to the long-term effects of international capital movements, need to be borne in mind when the pros and cons of the kind of Anglo-American investment partnership described in this book are evaluated from the perspective of UK economic policy.

ECONOMIC ADVANTAGES TO THE UNITED KINGDOM

General industrial development

The main conclusions of our study as dealt with at length in the preceding pages may now be briefly summarized. Apart from the fact that an added source of finance capital is usually made available, the main advantage which the presence of US-affiliated manufacturing subsidiaries brings to the UK is that the UK is able to derive benefits from the competitive and dynamic qualities of the American economy, and be directly linked to its industrial development and structural change. More especially, certain British firms, by enjoying full access to American research, manufacturing and managerial expertise, and by being in close contact with – if not actually governed by – American business attitudes, can utilize such advantages not only to their own profit but also to that of British industry as a whole. The results have been in evidence both in the introduction and development of new products and of new market structures more conducive to economic growth and competitiveness. New skills have been imported, and an increased impetus given to the application of technically superior methods of production and materials processing. The resultant impact has been both *horizontal* and *vertical* in character, affecting British competitors on the one hand and suppliers and consumers of US firms on the other. The directness of these associations and the contact which UK industry has been given with American industry has increased their receptiveness to new ideas, and has enabled the UK to adapt herself to her changing economic environment more quickly and with less frictional disturbance than would otherwise have been the case. Productivity has been raised in many spheres of industry and commerce, American managerial practices have been both publicized and assimilated, and the general tempo of industrial development advanced.

External trade and the balance of payments[8]

Any assessment of the amount of foreign currency – and in particular dollars – directly saved by the presence of US-affiliated firms in the UK must necessarily be subject to a wide margin of error. In 1954, about £500 million worth of the goods and services produced by American-controlled firms were consumed in the UK; of this amount between £25 and £30 million took the form of imported specialized components and materials from America. In fact, however, had the quantity of goods produced by US subsidiaries been imported from the US, it is unlikely that the total outlay would have remained the same. For as Chapter 8 has already shown, higher production costs, freight charges and tariffs would then have to be taken into account and, assuming the same profit margins, the UK consumer would probably have had to pay between £600 and £650 million for his purchases. In 1954, this would have represented a sum four times the total UK manufacturing imports from the US, or 15 per cent of the country's total import bill, of that year. And, as can be seen from Table 9.1, which shows the export trends of some of the newer UK industries in which US capital is concentrated, most of the commodities concerned were imported in 1939. To take two specific examples, the Fawley Refinery is thought to have saved the UK $300 million of oil imports between 1952 and 1955, and the manufacture of carbon black more than $10 million a year. Future savings are likely to be even greater as the British petrochemical and synthetic rubber industries develop. In both these fields, US capital is well represented.

It is, of course, true that many of these products would have been supplied by UK competitor firms in any case, while it is unlikely that the British balance of payments position would have supported the import of the remainder. This being so, to obtain a more positive picture of the role which US subsidiaries and Anglo-American concerns are playing in helping the UK to meet her external commitments, we must turn to consider their export achievements. In 1954, such firms exported £275 million worth of commodities, an amount equal to nearly 12 per cent of the total UK manufacturing exports for that year. Of this contribution, metal and engineering products – and most particularly motor vehicles, office machinery and farm implements – accounted for £225 million or *one-sixth* of total British exports. Of the newer industrial products only,[9] US-financed firms were responsible for about *one-third* of all UK exports, or – if motor-cars are included within this category – *two-fifths*. Pre-war, comparative exports were very small, not exceeding £15 million in value, or one-eighth of the 1954 volume. Then, they almost entirely consisted of motor-cars, sewing machines, agricultural tractors and specialized chemicals. Again Table 10.1 illustrates the net result of these trends. Prior to 1939, the selected industries there depicted cost the economy £34 million in foreign exchange, while in 1955 there was a net inflow of £231 million.

In actual fact, as Table 10.2 further illustrates, the average proportion exported by an American-affiliated engineering from in 1954 was 52 per cent of its total output that year and that of a non-engineering subsidiary 35 per cent. These figures are unweighted in that they make no allowance for the different sizes of the exporting firms. However, in general this is of little consequence, save that the percentage of engineering exports would be slightly higher – the larger firms in our sample recording rather more favourable achievements than the average. Twenty firms supplying sewing machines, radio sets, cotton textiles, agricultural tractors, refrigerating machinery components, oil-field equipment and mine safety equipment, export more than 75 per cent of their total output, and forty others in the electric tool, washing machine, dictating machine, razor-blade, accounting machine and pharmaceutical products industries more than 60 per cent. Export figures for subsidiaries established pre-1939 and post-1945 are also separately classified, and, as might be expected, the latter show much better results.

Compared with all British manufacturing exports, the percentage of output exported by US-affiliated companies is more than the average for their particular industry in two out of every three cases, and most noticeably by firms in the pharmaceutical, agricultural tractor, motor-car, office equipment, refrigerator, machine tool and radio industries. That this is at least partly due to the transatlantic associations enjoyed by these affiliates, as well as to the post-war shortage of dollar currency, is shown by the fact that in many cases the markets supplied are a replacement of those which were previously serviced by the American parent company. In like manner, the subsidiaries are able to benefit from the world-wide overseas sales and service facilities of the US organizations. And although it is true that the UK Board of Trade has granted permission for some American firms to

Table 10.1 Selected newer British industries in which US direct investment is concentrated: trade statistics, 1938–55 (£ million)

	Imports		Exports		Estimated share of US financed firms in total exports (1955)[1]
	1938	1955	1938	1955	
Engineering					
Agricultural machinery	0.5	2.4	0.1	17.7	C
Agricultural tractors	0.4	1.9	0.5	43.9	B
Cars and chassis	1.7	4.7	7.7	122.5	C
Electric portable power tools	n.a.	n.a.	–	2.3	B
Excavators and earth-moving equipment	0.2	3.9	0.5	18.9	C
Domestic refrigerators	0.2	0.2	Neg.	7.6	B
Scientific, industrial and aeronautical instruments	n.a.	3.1	Neg.	13.8	C[2]
Office machinery	1.4	8.9	0.5	14.7	B
Petroleum well-drilling machinery	–	–	–	2.2	A
Printing and bookbinding machinery	1.0	3.9	1.2	9.9	B
Packaging, packeting, bottling, machinery, etc.	n.a.	1.7	0.2	4.8	D
Sewing machines (and parts)	0.6	2.1	0.7	9.7	A
Washing machines and laundry equipment	Neg.	n.a.	0.1	7.5	B
Non-engineering					
Abrasives	0.6	3.2	0.4	2.5	B
Antibiotic drugs and sulphonamides[3]	–	0.4	–	7.8	A
Carbon black	0.6	1.9	–	0.5[4]	A
Refined petroleum	40.8	111.2	2.8	77.2	C
Synthetic detergents	–	–	–	6.7	A
Synthetic resin (including adhesives & plastic materials)	n.a.	12.0	0.3	22.9	D
Total (estimated)	48.0	161.5	15.0	393.1	40–45 per cent

Source: Board of Trade *Accounts relating to Trade and Navigation of the UK,* December 1938; 1937–8 (41–XI) xxii and December 1955: 1954–5 (41–XI) XVII.
Notes:
1 Key to Column 5: A = 75 per cent and over; B = 50–74 per cent; C = 35–49 per cent; D = 20–34 per cent.
2 Including British firms manufacturing under US licence.
3 Apart from penicillin.
4 1954 figure.

Table 10.2 Proportion of their total output exported by 152 American-affiliated subsidiaries in the UK, 1954–5

Per cent of output exported	Firms established in 1939 and earlier		Firms established since 1940		All firms			
	Engineering	Non-engineering	Engineering	Non-engineering	Engineering	Per cent of total	Non-engineering	Per cent of total
0–20	7	20	3	6	10	13.9	26	32.5
21–40	12	27	6	6	18	25.0	33	41.3
41–60	18	8	10	8	28	38.9	16	20.0
61–80	4	2	6	2	10	13.9	4	5.0
81–100	3	0	3	1	6	8.3	1	1.3
Total no. of firms in group	44	57	28	23	72	100.0	80	100.0
Average % exported	45.8	29.7	53.9	41.3	48.9	–	33.2	–

manufacture in Britain only because of their high export potential, it is also to be recalled that at least one in six US firms in the UK have other foreign direct investments.

In addition, a number of long-term factors are making for high exports. First, there is an increasing demand for the type of capital and consumer goods produced by US firms in the Commonwealth and underdeveloped areas, consequent upon the need for greater mechanization, and the accompanying improved living standards. Second, a growing number of parent and branch units are currently adopting a policy of product specialization: for example the entire world output of noiseless typewriters, industrial sewing machines, a range of comprehensive accounting equipment, washing machines, cigarette lighters, agricultural tractors and specialized refrigerating components is supplied by American manufacturing units in the UK, with the US itself being an important customer in several cases. And, third, the fact that the majority of subsidiaries are able to produce at lower costs than their parent concern has led to a deliberate encouragement of the British plant to supply non-US markets.

All these trends seem likely to continue in the future. Whereas a number of US-controlled firms, e.g. in the refrigeration, enamelling, industrial instrument, pump and kitchen equipment fields, claimed they competed with their parent companies, for the most part, there is some kind of pre-agreed division of export markets which varies, *inter alia*, according to the currency availability position of the buyers and the relative costs and convenience of the sellers. Thus, as might be expected, the UK branch unit or associate firm tends to specialize in servicing the European and Commonwealth (within the Sterling Area) markets, while the parent plant satisfies consumers in the Western Hemisphere.

At the same time, while at least 80 per cent of their exports are so directed, over one-half of the American-affiliated firms in our sample also supply direct to dollar markets. Between 1950 and 1956, while dollar sales of all UK manufacture exports grew by 65 per cent, those of US-affiliated companies doubled. The trend for the US alone is shown in Table 10.3. The reasons are mostly those already mentioned, but in addition, where US capital is invested in an existing British concern, the traditional product sometimes finds a market in America. Furthermore, where a different range of products are supplied in the UK plant, these may have a limited appeal in the Western Hemisphere, e.g. low horse-power cars, small-capacity refrigeration equipment, washing machines, food products, and cosmetics. One novel example is the scheme recently adopted by a well-known American tourist company to include within its scheduled cost for a visit to Britain, a 'souvenir' Ford car made at the Dagenham factory. In addition to motor vehicles, the US is also an important buyer of agricultural tractors, radio sets, cameras, calculating machines, typewriters and mine safety equipment from the UK. Principally, because of the favourable prices offered by subsidiaries, South America is supplied with razor-blades, electric tools, dictaphones and kitchen implements, while the Canadian market accepts duplicators, drill chucks, kitchen implements, refrigerators, locks and dental goods. Mexico is Britain's foremost purchaser of washing machines. All the same, it is sometimes difficult

Table 10.3 Export of selected commodities to the US by UK affiliates, 1950 and 1956 (£000s)

	United States		Estimated share of U.S.-financed firms in total $ exports
	1950	1956	(1955)[1]
Agricultural and tracklaying tractors	940	1,808	A
Agricultural implements		633	B[2]
Office machinery	Neg.	1,202	B
Sewing machines		1,874	A
Textile machinery	1,070	2,315	D
Printing and bookbinding machinery	Neg.	787	C
Road vehicles	6,320	16,182	C
Drugs and medicines	Neg.	966	D
Perfumery, soap and toilet preparations	Neg.	198	C
Scientific and industrial instruments, photographic equipment and watches and clocks	NSA[3]	1,591	C
	8,500	27,556	35–40 per cent

Source: Board of Trade *Accounts relating to Trade and Navigation of the UK*, December 1950, and December 1955; 1954–5 (41–XI) xvii.
Notes:
1 Key to Column 3: A = Over 75 per cent; B = 50–75 per cent; C = 35–49 per cent; D = 20–34 per cent.
2 Including that of an Anglo-Canadian firm.
3 Not separately available.

to counterbalance the prestige value of the hall-mark 'made in the USA'; for example, one subsidiary commented that, in spite of its product being identical in every way with that of its parent company, and sold at a 10 per cent discount, the Canadian customer still prefers to buy from the latter source.

By indirect means, too, British exports have also been advanced. Over £3 million worth of petroleum refinery equipment was sent overseas in 1955 for the construction of foreign refineries largely in the hands of American consultants, and contracts received through refinery consultants in the UK. In addition, component suppliers of US subsidiaries have earned valuable dollar contracts. One company is sending to the parent concern of its main UK customer over £250,000 of steel strip each year, another, substantial quantities of photographic paper and gelatine, and a third is responsible for one US subsidiary earning nearly $700,000 by exporting contact relays to the Canadian market. The same is true of exports of cast-iron, plastic parts, roller bearings and electrical equipment. Finally, there has been a general competitive stimulus of US firms in Britain, the effects of which, as described in Chapter 6, have been felt by a wide range of firms and industries. In this connection, one writer has suggested that had it not been for the presence of US motor vehicle subsidiaries in the UK, the attention paid by competitive British firms to the export market would not have been as marked.[10]

In all, then, US firms have played an important role in the UK's drive for external solvency since 1945. While, from the viewpoint of total trade, the contribution of US-financed firms may not seem to have been very marked, it has been unquestionably so on the British *balance* of imports and exports, which over the last five years has only averaged + £30 million. Moreover, the conversion value (i.e. value of exports less imports) of such products as office machinery, industrial instruments, specialized pharmaceuticals, photographic equipment, etc., is well above average for UK exports as a whole. The battle for external solvency has been essentially a *marginal* one and without the contribution of US-financed firms, the position might have been very different. Of course, it would be foolish to claim that the net inflow of foreign currency of nearly £250 million in 1954 was solely attributable to US direct investment in the UK. But in as much as (1) the American manufacturing and managerial expertise derived by them enabled their products to be made available at better quality and more cheaply than would otherwise have been the case, (2) for similar reasons, the *speed* of industrial development has been advanced and (3) as many of the export markets had already been exploited by US parent companies, there is a strong probability that a sizeable part of the increase in UK exports would not otherwise have been obtained.

Employment and industrial location

We have seen that one of the foremost results of US corporate investment in the UK has been the enlarged volume and variety of employment which it has created, and the subsequent repercussions which this has had on the economy as a whole. Right up to the Second World War, for example, American capital directly helped to utilize resources previously unemployed, though in magnitude the gain was comparatively small. During the 1919–39 period, over 140 new enterprises, giving employment to 60,000 people, were established, while those twenty-five firms already operating before 1914 expanded their labour force by 40,000. As these developments took place at a time of low effective demand and heavy structural unemployment, they were wholly to the good. Shortly after the Goodyear Rubber Company set up its factory in Wolverhampton in 1927, for example, the investment was reported as being of particular benefit in that it gave employment to disabled miners and created opportunities for a new industry in that area.[11] Around this time, too, factories were also being sited in the Distressed (or Special) Areas of South Wales, Mid-Scotland, North-West and North-East England, to produce toys, clothing, chemicals, cutlery and light engineering equipment. The generous wages policy adopted by some subsidiaries and the size of their investment, helped improve the economies of these regions especially as the industries in question were newly originated and growth-oriented.

Since 1939, the British economy has experienced a period of full or over-full employment, with its accompanying labour shortage: it has been suggested that the increasing permeation of US business capital has only aggravated the position, by raising the level of demand for real resources and forcing up wages and prices. The fact that wealthy US corporations have been subsidized by the lease of government factories in the Development Areas has led to a Parliamentary Committee raising objections.[12] Nevertheless, it is highly probable that the benefits resulting from the selectivity of the investment have more than outweighed the disadvantages. The argument that full employment would otherwise have been maintained is probably valid in the short period; at the same time it is more than likely that without the real resources provided by the American investors and the import-saving (or export-earning) content of their products, subsequent productivity and industrial development would have been retarded, and unemployment caused. In any event, American-affiliated companies have been subjected to precisely the same restrictions and controls on their UK activities, e.g. in respect of the raising of finance, allocation of materials, etc., as have domestic firms.[13] Both would-be new subsidiaries, and existing enterprises who have wished to expand, have been encouraged to set up their factories in the areas of above-average unemployment. Over 35,000 people are now employed by US firms in the newly named Development Areas, as compared with 15,000 before the war. In that the entire post-1945 investment has been within the newer and expanding industries involving new and unfamiliar production techniques, e.g. the introduction of light precision engineering to the Vale of Leven and Dundee, and of fine chemicals to South Wales and Merseyside, the trend towards the diversification and economic stability of these areas has been furthered. Furthermore, the industries in question are those which, so far as one can judge, are fast growing and their products serve a wide range of markets. In addition, they employ a comparatively high percentage of female labour. Most, if not all, these features were absent in the traditional trades of coal-mining, shipbuilding, iron and steel, and textiles, upon which such a large proportion of the population at one time depended for their livelihoods.

Such movements as these, however, are not confined to the Development Areas. A large new cosmetics factory at Eastleigh (Hampshire) aims to give employment to women workers in a town largely dependent on its railway engineering workshops. In Crewe, the production of refrigerating equipment is furthering industrial diversification in like manner, while on the outskirts of London, a post-war office equipment factory (now employing over 1,000 workers) has made new work available at Hemel Hempstead.

One cannot, of course, ignore the problems which the above trends have created. Skilled labour of the kind required by US affiliates has been a very scarce commodity since the war, and the tendency for many American subsidiaries to pay well above the current wage rates to attract the necessary numbers has caused certain older-established firms[14] to have some misgivings about the desirability of such investment, particularly when competitive wage spirals develop, to the detriment of the firms who can least afford to pay. However, this problem is – or should be – essentially short-term in character and, in any case, can only partly be attributed to the presence of US-financed companies, as the influx of new firms demanding unfamiliar production techniques and types of labour has been a general feature of the post-war industrial restructuring of such areas.

The clustering of new factories by American firms in the Development Areas continues. At the time of writing (March 1957), several new enterprises are scheduled for completion, as well as major expansions for branches of well-known American subsidiaries already producing in other parts of the country. Caterpillar Tractor, Remington Rand, Burroughs Adding Machine, Goodyear Rubber, International Business Machines, Ranco and Euclid, all have large extensions to their existing Scottish premises in hand while both the Heinz and Kraft food companies are building new factories in the Merseyside Development Area. Northern Ireland, with its attractions of a plentiful labour supply, government grants of up to 25 per cent of the cost of plant and equipment, subsidized rents, and special rebates on public utility prices is likely to become of more pronounced interest in the future.[15]

In addition to making available opportunities for employment and creating the demand for new skills, US-affiliated firms have measurably improved the lot of the worker in many trades, both through the normal course of competition, and by the attention they have paid to factory design and amenities, labour selection, holidays and wage incentives. Of course, it is not always possible to separate cause and effect, particularly where there are a cluster of firms in a limited geographical area. On the face of it, however, there is a regional competitive impact in such districts as those adjacent to the Great West Road and North Circular Road, where eighteen US firms within a radius of a mile employ 12,000 workers or 25 per cent of the total labour force. On the Slough industrial estate alone there are fourteen American-affiliated firms employing 3,400 of the 29,000 total workers. Clearly, such firms must have an influence on their geographical rivals and the standards and amenities which they offer.

The prosperity of the Ford Motor Company and the economy of Dagenham and its vicinity have gone hand in hand. The largest US employer of labour in this country, with a payroll of over 20,000, and drawing three-quarters or more of its labour supply from a radius within 4–5 miles, its influence has been, and is, far-reaching, not only through the normal course of labour turnover, but by the expenditure of over £280,000 in wages every week, and by the course of conversation and contact between employees and others in the area. Likewise, Vauxhall Motors, with its employment of 17,000 people, and proposed expansions in view, virtually encompasses the town of Luton, which has doubled its population since the initial investment by General Motors in 1927. The cumulative effects of such investment on retailing, housing and local government services are evident in this case, as with that of Dagenham. In the Dundee region, US firms employ 20 per cent of the *new* factory labour, and the two largest employers on the Vale of Leven Estate are American-financed, drawing between them a significant proportion of the total labour force of the surrounding district. *Àpropos* the former development, it is perhaps significant that the jute industry, which initially lost labour to such firms, has since raised its wages and bettered its working conditions, which improvements have been paid for by the introduction of new machinery and modern managerial methods.

Likewise, Briggs Motor Bodies, before 1939, and Esso Petroleum and A. C. Delco in post-war years, by their employment and wages policies have made their impact on the economy of Southampton and surrounding districts. The three companies pay over £130,000 in wages each week, which is spent mainly within the locality. Fawley Refinery recruits half of its labour from the Southampton region, and through its first-class working conditions and extremely good recreational facilities has undoubtedly helped raise local labour supply and general standards. With the projects and expansions planned by Regent Oil, Monsanto, International Synthetic Rubber, Standard Telephones & Cables, and Esso Petroleum, this part of the country is rapidly increasing its share of US investment capital.

The general relationships which these firms enjoy with the community in general are naturally varied. It is, for example, the rule rather than the exception that American-financed firms are members of UK Trade Associations: not all, however, play an important part, one firm going as far as to say: 'We have to join if we want to exhibit at the annual National Show.' Most of the subsidiaries and Anglo-American firms in our sample had members of their staff on the Executive Committees of such bodies, and at the time of our interviews, the Managing Directors of six firms happened to be the Presidents of their particular Trade Associations. By such means as these, new knowledge is promoted and publicized. On the other hand, because of its nationality, a US firm is not always allowed to become a member of a co-operative research association. Again, by being members of advisory, local productivity and management committees – one American director was given an annual award in association with the promotion of human relationships in industry – US executives cannot but have stimulated their colleagues by the viewpoints expressed, while public lectures given on such subjects as standard costing, personnel management, job evaluation, budgetary control have further publicized the applicability of American managerial techniques in British industry. Finally, factory visits are generally welcomed. Before the war, for example, the Shredded Wheat factory at Welwyn Garden City attracted over 10,000 visitors a year and in 1950 was allocating £1,750 a year to this same purpose.[16] Only one American firm in five actually discourages visitors over its plant; more than half, in fact, extend such a welcome to their competitors. Apparently, with one or two exceptions, this latter offer has not been reciprocated, and at least two important subsidiaries approached by us commented: 'Our competitors have not even bothered to come and see what we are doing in spite of our invitation.'

Economic ties with the US

That an expansion of American corporate investment in the UK strengthens the economic and – indirectly – strategic and political, ties between the two countries is axiomatic and need to be no more than mentioned.

Clearly, the fact that in 1955, US firms had a stake of $1,200 million in the industrial prosperity of the UK, and UK firms had a stake of around $1,500 million in the US,[17] suggests that there is a close economic and financial relationship between the two economies. While one does not wish to exaggerate this fact, in view of the small proportion of company assets in relation both to total British and American holdings which US-financed firms account for in this country, one must remember that it is the larger US corporations who are mainly the leading investors, and these can often exert considerable political influence in the American House of Representatives and Senate. To further this point: a recent supplement to *Fortune*[18] listed the 500 largest US companies. Of these, eighty-five had subsidiary manufacturing interests in the UK, and between them accounted for no less than 35.4 per cent of the total sales of the group, 35.2 per cent of the total assets and 43.3 per cent of the net profits. Of the largest 200 companies alone, fifty-five operated branch units in the UK.

Availability of investment capital

We have already touched upon the implications of this advantage in Chapter 1. One of the main reasons for the influx of American capital into the UK immediately following the First and Second World Wars was the insufficiency of domestic corporate or personal savings to secure an adequate rate of investment growth. Such foreign funds, by providing an additional source of capital and creating the demand for indigenous real resources, has helped increase the pace of British economic development. As an earlier survey has recalled,[19] this has been one of the chief attractions of US direct investment in Europe in recent years. Though, in general, the US contribution to the financing of UK industry is less important than once it was, it is interesting to note that between 1950 and 1956 the average growth of US net assets in UK manufacturing industry was 7.5 per cent of that for UK corporations as a whole.

ECONOMIC DISADVANTAGES TO THE UK

Long-term outflow of dollars

Dividend payments

The possibility that any substantial American investment will, in due course, lead to large dollar dividend outflow, which will inevitably have unfavourable repercussions on the UK balance of payments, is foremost among the reasons given by those who view the desirability of increasing the flow of US corporate capital into the UK with some misgivings. That, too, such investment is more likely than not to take the form of ploughed-back profits, rather than a net inflow of dollar capital only adds to this anxiety.

It is still too early to judge the force of this argument, as it is only in comparatively recent years that the volume of US investment in the UK has become of any real significance. According to a statement given in the House of Commons in 1954, the total amount of taxed profits remitted in 1953 by US-affiliated firms was £25 million, while technical service fees and royalties paid by British licensees

Table 10.4 Earnings and income[1] from US direct investment in UK industry, 1950–5 ($ million)

	Manufacturing industry			Petroleum refining and distribution			All industry		
	Investment	Earnings	Income	Investment	Earnings	Income	Investment	Earnings	Income
1950	542	103	53	131	11	Neg.	847	142	73
1951	610	118	49	158	13	6	961	164	74
1952	679	98	33	157	44	22	1,038	176	78
1953	745	116	45	170	45	21	1,131	187	90
1954	835	150	63	184	34	23	1,257	226	113
1955	941	163	71	216	76	50	1,420	278	149

Source: US Department of Commerce, Survey of Current Business, various issues.
Note:
1 Income is the sum of dividends, interest and branch profits: earnings is the sum of income and undistributed earnings. In both instances the figures quoted are net of UK taxation.

amounted to £13 million.[20] In 1955, the outflow of dividends (after tax deduction) was $149 million on a total capital invested of $1,420, while, at that time, the profits reinvested amounted to $129 million. The respective figures for manufacturing alone (on a capital invested of $941 million) were $71 million and $92 million.[21] It might, however, be fairly assumed that sooner or later profits at least equal to – and most likely more than – these latter sums will be required from the American parent companies as a reward for their investment. This would seem both inevitable, unless the capital is itself repatriated, and cumulative inasmuch as the amount invested is growing all the time. Yet, because the UK branch units frequently represent only a small part of their US associates' total commitments, the latter may be less anxious to obtain quick profits than would otherwise be the case. Meanwhile, royalty payments may be expected to increase. We have already seen that nearly half of American-financed firms at present make some kind of payment (in the form of royalties and fees) for US manufacturing and research expertise (a larger number than before the war), and there has been a gradual movement by parent concerns to ask for more payments since profits are being reinvested to such a great extent. A recent case is that of the Heinz subsidiary, which, because of the increasing value of the know-how received from its parent company, was recently asked to pay a royalty on the basis of a fixed percentage of turnover.

Partially offsetting these trends is another. As a US-financed company develops, the likelihood that it will obtain the greater percentage of its additional capital from British shareholders increases. More important, it is necessary to relate the whole question of dividend payments to incoming capital flows and the export-earning or import replacement achievements of American firms. The impact of American investment on the gross national product of the UK must also be taken into account. Only when this is shown to be less favourable than it would otherwise have been, is the question of dividend payments seriously considered. Certainly, if one wishes to encourage US investment, it seems imperative that no restrictions should be placed on the remission of such payments.

Finally, a distinction should perhaps be made between the short-term and the long-term effects insofar as the present high export achievements of American firms in the UK are concerned. To what extent, for example, are such exports due to a more favourable comparative cost situation, and to what extent to what *may* be a merely temporary world shortage of dollars? If this latter be the case, then it might well be that future exports may fall, and thus the balance of payments situation further aggravated.

Capital repatriation

The possibility that US-affiliated firms might need to make sudden and large withdrawals of capital, sell out their UK interests or go into voluntary liquidation, should also be considered as a potential danger to the balance of payments situation. Both the British and American economic and political environment, their respective governments' attitudes towards investment, the prosperity of the

US parent concern and the Sherman Anti-Trust Acts are the main factors likely to influence developments in this direction. It may be argued, of course, that the possibility of effective capital repatriation is not in itself of any great significance, as it is always possible to check this by placing an embargo or blocking the exchange of sterling if need be. In so far as the likelihood of such a course would be a major deterrent to the free flow of international finance, however, it may be worth while to examine some of the factors which have, in the past, caused the repatriation of US interests in Britain.

In reality, the number of American firms which have sold out their British interests lock, stock and barrel is comparatively small. While a US firm may sometimes surrender its financial control, it will not, as a general rule, reduce its holding absolutely. For the most part, those companies which repatriated their capital in the inter-war years did so more because of the depressed economic conditions in the US than those in the UK. The withdrawals of the United Drug Company's shareholding in Boots, of the Theodore Gary Group in Automatic Telephone, and of Willys Overland in Willys Overland Crossley are typical examples. There is always the possibility of such a danger recurring. Thus, should a good deal of surplus capacity develop in the parent plant, the American company might well be forced to curtail the output of its UK branch, and serve the export markets from the US.

Since 1945, other factors have assumed greater significance. First, the Sherman Anti-Trust Acts have been a potent cause of the repatriation of capital holdings.[22] Second, the unfavourable view taken of the British political situation, coupled with the fear of nationalization and expropriation, have led to a score or more US firms selling out their manufacturing interests. Third, the tendency for a subsidiary to develop independently of its parent concern and for the relationship between the two companies to become more distant was greatly accentuated by the war, during which time such subsidiaries not only came under the control of British nationals but evolved separate product lines of their own: more than a dozen branch units, including the Pyrene, National Marking and Ruberoid Companies, have since repatriated their UK interests for these reasons. Indeed, because of the very uncertain investment outlook in 1939, some US companies wrote off their European assets completely.

Apart from such instances as these, which are in a minority, the American company will usually retain its initial investment in the British concern, though leave it to domestic sources to finance additional expansions over and above those made possible by capital profits of their own.

Domination of British industry

The recent Trinidad oil dispute and large-scale buying of British industrial equities by American investors[23] has led to a reiteration of the argument – less commonly expressed in recent years than in pre-war days – that, on present trends there is a danger of whole sections of UK industry passing into US hands, the implication being that this is necessarily a thing to be avoided. Undoubtedly, the very prosperous conditions of recent times and the need to attract an additional source of investment capital in certain industries, have veiled the growing influence exerted from the other side of the Atlantic.

Prior to 1939, this question was principally discussed in terms of *portfolio* investments; and as we have already seen, in the late 1920s, firms in the electrical, rubber and aircraft industries all made stipulations that American shareholders could hold only up to a certain limit on shares, and that their voting rights were strictly limited.[24] The infiltration of US *corporate* investment was largely ignored, mainly because it was directed to the newer trades which, at that time, contributed but little to the total industrial output. This is no longer the case – the infant industries of yesterday are among the leaders in our economy today.

The purely nationalistic argument that *because* an industry is mainly in the hands of a foreign country it is *necessarily* a bad thing, and the fear that certain of the less desirable elements of the American way of life will further permeate into the UK, may be largely discounted for the purposes of our present argument. In any event, compared with the influence exerted by other media, e.g. films, literature, tourism, etc., it is of negligible account, and there is no evidence to suggest that employees of US-affiliated firms become Americanized in any respect, save perhaps as regards their attitudes towards their jobs and employers.

The real issues are two-fold: (1) whether or not, as a direct result of the influence exerted by US firms, British industrial development has been adversely affected or the consumer exploited, and (2) whether, if a situation arose which either necessitated the repatriation of US capital, the UK economy would find itself handicapped in the particular line of business which had previously relied heavily on American expertise.

As regards the first issue, it is, of course, inevitable that the presence of American firms has had detrimental repercussions on their less efficient competitors, and through high-pressure marketing methods, consumers may well have been adversely affected. Exclusive dealing is a two-edged weapon, though there is nothing specifically American in its implementation, even if in certain fields US firms have been the first to introduce the practice. To the extent that many of the products which American firms advertise are demanded frequently, it might be fairly argued that advertising cannot force a consumer to buy a good which he has previously found to be unsatisfactory. Yet resources may still be misplaced in this respect. Possibly the critic might point out that US firms have been among the chief culprits in encouraging unnecessary and exaggerated product differentiation (e.g. in the case of toilet preparations, proprietary medicines, various processed foods, etc.); but, no less, has their contribution been the trend towards the standardization and simplification of products, e.g. motor-car components, agricultural implements, rubber tyres, razor-blades, petroleum refinery equipment, soft drink bottles, industrial instruments. At the same time, it is a fact that before the Second World War certain US companies, secure in the financial backing of their parent concerns, were among the leaders in cut-throat competitive practices, e.g. price and profit margin slashing, deferred rebates, the operation of fighting companies, etc.,[25] and though such practices are less evident in today's situation of full employment, there is no guarantee that they might not be repeated in a time of excess capacity and reduced demand.

How far the swallowing up of small firms by US subsidiaries during the course of their growth is disadvantageous to industrial competitiveness and progress, is also a moot point; it may be that any increase in technical efficiency has been sufficient to compensate for any adverse monopolistic tendencies, or the opposite may be true. That there are a number of potential drawbacks following from the introduction of less desirable American business practices would be foolish to deny. But there is no reason to suppose, however, that these are *inherent* in the investment itself, and being similar in kind to those of their British counterparts, present no *special* problems. A number of US-affiliated firms, in fact, have already come within the purview of the Monopolies Commission in the normal course of its duties, and though this possibility, even if it is an unlikely one, might be a deterrent to new investment, it does provide a safeguard to the UK consumer against unacceptable American influences.

Further, in recent months some of the US drug houses have been accused of making large profits out of the National Health Service and repatriating these to the US: in fact, one medical authority claims the amount of dollars remitted in profits as being equivalent to 50 per cent of the total cost of the drugs supplied.[26] However, while it is true that more than one-half of the £29 million worth of medical proprietaries bought by the National Health Service in 1955 were produced by US-controlled subsidiaries, it is very unlikely, even assuming that such companies were making substantial profits and without arguing the ethics of the matter, that the dollar drain directly attributable to such drugs (which in the main represent the various antibiotic proprietaries) would have been more than one-tenth of this amount. For, first, allowance must be made for that part of the gross profits earned by the subsidiaries ploughed back in plant investment and research and development, and in 1955 most of the larger branch units had large expansion programmes in hand. Second, the residue is subject to the normal rate of UK corporate tax: hence the Minister of Health's loss is partly the Chancellor of the Exchequer's gain! To put the matter in its right perspective, between 1954 and 1955, the net gain in foreign currency as a result of reduced British imports and increased exports of antibiotic drugs amounted to £5.4 million, while the net increase in profits remitted to the US from all American-controlled companies in manufacturing industry was only £2.9 million.[27]

The second possible danger of over-dependence on American investment is, however, more important, and should be constantly monitored. In certain cases, too much reliance on the research and development department of the American concern could well mean that its British competitors refrain from independent research which, in the long run, might prove to be to the disadvantage of the UK economy. Alternatively, the withdrawal of US capital may deprive the UK of research facilities which, left to itself, it might otherwise have built up. Finally, too much dependency on US technological and managerial knowledge may result in a reduction in the domestic demand for skilled labour, scientists and professional personnel to the ultimate detriment of the UK's industrial competitiveness.

THE ADVANTAGES TO THE UNITED STATES

Beside the benefits of international investment which accrue to any country which has a substantial export surplus, there are a number of specific advantages which the US derives from her business investments in British manufacturing industry.

Profitability of investment

The past experience of American-financed companies in the UK as regards the profits earned on investments has been favourable. Figures for manufacturing industry are not separately given, but the rate of profit earned by all US direct investments in the UK during the 1930s was above that earned by similar enterprises in the US. More recently, the US Department of Commerce estimated that the earnings of US companies in Britain totalled over $278 million in 1955: the average rate of return in that year was shown to be over 19 per cent compared with an average profit on all their foreign investment of 15 per cent and domestic investments of 10 per cent.[28] As the most profitable outlet for US business capital, Britain is exceeded only by the returns offered by the petroleum and raw material investments in the Middle and Far East. Again, it is true that much of this profit is currently reinvested in the businesses concerned (between 1950 and 1955, the figure was 55 per cent of gross income earned), but, nevertheless, the post-war experiences of US corporations in Britain is highly encouraging to would-be owners of overseas assets. Looking to the future, such profits on foreign investments are likely to play an increasing role in financing the rising value of American imports at a time when competition for that country's manufacturing exports is becoming more pronounced.

Maintenance and expansion of export markets

To the extent that the products supplied by branch subsidiaries would not have been imported from America, due to the shortage of dollar currency, it is clearly an advantage to a US company to operate a manufacturing unit in a country the supply of whose currency is relatively plentiful, and satisfy overseas markets from there. A variety of geographic, linguistic, political and cultural reasons combine to make the UK an obvious first choice. With sterling in comparatively plentiful supply, it is possible to serve markets previously satisfied from the US from a UK location. As has been described earlier in this chapter, American-financed firms exported £275 million worth of goods in 1954; in fact, in relation to its sales the average US subsidiary exported twice as much as the average parent concern in that year. Several companies depend almost exclusively on their subsidiaries to supply their foreign outlets, as a result of which the UK is now one of the largest suppliers in the world of American-designed goods. In essence, it has been found that the *average* cost of producing for export is less in this country than the *marginal* cost of expanding production in the US, and as American factories approach capacity point through a growing home demand, this factor is likely to become more and more significant. The position might, however, be very different should there arise a recession in the American domestic market; in such a case, assuming dollars were more plentiful, it might pay the parent concerns themselves to meet the demands previously satisfied by their overseas manufacturing outlets.

At the present time, then, a sizeable proportion of the profits earned by US subsidiaries is a direct consequence of their high export achievements and, with the proviso that the relative cost and efficiency trends do not move markedly in favour of the US away from the UK, it would seem that the larger share of the non-dollar US markets will continue to be supplied from the latter country. At any rate, this is partly the reason for Britain's expanding share in the world trade of certain commodities. Of her newer industrial products, in 1938 the UK exported 3 per cent of the comparable US volume; this figure had risen by 1948 to 15 per cent and by 1955 to 53 per cent; of this latter amount the US subsidiaries were responsible for about 35 per cent.[29]

Comparative costs

Partly, at least, the high rates of return recorded by American-financed firms in the UK reflect the favourable structure of manufacturing costs in that country *vis-à-vis* the USA. Lower costs of production and distribution enable lower prices to be charged, thereby extending the market and allowing higher earnings to be made than otherwise would have been the case. This is essentially a long-term trend, and the decision to relocate production to achieve these gains is becoming an increasingly important component of US business strategy. The fact that certain products manufactured under UK conditions are charged at US prices in overseas markets only adds force to the argument.

This, however, is not to argue that those affiliated firms which have the greatest cost advantages over their US parents are also those which earn the highest profits, for these latter depend as much on the degree of competition in the selling country as on costs of production in American and British factories. The motor-car and pharmaceutical subsidiaries, for example, retain the best profits on the capital invested, yet, at the same time, they are faced with a relatively (i.e. compared with other industries) less favourable production environment than their parent companies.

The result is shown in an increasing tendency for parents and subsidiaries to specialize in certain types of research and production in order to maximize joint profits. We have seen that a number of US firms already practise such inter-plant specialization; and the probability is that, were it not for the monetary difficulties fluctuating exchange rates and trade barriers which discourage the rationalization of cross-border activity, this would be more widespread. There are instances too where it would be possible for the subsidiary to sell to the American market at a price below that charged by the parent company, but this is not done because it might create problems for its labour force in the USA.

New knowledge passed back

The flow of research, development and managerial expertise, though primarily from the parent company to its British subsidiary, is by no means solely in that direction. The fact that important technological and other gains that have accrued to American firms as a result of their UK interests is not always publicized as well as it might be. In the limited number of instances where there is some international specialization of research effort, the advantages offered are self-evident, but in others, important discoveries or suggestions have been made which have later been taken up by the US associate. One of the earliest cases in point is that of the International General Electric Company's investment in the Associated Electrical Industries Group. For several years prior to its capital repatriation, knowledge had flowed in both directions, and though the American company forged well ahead during the Second World War, since that time research and manufacturing knowledge on diesel engines and turbines, etc., has been returned to the US. Another example is that of the first harbour radar installation in the world set up at Liverpool in 1948, the principles of which were used beneficially by the US Sperry Company when obtaining a commission to install harbour supervision at Long-Beach, California.

New knowledge has also been passed back to the US in respect of phenolics and laminated plastics, materials for cinematic equipment and mechanical handling techniques. In one or two cases, the presence of a smaller manufacturing plant in the UK has meant that new processes and products could be tried out with less capital outlay (and hence risk) than would have been required in the US. In those companies which do a limited amount of basic research and development, the total value of such information is fairly small and in the main confined to technical details.

Finally, US subsidiaries in the UK have provided their parent companies with important insights into various aspects of UK commercial life, and of the nature and character of UK and foreign markets served by them.

OBSTACLES TO US INVESTMENT IN BRITAIN

The important point to be remembered in this connection is that the US exports the equivalent of only 6 per cent of her gross domestic product (compared with approximately 25 per cent in the case of the UK) and currently invests abroad only 4 per cent of her domestic capital formation. In consequence, she has not the same concern in international capital movements as have other countries; indeed, the vast majority of business corporations are just not interested either in establishing branch units overseas or in exploiting foreign markets by more direct means. Of the 250 manufacturing companies in Britain in June 1954, 85 per cent were controlled by parent concerns which employed more than 1,000 workers.

In so far as American companies do consider investing in the UK, the potential drawbacks can best be looked at from the viewpoint of the *opportunity cost* of the contemplated investment. That is to say, assuming that it is desired to allocate capital in the most profitable way, to what extent does investment in British manufacturing industry best satisfy this criterion? We have seen that the pecuniary rate of return is likely to be favourable; what of the possible disadvantages?

Investment opportunities in the US and Canada

Without doubt, the counter-attraction of domestic and Canadian investment opportunities has discouraged more interest from being shown by American firms in European industry in recent years. Why incur risks by exporting capital when a good and safe profit can be made at home? The rate at which the American economy has been expanding since the war and the channels for remunerative deployment of capital have, in general, been more than sufficient to meet the savings available. Moreover, due to greater publicity, it is often easier to sell and buy securities on the American Stock Exchange, and every day new issues are brought to the attention of would-be investors by enthusiastic salesmen.[30] In contrast to the position in other countries, full financial and economic data are normally available to the US investor; moreover, he knows that he can sell any stock or share at any time without the restrictions placed upon such sales in the United Kingdom. Substantially the same reasoning holds good with respect to US manufacturing investments in Canada, which, in volume, have exceeded those in Western Europe by over four times in the past ten years. Indeed, to quote from an American business representative at an OEEC Conference on Private US Overseas Investment held in 1953, 'We regard Canadian investment as fully as attractive as domestic. We feel that the Canadians understand us and we understand them.'[31]

Thus, however attractive the prospects of a British investment may appear, there is a point above which an American investor, private or corporate, is just not prepared to countenance whether he can get more profits, if elsewhere his capital is remuneratively employed. Moreover, since the investment is almost always in a *new* industrial venture, rather than the expansion of an existing one, the would-be investor is likely to have to wait much longer for his capital to be realized, for though the total profits earned on UK assets may be higher than on US assets, the dividends distributed may not be.

Risk of UK exchange control and government interference

Post-war US investment trends in Britain may be conveniently divided into two periods – 1945–9 and 1950 onwards. The feature of these earlier years was that almost all the capital flows were of a kind which aimed at nullifying exchange control restrictions and protecting previously established sales outlets. There was very little investment for pioneering of untapped or unfamiliar markets; the cloud of uncertainty which, in American eyes at least, hung over the economic and political security of the UK (and in particular the risk of exchange control and devaluation of sterling) weighed heavily against those advantages cited earlier. The fear, too, of nationalization and expropriation, of sudden shifts in economic policies and regulations, and of the wider possibility of a Third World War, was cited by more than a score of established American companies we interviewed, as the main reason for the repatriation of their British interests during this period.

Since 1950, however, UK and European economic and political conditions have become more settled, and US firms attracted by the long-term opportunities offered in Britain have increased their financial stake, both by establishing green-field ventures and by joining with British companies to form Anglo-American ventures. The disadvantages have appeared less formidable, and during the last five years the number of new investments in Britain has been steadily growing each year.

A number of other circumstances have also combined to induce a greater outflow of US business capital to Britain. First, from January, 1950, it has been possible for all new American investments in *approved projects* to be repatriated in US dollars on demand, a concession which was extended in February 1953 to include all capital profits subsequently earned. Second, the granting of ECA investment guarantees aimed to protect US investors against expropriation of assets and currency inconvertibility have given potential investors an added sense of security; and since 1948 over twenty firms have taken advantage of this scheme.[32] Third, the easing of world trading conditions, the relaxation of physical controls and import quotas and the return of a Conservative government in the UK have all been welcomed by American firms. Fourth, in 1954 the UK was added to the list of countries scheduled under the Randall Act (US) which legislated that American overseas companies, earning 95 per cent or more of their income outside the US, should pay tax of 38 per cent instead of the domestic rate of 52 per cent. And, fifth, the continuing profitability of existing investments in the UK compared with those in the US and Canada, together with a growing understanding of the advantages which a stake in British industry has to offer, have made for an increasing flow of capital across the Atlantic. For example, the *Anglo-American News* alone reported that fifteen new firms established themselves in 1950 and 1951, twenty in 1952, and 1953, and thirty in 1954 and 1955.

Attitudes of the US government

Two points are worthy of comment in this connection. First, in Part II of a report – 'Factors Limiting U.S. Investment Abroad' – published by the US Department of Commerce in 1954, and based on statements made by officials of over 350 American corporations, it was concluded that, for the most part, the US govern-ment's attitude gave little tangible encouragement to US corporations wishing to invest abroad. The Report, in fact, made three points to support this argument – (1) US tax policies provide no incentive for investment overseas – in fact, if anything, they tend to counteract the concessions made by other countries to attract capital,[33] (2) little direct support is given to US investors in the protection of their property and contractual rights from seizure or discriminatory treatment abroad and (3) information services are inadequate and the US Foreign Service presents a negative attitude towards assisting with the general problem of overseas investment.

Second, the application and execution of Sherman Anti-Trust legislation must be held responsible both for destroying existing US investments in the UK, and for hampering the flow of new funds to the UK. The repatriation of the American interests in British American Tobacco, Electric & Musical Industries, Associated Electrical Industries and British Timken Ltd are past examples of the effects of such legislation. More recently, this matter has been extensively discussed by the American Chamber of Commerce in London, in a booklet entitled *The American Anti-Trust Laws and American Business Abroad*.[34] Two cases cited by this publication may be quoted. The first refers to the effects of the withdrawal of an existing investment, and the second to that of a prospective capital flow:

1 The result has been loss of the benefits to both participants from a pooling of research, experience and skills and of profit to the American concern from its investment in the British company. There has also been a wider deterioration of relationships. Customers of the British manufacturer, finding that it no longer has access to American methods and the fruits of American research, now propose to deal with manufacturers on the Continent which have developed new methods of their own. This threat may well force the British manufacturer to make its own alliance with a Continental manufacturer as a substitute for the previous arrangement with its American partner. As a result, American trade suffers a substantial loss.[35]

2 An American manufacturer wished to pool its production techniques and experience, and the fruits of its own research relating to certain products with the research and distributing organization of a British concern. It was proposed that a joint company be formed in Great Britain, and that each party put up half the required capital, own half the shares and appoint half the directors. Although the venture was to be limited to certain products and to the United Kingdom, the American company was advised that the underlying agreement by the parent companies not to compete with each other in the British market in the products concerned would probably violate the Sherman Act. In view of the Anti-Trust uncertainties involved, the American company decided not to go ahead. The British company and the economy were thus deprived of the benefit of a commercial association with an important American manufacturer in an important line of goods.[36]

Such deterrents to the American investor have shown themselves to be very powerful. Indifferent publicity and advertising by the countries wishing to attract investment has done little to help.[37] The average US investor lacks familiarity with European conditions, and often has insufficient knowledge of the opportunities for investment. The major exceptions are the public relations efforts of Scotland, through the agency of the Scottish Council; of the Netherlands, which at home has a public office to co-ordinate the activities of the various authorities concerned with incoming investment, while in the US a private body, the Institute for Netherlands–American Industrial Co-operation, operates an information bureau for prospective US investors; and of Northern Ireland, which recently set up a liaison group consisting of ten US industrialists and bankers in New York to encourage US industries to establish branch plants in that area.[38] It would seem, however, that if the rest of the UK is to attract more American firms, then both the scope of its public relations, and that of its authorization and administrative procedures need to be further scrutinized.

CONCLUSIONS

The law of comparative costs and the internationalization of industry

What may one conclude from this study? Are UK economic conditions in the future likely to favour more inward investment by US corporations? Should the existing investment more be closely screened? In examining the main advantages which American-affiliated firms have brought to the UK economy, the two which we have shown to be of unquestionable benefit to industrial development and efficiency are those associated with American research and development know-how and managerial attitudes on the one hand, and the improvement of the UK balance of payments on the other. These are gains which may be specifically ascribed to the transatlantic connections fostered by US firms. It is, however, one thing to say this but quite another to argue that more efforts should be made to increase the participation of US firms in British industry.

At the time this chapter is being written (March 1957), the British economy is operating at full, or near full, capacity. Apart from a few regions like Northern Ireland, it is difficult enough to satisfy the demands of indigenous firms for labour without encouraging foreign investors to the economy. In itself, however, the attainment of full employment is not a sufficient reason for discouraging more US investment, for if such investment ultimately leads to more efficiency and an accelerated rate of industrial development, this might counteract any short-run inflationary consequences. Indeed a *redistribution* of *existing* resources on these lines may be very much desired. At the same time, it is likely that the American industrialists have already established themselves in most of the fields where there is a major unsatisfied demand for US-type goods, and – apart from specialist firms and selected Anglo-American agreements – subsequent developments seem set to follow along those lines, where, for one reason or another, the US has a comparative innovating advantage over the UK, and this advantage is best transferred by foreign investment. For inasmuch as the US investment stake in British industry has followed its own domestic pattern established some years previously, then the gap which exists between the stages of growth in the two countries, as regards most industries, has been largely filled. As new techniques develop, e.g. in the field of electronic office equipment and industrial instruments, these will be introduced via their existing subsidiaries, though it would seem unlikely that there will be any substantial new capital flows from America in this type of investment. As to the major developments which are now taking place in the aircraft, electronics and atomic power industries, these are almost as new to the US as to the UK, and it will be a long time before the domestic markets of the former are sufficiently exploited and the American industrialist needs to turn overseas for additional sales outlets. At the same time, it is interesting to observe that at the moment all these industries are in that phase of growth which most suits the UK's resources and capabilities and it may well be that, as the application and commercialization of their products widen, the US will assume the lead. But by a close contact between British and American firms of the kind described, the UK would be able to share in such developments right from the start.

The opportunities and prospects for further output and product diversification in the UK by US-owned firms are favourable. In most cases, the market potential satisfied by them is relatively small. As living standards improve, and the British economy develops an industrial structure similar to that of America, the share of the type of products supplied by US subsidiaries will almost certainly grow. Further, one has only to examine the advertisements of the parent companies of these concerns, e.g. in the foodstuffs, toilet preparation and household goods industries, to realize how much greater is the range of products supplied in that country as compared with that in the UK, and how promising is the scope for development in these fields also.

The volume and direction of US participation in British industry should theoretically comply with the law of comparative costs and ought in no way to contradict the proposition that each country should produce those goods and services to which its resources and capabilities are comparatively the most suited, and trade these for others for which it is least suited to produce. That US firms engaging in some activities more cheaply in the UK than their parent concerns are able to do only confirms this fact. For what in essence has happened in that the principles behind the law have been extended to cover the different *stages of the manufacturing process* as well as the *specialization of end products*. Generalizing, we might say that the UK *vis-à-vis* the US has a *relative* advantage in the discovery of new ideas and in labour intensive manufacturing activities, while the US has a *relative* advantage in the development and application of ideas up to the latter part of the production chain, and sometimes in their post-manufacturing commercialization. This means that the close association between the two countries occasioned by international investment of the kind described in this book is of mutual benefit. But this of course demands much more of the international, political and social relations of the two countries than that of the trade of goods each produced in the separate countries. It implies both an increased willingness to pool and share knowledge and information, and an acceptance of the fact that economic activity should be allocated between the two countries according to the pattern of resources and capabilities available.

The fact that the American and British economies are as *complementary* to one another as they are *competitive* needs to be better recognized and taken advantage of. Providing we can contain our own inflationary tendencies, as America's living standards further improve, there will be an inevitable tendency for her labour costs to outstrip UK labour costs, and for the proposition argued to assume even greater validity. That any move towards a closer economic association between the two countries can bring more good than harm can surely not be disputed. For if this country does not welcome American investment, other European nations will surely do so to the ultimate detriment of UK competitiveness and long-term growth.[39]

Yet some definite, clear-cut and well-defined policy, on the part of the UK authorities would seem desirable. That a selective screening of potential American investors must continue as at present and that any uncontrolled influx of capital is undesirable is hardly debatable. But once such a policy has been agreed upon, there is much to be said for a centralized and more simplified procedure of negotiation, for more aggressive and dynamic publicity, and for more careful advice as to the form which investment should take so that it can be of optimum benefit to the host country. Should, for example, the US company be encouraged to establish a new wholly-owned subsidiary, purchase outright an existing British concern or join with an existing UK firm to set up a joint enterprise – or would, in fact, a licensing agreement be the best proposition? What has the American philosophy of management to offer the particular industry in question? How far should existing subsidiaries be encouraged to finance their expansion by drawing on UK capital?

In such ways as these then, the competitiveness and industrial development of both countries may be related to the best which each has to offer. Given that the partnership is on an equal footing, and the UK is not a satellite of the US industrial machine, there is no reason why, given peace, this country should not look forward with confidence to a period of continued industrial growth and prosperity, possessed only of a healthy fear of foreign competition in her fight for world manufacturing markets.

11 Forty years on

American investment in British industry revisited

INTRODUCTION

The contents of this volume were first published by Allen & Unwin in June 1958.
As mentioned in the preface, the monograph was the outcome of a three-year
research project financed by a grant from the (UK) Board of Trade under the
Conditional Aid Scheme for the use of counterpart funds derived from US
economic aid.[1] Its purpose was to evaluate the ways in which, and the extent
to which, US direct investment in UK manufacturing industry in the mid-1950s
was helping to increase the productivity of indigenous resources and capabilities,
and the competitiveness of UK firms.

The stimulus for this study came from two sources. The first were the findings of
a series of some sixty-six studies on the comparative productivity of British and US
industries, conducted by the Anglo-American Council on Productivity (AACP)
between 1949 and 1952.[2] *Inter alia*, these studies, like those of E. Rothbarth and
Laslo Rostas in the 1940s[3] revealed that the productivity of the average US
industrial worker was universally between two and four times higher than his
UK counterpart.[4] The second was an observation, by myself, on a visit to Scotland in 1952, of a concentrated agglomeration of US manufacturing subsidiaries
within a 15-mile radius of Dundee and Glasgow, and the apparent impact such a
presence was having on the employment, productivity and exports of the region.[5]

The key question which particularly intrigued me was this:

> Given that, across the board, US-owned firms in the US were more productive
> than UK-owned firms in the UK, would this generalization still hold good if
> US-owned firms were located in the UK or UK-owned firms were located in
> the US?

In other words, was the higher productivity of US firms in the US due to the
better quality of American technology and/or management and organizational
techniques which might be readily transferred to the UK, or was it a reflection of
superior, but immobile, factor endowments and/or markets of the US economy?

In seeking an answer to this question, I distinguished between country- and
firm-specific differences in productivity, or between (what I later came to call)
location-specific and *ownership*-specific advantages facing potential foreign investors,

viz. those specific to a country or region independently of the ownership of firms, and those specific to the ownership of firms independently of their location. If, for example, most differences in Anglo-American productivity were location-specific, then, insofar as most of these were not transferable across space, Anglo-US productivity differences could be regarded as largely unavoidable. If, on the other hand, they were primarily due to the higher efficiency of US intellectual capital – including managerial capabilities – and such assets were readily transferable to the UK, then US subsidiaries would show superior performance relative to their indigenous, i.e. UK, counterparts.

It seemed to me, then, that a study of US business investment in the UK afforded a unique opportunity to put this proposition to the test; and, as described in Chapter 4 of this volume, we did our best to make productivity comparisons both between US parent firms and their UK subsidiaries, and between the US subsidiaries and their UK-owned competitors. Having demonstrated that some, at least, of the competitive advantages of US firms were transferable, we then sought to examine *which* of these were exported across the Atlantic, and *how* they were assimilated into the UK economy; and in particular, how they helped upgrade the productivity of UK resources and location-bound capabilities, and the competitiveness of UK firms.

In the final chapter of this volume, we seek to do three main things. First, we compare and contrast the level, structure and significance of US foreign direct investment (fdi) in UK manufacturing industry in the early 1990s with that of forty years ago. In the following section, we revisit some of the ideas and data presented in our earlier study, but view them through the analytical lens of contemporary scholars; in other words, had I been writing the 1958 monograph today, what changes might I wish to make? The third objective, drawing upon the data set out in the previous section, is to establish how different might be our explanations of the economic determinants and effects of US fdi in the UK in the 1990s, as compared with those put forward in the 1950s. The chapter concludes by taking an exploratory glimpse into the likely future of US participation in British industry.

'THEN' AND 'NOW': THE LEVEL, PATTERN AND SIGNIFICANCE OF US PARTICIPATION IN UK INDUSTRY

As Chapter 2 has shown, even in the mid-1950s the UK was the most popular destination for US manufacturing fdi outside Canada. In 1955, it accounted for 57.7 per cent of the stock of US fdi in Europe and 14.9 per cent of that in all countries. Although, in 1953, it was estimated that the sales of US manufacturing subsidiaries in the UK were only 4.8 per cent of all manufacturing sales, this percentage was at least double in the case of technology-intensive and branded consumer goods.

While, in the mid-1950s, most US fdi in the UK replaced imports from the US, between 35 per cent and 40 per cent of the sales of US manufacturing subsidiaries at that time were exported. In spite of quite high intra-European tariff and non-tariff barriers, the UK was regarded by US firms as a bridgehead to both Continental European and to Commonwealth markets – especially in the case of newer industrial exports.[6] The productivity (output per employee) of US manufacturing subsidiaries was estimated to be about one-third higher than that of their indigenous competitors. While, as Chapter 6 has shown, this was partly due to the concentration of US fdi in the more productive UK sectors, in each of the manufacturing sectors about which data were available, US subsidiaries outperformed their UK competitors.[7]

Table 11.1 sets out further details, and also compares and contrasts the situation in the 1950s with that of forty years later. Appendix 2 also presents some data on the role of US affiliates in the UK in the intervening period. Here we might highlight five points:

- First, the contribution of US affiliates to British manufacturing output and employment has risen significantly over the last forty years; in 1992 it stood at 8.6 per cent and 14.7 per cent respectively. At the same time, the share of the total inbound fdi stock into the UK accounted for by US direct investors has fallen from around four-fifths in the early 1950s to 41.4 per cent in 1994. This is mainly the result of a sharp growth of intra-EC fdi (under 10 per cent in 1953 to 30.9 per cent in 1994), and of Japanese fdi (from 0 per cent in 1953 to 4.5 per cent in 1994) (Central Statistical Office 1997).

- Second, the industrial distribution of the activities of US subsidiaries[8] suggests that, over the past four decades, the growth in employment has been most marked in the chemical and allied trades (especially drugs), food and drink products, instruments, electrical products, and paper products sectors; and least in the mechanical engineering, rubber goods and transportation sectors. However, relating these data to those of total UK employment suggests that, compared with 1953, the US concentration quotient has risen in nine of the twelve industrial sectors identified in Table 11.1, and has fallen in the remaining three. The representation of US affiliates is currently most marked in the chemicals, precision instruments and electrical goods sectors; and, in the 1990s, as in the 1950s and 1960s, their share of total UK production is concentrated in the high to medium knowledge-intensive sectors, and in those producing high-quality branded consumer goods.

- Third, there is some reason to suppose that, whereas in the 1950s US investors were locating their value-adding facilities in the UK to overcome barriers to exports from their US factories,[9] in the 1990s, not only are US fdi in, and US exports to, the UK complementary to, rather than substitutes for each other,[10] but a significant (and growing) proportion of UK-based activity by US firms is geared towards protecting or augmenting their core competitive advantages rather than exploiting these advantages. Earlier in this volume, we gave several examples of new knowledge passed back from the US subsidiaries to their parent companies.[11] Over the past forty years, not only has the research and development (R&D) intensity of US subsidiaries in the UK substantially increased,[12] but so has the propensity of these subsidiaries both to undertake

Table 11.1 US direct investment in UK manufacturing industry, 1953 and 1994

	1953		1994	
US direct investment stock in manufacturing ($ million)	941[1]		26,742	
% of UK GNP	(2.3)		(3.0)	
% of all US fdi stock in UK	(66.3)		(24.0)	
% of all fdi manufacturing stock in UK	(80+)		(41.4)	
% of all US fdi stock in European manufacturing	(57.7)		(24.9)	
Number of US manufacturing subsidiaries in the UK	246		624[2]	
Manufacturing sales of US subsidiaries ($ million)	1,709		96,081	
% of all manufacturing sales in UK	(4.8)		(14.7)[2]	
Manufacturing employment of US subsidiaries	262,200		374,800[2]	
% of all manufacturing employment in UK	(2.8)		(8.6)[2]	
% of manufacturing employment of US subsidiaries in Europe	(n.k.)		(26.4)	
Manufacturing exports ($ million)	660		33,000	
% of all UK manufacturing exports	(12.0)		(17.0)	
% of all manufacturing sales of US subsidiaries in UK	(38.6)		(33.8)	

Industrial distribution of employment in US subsidiaries

	%	CQ[3]	%	CQ
Chemicals and allied trades	12.7	2.23	17.8	2.48
Food, drink and tobacco	6.7	0.69	14.5	1.27
Metal manufacturing	3.4	0.52	3.4	0.32
Non-electrical and engineering	31.3	1.70	16.5	1.69
Electrical goods and machinery	5.5	1.45	8.4	1.07
Vehicles	22.7	1.77	18.9	2.18
Metal goods not otherwise specified	1.0	0.18	1.6	0.50
Precision instruments	6.6	4.13	6.5	1.82
Textiles and clothing	1.6	0.06	1.4	0.16

Table 11.1 Continued

	1953		1994	
Wood, cork, paper, etc.	1.8	0.53	7.4	0.53
Other manufacturing industries	6.7	0.48	3.7	0.25
Total manufacturing industries	100.0		100.0	

Sources: Earlier tables and references in this volume, especially Chapter 2; US Department of Commerce, *US Direct Investments Abroad*; *Benchmark Survey 1994*, Washington: US Government Printing Office 1996; Central Statistical Office (CSO), *Abstract of Statistics*, London: CSO, 1997; Central Statistical Office (CSO) *Report of the Census of Production 1992*, *Business Monitor P1002*, London: CSO, 1996; Central Statistical Office (UK), *Overseas Direct Investment, Business Monitor MA4*, London: CSO, 1997.
Notes:
1 1955.
2 1992.
3 CQ = US concentration quotient = the share of the total manufacturing employment accounted for by US subsidiaries in a particular sector divided by the share of total manufacturing employment accounted for by all UK firms.
n.k. = not known.

R&D on behalf of their parent companies[13] and to act as vehicle for tapping into innovatory activities undertaken by British firms. In a recent survey on the geographical origins of the competitive advantage of 144 of the world's largest industrial enterprises,[14] the UK was named as the second most important source country for augmenting managerial and technological assets. It is also worth noting that the greater part of US direct investment in the UK since the early 1980s has taken the form of acquisitions and mergers (A&Ms);[15] and that the major motive for many of these has been to acquire new sources of knowledge, and to gain access to new markets, as much as to exploit the existing stock of such knowledge and markets.

- Fourth, as in the 1950s, a substantial proportion of the output of the UK manufacturing subsidiaries of US firms is exported. In 1953, we estimated this proportion to be 38.6 per cent; and that, at that time, US subsidiaries accounted for 12.0 per cent of all UK manufacturing exports.[16] The great majority of these exports went either to the rest of Europe or to Commonwealth countries. In 1994, according to US cited in Table 11.1, UK manufacturing subsidiaries exported 27.6 per cent of their output, and accounted for 33.8 per cent of all UK manufacturing exports. No data on the imports of affiliates are available except those from the US. In 1994, these accounted for about 6 per cent of total sales, a very considerable increase on the 3–4 per cent estimated for 1954.[17]

- Fifth, there has been some geographical decentralization of intra-UK inward fdi since the mid-1950s. In 1953, 57.9 per cent of all the total manufacturing employment of US firms was in London and the South East and in the eastern counties of England. For *all* foreign-owned firms, the corresponding figure for

1992 was 30.9 per cent.[18] Among the regions which have attracted a larger inbound share of fdi are the North and North-West England (up from 7.1 per cent to 18.8 per cent), the Midlands (up from 10.1 per cent to 18.4 per cent) and Wales (up from 2.8 per cent to 6.5 per cent). Among the regions which have lost ground are Scotland (down from 12.1 per cent to 10.1 per cent) and the South and South-West England (down from 6.5 per cent to 5.4 per cent). However, whereas the share of employment of foreign firms in Assisted (previously Development) Areas was only slightly less than that for all UK firms (40.9 per cent compared with 43.1 per cent in 1953), that of US subsidiaries (22.0 per cent) was considerably lower than that of all UK firms (34.6 per cent). There is, indeed, some evidence that foreign firms – and particularly, in the last decade, Japanese firms – have encouraged the development of new clusters of industrial activity, especially in those regions whose development agencies have been particularly active in their marketing campaigns to attract new investment.[19]

THE DETERMINANTS AND EFFECTS OF US FDI IN UK MANUFACTURING (CIRCA 1953)

So much for some general facts and figures, the main conclusions of which are twofold: (1) the contribution of US subsidiaries and Anglo-US firms to UK manufacturing output – and particularly in the high to medium technology sectors – has continued to increase over the past forty years, but this contribution, relative to that of other foreign direct investors, is less significant than it used to be, and (2) although there has been some diversification in both the industrial structure and the locational pattern of US-owned manufacturing affiliates relative to that of indigenous UK firms, the activities of these affiliates continue to be concentrated in knowledge- and scale-intensive sectors, and in those supplying branded consumer goods with a relatively high income elasticity of demand. US subsidiaries also tend to cluster in or around large urban areas, notably London, Cardiff and Glasgow; and, more recently, Sunderland and Derby.

We now turn to consider (what we perceive to be) the main analytical thrust of our earlier research and of how, if we were writing *American Investment* today (but viewed from the perspective of the 1950s), this would be different, and of how, if we were applying our analysis to the contemporary economic and political milieu, we would wish to modify our earlier findings. In the following subsection (a) we shall consider the *determinants* of US fdi in the UK; and in subsection (b) the *effects* of US fdi on the technical and allocative efficiency of the UK manufacturing sector.

(a) Determinants

In our original study, we were not primarily concerned with the determinants of US fdi in the UK. But in our survey of its historical development, and of its industrial composition in 1953 (Chapters 1 and 2), we did consider some of the major attractions of the UK (and/or major disadvantages of the US) as a manufacturing base for supplying the UK, other European and Commonwealth markets with US goods and services.[20] Moreover, in these same chapters, and more specifically in Chapter 6 in the section entitled 'The competitive advantages of American technical expertise and management philosophy', we detailed the main competitive (later[21] to be called ownership-specific) (O) advantages of US-owned firms;[22] and the reasons – which were largely reflected in the different economic environments of the US and the UK – why this was so.[23]

The kind of country (viz. US)-specific competitive or O advantages we identified in the mid-1950s are documented in several places in this volume.[24] We would like to reiterate here just four of the more important of these advantages:

1 American representation (in the UK) is highly concentrated in the 'newer' – though not 'brand new' – British industries. Yet, though new to this country, most of the industries concerned had been previously well established in the United States. In the main, they embrace technologies, trades and skills which, if not discovered by, were first exploited on any scale in, the United States, and/ or those which the comparative advantage of production in the past – if not at present – has favoured that country (pp. 52–3).

2 With one or two minor exceptions, all subsidiaries and Anglo-American concerns are able to draw upon the research and development output and facilities of their US associates, and this gives them an important advantage over most of their native competitors. To the extent that an American subsidiary can freely draw upon such knowledge and in most cases adapt it to the specialized needs of the markets it services and with little difficulty, it is afforded a vital competitive advantage – an advantage which is further underlined by the fact that it is also able to send back to the parent company any ideas for experimentation, development or commercialization (pp. 122–3).

3 The manufacturing expertise of the parent plant available to US-affiliated concerns is, in most cases, the result of many years' accumulated learning and experience. Coupled with the fact that the economic environment in America is frequently more favourable to the development of those industries in which there is strong American representation in the UK, the gains which inward direct investment might bring are substantial. The more marked the differences between current British and American production methods, the greater the potential benefits likely to result from such associations of this kind (p. 129).

4 Because of these factors – educational, cultural and economic – it is not surprising that the United States should lead the world in the development of management techniques, and that it should have a larger measure of ability both to take decisions and to administer them more effectively. But there is also the question of the attitude towards entrepreneurship and management, the dynamism and inventiveness of which, in America, so much impressed the Productivity Teams, who strongly argued it should be emulated by British management. Even here, however, it is difficult to argue that this should always

be the case, for to benefit from a particular managerial technique it may be that a whole set of conditions have to be brought about which are not, in themselves, economically justifiable (p. 192).

In several places in our study we also acknowledged that fdi was just one way by which the competitive advantages of US firms might be channelled to the UK.[25] However, at the time, we made no attempt explicitly to identify the conditions under which fdi might be preferred to licensing and other non-equity entry modes. This point was taken up later in another of my contributions; but, even then (in 1973), it was acknowledged that, although the literature was full of examples of when licensing was likely to be preferred to fdi or exports as a means of exploiting foreign markets, there was 'little systematic attempt to formalize these into a theory of marketing'.[26]

If I were writing *American Investment* today, the main change I would make is to give its contents a more formal analytical framework. As might be expected, I would use that of the eclectic, or OLI, paradigm of international production, as set out in various of my recent writings,[27] and also in a study of Japanese fdi in UK manufacturing industry conducted in the early 1980s.[28]

In brief, the eclectic paradigm asserts that the participation of firms from one country in the value-adding activities of another country is determined by:

(i)   the extent and characteristics of the competitive or *ownership* (O)-specific advantages of the investing (or potentially investing) firms, relative to those headquartered in the recipient or host country;

(ii) the *locational* (L) attractions of the recipient country, relative to those other countries – including the investing country – especially in respect of the value-added activities necessary to optimize the economic rent on the O-specific advantages of the investing firms;

(iii) the extent to which it is in the best interests of the foreign firm to *internalize* (I) the cross-border market for its O-specific tangible and intangible assets, rather than choose another organizational mode, e.g. licensing, management contracts, franchising, etc., by which these assets, or the rights to their use, are transferred; or by which their value may be protected or augmented.

The paradigm further asserts that the structure of the OLI advantages facing a particular firm will vary according to a number of contextual variables, including the nature of the value-added activities of the firm, its country of origin, and a range of firm-specific characteristics, such as age, size and strategic focus, and its relation to its competitors or potential competitors.[29] The determinants of fdi will also vary according to the *raison d'être* for such investments. Is it, for example, primarily intended to supply products for sale in local or adjacent markets? Or is it seeking a secure supply of natural resources or to take advantage of lower real labour costs? Or is its purpose to rationalize or restructure its portfolio of existing foreign assets, or to augment the firm's global competitive advantages – so-called strategic assets-seeking fdi?

Table 11.2 Some determinants of US direct investment in UK manufacturing industry: the early 1950s and the mid-1990s

			In early 1950s	*In mid-1990s*
1		O-specific advantages (of the investing firms)	(a) * Manufacturing techniques and marketing experience of US parent companies	As (a) to (d) in early 1950s
(i)		Property right and/ or intangible asset advantage (Oa)	(b) * Access to US product and production technology; and innovatory capacity	(e) Knowledge gained about the UK (and other European) commercial and legal infrastructure, supply and marketing conditions; human resource management, consumer culture, and government policies and regulations
			(c) * Access to US managerial philosophy, attitudes and techniques; and 'bank' of human learning, expertise and experience	(f) Ability to identify, access and harness resources from throughout the world; and capability to reconcile global market needs with those of particular regional and national markets
			(d) * Privileged possession of patents, trade-marks and/ or brandnames	
(ii)		Advantages of common governance, learning experiences, and organiz-ational competence (Ot)	(a) * Those that branch plants of established enterprises enjoy c.f. *de novo* firms, e.g. those associated with size, economies of scope, spreading of overhead costs and product diversification of parent companies; those which allow affiliates access to resources and experience of parent companies at marginal cost; and synergistic economies (not only in production, but in R&D purchasing, marketing and finance)	As (a) in early 1950s
				(b) Those which specifically result from the multinationality of a company. Multinationality enhances the operational flexibility of the investing firms by offering (a) wider opportunities for arbitraging, production shifting and global sourcing of inputs, (b) more favoured access to and/or better knowledge about international markets, e.g. for information, finance, labour, etc., (c) an ability (i) to take advantage of geographic differences in factor endowments, government intervention, markets, etc.; and (ii) diversified or reduced risks, e.g., in different currency areas, and creation of options and/ or political and cultural scenarios, (d) an ability to learn from societal differences in organizational and managerial processes and systems, and (e) opportunities to balance the economies of integration and a speedy response to changes in country-specific needs and advantages

Table 11.2 Continued

	In early 1950s	*In mid-1990s*
		(c) Those which arise from co-ordinating the firm's Oa advantages with those of other firms, and achieving an optimum profile of L-specific assets. Such co-ordination embraces cross-border vertical and horizontal strategic alliances (e.g. with suppliers and competitors) and networks of similar firms; it also includes the ability of firms to recognize whether and when they need to augment or use their own O-specific advantages with those of the immobile assets located in foreign countries

2 Location-specific advantages (of the UK, relative to other locations, for value-added activities of US-owned firms)	(a) * Tariff and non-tariff barriers (both to US exports to Europe and intra-European trade)
	
	(b) * Exchange controls
	
	(c) * Limitations on dividend, remission and capital repatriation
	
	(d) * Transatlantic transport and communication costs
	
	(e) * Real production costs (including labour, material costs, etc.)
	
	(f) * Domestic market size and growth potential
	
	(g) * Government economic policies
	   (i) general
	   (ii) specific to inbound fdi
	
	(h) Costs of setting up and organizing and monitoring a foreign value-adding operation
	
	(i) * Presence of related firms, including other foreign affiliates
		As (d), (e) and (h) in early 1950s
		
		(j) Quality of human and physical infrastructure
		
		(k) Exchange rates
		
		(l) Availability of complementary assets (e.g. supplier capability, local technological base agglomeration economies)
		
		(m) Investment incentives (offered by both national and sub-national governments in Europe)
		
		(n) Need to acquire or tap into the O advantages of European firms, especially in knowledge-intensive sectors

Table 11.2 Continued

	In early 1950s	In mid-1990s
3 Internalization incentive advantages (of the investing firms or potential investors)	(a) Avoidance of search and negotiating costs (b) To avoid costs of moral hazard, information asymmetries and adverse selection; and to protect reputation of internalizing firm (c) * To avoid cost of broken contracts and ensuing litigation (d) Buyer uncertainty (about nature and value of inputs (e.g. technology) being sold) (e) When market does not permit price discrimination (f) * Need of seller to protect quality of intermediate or final products (g) To capture economies of interdependent activities (see b below) (h) To compensate for absence of future markets (i) To avoid or exploit government intervention (e.g. quotas, tariffs, price controls, tax differences, etc.) (j) * To control supplies and conditions of sale of inputs (including technology) (k) To control market outlets (including those which might be used by competitors) (l) To be able to engage in practices, e.g. cross-subsidization, predatory pricing, leads and lags, transfer pricing, etc. as competitive (or anti-competitive) strategies	As in early 1950s, but (f), (j), (k) and (l) are relatively more significant today than they were in the 1950s (m) While, in some cases, time-limited inter-firm co-operative relationships may be a substitute for fdi in others, they may add to the I-incentive advantages of the participating firms. R&D alliances may help strengthen the overall competitiveness of the participating firms. In addition, the growing structural integration of the world economy is requiring firms to go outside their immediate boundaries to capture the complex realities of know-how creation and knowledge exchange, particularly where intangible assets are tacit, and there is a need to speedily adapt competitive-enhancing strategies to structural change (n) Alliances or network-related advantages are those which prompt a 'voice' rather than an 'exit' response to market failure; they also allow many of the advantages of internalization without the inflexibility, bureaucratic or risk-related costs associated with it. Such quasi-internalization is likely to be most successful in cultures in which trust, forbearance, reciprocity and consensus politics are highly valued

Notes:
* Indicates those advantages identified in *American Investment*.

Table 11.2 uses this framework to explain US fdi in UK manufacturing industry in the 1950s. Before commenting on this table, we would observe that, at that time, the great majority of inbound US investment was of a market-seeking variety. However, in choosing the UK rather than some other European country as a location for production – particularly when it was intended to supply the European market as a whole – supply side considerations – notably input costs and culture/psychic distance variables, e.g. language, business customs, etc. – played a critical role. But generally, because of trade barriers, there was little efficiency-seeking, i.e. rationalized, US investment in Europe; nor, except perhaps in the pharmaceutical industry,[30] was there any explicit attempt by US firms to augment their existing O-specific advantages by tapping into European intellectual or physical capital.

In Table 11.2, in column 1, we have asterisked the kind of country- and firm-specific O and L advantages identified in this volume.[31] Those not asterisked are those which scholars, over the last four decades, have identified as being significant determinants of fdi by market-seeking MNEs – and particularly US MNEs. It is to be noted that the OLI variables thought to influence other kinds of contemporary fdi, e.g. that of a strategic asset-seeking kind, are included. The components of column 2 of Table 11.2 are explained in a later section of this chapter.

The obvious lacunae of our original study in identifying the determinants of fdi was that it did not explain – indeed, it did not seek to explain – why, given the O advantages of the investing or potential investing US firms, and the L advantages of the UK as a production outlet relative to those of the US firms, should choose to internalize the transatlantic market for these assets, rather than engage in licensing, technical service, franchising, subcontracting or other non-equity arrangements with UK firms. Contemporary theory would suggest that this was because the transaction and co-ordinating costs of using the cross-border intermediate product market for the transfer of technology and other intangible assets were greater than those associated with their transfer and usage within the firm possessing these advantages.[32]

A contemporary reading of the findings of our 1958 study suggests that the costs associated with the transfer of intangible assets between independent US and UK firms in the early 1950s were five-fold. These were:

1 search and negotiating costs prior to the transatlantic transfer of intangible assets or rights to assets,
2 the need to protect the quality of intermediate or final products arising from these assets,
3 the costs of moral hazard and adverse selection,
4 the absence, or inadequacy, of futures markets, and
5 some degree of buyer uncertainty, e.g. about the value of the technology being sold.

In the absence of these and other market-related transaction costs identified in Table 11.2, it is probably that US fdi in the UK would have been less, and licensing and other non-equity agreements between US and UK firms more in the 1950s.

In summary, in the 1950s, the main determinants of US fdi in UK manufacturing industry were, first, the privileged possession of US-specific intangible assets – and particularly technology, managerial expertise and marketing skills; second, the (perceived) lower production and/or transfer costs of adding value to these assets in the UK rather than in the US or elsewhere; and third, the belief by US producers that, due to the (perceived) high transaction and co-ordinating costs of using the transatlantic market for the direct sale of these assets, or the right to their use to UK firms, they could more profitably exploit these by establishing their own production facilities in the UK.

(b) Effects

Forty years ago, we were primarily interested in identifying:

(1) the extent to which the kind of competitive or O advantages of US firms earlier identified by the Graham Hutton and the Anglo-American Productivity Teams could be economically transplanted to the UK, and (2) how far such advantages have helped upgrade and raise the productivity of US subsidiaries as compared with that of both their parent companies and their UK competitors.

On the first point we concluded (on p. 112) that:

> the labour efficiency of (US) branch plants approaches closely to that of their parent concerns. This being so, assuming the order of our productivity estimates (based on data published by the US subsidiaries) to be substantially correct, they would suggest that it is possible for British firms in like industries to reach a plant productivity at least three-quarters of their American counterparts.

At the same time, we also found that a number of indices[33] suggested that US subsidiaries in the UK turned in better performances than their indigenous competitors. Indeed, we averred (on p. 138) that

> the evidence, such as it is, would strongly suggest that the US affiliates are more efficient than their competitors – and particularly so in the foodstuff, tools and cutlery and pharmaceutical industries. (Overall), in only six cases out of fifty-five[34] are there indications to the contrary.

We would, then, conclude that, bearing in mind that the Anglo-American team studies showed that UK industrial productivity was one-half or less than that of its US counterpart, it would seem that many of the competitive advantages of US firms are not US bound in their usage, but can be successfully transferred to a UK location. Furthermore, were we writing *American Investment* today, it is unlikely we would adopt a different methodological approach, except, perhaps, to extend our productivity measure[35] to embrace an index of total factor productivity, and to consider value-added as well as net selling value (i.e. sales) as our measure of output.[36]

As to the impact of US direct investment on UK industrial productivity, we believe the methodology we adopted in the 1950s holds good today, although later econometric studies by Steve Globerman, the present author and Stephen Davies and David Petts (on the comparative structure and efficiency of US subsidiaries in the UK and that of their indigenous competitors), and work by Magnus Blomstrom and UNCTAD on the spillover effects of fdi on the economies of other countries, has added more rigour to that methodology.[37]

In our 1958 study, the main approach we used for evaluating the economic effects of US direct investment was to distinguish between (a) the direct contribution of US affiliates to *technical* and *allocative* efficiency by comparing the performance of US affiliates with that of their UK competitors *in a given sector*, and also the *industrial structure* of their activities, and (b) the 'spillover' effects of these activities on the productivity of their UK competitors, suppliers and customers.

On (a), as indicated earlier (p. 251 of this chapter), we calculated US concentration quotients[38] for each of the main manufacturing sectors. However, it was not until later[39] that we were able to make these comparisons at a three-digit sic[40] level, and to relate the coefficients to a variety of measures of technical and allocative efficiency. *Inter alia*, these data, based on a follow-up survey by the author, of US direct investment in UK manufacturing, showed that, in all but one of thirty-seven sectors identified, US firms recorded a higher total factor productivity than all UK firms (including US subsidiaries), while 72.1 per cent of the sales of US affiliates (cf. 48.5 per cent of all UK firms) was concentrated in sectors recording an above-average growth in output between 1958 and 1970. And it was not until our 1985 monograph,[41] that we were able to do any econometric analysis on these and related variables, but, had such techniques (and data) been at our disposal in the 1950s, we believe they would have yielded similar (albeit statistically more refined) results to those which we obtained.

On the spillover effects of US fdi, the findings set out in earlier chapters of this volume are largely qualitative, and based upon surveys and/or interviews with competitors, suppliers and competitors. A taste of these findings are set out in some quotes in Chapters 6–8, which have been echoed and re-echoed throughout the past forty years by scholars using more rigorous investigative techniques than those available in the 1950s.

If I were writing *American Investment* today, I would make only two modifications to my analysis. The first is that I would set it more systematically within the framework of the eclectic paradigm, and then formulate more specific hypotheses which are both quantifiably and qualitatively testable, about the likely impact of inbound fdi on the efficiency of related firms in the host country. The second modification is that I would give more attention to the contextual variables likely to influence the impact of US fdi in the UK.

During the 1960s and 1970s, a whole range of country-, industry- and firm-specific studies have attempted to do just this. The consensus of the great majority of those[42] is that the contribution of fdi to the upgrading and increased productivity of the host country's resources and firms is strongly conditional on the motives for the investment, the size, nationality and degree of multinationality of the investing companies, the human and physical infrastructure and market structure of the host country, the form of entry by the foreign affiliate, the nature of the products, the characteristics of related firms (e.g. competitors, suppliers, etc.), and the entrepreneurial ethos and strategies of both the investing companies and indigenous competitors in the host country. Most of these follow-up studies, indeed, have tried to evaluate how one or other (or a group) of these variables influences the economic impact of inbound fdi, and of how (host) government actions may either hinder or assist the efficient transmission and absorption of the O-specific advantages of foreign firms.

In summary, over the past four decades there have been a plethora of empirical studies on the determinants and effects of fdi, viewed from the perspective of host countries. In addition, statistical data and information about individual firms and industries – especially that unearthed by business historians – have improved considerably.[43] We believe that applying contemporary analytical tools on fdi-related issues to the situation in the 1950s would not dramatically alter our findings, but what it would do is to give it a sounder theoretical base, and to enable a range of firm-, sector- and country-specific issues to be explored more rigorously and with greater accuracy.

THE DETERMINANTS AND EFFECTS OF US FDI IN UK MANUFACTURING (CIRCA 1993)

The next part of this chapter considers the contemporary situation of US fdi in UK manufacturing, and asks how its determinants and effects differ from that described in the previous section. Or, put another way, if I were writing a study of US fdi in the mid-1990s, what changes would I make to the contents of this volume?

A clue to the answer to this question is given in my approach to explaining the reasons for, and consequences of, Japanese fdi in UK manufacturing industry in the 1970s and 1980s.[44] Here, I explicitly used the eclectic paradigm, first put forward in 1976, as my conceptual framework, and I believe this, suitably modified to take account of the changing world economic scenario – and particularly the emergence of alliance capitalism in the last decade or so –[45] would serve as a useful starting point.[46]

Rather than set out the current tenets of the eclectic paradigm, let me indicate some of the critical changes which have occurred in the motivation and/or characteristics of inbound (and particularly US) fdi into the UK over the past four decades, and which might be expected to affect the determinants and effects of such investment.

I would highlight three such changes:

1 The degree of multinationality of most of the leading US investors in the UK – and especially their participation in other European countries – has greatly increased since the mid-1950s, as, indeed, has the range of products supplied by them. This, together with the trend towards deeper European economic

integration, has caused US MNEs increasingly to adopt an efficiency-seeking or rationalized strategy towards their European manufacturing operations in place of the 'stand alone' or multi-domestic strategies they pursued in the 1950s. These factors, in turn, have led to the emergence of a new set of firm-specific competitive advantages, which primarily reflect the ability of investing firms to co-ordinate multiple activities in multiple locations – or what, in our various writings, have been termed transaction cost-minimizing O advantages (O_t).[47] Many of these advantages can *only* be fully realized through fdi, though it would appear that at least some economies of scale, scope, common governance and knowledge-sharing are being achieved through a variety of co-operative agreements, including strategic alliances and inter-firm networks.

2 Since the early 1980s, acquisitions and mergers (A&Ms) have become an important modality of MNE activity. Between 1985 and 1994 they are believed to have accounted for betwen 50 per cent and 60 per cent of all new foreign direct investment.[48] In analysing the reasons for these A&Ms, it is clear that many were motivated not so much to exploit existing O-specific advantages as to protect and/ or augment such advantages. There is, indeed, a good deal of other evidence to support this view. According, for example, to a survey of 144 of the world's largest industrial companies in 1994/5, a substantial proportion (upwards of one-third – and over one-half in the case of the most multinational of firms) of their technology-based competitive advantages were perceived to be derived directly as a result of their foreign-based activities.[49] Scholars are also generally agreed that the pace of technological development and the globalization of markets has compelled large and medium-sized firms – particularly in knowledge-intensive industries – to conclude cross-border A&Ms and strategic alliances, both to capture various economies of synergy, and to truncate the research and development time for innovations. The implication of these, and other features of alliance capitalism, is that not only do MNEs need O-specific advantages to penetrate international markets, but, to utilize these profitably, they also need to gain access to a variety of complementary assets, both owned by indigenous firms and those more generally available, but location-bound (e.g. human and physical infrastructure), in foreign countries.

3 Third, there is increasing evidence that the foreign activities of MNEs are becoming more embedded in many host countries. As Chapter 6 has shown, in 1953, 77 of the 205 US subsidiaries in the UK had been established for 24 years or more and 64 per cent undertook some form of R&D.[50] But, in general, the innovatory activities of US MNEs were confined to their home countries. For example, only 6.5 per cent of the R&D expenditures by US MNEs were undertaken outside the US, while over the period 1969–1972, the patents registered by US firms in the US attributable to research carried out in foreign locations was 5.0 per cent. Throughout the 1970s, these figures increased only marginally, but the latest statistics (1994 for R&D expenditures and 1991–5 for patents) give respective proportions of 13.2 per cent and 8.6 per cent.[51] Data on the location of innovatory activities of MNEs from France, Germany, the Netherlands and the UK point to broadly comparable trends.[52] We conclude that while the

globalization and/or rationalization of R&D activities remains well below that of other value-added activities of MNEs,[53] it is rising quite speedily.

These (and other) changes in the world economic scenario have caused scholars (including myself) to reappraise their theorizing on the reasons for international business activities and their consequences for host countries. However, to the best of our knowledge, there has not been any systematic attempt to evaluate the ways in which US fdi in the UK has been affected by these changes.[54] While such a task is well beyond the scope of this chapter, it is possible to identify some of the ways in which the configuration of OLI advantages facing US and other foreign investors in the 1990s is different from that in the 1950s; and of how these differences have affected both the structure and the impact of US fdi in the UK manufacturing sector.

The second column of Table 11.2 sets out the main OLI advantages in respect of the three main types of US fdi in UK manufacturing industry, viz. market seeking, efficiency seeking and strategic asset seeking, in the 1990s. Compared with those listed in the first column, we see four main differences.

1 Knowledge-based O_a advantages and most kinds of O_t advantages have become more important components of the core competencies of US foreign investors (or potential investors) relative to those O_a advantages most prevalent in the 1950s. In general, the former advantages are less *country* (US)-specific and more *firm*-specific than the latter. They also tend to reflect the degree of multi-nationality of the investing firms as much as, or more than, their country of ownership.

2 The value of the core competencies of particular investing firms are increasingly influenced by their ease of access to complementary assets of foreign firms or public authorities, and their ability to co-ordinate these efficiently with their own O-specific advantages.

3 The location (L) attractions of countries to mobile investors is increasingly viewed by the latter in terms of the ability of indigenous firms and governments to offer the kinds of human and physical infrastructure and other support facilities necessary for their O-specific advantages to be efficiently exploited.

4 There have been a number of changes in the factors influencing foreign entry modes by firms, and particularly the choice between cross-border licensing (and other non-equity agreements) and fdi. On the one hand, transport and communication advances have reduced some transaction and co-ordination costs of cross-border markets.[55] On the other, the intra-firm benefits derived from effectively co-ordinating the use of multiple assets – both external and internal to the firm – in different locations have risen as the world economy has become technologically and organizationally more complex.

These differences in the OLI characteristics of firms would suggest a rather different structure of inbound fdi in the UK in the 1990s, relative to that in the 1950s. They also suggest that home countries which are more successful in generating the conditions for their MNEs to be successful organizers of multiple economic activities and co-ordinators of disparate assets (including those which are culture-specific) are those likely to be the most successful foreign investors in the late twentieth century.

Japan is often cited as a country which offers its corporations a supportive infrastructure and a competitive ethos well suited to the needs of global investors. To what extent this is the case is not for this chapter to consider, but there can be little doubt that, in some sectors – notably autos and consumer electronics – Japanese foreign direct investors have taken some UK and European markets away from US subsidiaries over the past two decades. This, together with the growth of intra-European Union (Community) fdi following the completion of the European Internal Market, is the main reason why the US share of the foreign direct investment stock in the UK fell from 74.1 per cent in 1962 to 41.4 per cent in 1993.

An analysis of the published statistics of US fdi in UK manufacturing industry gives little hint of the changing rationale behind such investment. Such evidence as we have mainly comes from a variety of academic and business surveys conducted on both sides of the Atlantic; and from the records of the Invest in Britain Bureau[56] and various regional development agencies. Most of this, though fragmentary, does point to a reconfiguration in the perception of US investors as to their locational needs, which, itself, partly reflects the changing character of their O-specific advantages, and partly the benefits to be derived from internalizing the transatlantic market for (some) intangible assets as compared to selling these (or their rights) to independent UK firms. One fairly clear conclusion from these surveys, and from the actions of individual US and other investors, is that, in the emerging knowledge-based globalizing economy, firms increasingly view their core competencies as their ability to create, harness and effectively utilize technological and human assets drawn from multiple geographical sources. Moreover, in looking both for the most appropriate ways to achieve this goal and for the right location to undertake value-added activities pursuant to it, they seek the external assets which, when combined with their own, will help them to augment and deploy their resources in the most cost-effective manner.

It would seem, too, that over the last forty years, there has been some convergence in the structure of the value-adding activities of US manufacturing subsidiaries and that of their UK competitors. Partly, this reflects the response of UK firms to the example and stimulus of past inbound US investment,[57] and partly the fact that in the 1990s the main UK competitors to US subsidiaries are, themselves, among the leading global players and have to meet similar demands in the international marketplace. Indeed, we would suggest that it is the *degree* of multinationality rather than *nationality* of ownership which is becoming the main distinguishing feature between large firms in internationally oriented sectors. If this is the case, then *industry-* and *country*-specific factors in determining differences in the pattern of O and L advantage between foreign-owned and domestic firms are becoming less important, and firm-specific factors increasingly so.

Similar considerations are apt to apply to the likely impact of inbound US investment on the UK economy. In a very real sense, the wheel has turned full circle over the last four decades. In the 1950s, the main focus of attention was on contribution to raising the productivity of UK resources and firms – which is exactly the same as it is in the mid-1990s, except that the word 'competitiveness' has replaced the word 'productivity'. And for the most part, too, the factors contributing to the upgrading of productivity are the same today as they were in the 1950s, and are well described in UNCTAD's *World Investment Report* for 1995.

However, two distinctive features of the way in which the O advantages of US firms (via their UK subsidiaries) interface with, and affect, the L advantages of the UK and the O advantages of UK firms in the 1990s are worthy of note. The first is – and this follows the observation made a little earlier in the chapter – that the intangible assets and other O advantages specific to US MNEs are now increasingly the outcome of their global, as distinct from their home-based, activities (e.g. harnessing of global technology, human resources, access to foreign markets, etc.). In other words, US affiliates which are part of an integrated global or regional strategy operated by their parent companies are likely to have a rather different impact on the host countries in which they operate than those which are part of MNEs which pursue an 'every tub on its bottom' strategy. The second is that the advantages associated with the acquisition and efficient co-ordination of diverse assets sited in multiple locations, and the efficient search for, and exploitation of, new markets reflect those associated with a more knowledge-based and dynamic world economy than that which existed in the 1950s.

If I were then preparing a study of the contemporary impact of US direct investment on the productivity of the UK economy, I would take account of these additional elements of MNE activity, which, in the main, reflect the contemporary world economy. I would also need to give more attention to the implications of the growth of non-equity strategic alliances; and how, in particular, these affect the core competencies of the investing firms and the kind of locational attractions necessary to create and exploit these competencies, which are specifically germane to the upgrading of the innovatory capabilities of the UK economy. Such attractions include the formation and growth of sub-national spatial clusters of related value activities.[58]

A GLIMPSE INTO THE FUTURE

Although, over the past forty years, the share of UK manufacturing output accounted for by US subsidiaries has continued to rise – albeit at a much slower rate since the mid-1970s – several of the unique characteristics of US direct investment described in this volume have evaporated. This is mainly because the kind of O-specific advantages ascribed to US subsidiaries have been assimilated by UK and other foreign firms producing in the UK; and, that contemporary 'best practice' manufacturing, managerial and marketing techniques are fairly standardized practices among the most efficient firms, whatever their nationality. Indeed, names of US subsidiaries, which in the 1950s were recognized as being distinctly American, are now predominantly thought of as British – or at least an integral part of the Britich industrial scene. Moreover, as more firms compete in the global marketplace, almost inevitably there is a convergence in cross-border competitive advantages which reduces the significance of nationality of ownership as a variable affecting competitiveness. Indeed, as we have argued elsewhere,[59] in the 1990s the extent and character of a firm's multinationality might be a more significant determinant of its competitiveness than its country of ownership.

We would not, however, want to press this point too far. Among 'best practice' firms, there continues to be at least some of those attributes which reflect their country of ownership. National innovatory systems, for example, are not irrelevant in explaining why firms from some countries and in some sectors are more successful innovators. The business culture in Japan and other Asian countries continues to offer the MNEs from these countries considerable transaction-related advantages in the emerging age of alliance capitalism, *vis-à-vis* their Western counterparts. That these country-specific advantages will continue to be of some importance – especially in cutting-edge technologies, and in human resource management – we have no doubt; but we do not believe these will be the critical O-specific advantages of foreign (including) US firms in the future.

All this should not be taken to mean that the UK will not continue to welcome US direct investment as it has done in the past; but this will primarily be because of the added source of firm-specific created assets and markets it brings rather than those which reflect the national resource endowments of the US economy. Nor should it be inferred that investors will not find the UK an attractive location in which to engage in value-added activities. But, like other mobile investors, including UK-owned firms, they will only invest in the UK relative to other countries (particularly European countries) if they perceive it is in their best interests to do so; and it is our opinion that the economic demands of potential investors in the global economy of the 1990s are much more stringent than they were in the 1950s.

Relative to that of other foreign-owned firms, we foresee a further fall in the participation of US investment in UK industry in the years ahead. By contrast, we envisage a major increase in the share of Japanese investment and that from other Asian developing countries, and a modest rise in intra-European fdi. It is, perhaps, worth observing that, in stark contrast to their Japanese counterparts, the share of the global sales of US MNEs accounted for by their foreign affiliates has remained fairly constant over the past decade.[60] We think this might increase marginally in the next decade in the faster growing developing countries, and perhaps also in Japan, but only if the rate of European economic growth were to exceed that of the US (which, at the moment, seems improbable) would the European share of the global sales of US foreign direct investors seem likely to rise.

Are US MNEs likely to give (relatively) more attention to the European market? Over the past three decades, US participation in UK industry has grown from adolescence to maturity. This, however, is not to say there are no opportunities for the UK to divert new US investment away from the European mainland to supply the European market. (Of course, the reverse could also happen!) But, in general, and except in the short run, we do not see substantial gains arising from intra-EU investment diversion. It is true that Britain's future stance on European Monetary Union (EMU) could be a critical factor here. Most (but not all) US MNEs the UK's entry into the EMU, partly because it would lower the transaction costs of doing intra-EU business, but mostly because they perceive (rightly or wrongly) that, by remaining outside the EMU, the UK would lose many of its competitive advantages relative to those of its Continental European rivals. Whether or not this is a correct assessment depends on the extent to which, by joining the EMU, the UK would have to commit herself to other economic and social policies of the EU, e.g. the social chapter, which might raise the production and/or transaction costs of her firms.

It is a fact that the completion of the European Internal Market Programme (IMP) has affected some industrial sectors more than others. Moreover, the evidence[61] suggests that not only has the UK been one of the chief gainers of inward fdi as a consequence of the IMP,[62] but that this gain has been concentrated in sectors in which the UK already had a comparative advantage.[63] Moreover, it is in these same sectors where it is most likely that the reduction in transaction costs and the gains to be derived from intra-EU rationalized production will outweigh any additional costs following the adherence to European labour and other standards. In any case, the consensus among the more efficient US MNEs (as, indeed, among their UK and European counterparts) is that they are already providing the wages and working conditions well in excess of the minimum laid down by the European social chapter. And, certainly, the UK's environmental standards match up well to their major competitors for US investment on the Continent.

What does all this imply concerning policy towards inward direct investment? In the 1950s, I was advocating a constructive and liberal approach, and have continued to do so in my various writings over the last forty years. However, I have also come to appreciate the critical role of national governments in setting the right economic and political climate for inbound MNE activity. This they may do by reducing information asymmetries and uncertainties; by fostering the right ethos for entrepreneurship and competitiveness among their national constituents; by ensuring, through appropriate macro-economic and micro-management policies that the market system works as efficiently and fairly as it can. It is surely no coincidence that since the early 1980s, when market-oriented policies were vigorously pursued by the Conservative government – and, in the 1990s, are essentially being largely replicated by the Labour government – that the UK has become such a favoured European location for inbound (including US) investment.[64]

At the same time, recent surveys[65] have shown that mobile investors are increasingly preferring to locate their activities in countries or regions which not only provide the right fiscal and other incentives but offer the kind of location-bound real resources which the firms need if they are efficiently to exploit, and/or complement, their own O-specific advantages. Countries and regions which are successful in promoting their *distinctive* locational advantages are likely to be those most attractive to inward direct investment. It is, then, no longer sufficient for the UK just to provide a first-rate physical infrastructure and educational facilities. It also needs to evolve a portfolio of customized assets which are not possessed by its competitors and not easily imitable by them.[66]

Such advantages may embrace a whole set of market-facilitating actions designed to promote the static and dynamic efficiency of the private sector; but again it is not accidental that those countries (or regions within countries) which have been the most successful in attracting mobile investment are those which promote and publicize their competitive advantages the most aggressively, and which offer inward innovators informative 'hassle-free' and speedy administrative procedures.[67] In this respect, the setting up of the Invest in Britain Bureau in 1977 was an important step forward in the UK's efforts to upgrade its profile to foreign investors; and, as location decisions are increasingly being taken at a sub-national, i.e. micro-regional level, the incentives offered by regional authorities are no less important. Here, of course, national governments have to draw a fine line between encouraging inter-regional competition, while avoiding wasteful locational tournaments between the regions within their jurisdiction.

We would make one final point. In Chapter 11 of this book, and in a later study, we have made some reference to US firms investing in the UK to gain access to UK technology and certain types of professional and skilled labour. Such asset-seeking investment, particularly among advanced industrialized countries, has become much more common in recent years. It certainly explains a good deal of the acquisition of US firms by European investors over the last decade. As and when the UK increases her competitiveness, one might expect rather more of this type of US direct investment. As argued in my 1970 volume,[68] I do not believe one should be unduly concerned about this kind of inward investment, partly because it is a two-way phenomenon, and partly because the evidence suggests that, far from exporting technology from the UK, inbound investors are helping to build up the UK's innovatory capabilities – particularly *vis-à-vis* their Continental European competitors.[69] Finally, in judging the economic merits of any acquisition, its price should reflect its true social worth and this should include, *inter alia*, any future costs and benefits directly resulting from the acquisition.[70]

CONCLUSIONS

As might be expected, there are many similarities between the structure of US fdi in the UK manufacturing sector, its determinants and its consequences for UK industrial productivity in the 1950s and 1990s. But there are some noticeable differences, which are the result, first, of changing economic circumstances – notably that of technological advances and the liberalization of markets – and second, the emergence of new analytical tools available to international business scholars, business historians and geographers. In conclusion, let us summarize four of the more important of these.

1 Though US subsidiaries now account for a larger share of total UK manufacturing output than they did in the 1950s, their share of the contribution of all foreign firms has fallen quite significantly.

2 Any contemporary explanation of US fdi in the 1950s would benefit from a more rigorous analytical base than was available to scholars (or at least than the one I adopted!) at that time.

3 In the UK in the 1990s, compared with in the 1950s, the extent and configuration of OLI advantages facing foreign firms (*vis-à-vis* their indigenous competitors) has undergone a number of changes as a result of the emergence of alliance capitalism and the knowledge-based economy, and of the growing multinationalization of the leading foreign direct investors. *Inter alia*, this has led to more strategic asset-seeking fdi and cross-border co-operative ventures by US firms, and a different set of locational needs by them. More particularly, O advantages which relate to the economies of common governance and the efficient co-ordination of a diverse portfolio of international activities have become more important. At the same time, non-equity co-operative ventures between US firms and their UK competitors, suppliers and customers, have helped complement fdi as a critical avenue for both gaining and exploiting firm-specific advantages.

4 From a policy perspective, there is less reason in the 1990s for US foreign direct investors in the UK to be favoured or discriminated against *vis-à-vis* their indigenous competitors than there was in the 1950s. In today's more liberalized market economy, UK economic policy[71] should be principally directed to providing the right kind of macro-organizational environment so that (a) the kind of inbound fdi most conducive to advancing the long-term and dynamic comparative advantage of the UK can be attracted to the UK and (b) that it should have the greatest net benefit[72] in promoting the upgrading of domestic resources and capabilities, and the competitiveness of UK firms.

In conclusion, we would emphasize that this chapter has not attempted to present a developmental view of US fdi in the UK since the 1950s or to trace the main landmarks in its recent economic history. However, the tables presented in Appendix 3 do give the reader a sense of what has happened over this period, and particularly the significance of US manufacturing subsidiaries relative to that of other foreign firms and of indigenous UK companies. It also sets out the changing share of US fdi directed to the UK compared to that of other European countries.

Appendix 1

US affiliates known to be operating in British manufacturing industry, December 1956[1]

KEY TO FINANCIAL CLASSIFICATION

A = Fully-owned US subsidiary or branch plant (apart from qualifying shares held by UK directors).

B = Anglo-American-financed firms with 25 per cent or more of its equity share capital US-owned.

C = UK subsidiary of, or firms partially financed by, A or B above.

Name of UK company or US branch	*Financial classification (see key above)*	*Products manufactured*
A.C.-Delco Division of General Motors Ltd	A	Automobile accessories
Abbott Laboratories Ltd	A	Pharmaceuticals
Acheson Colloids Ltd	A	Colloidal graphite dispersions
Addressograph-Multigraph Ltd	A	Office machinery
Aircraft Marine Products Ltd	A	Solderless electrical terminals
Air Trainers Ltd	B	Aircrew training equipment
Akerman, Simon Ltd	A	Clothing
Aladdin Industries Ltd	B	Heating and lighting appliances
Allcock Products Ltd	B	Medicinal products
Allis-Chalmers Great Britain Ltd	A	Agricultural tractors and implements
Angier Chemical Co. Ltd	C	Medicinal products
Arabol Manufacturing Co. Ltd	A	Adhesives
Arden, Elizabeth Ltd	A	Toilet and beauty preparations
Armco Ltd	A	'Armco' ingot iron products and 'Bundy' tubing
Armour & Co. Ltd	A	Hormones
Armstrong Cork Ltd	A	Cork products

Name of UK company or US branch	*Financial classification (see key above)*	*Products manufactured*
Arrow Electric Switches Ltd	A	Electrical switchgear
Art Metal Construction Co	A	Office furniture (steel)
B. B. Chemical Co. Ltd	C	Shoe and leather dressings, industrial adhesives, etc.
Bakelite Ltd	B	Plastic materials, etc.
Baker Platinum Ltd	A	Refined platinum
Barber & Colman Ltd	B	Textile machinery
Barber Greene Olding & Co. Ltd	B	Road-making machinery and materials handling equipment
Barcley Corsets Ltd	A	Surgical and foundation garments
Barry-Wehmiller Machinery Co. Ltd	B	Brewing and bottling machinery
Bayer Products Ltd	A	Pharmaceuticals
Behr-Manning Ltd	A	Coated abrasives
Berkshire Knitting (Ulster) Ltd*	A	Hosiery and knitwear
Bird, Alfred & Sons Ltd	A	Food products
Black & Decker Ltd	A	Portable electric tools
Blaw Knox Ltd	B	Construction and earth-moving equipment
Bliss, E. W. (England) Ltd	B	Mechanical presses, rolling mill, can-making equipment
Borg-Warner Ltd	A	Power transmission chain drives, etc.
Bowater-Scott Ltd	B	Paper products
Boyle, A. S., Co. Ltd	C	Pharmaceuticals
Briggs Motor Bodies Ltd	C	Motor bodies, etc.
Brillo Mfg Co. of Great Britain Ltd	A	Steel wool
Bristol Myers Co. Ltd	A	Medicinal products and toilet preparations
British Acheson Electrodes Ltd	B	Electrodes
British American Optical Co. Ltd	A	Ophthalmic supplies
British Driver-Harris Co. Ltd	B	Nickel alloys
British Geon Ltd	B	'Geon' and 'Hycar' materials
British Jeffrey-Diamond Ltd	A	Mining machinery
British Laundry Machinery Co. Ltd	A	Laundry and dry cleaning machinery
British Miller Hydro Co. Ltd	A	Bottling machinery
British Oilfield Equipment Co. Ltd	A	Oilfield equipment

Name of UK company or US branch	Financial classification (see key above)	Products manufactured
British Oxygen Aro Equipment Ltd	A	Liquid oxygen and nitrogen equipment
British Sisalkraft Ltd	B	Reinforced waterproof building paper
British United Shoe Machinery Co. Ltd	B	Boot and shoe machinery
Brown & Polson Ltd	A	Food products
Burroughs Adding Machine Ltd	A	Office machinery
Cabot Carbon Ltd	A	Carbon black
Camp, S. H. & Co. Ltd	B	Surgical belts and supports
Carborundum Co. Ltd	A	Abrasives and refractories
Carr Fastener & Co. Ltd	B	Press and slide fasteners
Caterpillar Tractor Co. Ltd	A	Tractors and earth-moving equipment
Celotex Ltd	A	Insulating and hardboard
Cellucutton Products Ltd	A	Personal products
Champion (Scissors) Ltd	C	Scissors
Champion Sparking Plug Co. Ltd	A	Sparking plugs, etc.
Chappie Bros. Ltd	C	Canned animal food, etc.
Chemstrand Ltd*	A	Acrylic fibre
Chesebrough-Ponds Ltd	B	Proprietary articles and toilet preparations
Cincinnati Milling Machines Ltd	A	Machine tools
Clark Bros. Co.	A	Engines and compressors
Cleveland Twist Drill Co. Ltd	A	High-speed twist drills
Cobble Brothers Machinery Ltd	A	Carpet-tufting machinery
Coca-Cola Export Corporation	A	Beverages
Cocker Chemical Co. Ltd	C	Toxyphine
Colgate-Palmolive Ltd	A	Proprietary articles and toilet preparations
Colly Products Ltd	C	Cutlery ware
Columbia Ribbon & Carbon Mfng Co. Ltd	A	Inked ribbons and carbon papers
Consolidated Pneumatic Tool Co. Ltd	A	Pneumatic tools, air compressors, etc.
Construction Machinery Ltd	A	Motor graders
Crane Ltd	A	Valves, boilers and radiators
Cummins Engine Co. Ltd	A	High-speed diesel engines
Cyanamid Products Ltd	A	Pharmaceuticals
Dalex Ltd	B	Container sealing compounds

Name of UK company or US branch	Financial classification (see key above)	Products manufactured
Delco-Remy Div. of General Motors Ltd	A	Automobile accessories
Dennison Mfg Co. Ltd	A	Crepe paper, tags, etc.
Denver Chemical Mfng Co.	A	Pharmaceuticals
'Diamond H' Switches Ltd	A	Switchgear and thermostat products
Dictaphone Co. Ltd	A	Dictating and recording machines
Du Pont Co. (United Kingdom) Ltd	A	Chemical products
Durham Duplex Razor Co. Ltd	A	Safety razors and blades
Dzus Fastener Europe, Ltd	B	Metal fasteners
Eagle Pencil Co.	A	Pencils
East Anglian Engineering Co. Ltd	C	Boot and shoe machinery
Edison, Thos. A., Ltd	A	Miners' caps, lamps, etc.
Eimco (Great Britain) Ltd	A	Mining equipment
Elliott Brothers (London) Ltd	B	Industrial instruments and control gear
Emsco Engineering Co. Ltd	B	Oil-well machinery
Erie Resistor Ltd	A	Radio components
Esso Petroleum Co. Ltd	A	Petroleum products
Esterbrook-Hazell Ltd	B	Fountain pens, desk sets, etc.
Ethicon Sutures Laboratories Ltd	A	Sutures
Euclid (Great Britain) Ltd	A	Earth-moving equipment
Eutetic Welding Alloys Co. Ltd	A	Low-temperature welding alloys
Evans Chemicals Ltd	B	Medicinal products
Ever-Ready Razor Products Ltd	A	Razors and accessories
Eversharp Ltd	A	Pens and pencils
Ex-Cello-O Corp. (Machine Tools) Ltd	A	Machine tools
Factor, Max, & Co.	A	Cosmetics
Felt & Tarrant Ltd	A	Office appliances
Ferro Enamels Ltd	A	Vitreous enamels
Firestone Tyre & Rubber Co. Ltd	A	Motor tyres and accessories
Ford Motor Co. Ltd	B	Motor vehicles
Forth Chemicals Ltd	C	Styrene monomer
Foster McClellan Co.	A	Medicinal products

Name of UK company or US branch	Financial classification (see key above)	Products manufactured
Foster Wheeler Ltd	A	Marine and oil refinery equipment
Foxboro-Yoxall Ltd	B	Industrial instruments
Frigidaire Div. of General Motors Ltd	A	Refrigerating machinery
Gemec Chemical Co. (A Division of Union Carbide Ltd)	B	Chemicals
General Milk Products Ltd	A	Canned evaporated milk
Gillette Industries Ltd	A	Safety razors and blades, etc.
Goodyear Tyre & Rubber Co. (Great Britain) Ltd	A	Motor tyres and accessories
Goss Printing Press Co. Ltd	B	Printing machinery,
Grange Chemicals Ltd	B	Synthetic chemicals
Graton & Knight Ltd	A	Leather belting, etc.
Gray, Dorothy, Ltd	A	Beauty preparations
Hardinge Machine Tools Ltd	B	Machine tools
Hedley, Thomas & Co. Ltd	A	Soap products
Heinz, H. J., Co. Ltd	B	Food products
Hercules Powder Co. Ltd	A	Paper-makers' chemicals, etc.
Hobart Mfg Co. Ltd	B	Food and dishwashing machinery
Holden Vale Mfg Co. Ltd	C	Bleached cotton
Honeywell-Atlas Ltd	B	Sorbitol and surface active agents
Honeywell-Brown Ltd	A	Industrial instruments
Hoover Ltd	B	Domestic electrical appliances
Hudnut, Richard, Ltd	C	Cosmetics
Hughes Brushes Ltd	A	Hair and toothbrushes
Hughes Tool Co. Ltd*	A	Rock drilling bits
Hygienic Drinking Straws Co. Ltd	A	Drinking straws
Hyster Co. Ltd	A	Mechanical handling equipment
IBM United Kingdom Ltd	A	Office appliances, time recorders and electrical clocks
Ideal Boilers & Radiators Ltd	A	Heating appliances and sanitary fitments
Ingersoll Rand Co. Ltd	A	Compressors, rock drills, etc.
Integra, Leeds & Northrup Ltd	B	Industrial instruments
International Chemical Co. Ltd	A	Manufacturing chemists

Name of UK company or US branch	Financial classification (see key above)	Products manufactured
International Harvester Co. of Great Britain Ltd	A	Agricultural machinery and tractors
International Latex Corporation	A	Foundation garments
Irving Air Chute of Great Britain Ltd	A	Parachutes
Jacobs Mfg Co. Ltd	B	Engineers' small tools
Jantzen Ltd	A	Swimwear and sportswear
Jobling, James A. & Co., Ltd	B	'Pyrex' glassware
Johnson & Johnson (Great Britain) Ltd	A	Surgical dressings, etc., and baby products
Johnson, S. C., & Son Ltd	A	Wax polish
Joy-Sullivan Ltd	A	Mining machinery
Kellogg Co., of Great Britain Ltd	B	Food products
Kelsey-Hayes Wheel Co. Ltd	C	Automobile accessories
Kemet Products Ltd	B	Metallurgical and electrochemical products
Kenwood Silver Co. Ltd	A	Silversmiths
Ketay Ltd	B	Electronic instruments and control gear
Kidde, The Walter, Co. Ltd	A	Fire protection equipment
Kodak Ltd	A	Films and photograph equipment
Kraft Foods Ltd	A	Food products
Lambert Chemical Co. Ltd	C	Medicinal products
Lapointe Machine Tool Co. Ltd	A	Broaching machines and tools
Lehn & Fink Products Ltd	A	Toilet creams, deodorants, etc.
Leicester Lovell & Co. Ltd	A	Synthetic resins and glue products
Libby McNeill & Libby Ltd	A	Canned evaporated milk
Lilly, Eli, & Co. Ltd	A	Pharmaceuticals
Linotype & Machinery Ltd	A	Type composing and printer's machinery
Luft-Tangee (London) Ltd	A	Cosmetics
Mallory Metallurgical Products Ltd	B	Metallurgical engineers
Marinite Ltd	B	Incombustible marine board
Mars Ltd	A	Confectionery
Marx, Louis & Co. Ltd	A	Toys
Mentholatum Co. Ltd	A	Medicinal products
Merck-Sharp & Dohme Ltd	A	Pharmaceuticals

Name of UK company or US branch	Financial classification (see key above)	Products manufactured
Metallizing Equipment Co. Ltd	B	Metal spraying plant
Meyer Dumore Bottler's Equipment Ltd	A	Bottlers' and brewers' equipment
Midland Silicones Ltd	B	Silicone fluids, greases, etc.
Miles Laboratories Ltd	A	Proprietary medicines
Miller Last, O. A., Co. Ltd	C	Shoe-makers' lasts, etc.
Mine Safety Appliances Co. Ltd	A	Safety equipment for mines
Minnesota Mining & Mfg Co. Ltd	B	Coated abrasives
Mobil Oil Co. Ltd	A	Oil products
Monsanto Chemicals Ltd	B	Chemicals
Nabisco Foods Ltd	A	Food products
Nash Kelvinator Ltd	A	Refrigerating machinery
National Adhesives Ltd	B	Adhesives
National Cash Register Ltd	A	Office appliances, cash registers, etc.
Nelson's Acetate Ltd	C	Cellulose acetate
Neusso Hesslein Kemptar Ltd	A	Cotton piece goods
New Holland Machine Co. Ltd	C	Hay and straw balers
North British Rubber Co. Ltd	B	Motor tyres and rubber products
Norton Grinding Wheel Co. Ltd	A	Grinding wheels and abrasives
Oil Well Engineering Co. Ltd	B	Oilfield drilling equipment
Oreole Records Ltd	B	Gramophone records
Ortho Pharmaceutical Ltd	A	Gynaecological specialities
Pal Personna Blades Ltd	C	Safety razor-blades and cutlery
Parke-Davis & Co. Ltd	A	Pharmaceuticals
Parsons Chain Co. Ltd	A	Electrically welded steel chain
Pepsi-Cola Ltd	B	Soft drinks
Perry Bevan & Co. Ltd	C	Art metalwork
Peterhead Gear Manufacturing Co. Ltd	C	Gears and circular components
Pfizer Ltd	A	Pharmaceuticals
Philco (Overseas) Ltd	A	Radio and television products
Phillips, The Chas. H., Chemical Co. Ltd	A	Proprietary articles, medicines, etc.
Plibrico Co. Ltd	A	Refractory products
Prestige Group Ltd	B	Cutlery and hardware products
Quaker Oats Ltd	A	Food products

Name of UK company or US branch	Financial classification (see key above)	Products manufactured
Ralph-Kamborian Shoe Machinery Co. Ltd	B	Boot and shoe machinery
Ranco Ltd	A	Electrical switches, thermostats
Rank-Xerox Ltd	B	Xerography products
Raybestos-Belaco Ltd	B	Brake and clutch linings
Remington Rand Ltd	A	Office appliances and business equipment
Revlon International Corporation	A	Cosmetics
Rheem Lysaght Ltd	B	Metal containers
Robertson Thain Ltd	A	Roofing and ventilation equipment
Rockware Glass (Wheaton) Ltd	B	Glass containers
Ronson Products Ltd	A	Cigarette lighters
Rubinstein, Helena Ltd	A	Cosmetics
Ruston-Bucyrus Ltd	B	Mechanical handling equipment
S. F. Appliances Ltd	A	Cooling, lighting and heating appliances
Sangamo Weston Ltd	B	Electrical instruments and meters
Scherer, R. P., Ltd	A	Filled gelatin capsules
Scholl Mfg Co. Ltd	A	Foot comfort service
Schrader's, A., Son, Division of Scovill Mfg Co	A	Motor tyre accessories, tyre pressure gauges, etc.
Seager-Evans & Co. Ltd	B	Whisky distilling
Signode Ltd	A	Steel strapping systems
Simplicity Patterns Ltd	A	Dress patterns, etc.
Singer Sewing Machine Co. Ltd	B	Sewing machines and accessories
Siris, A. J., Products, Ltd	B	Cosmetics and toilet articles
Spauldings Ltd	B	Insulating materials
Spencer (Banbury) Ltd	A	Foundation garments
Sperry Gyroscope Co. Ltd	B	Scientific instruments
Spirella Co. of Great Britain Ltd	B	Foundation garments
Squibb, E. R., & Sons Ltd	A	Pharmaceuticals
Stafford-Miller Ltd	A	Dental fixatives
Standard Brands Ltd	A	Food products
Standard Telephones & Cables Ltd	A	Telecommunication equipment

Name of UK company or US branch	Financial classification (see key above)	Products manufactured
Stanley Works (Great Britain) Ltd	B	Joiners' and carpenters' tools
Sunbeam Electric Ltd	A	Domestic electrical appliances
Swift & Company Ltd	A	Meat products and processed cheese
Sylvania-Thorn Colour Laboratories Ltd	B	Cathode ray tubes
Tampax Ltd	B	Surgical tampons, etc.
Taylor-Short & Mason Ltd	A	Industrial instruments
Thor Power Tool Co. Ltd	A	Pneumatic and electrical tools
Tokalon Ltd	C	Cosmetics and beauty preparations
Toni-Cosmetics Ltd	C	Cosmetics, hair shampoos, etc.
Torrington Co. Ltd	A	Boot and shoe findings, etc.
Trico-Folberth Ltd	B	Motor-car accessories
Tucker Eyelet, George, Co. Ltd	C	Light metal pressings
UK Optical Bausch & Lamb Ltd	B	Ophthalmic products
UK Time Ltd	A	Watches
Underwood Business Machines Ltd	A	Office appliances
Union Carbide Ltd	A	Refined metals, chemicals, etc.
Upjohn of England Ltd	A	Pharmaceuticals
Valentine Pen Co. Ltd	C	Fountain pens
Varley-FMC Ltd	B	Hydraulic and general engineers
Vauxhall Motors Ltd	A	Motor vehicles
Veeder Root Ltd	B	Measure and counting instruments
Venus Pencil Co. Ltd	A	Pencils
Vick International Ltd	A	Medicinal products
Wallace & Turner Ltd	A	Water sterilizing equipment
Warner Bros. (Corsets) Ltd	A	Foundation garments
Warner, W. R., & Co. Ltd	A	Medicinal products
Waterman Pen Co. Ltd	B	Pens, pencils and writing accessories
Waygood-Otis Ltd	B	Lifts and escalators
Wayne Tank & Pump Co. Ltd	A	Petrol and oil storage systems
Webb Jervis, J. B., Ltd	A	Materials handling equipment
Westclox Ltd	A	Alarm clocks
Westrex Co. Ltd	A	Cinematograph projection apparatus

Name of UK company or US branch	Financial classification (see key above)	Products manufactured
White Laboratories Ltd	A	Pharmaceuticals
White, S. S., Co. (Great Britain) Ltd	A	Dental goods
Whitfield, Hodgson & Brough Ltd	C	Shoe repairing machinery
Wilcox & Gibbs Sewing Machine Co. Ltd	A	Industrial sewing machines
Winget-Syncro Ltd	B	Wire and cable-making machinery
Wix, J., & Son Ltd	A	Cigarettes
Wizard Lightfoot Co. Ltd	B	Arch supports
Wrigley Products Ltd	A	Chewing gum
Wyeth, John, & Brothers Ltd	C	Pharmaceuticals
Yale & Towne Mfg Co	A	Yale locks, mechanical handling equipment, etc.
York-Shipley Ltd	A	Refrigeration and air-conditioning machinery
Zimmer Orthopaedic Ltd	A	Surgical equipment

* Located in Northern Ireland.

Appendix 2

The fifty largest US affiliates and Anglo-US financed firms in UK industry, 1995

	Name of company	Products supplied	Capital employed £000	Sales turnover £000
1	(37) Esso UK	Oil, gas and nuclear fuels	3,809,000	3,674,600
2	(49) Smith Kline Beecham	Health and household	3,141,000	6,492,000
3	(55) Rank Xerox	Electronics	2,798,000	3,309,000
4	(59) Conoco	Oil, gas and nuclear fuels	2,622,300	2,714,800
5	(73) Ford Motor Co.	Motor vehicles	2,256,000	5,327,000
6	(108) IBM UK Holdings	Electronics	1,437,300	4,057,100
7	(132) Chevron UK	Oil, gas and nuclear fuels	1,099,136	1,023,097
8	(153) Texaco	Oil, gas and nuclear fuels	929,039	3,832,496
9	(155) Vauxhall Motors	Motor vehicles	923,100	3,100,900
10	(273) Kodak	Engineering, instruments, films	425,100	1,109,600
11	(289) Mobil Oil Co.	Oil, gas and nuclear fuels	389,480	1,196,476
12	(293) Procter and Gamble	Health and household	381,467	1,377,102
13	(301) Kellogg Co. of Great Britain	Food manufacturing	366,991	589,228
14	(331) Hewlett Packard	Electronics	328,227	1,313,989
15	(354) Merck Sharp and Dohme	Health and household	284,687	291,278
16	(355) Pfizer Group	Health and household	284,224	170,895
17	(356) Kimberly-Clark	Packaging, paper and printing	282,744	286,408
18	(359) General Foods	Food manufacturing	280,722	364,550

		Name of company	*Products supplied*	*Capital employed* £000	*Sales turnover* £000
19	(363)	3M UK Holdings	Chemicals	276,653	617,539
20	(368)	Toys 'R' Us Holdings	Toys	272,018	252,604
21	(370)	Exxon Chemical	Chemicals	270,691	456,229
22	(377)	AT&T (UK) Holdings	Telecommunications	265,625	460,308
23	(386)	H. J. Heinz	Food manufacturing	257,636	501,537
24	(391)	Compaq Computer	Electronics	255,952	690,662
25	(393)	Baker Hughes	Oil, gas and nuclear fuels	255,634	298,124
26	(400)	Black and Decker	Electronics	251,629	398,955
27	(401)	Digital Equipment Scotland	Electronics	250,833	648,374
28	(404)	Phillips Petroleum Co. UK	Oil, gas and nuclear fuels	248,417	608,921
29	(427)	Union Texas Petroleum	Oil, gas and nuclear fuels	228,657	140,527
30	(431)	Gillette Industries	Health and household	223,784	361,114
31	(458)	Cummins UK	Engineering – general	201,998	595,548
32	(466)	Eli Lilly Group	Health and household	197,793	258,424
33	(475)	Superior Oil (UK)	Oil, gas and nuclear fuels	191,836	76,021
34	(483)	Coca-Cola Holdings (UK)	Soft drinks	187,701	94,814
35	(486)	Air Products	Chemicals	185,705	245,630
36	(490)	Del Monte Foods	Food manufacturing	184,343	226,809
37	(494)	Scott Paper (UK)	Packaging, paper, etc.	182,142	301,599
38	(520)	Goodyear Great Britain	Industrial materials, tyres	167,395	432,506
39	(527)	United Technology Holdings	Engineering – general	159,135	302,627
40	(581)	Rohm and Haas (UK)	Chemicals	137,695	229,169
41	(595)	CPC (UK)	Food manufacturing	133,169	252,362

Name of company	Products supplied	Capital employed £000	Sales turnover £000
42 (617) Warner Lambert (UK)	Health and household	125,860	207,914
43 (620) Ingersoll-Rand Holdings	Engineering – general	125,306	178,180
44 (632) Cyanamid (UK) Holdings	Health and household	121,387	255,192
45 (648) Bristol-Myers Squibb	Health and household	115,747	370,105
46 (661) Duracell Holdings UK	Batteries, miscellaneous	112,385	135,405
47 (665) Sterling-Winthrop Group	Chemicals	111,972	64,317
48 (681) National Semiconductor (UK)	Electronics	107,971	402,356
49 (693) Dow Corning	Glassware, etc.	104,570	182,627
50 (705) Honeywell	Electronics	102,316	230,939

Source: List extracted by author *The Times 1000, 1996*, London: Times Book 1995. Later editions of this yearly publication do not include foreign-owned companies. Figures in brackets represent the positioning of the company in *The Times* largest 1000 companies. This list includes some non-industrial companies. Companies which were US-owned in 1995 but are no longer US-owned (in 1998) are excluded. Capital employed = Total assets less current liabilities (book value) as reported in company accounts. All data relate to the financial year (or end of financial year) 1994/5 or 1995.

Appendix 3

US direct investment in UK manufacturing industry 1950–95. Statistical annexe

TABLE

INTRODUCTORY NOTE

In this appendix we give some statistical data on the growth, composition and significance of US foreign direct investment in UK manufacturing industry over the past forty years. We have drawn our data from both US and UK sources. The first three tables present the broad picture, and compare trends of the US capital stake in the UK with that in Western Europe and also with the UK stake in the US. The changing significance of the US capital stake as a proportion of the UK's gross national product is documented in Table A.1, while Table A.4 compares the changing share of US capital stake in the UK with that of Western European and Japanese investors.

Tables A.5 to A.10 set out particulars of changes in the output, productivity, employment and wage bill of US affiliates manufacturing in the UK over the past three decades, and also of the industrial composition of their assets and/or sales.

Table A.11 compares and contrasts the changing profitability of US manufacturing affiliates in the UK with that of their counterparts in Western Europe and in all countries.

Tables A.12 to A.18 present some statistics on the innovatory capabilities of US affiliates in the UK, using both R&D and patent data. Where possible, these data are given over time and compared with the innovatory capabilities of all firms, and with those of US affiliates in Western Europe.

Tables A.20 and A.21 set out some details on the export performance of US manufacturing affiliates in the UK. The two tables which follow (A.22 and A.23) reproduce some data on the regional distribution of the employment of *all* foreign firms in the UK (data on US-owned firms are not separately available). Finally, Table A.24 documents some data on the acquisitions and mergers of UK companies by US companies over the period 1987–95.

Table A.1 US direct capital stake in the UK,[1] 1950–95 (£ million)

	Direct capital stake	as % of UK GNP[2]
1950	303	2.60
1957	705	3.60
1960	1,154	5.00
1965	1,943	5.70
1970	3,348	7.50
1975	6,883	7.10
1980	11,994	6.00
1985	23,583	6.60
1990	37,711	6.84
1991	42,668	7.41
1992	56,333	9.41
1993	73,729	11.69
1994	77,645	11.63
1995	79,205	11.31

Sources: US Department of Commerce, *Survey of Current Business* and (UK) Central Statistical Office, *Abstract of Annual Statistics* (various issues).
Notes:
1 Defined as the book value of the net assets of US affiliates in the UK owned by the US parent or associated companies.
2 Gross national product.

Commentary:

1 As a proportion of the UK's gross national product, the significance of the *total* US direct investment stake in the UK steadily increased between 1950 and 1970. After declining from 7.5% in 1970 to 6.0% in 1980 it rose marginally in the 1980s and then very markedly in the 1990s. In 1995, it was over four times as significant as in 1950.

Table A.2 US capital stake in UK manufacturing industry and UK capital stake in US manufacturing industry, 1950–95 ($ million)

	US stake in the UK	UK stake in the US	Ratio UK/US
1950	542	337	1.61
1957	914	510	1.79
1960	2,164	722	3.00
1965	3,306	839	3.94
1970	4,909	1,391	3.53
1975	7,555	1.883	4.01
1980	13,893	6,159	2.26
1985	12,560	11.884	1.06
1990	22,967	42,365	0.54
1991	23,591	42,259	0.56
1992	20,328	42,208	0.48
1993	23,619	42,485	0.56
1994	26,742	48,427	0.55
1995	27,865	56,897	0.49

Source: US Department of Commerce, *Survey of Current Business*. Annual Surveys of *US Foreign Direct Investment*, and *Foreign Direct Investment in the US*, usually published in August, September or October issues.

Commentary:

1 Between 1950 and 1975 the US direct investment stake in manufacturing industry grew considerably faster than the UK direct investment stake in US manufacturing industry. Thereafter the reverse movement took place, and in 1995 the UK was a net investor in the US to the tune of $29 billion. However, since 1990, the proportionate increases in two way transatlantic investment flows have, on average, been broadly comparable.

Table A.3 US direct capital stake in UK manufacturing industry, 1950–95 ($ million)

	1 *Value $ mil.*	*2* *As a % of all US* *stake in UK*	*3* *As a % of US* *stake in Western* *Europe*	*4* *As a % of US* *stake in all areas*
1950	542	64.0	58.1	14.9
1957	1,234	62.6	55.3	15.1
1963	2,731	62.6	55.3	15.1
1970	4,909	61.2	35.5	15.8
1975	7,555	54.2	29.1	13.5
1980	13,893	48.6	30.6	15.6
1985	12,560	36.9	27.8	13.1
1989	22,097	36.3	34.4	14.1
1990	22,967	31.7	27.2	13.7
1991	23,591	30.2	25.4	13.1
1992	20,328	26.1	21.7	10.9
1993	23,619	21.8	24.9	12.3
1994	26,742	24.0	24.9	12.3
1995	27,875	23.2	21.3	10.8

Source: US Department of Commerce, *Survey of Current Business*. Annual articles on the *US's International Investment Position*, usually published in August or September each year.

Commentary:

1 Although the significance of US direct investment to the UK economy has increased over the last forty years, the share of manufacturing industry has markedly declined as services, notably finance, banking and insurance, business services and trade have become more important.

2 Relative to the rest of Europe, the UK's share of US manufacturing investment has fallen by more than one-half over the last thirty years. However, its share of fdi throughout the world has remained fairly stable. The falling share in Europe has been particularly significant since the later 1980s, consequential upon the completion of the European Internal Market.

Table A.4 US, Western European, Japanese and total foreign direct capital stake in UK manufacturing industry, 1965–95 (£ million)

	US	Western European	Japanese	World
1965	1,117	300	–	1,643
	(68.0)	(18.3)	(0.0)	(100.0)
1968	1,556	474	–	2,263
	(68.8)	(20.9)	(0.0)	(100.0)
1971	2,128	739	–	3,180
	(66.9)	(23.2)	(0.0)	(100.0)
1974	3,129	1,171	–	4,701
	(66.6)	(24.9)	(0.0)	(100.0)
1978	5,420	2,148	neg.	8,118
	(66.8)	(26.5)	(neg.)	(100.0)
1981	8,160	2,850	44	12,188
	(67.0)	(23.3)	(0.4)	(100.0)
1984	10,074	3,995	104	15,694
	(64.2)	(25.5)	(0.7)	(100.0)
1987	12,115	4,806	298	19,779
	(61.2)	(24.3)	(1.5)	(100.0)
1990	22,509	11,138	676	40,491
	(55.6)	(27.5)	(1.7)	(100.0)
1992	18,420	12,528	1,272	39,538
	(46.5)	(30.2)	(3.2)	(100.0)
1994	16,122	13,586	1,579	39,938
	(46.4)	(34.0)	(4.0)	(100.0)
1995	18,546	13,244	1,039	41,449
	(44.7)	(32.0)	(2.5)	(100.0)

Sources: Central Statistical Office (CSO) and Office for National Statistics (ONS), *Overseas Direct Investment* and *Book Values of Overseas Investment*, various editions, London: CSO and ONS.

Commentary:

1 The share of the total foreign net assets in UK manufacturing industry accounted for by US firms has steadily fallen since 1965, but particularly so since the mid-1980s. By contrast that of European and Japanese investors has risen from 18.3% in 1965 to 26.2% in 1984 to 34.5% in 1995.

Table A.5 Number of US and other foreign-owned enterprises and establishments in UK manufacturing industry, 1963–92

(a) Enterprises

Year	1 US	2 EC(EU)	3 Japan	4 Total foreign	5 All enterprises	6 1 as % of 4	7 1 as % of 5
1963	369	93	–	502	63,865	73.5	0.58
1968	488	124	–	667	61,078	73.2	0.80
1973	760	173	–	1,094	n.a.	69.5	n.a.
1977	788	291	7	1,370	89,822	57.5	0.88
1981	827	340	17	1,522	90,068	54.3	0.92
1985	777	364	31	1,515	127,430	51.3	0.61
1986	689	326	28	1,300	130,243	53.0	0.53
1987	690	344	33	1,355	133,140	50.9	0.52
1988	640	321	38	1,291	135,405	49.6	0.47
1989	633	347	86	1,356	139,879	46.7	0.45
1990	642	391	104	1,443	132,940	44.5	0.48
1991	608	438	115	1,470	127,907	41.4	0.48
1992	624	458	117	1,507	130,936	41.4	0.48

(b) Establishments

Year	US	EC(EU)	Japan	Total foreign	All enterprises	1 as % of 4	1 as % of 5
1963	813	195	–	1,098	83,774	74.0	0.97
1968	1,144	301	–	1,573	82,343	72.7	1.39
1973	1,094	290	–	1,677	93,952	65.2	1.16
1977	1,592	495	7	2,654	107,691	60.0	1.48
1981	1,510	575	19	2,825	108,276	53.4	1.39
1985	1,259	532	32	2,562	142,553	49.1	0.88
1986	1,226	518	29	2,372	148,852	51.7	0.82
1987	1,161	497	34	2,283	145,493	50.8	0.80
1988	1,074	471	40	2,223	147,608	48.3	0.73
1989	1,058	557	89	2,330	151,393	45.4	0.70
1990	1,047	637	110	2,419	143,371	43.3	0.73
1991	997	705	124	2,462	137,415	40.5	0.73
1992	1,012	775	128	2,523	139,693	40.1	0.72

Source: COI, *UK Census of Production (PA 1002)*, London: Central Statistical Office, various dates.

Commentary:

1 From the 1950s through to the late 1970s the number of US-owned enterprises and establishments continued to increase. (In 1979 the number of enterprises peaked at 1,234.) Throughout the 1980s the number steadily declined, but in the 1990s it appears to have stabilized.

2 The share of all UK manufacturing enterprises of establishments accounted for by US firms is a very small one, and in 1992 was only slightly less than in 1963. However, one of the most noticable features of Table A.4 is the growth of EC- and Japanese-owned firms since the mid-1980s. This partly reflects the completion of the European Internal Market, and partly the emergence of Japanese firms as important inward direct investors.

3 Combining the data with those in Table A.5, it can be seen that, in 1992, the average employment of a US manufacturing enterprise (at 600) was somewhat greater than that of other foreign-owned firms (at 463), and nearly 20 times greater than that of all UK enterprises (at 33). The corresponding figures for employment per establishment in that year were 370, 270 and (31).

4 The average number of plants of US manufacturing subsidiaries in the UK in 1992 was 1.62 compared with 1.69 for European affiliates, 1.09 for Japanese affiliates and 1.07 for all UK-based firms. Rather surprisingly, the number of plants per US and European firm has fallen noticeably since 1977 (when it was 2.02) and marginally since the late 1980s. This suggests that US and other foreign-owned firms are tending to concentrate their output in one or two locations in the UK.

Table A.6 Output of US and other foreign-owned subsidiaries in UK manufacturing industry, 1963–92 (£ million)

(a) Gross output[1]

Year	1 US	2 EC(EU)	3 Japan	4 Total foreign	5 All enterprises	6 1 as % of 4	7 1 as % of 5
1963	1,944.4	171.2	–	2,525.7	27,698.1	77.0	7.0
1968			–				
1973	7,506.3	944.6		9,688.8	60,398.8	77.5	12.4
1977	19,180.1	4,871.0	35.9	27,963.3	125,321.7	69.0	15.3
1981	21,797.9	4,565.3	127.4	31,909.5	165,471.0	68.3	13.2
1985	29,891.3	5,332.3	450.8	44,626.2	219,678.5	67.0	13.6
1986	29,792.9	5,566.5	628.3	43.988.3	227,038.0	67.7	13.1
1987	33,112.0	7,007.6	1,082.6	50,935.9	242,840.9	65.0	13.6
1988	35,868.8	8,024.5	1,845.0	57,240.4	276,345.5	62.7	13.0
1989	42,731.5	12,061.7	2,936.8	72,662.5	302,191.1	58.8	14.1
1990	45,264.5	13,741.8	4,696.3	80,352.6	318,121.9	56.3	14.2
1991	41,667.9	14,252.4	5,426.4	78,234.3	307,713.0	53.3	13.5
1992	46,682.3	6,220.0	6,219.8	86,104.8	318,360.8	54.2	14.7

(b) Net output

Year	1 US	2 EC(EU)	3 Japan	4 Total foreign	5 All enterprises	6 1 as % of 4	7 1 as % of 5
1963	867.2	129.8	–	1,105.7	10,470.0	78.4	8.3
1968	1,479.6	288.5	–				
1973	3,028.3	423.2	–	3,884.1	25,377.0	78.0	11.9
1977	6,686.9	1,589.4	11.0	9,650.6	48,578.2	69.3	13.8
1981	9,115.9	1,721.1	37.1	13,099.3	70,614.5	69.6	12.9
1985	11,272.2	2,246.8	112.0	17,279.3	91,706.1	65.2	12.3
1986	11,465.3	2,441.0	146.5	17,392.2	98,183.5	65.9	11.7
1987	12,899.3	3,177.6	226.5	20,298.1	106,534.9	63.5	12.1
1988	13,920.7	3,272.1	448,7	22,385.6	120,863.9	62.2	11.5
1989	17,045.7	4,600.9	797.7	28,430.8	132,355.2	60.0	12.9
1990	17,340.5	5,378.4	1,758.0	31,115.7	138,984.4	55.7	12.5
1991	15,852,1	5,642.8	2,137.0	30,474.9	135,208.4	52.0	11.7
1992	17,278.2	7,082.9	2,546.9	33,749.1	139,679.7	51.2	12.4

Source: As for Table A.4.
Note:
1 Sales figures for 1963 and 1968.

Commentary:
1 US subsidiaries continued to increase their share of UK production until the later 1970s, since when it has stabilized.
2 Their share of value added (net output) is slightly less than their share of gross output; this indicates that they are marginally less vertically integrated than other foreign-owned and indigenous competitors.
3 The share of all foreign-owned manufacturing output accounted for by US subsidiaries has steadily fallen throughout the last three decades with the sharpest fall occurring between 1987 and 1991 following the announcement of the completion of the European Internal Market in January 1993. Between 1986 and 1992 EC (EU) investors increased their stake in the foreign-owned (gross) manufacturing output in the UK from 12.7% to 18.8%. At the same time the corresponding share of Japanese-owned companies rose from 1.4% to 7.2%.

Table A.7 Net output per head of US and other foreign subsidiaries in UK manufacturing industry, 1963–92 (£ million)

Year	*1* US	*2* EC(EU)	*3* Japan	*4* Total foreign	*5* All enterprises	*6* 1 as % of 4	*7* 1 as % of 5
1963	2,157	1,614		2,051	1,363	105.2	158.3
1968	2,772	2,279		2,693	1,954	102.9	141.9
1973	4,855	3,964		4,728	3,493	102.7	139.0
1977	9,394	11,619	9,847	9,519	6,986	98.7	134.5
1981	16,046	13,505	12,519	15,265	12,170	105.1	131.8
1985	27,078	23,619	17,741	25,519	18,937	106.1	143.0
1986	29,793	26,434	18,819	28,003	20,563	106.4	144.9
1987	33,565	31,691	21,577	32,491	22,802	103.3	147.2
1988	37,358	31,484	25,609	35,240	24,955	106.0	149.7
1989	43,153	34,453	29,326	39,264	27,157	109.9	158.9
1990	43,125	34,752	42,990	40,144	28,907	107.4	149.2
1991	42,384	33,948	37,725	39,334	30,003	107.8	141.3
1992	46,097	37,214	43,904	43,055	32,175	107.1	143.3

Source: As for Table A.1.

Commentary:

1 Throughout the past three decades US-owned manufacturing subsidiaries have recorded a productivity between 32% and 59% higher than that of all UK enterprises. Most certainly this is partly due to the concentration of US affiliates in sectors which record a higher than average productivity (see also Table A.9). These data offer little support for the hypothesis that indigenous UK firms have, over the years, improved their performance relative to their US-financed competitors.

2 However, column 6 of this table shows that the superior performance of US subsidiaries may not be primarily a US-specific factor, but one common to all foreign firms. For example, only marginally do US-owned firms seem to perform better than EU-owned firms. Another interesting feature of this table is the very marked increase in the net output per head in the 1990s. This represents their deeper embeddedness in the UK economy – particularly in the auto and electronics sectors.

Table A.8 Employment and employee compensation of US and other foreign-owned affiliates in UK manufacturing industry, 1963–92

(a) Employment total (000s)

Year	1 US	2 EC(EU)	3 Japan	4 Total foreign	5 All enterprises	6 1 as % of 4	7 1 as % of 5
1963	406.2	80.8	–	539.0	7,695.0	75.4	5.3
1968	533.8	126.6	–	703.5	7,249.0	75.9	7.4
1973	623.8	106.8	–	714.8	7,268.3	87.3	8.6
1977	711.8	136.8	1.1	1,013.8	6,883.4	70.2	10.3
1981	568.1	127.4	3.0	858.1	5,777.9	66.2	9.8
1985	416.3	95.1	6.3	677.1	4,842.8	61.5	8.6
1986	394.0	92.3	7.8	621.1	4,774.8	63.4	8.3
1987	384.3	100.3	10.5	624.7	4,672.6	61.5	8.2
1988	372.6	103.9	17.5	635.2	4,843.2	58.7	7.7
1989	395.0	133.5	27.2	724.1	4,873.6	54.6	8.1
1990	402.1	154.8	40.9	775.1	4,808.0	51.9	8.4
1991	374.0	166.2	56.6	774.8	4,506.4	48.3	8.3
1992	374.8	190.3	58.0	784.2	4,341.3	47.8	8.6

(b) Employee compensation per head (£)

Year	1 US	2 EC(EU)	3 Japan	4 Total foreign	5 All enterprises	6 1 as % of 4	7 1 as % of 5
1963	n.a.	n.a.	n.a.	n.a.	n.a.	–	–
1968	n.a.	n.a.	n.a.	n.a.	n.a.	–	–
1973	2,004	1,672	–	1,951	1,673	102.7	99.9
1977	3,740	3,618	2,636	3,696	2,260	101.2	160.1
1981	6,892	6,539	4,800	6,768	5,916	101.8	110.5
1985	10,068	9,247	6,667	9,941	8,259	101.3	112.0
1986	10,841	9,891	7,385	10,591	8,870	102.4	111.5
1987	11,644	10,498	8,381	11,370	9,441	102.4	111.2
1988	12,759	11,212	10,131	12,334	10,233	103.4	109.6
1989	14,155	12,645	10,985	13,455	11,168	105.2	113.2
1990	15,628	13,739	11,980	14,768	12,338	105.8	111.4
1991	16,922	14,789	15,023	15,999	13,401	105.8	110.4
1992	17,968	15,745	16,456	17,074	14,131	105.2	111.4

Source: As for Table A.1.

Commentary:
1 The share of total manufacturing employment of US-affiliated firms reached its peak of 10.3% in 1977, since when it has declined slightly. But as a percentage of employment in all foreign firms it has dramatically fallen from 87.3% in 1992. Other data reveal that the US affiliates' share of all UK administrative and other non-operative workers was about one-quarter higher than its share of operative workers (10.5% compared with 7.9% in 1992).
2 The average employee compensation in US affiliates has varied between 10 and 20% higher than paid by all UK firms, and up to 5% higher than that paid by all foreign-owned firms. Table A.4 shows that, of the latter group of firms, the Japanese recorded the lowest average wages and salaries, but that the wage 'gap' between them and US affiliates has considerably lessened in recent years. Again, to be fully meaningful, these data need to be broken down both by industry and by sex of employee.

Table A.9 Percentage distribution of net book value of foreign affiliates in UK manufacturing industry by nationality of firm and sector, 1968–95

		Food, drink & tobacco	Chemicals	Metals	Mechanical engineering	Electrical engineering	Transport equipment	Paper	Other manufacturing	All industry	Valuation (£mill)
1968	US	12.6	13.2	5.0	25.2	11.3	18.7	2.5	11.5	100	1,556
	Western Europe	12.0	15.2	4.1	14.6	31.1	1.7	2.6	18.7	100	474
	All	13.4	14.2	7.7	20.8	14.3	15.6	2.7	10.9	100	2,263
1971	US	11.3	12.2	4.5	25.8	13.7	17.6	2.7	12.2	100	2,128
	Western Europe	12.7	23.7	3.1	9.5	23.6	1.1	2.0	24.3	100	739
	All	12.3	14.5	8.1	21.5	14.7	12.1	2.9	13.9	100	3,180
1978	US	12.6	16.3	1.2	25.8	15.1	15.0	2.6	11.4	100	5,420
	Western Europe	18.4	17.0	13.8	9.8	15.5	nsa	4.4	21.1	100	2,148
	All	14.1	16.1	4.6	21.8	14.4	10.7	5.0	13.7	100	8,819
1984	US	15.4	19.9	1.7	17.4	17.2	14.2	4.4	9.8	100	10,074
	Western Europe	12.8	23.3	15.7	10.3	19.1	2.4	4.5	11.8	100	3,995
	Japan	neg.	neg.	neg.	nsa	58.7	neg.	neg.	nsa	100	104
	All	15.2	20.7	6.4	15.2	16.8	9.8	5.1	10.8	100	15,694
1990	North America[1]	13.5	17.9	3.3	13.6	17.2	23.1	5.7	5.6	100	24,217
	Western Europe	14.4	19.1	4.9	11.9	14.8	5.0	12.9	16.9	100	11,138
	Japan	neg.	neg.	neg.	11.5	49.4	31.5	neg.	7.6	100	676
	All	12.1	16.1	3.7	11.7	15.3	15.7	16.8	8.5	100	40,491

Table A.9 Continued

		Food, drink & tobacco	Chemicals	Metals	Mechanical engineering	Electrical engineering	Transport equipment	Paper	Other manufacturing	All industry	Net assets (£mill)
1995	US	16.1	19.3	0.9	20.7	17.4	9.0	5.2	9.5	100	18,546
	Western Europe	18.0	11.7	6.5	10.2	22.0	4.1	12.6	16.8	100	13,244
	Japan	neg.	neg.	neg.	20.9	41.5	19.5	neg.	11.8	100	1,039
	All	15.2	12.5	3.3	13.0	18.2	6.3	21.0	10.5	100	41,449

Source: Central Statistical Office, Business Monitor, MA4/M4, Overseas Transactions, various dates.

Note:
1 Canada and USA

Commentary:

1 The industrial structure of US fdi in UK manufacturing has remained broadly the same since 1968, although the food, drink and tobacco, chemicals, electrical engineering and paper sectors have gained relative to metals, mechanical engineering and transport equipment sectors.

2 In 1995, relative to European-owned counterparts the comparative investing advantage of US affiliates was most pronounced in the chemicals, mechanical engineering and transport equipment and least pronounced in metals, electrical engineering and paper products. In that same year, Japanese fdi in the UK was most concentrated in electrical engineering, motor vehicles (where the Japanese affiliates have taken over from US affiliates as the leading investors) and mechanical engineering. There was very little Japanese fdi in food products or chemicals, which sectors accounted for 35.4% of the net book value of US affiliates in 1995.

Table A.10 Sales by majority-owned US foreign affiliates in the UK by major industry, 1957–94 ($ million)

	1957	%	1966	%	1977	%	1982	%	1989	%	1992	%	1994	%
Food products	732	9.1	907	11.0	2,789	10.5	5,417	13.4	6,789	8.6	9,366	10.3	10,009	10.2
Chemical products	1,378	17.2	1,365	16.5	3,945	14.8	6,540	16.1	11,798	14.9	14,785	16.3	16,199	16.6
Primary and fabricated metals	941	11.7	781	9.4	1,535	5.8	2,539	6.3	3,072	3.9	3,600	4.0	3,712	3.8
Machinery	1,658	20.7	(d)[1]	49.4	4,868	18.3	6,689	16.5	18,419	23.3	22,192	24.5	23,783	24.3
Electrical equipment	245	3.1	NA[2]		1,999	7.5	2,357	5.8	5,659	7.1	4,518	5.0	7,474	7.6
Transportation equipment			(d)		6,699	25.2	9,040	22.3	16,709	21.1	19,439	21.5	20,054	20.5
Other manufacturing	2,106	26.3	1,213	14.7	4,763	17.9	7,976	19.7	16,772	21.2	16,619	18.4	16,500	16.9
Total	8,069	100.0	8,275	100.0	26,599	100.0	40,556	100.0	79,218	100.0	90,520	100.0	97,731	100.0

Source: US Department of Commerce, Survey of Current Business, various issues, and Benchmark Surveys on US Direct Investment Abroad, various dates.

Notes:
1 (d) Suppressed to avoid disclosure of data of individual companies.
2 NA = Net Assets: sales are not available for that year.

Commentary:
1 As noted in Chapter 2 of this volume, US direct investment in the UK has always tended to favour high technology sectors, or those producing branded products with an above-average income elasticity of demand. In 1994 the former sectors – viz. chemical products, machinery, electrical equipment and transportation equipment sectors – accounted for 69.0% of the sales of US manufacturing subsidiaries compared with 66.4% in 1989, 65.8% in 1977, 65.8% in 1966 and 41.0% in 1957.

Table A.11 Profitability of US direct investment in manufacturing industry in the UK, Western Europe and all countries, 1957–95

Year	Earnings[1] ($m)		Direct Investment Stake[2] ($m)	Profitability (%)
1957	United Kingdom	165	1,201	13.74
	Europe	269	2,077	12.95
	All countries	852	7,918	10.76
1960	United Kingdom	251	2,164	11.60
	Europe	487	3,797	12.83
	All countries	1,176	11,152	10.55
1970	United Kingdom	463	4,988	9.28
	Europe	1,662	13,703	12.13
	All countries	3,324	32,231	10.31
1980	United Kingdom	1,836	13,833	13.27
	Europe	8,804	45,287	19.44
	All countries	11,263	89,290	12.61
1985	United Kingdom	1,673	13,103	12.77
	Europe	5,971	46,248	12.91
	All countries	11,462	96,741	11.85
1990	United Kingdom	3,242	22,967	14.12
	Europe	14,491	84,355	17.18
	All countries	24,553	167,993	14.62
1995	United Kingdom	3,578	27,865	12.84
	Europe	16,905	131,100	12.89
	All countries	35,775	257,589	13.89

Source: As for Table A.10.
Notes:
1 Earnings is the sum of income (sum of dividends, interest and branch profits) and undistributed subsidiary earning, less taxation and depreciation.
2 Direct Investment Stake is the total foreign owned assets (book value) of US firms less their current liabilities (i.e. net assets).

Commentary:
1 Over the past four decades the profitability of US manufacturing subsidiaries in the UK has fluctuated between 9.3% and 17.5% around an average of 13.2%. These fluctuations largely reflect the general economic conditions in the UK, Europe and the rest of the world.
2 The UK's attractiveness as a location for US investment in Continental Europe has also fluctuated, but *vis-à-vis* the rest of the world it has deteriorated over the last decade.

Table A.12 Expenditures and employment in R&D activities of US affiliates in the UK, 1995

	Expenditures (£ millions)	%	Employment (1000)	%
US affiliates	1,385	14.8	20	13.5
EU affiliates	736	7.5	11	7.4
Japanese affiliates	296	3.2	4	2.7
Other foreign affiliates	1,099	11.7	18	12.1
All foreign affiliates	3,516	37.5	53	35.8
UK-owned firms	5,863	62.5	95	64.2
All firms	9,379	100.0	148	100.0

Source: (UK) Office for National Statistics, *Survey of Business Enterprise R&D 1995.*

Commentary:
1 In 1995, US affiliates accounted for 14.8% of the research and development (R&D) performed in the UK, and 39.4% of the R&D undertaken by all foreign affiliates. Coupled with data set out in earlier tables, each of these percentages indicates that foreign affiliates, relative to indigenous UK firms, tend to be more concentrated in R&D-intensive sectors.

Table A.13 R&D expenditures by US manufacturing subsidiaries in the UK, 1966–94 ($ million)

	1966 $	1966 %[1]	1977 $	1977 %[1]	1982 $	1982 %[1]	1989 $	1989 %[1]	1992 $	1992 %[1]	1994 $	1994 %[1]
Food products	9	1.0	14	0.5	43	0.8	60	0.9	(d)	NA	77	0.8
Chemical products	20	1.5	65	1.6	182	2.8	419	3.6	561	3.8	616	3.8
Primary and fabricated metals	2	0.3	7	0.5	16	0.6	15	0.5	25	0.7	25	0.7
Machinery	41	NA	40	0.8	54	0.8	92	0.5	210	0.9	433	1.8
Electrical equipment	NA	NA	44	2.2	39	1.7	(d)	NA	50	1.1	(d)	NA
Transportation equipment	(d)*	NA	131	2.0	160	1.8	(d)	NA	(d)	NA	(d)	NA
Other manufacturing	(d)	NA	51	1.1	216	2.7	(d)	NA	190	1.1	(d)	NA
Total	124	0.9	352	1.2	711	1.6	1195	1.4	1452	1.5	1938	1.8
As a % of total R&D performed in UK businesses[2]	8.00		9.78		14.08		12.60		13.02		18.53	

Sources: US Department of Commerce, Benchmark Surveys on US Direct Investment Abroad and (UK) Office for National Statistics, Survey of Business Enterprise R&D 1995.

Note:

(d) Suppressed to avoid disclosure of data of individual companies

Commentary:

1 As a percentage of total R&D undertaken in manufacturing industry in the UK over the past decade, the research and development expenditure of US manufacturing subsidiaries has doubled, with the most noticeable increases occurring in the chemicals and metal sectors. However the R&D intensity of US in the food products industry has little changed, while that in the electrical equipment industry has fallen.

2 Since the early 1980s the share of total R&D undertaken by UK-based businesses accounted for by US affiliates has steadily increased. Other data not presented here suggest that the share of total R&D undertaken by US subsidiaries has risen the most rapidly in the machinery (non-electrical engineering) sector. Also, in the table, 1983 data for UK total R&D expenditures are used as a proxy for 1982 data.

Table A.14 R&D expenditures of US manufacturing subsidiaries in the UK, Germany and the rest of Europe as a percentage of their total sales, 1982–94

	1982		1989		1994	
	R&D of US sub. ($m)	R&D/ total sales of affiliates (%)	R&D of US sub. ($m)	R&D/ total sales of affiliates (%)	R&D of US sub. ($m)	R&D/ total sales of affiliates (%)
Food products						
UK	43	0.79	60	0.89	77	0.58
Germany	15	0.52	33	0.56	25	0.16
Rest of Europe	24	0.28	49	0.29	64	0.11
Chemical products						
UK	182	2.78	419	3.57	616	3.16
Germany	81	1.35	201	1.90	295	1.56
Rest of Europe	252	1.39	532	1.41	1,293	1.76
Primary fabricated metals						
UK	16	0.63	15	0.53	25	0.72
Germany	11	0.42	19	0.40	23	0.58
Rest of Europe	7	0.21	20	0.44	19	0.23
Machinery						
UK	54	0.81	92	(d)[1]	433	1.63
Germany	55	0.80	133	(d)	530	2.27
Rest of Europe	83	0.61	300	0.90	637	0.88
Electrical equipment						
UK	39	1.65	(d)	(d)	(d)	(d)
Germany	179	5.12	102	2.79	128	(d)
Rest of Europe	128	2.12	(d)	(d)	(d)	(d)
Transportation equipment						
UK	160	1.77	(d)	(d)	(d)	(d)
Germany	443	3.82	843	3.38	1,435	0.37
Rest of Europe	12	0.25	(d)	(d)	(d)	(d)
Other manufacturing						
UK	216	2.71	(d)	(d)	(d)	(d)
Germany	62	1.35	130	(d)	193	1.33
Rest of Europe	111	0.94	(d)	(d)	(d)	(d)
Total manufacturing						
UK	711	1.75	1,195	1.55	1,938	1.52
Germany	847	2.23	1,459	2.10	2,630	2.16
Rest of Europe	741	1.12	1,549	1.14	(d)	(d)

Source: US Department of Commerce, *Benchmark Surveys on US Direct Investment Abroad*, 1982, 1989, 1994.
Note:
1 (d) Suppressed to avoid disclosure of data of individual companies.

Commentary:
1 Such fragmentary data as are available on the R&D expenditures of US affiliates in Europe suggest that between 1982 and 1994 these have broadly kept pace with sales in the UK and the rest of Europe, apart from in Germany, where they have declined slightly.
2 The most noticeable increase in research intensity of US firms has occurred in the chemical products sector. However, in most metal-using sectors, it has remained stable or declined.

Table A.15 The share of US patents of the largest US firms attributable to their research activities in the UK as a proportion of all patenting by UK firms in the UK, 1969–95 (%)

	1969–72	*1973–77*	*1978–82*	*1983–86*	*1987–90*	*1991–95*
Food, drink and tobacco	10.50	11.95	11.39	10.24	9.89	19.50
Chemicals and pharmaceuticals	16.11	19.18	21.66	25.63	28.08	29.63
Metals and mechanical engineering	20.36	22.94	22.87	31.92	32.55	45.73
Electrical equipment and computing	30.53	35.45	34.69	31.92	18.52	29.66
Motor vehicles	10.13	7.23	9.04	14.80	17.56	28.42
Aircraft and aerospace	13.50	15.02	12.82	7.17	4.26	3.61
Other transport equipment	0.00	0.00	0.00	0.00	0.00	11.11
Textiles and clothing	0.00	0.00	0.00	0.00	0.00	0.00
Paper products and publishing	2.70	2.27	4.55	24.24	17.24	21.21
Rubber and plastic products	12.39	14.54	13.89	4.00	4.26	0.00
Non-metallic mineral products	16.09	22.70	20.31	32.00	31.40	71.43
Coal and petroleum products	11.11	12.44	18.15	10.95	12.70	17.07
Professional and scientific instruments	92.41	90.70	97.67	84.09	72.73	96.10
Other manufacturing	78.16	43.71	21.38	26.21	36.84	60.47
Total manufacturing industry	20.01	20.93	22.10	24.20	21.73	29.89

Source: The data in Tables A.15–18 on the geographical origins and industrial distribution of patents granted in the USA to 770 of the world's largest industrial firms have been compiled by John Cantwell at the University of Reading with the support of the US Patent and Trademark Office. For further details see, for example, John Cantwell, 'The Globalisation of Technology: What Remains of the Product Cycle?' *Cambridge Journal of Economics* 19, 1995, pp. 155–74.

Commentary:

1 Consistent with data in earlier tables (see e.g. Tables A.1, A.6 and A.13) the share of the total patents, registered in the US by UK firms, but accounted for by the UK affiliates of US firms, has steadily increased since 1969–72, but most markedly so since 1990.

2 Apart from in the rubber and plastic product sectors – there no longer is any US fdi in the UK rubber industry – aircraft and aerospace, and electrical equipment and computing sectors, US affiliates have increased their share of total UK patenting. This increase has been particularly noticeable in the paper products, food, drink and tobacco and metals and mechanical engineering sectors, and, in part at least, reflects several large acquisitions of UK firms by US corporations over the last 25 years.

Table A.16 The share of US patents of the largest US firms attributable to their research activities in the UK, as a proportion of the number due to their research activities in Western Europe, 1969–95 (%)

	1969–72	1973–77	1978–82	1983–86	1987–90	1991–95
Food, drink and tobacco	44.68	46.67	45.71	37.14	37.14	26.50
Chemicals and pharmaceuticals	37.38	39.53	45.41	40.68	43.06	41.20
Metals and mechanical engineering	40.22	37.80	37.53	37.79	34.69	35.97
Electrical equipment and computing	32.70	31.47	29.64	23.98	22.94	22.51
Motor vehicles	55.28	41.44	43.26	34.42	22.57	48.40
Aircraft and aerospace	67.50	39.81	34.31	20.41	13.68	13.89
Other transport equipment	0.00	0.00	N/A	0.00	N/A	100.00
Textiles and clothing	N/A	0.00	N/A	N/A	N/A	N/A
Paper products and publishing	11.11	7.69	11.11	25.81	18.52	31.82
Rubber and plastic products	31.03	26.19	21.51	4.35	3.28	0.00
Non-metallic mineral products	54.90	35.24	20.16	27.12	13.92	22.28
Coal and petroleum products	29.63	23.15	28.98	18.75	31.50	31.21
Professional and scientific instruments	32.30	26.17	34.43	36.27	34.78	40.44
Other manufacturing	57.63	42.86	17.82	17.42	14.69	26.00
Total manufacturing industry	37.33	34.88	34.69	30.05	29.38	32.07

Note:
N/A – not available.

Commentary:
1 The UK has retained its position as one of the premier locations for the innovatory activities of US manufacturing subsidiaries in Western Europe. Though its share of the patents registered by US subsidiaries in Europe has fallen slightly since the early 1970s, it has not been so marked as that of the total US capital stake in UK industry (see Table A.3).
2 While in some sectors, e.g. chemicals and pharmaceuticals, paper products, and professional and scientific instruments, the UK's share of European registered patents has risen over the last two decades, in others, notably electrical equipment, rubber and plastic products and other manufacturing, it has fallen – and in some cases quite sharply.

Table A.17 The share of US patents of the largest US firms attributable to their research activities in the UK, as a proportion of the number attributable to their research activities in the US, 1969–95 (%)

	1969–72	1973–77	1978–82	1983–86	1987–90	1991–95
Food, drink and tobacco	1.00	1.52	2.15	1.93	1.84	2.24
Chemicals and pharmaceuticals	1.56	2.44	2.81	2.92	3.52	3.60
Metals and mechanical engineering	1.41	1.59	1.85	2.83	3.32	3.02
Electrical equipment and computing	1.85	1.87	1.96	1.80	1.29	1.06
Motor vehicles	1.57	1.32	1.59	2.39	2.39	2.21
Aircraft and aerospace	0.79	0.56	0.57	0.35	0.19	0.17
Other transport equipment	0.00	0.00	0.00	0.00	0.00	5.88
Textiles and clothing	0.00	0.00	0.00	0.00	0.00	0.00
Paper products and publishing	0.09	0.07	0.08	0.81	0.49	0.59
Rubber and plastic products	1.75	1.91	1.68	0.23	0.25	0.00
Non-metallic mineral products	2.03	2.64	2.42	3.83	3.81	6.96
Coal and petroleum products	0.37	0.40	0.49	0.33	0.53	0.56
Professional and scientific instruments	2.35	1.30	1.54	1.79	0.93	2.82
Other manufacturing	2.14	2.24	1.37	1.52	1.38	1.54
Total manufacturing industry	1.45	1.61	1.76	1.80	1.73	1.73

Commentary:

1 Although the share of domestically registered patents by US firms accounted for by their UK affiliates is very small, it has steadily increased since the early 1970s.

2 The relative significance of patenting in the UK affiliates of US firms has risen most markedly in the food, drink and tobacco, chemicals, non-metallic minerals and paper products sectors; by contrast, in the rubber and plastic products and electrical equipment and computing sectors it has fallen quite sharply.

Table A.18 The ratio of US patents of the largest US firms attributable to their research activities in the UK to the equivalent for UK firms in the US, 1969–95

	1969–72	1973–77	1978–82	1983–86	1987–90	1991–95
Food, drink and tobacco	0.08	0.09	0.11	0.09	0.10	0.12
Chemicals and pharmaceuticals	0.67	1.09	1.79	2.31	1.27	1.32
Metals and mechanical engineering	0.30	0.59	0.70	0.88	0.70	0.62
Electrical equipment and computing	1.65	1.61	2.16	2.97	1.01	1.75
Motor vehicles	6.85	3.41	2.77	2.00	0.94	2.00
Aircraft and aerospace	27.00	N/A[1]	35.00	1.43	1.30	1.15
Other transport equipment	N/A	N/A	N/A	N/A	N/A	N/A
Textiles and clothing	0.00	0.00	0.00	0.00	0.00	0.00
Paper products and publishing	0.05	0.03	0.04	0.14	0.10	1.75
Rubber and plastic products	13.50	33.00	10.00	N/A	N/A	N/A
Non-metallic mineral products	2.33	1.61	1.86	1.88	4.50	2.65
Coal and petroleum products	0.03	0.05	0.06	0.03	0.04	0.05
Professional and scientific instruments	24.33	9.75	14.00	18.50	4.00	148.00
Other manufacturing	N/A	N/A	10.33	3.38	N/A	26.00
Total manufacturing industry	0.48	0.59	0.69	0.64	0.50	0.65

Note:
1 N/A – not available.

Commentary:
1 Overall, UK affiliates in the US registered more patents in the US than did US affiliates in the UK for each of the periods identified in Table A.18.
2 The relative significance of patents attributed to US affiliates in UK manufacturing *vis-à-vis* those attributed to UK affiliates in US manufacturing have marginally increased since the early 1970s. This is rather surprising as the UK capital stake in the US has risen faster than the US capital stake in the UK over these years. The industrial composition of the data would, however, suggest that US affiliates in the UK are more R&D intensive sectors than are UK affiliates in the US.
3 Apart from in metals and mechanical engineering, the patenting advantage of US affiliates in the UK is strongly concentrated in the technology-intensive sectors, whereas the comparative patenting advantage of UK affiliates in the US is most marked in the food, drink and tobacco and petroleum product sectors. In the great majority of sectors, however, the growth of UK-registered patents by US affiliates has exceeded that of US-registered patents by UK affiliates.

Table A.19 Anglo-US royalties and licence fees, 1956–96

Year	Receipts (by US from UK firms)			Payments (by US from UK firms)		
	Affiliated	Non-Affiliated	Aff/Non-Aff	Affiliated	Non-Affiliated	Aff/Non-Aff
1956	22	29	0.76	7	9	0.78
1960	51	40	1.28	8	9	0.89
1965	140	57	2.46	11	18	0.61
1970	217	56	3.88	19	35	0.54
1975	444	79	5.62	27	76	0.36
1986	747	113	6.61	124	76	1.63
1987	1,002	112	8.95	300	96	3.13
1988	1,244	134	9.28	282	155	1.82
1989	1,290	215	6.00	404	174	2.32
1990	1,523	262	5.81	507	199	2.55
1991	1,670	196	8.52	874	201	4.35
1992	1,760	224	7.86	975	221	4.41
1993	1,584	230	6.89	1,036	246	4.21
1994	1,766	247	7.15	1,105	266	4.15
1995	1,849	266	6.95	1,387	316	4.39
1996	2,042	290	7.04	1,432	303	4.73

Source: US Development of Commerce, *Survey of Current Business*, October 1997, September 1994, September 1991, January 1980, December 1973.

Commentary:

1 The royalties and fees paid by UK to US firms for technology, managerial expertise and administrative services rose 46 times (in money terms) between 1956 and 1996, while payments made by US to UK firms rose by 108 times. While the rise in the former flows has been quite steady, substantial payments by US to UK firms have only occurred since the 1980s.

2 In 1996, 87.6% of royalties and fees received by US from UK firms were intra-firm, i.e. paid by the US subsidiaries to their US parent companies. This proportion represented a considerable increase over the figure forty years earlier. A similar trend towards more internalized royalties and fees occurred with respect to US payments to UK firms.

3 Until the late 1970s, the value of royalties and fees paid by UK to US firms exceeded payments made by US to UK firms by a rate of 5 to 1 or more. Throughout the 1980s and early 1990s, as UK fdi in the US increased markedly (see Table A.2) this ratio fell steadily, and in 1996 it was 1.34 to 1.

4 Comparing data in Table A.19 (column 1) with those in Table A.11, it can be seen that the royalties and fees paid by US subsidiaries to their parent concerns have risen faster than the earnings of US manufacturing affiliates in the UK. For example, betwen 1970 and 1995, while these earnings increased by 7.7 times, royalties and fees increased by 9.4 times. *Inter alia*, this suggests that either the knowledge content of US direct investment in the UK has more than kept pace with its financial content, or that US subsidiaries are being charged more for the technology, managerial and administrative services provided by their parent companies.

Table A.20 Percentage of all UK manufacturing exports accounted for by US subsidiaries, 1957–94 (£ million)

	(1) US affiliates	1982 = 100.0	(2) UK exports	1982 = 100.0	(1)/(2) %
1957	296	3.0	2,971	7.4	9.96
1966	639	8.4	4,772	11.9	13.39
1973	1,839	24.2	11,589	29.0	15.87
1977	4,365	57.6	25,824	64.4	16.90
1982	7,576	100.0	40,087	100.0	18.90
1989	14,094	186.0	76,361	190.9	18.46
1990	16,253	214.5	84,166	210.4	19.31
1991	18,633	249.5	86,062	215.2	21.65
1992	23,964	316.3	88,796	222.0	26.99
1993	23,651	312.2	98,090	245.0	24.11
1994	24,350	321.4	112,078	280.2	21.73

Sources: US Department of Commerce, *Survey of Current Business* (various issues) and (UK) Central Statistical Office, *Abstract of Annual Statistics* (various issues).

Commentary:

1 Between 1957 and 1992, US affiliates accounted for a steadily increasing share of all UK manufacturing exports. In the last two years for which data are available, this share has fallen slightly.

Table A.21 Export sales of US manufacturing affiliates in the UK, 1966–94

(a) Value of manufacturing exports ($ millions)

	1966	1977	1982	1989	1992	1994
Food products	49	(d)	462	(d)	(d)	1,284
Chemical products	(d)*	1,033	1,966	3,774	5,230	5,692
Primary fabricated metals	135	342	660	(d)	(d)	1,363
Machinery	719	2,089	2,619	4,110	11,464	13,511
Electrical equipment	N/A[2]	(d)	548	1,555	1,264	1,187
Transportation equipment	(d)	(d)	2,218	3,139	6,549	5,481
Other manufacturing	(d)	1,182	2,564	2,861	4,612	4,493
Total	1,920	7,773	11,138	17,342	31,554	33,012

(b) Percentage of UK exports accounted for by US affiliates

Food products	5.4	N/A	N/A	N/A	N/A	12.8
Chemical products	N/A	26.2	30.1	32.0	35.4	35.7
Primary fabricated metals	17.3	22.3	26.0	N/A	N/A	36.7
Machinery	N/A	42.9	39.2	22.3	51.7	56.8
Electrical equipment	N/A	N/A	27.5	27.5	28.0	15.9
Transportation equipment	N/A	N/A	24.5	18.8	33.7	27.3
Other manufacturing	N/A	24.8	N/A	17.1	27.8	27.2
Total	25.1	29.05	29.46	23.54	35.32	30.34

Sources: US Department of Commerce, *Survey of Current Business* and *Benchmark Surveys of US Direct Investment Abroad*.
Notes:
1 (d) Suppressed to avoid disclosure of data of individual companies
2 N/A = not available.

Commentary:
1 The exports of US manufacturing subsidiaries in the UK are largely concentrated in the high or medium technology-intensive sectors, with the fastest rates of growth (since 1977) being recorded by the machinery sector.
2 The machinery sector is also the most export-intensive among US affiliates, with electrical equipment becoming significantly less export-intensive over the years. There is some suggestion that the completion of the European Internal Market may have modestly contributed to the export propensity of US affiliates in the UK.

Table A.22 Distribution of total employment in manufacturing of foreign-owned firms in the UK, by region, 1971–92 (selected years)

	1971	1979	1984	1992
More prosperous regions[1]	60.3	56.3	58.5	54.7
East Midlands	3.5	4.4	4.5	6.3
East Anglia	4.1	4.3	4.4	4.0
South East	41.1	35.3	36.1	26.9
South West	2.6	4.3	5.6	5.4
West Midlands	9.0	8.0	7.9	12.1
Less prosperous regions	39.7	43.7	41.5	45.3
North	3.3	5.0	5.4	6.3
Yorkshire & Humberside	3.3	6.5	5.4	6.8
North West	13.2	13.8	13.2	12.5
Wales	4.8	5.5	5.7	6.5
Scotland	11.1	9.8	8.9	10.1
Northern Ireland	4.0	3.0	2.7	3.1
UK	100.0	100.0	100.0	100.0

Source: *UK Census of Production (PA1002)*, London: Central Statistical Office, various dates.
Note:
More prosperous regions are defined as those which have an average or a below average unemployment record for the period 1971–92. Less prosperous regions are the rest.

Commentary:

1 There are no published data on the spatial distribution of US-owned manufacturing activity in the UK. However, data on the regional distribution of employment by all foreign-owned firms suggest that, between 1971 and 1992, there was some dispersion of manufacturing activity away from the more prosperous regions of the UK (especially South-East England) towards the less prosperous regions. Part of this spatial restructuring of the activity most certainly reflects the propensity of new Japanese foreign direct investment to favour Wales and the North East of England – but also, since the late 1980s, the Midlands.

Table A.23 Location quotients[1] of foreign firms in UK manufacturing industry, 1971–92 (selected years)

		1971	1979	1981	1984	1992
North	% foreign	3.30	5.00	4.90	5.40	6.30
	% all UK	5.70	5.90	5.80	5.50	5.60
	Location quotient	0.58	0.85	0.84	0.98	1.12
Yorkshire &	% foreign	3.30	6.50	5.80	5.40	6.80
Humberside	% all UK	9.80	9.90	9.60	9.30	9.80
	Location quotient	0.34	0.66	0.60	0.58	0.69
East Midlands	% foreign	3.50	4.40	4.80	4.50	6.30
	% all UK	7.40	8.20	8.30	9.00	9.80
	Location quotient	0.47	0.54	0.58	0.50	0.64
East Anglia	% foreign	4.10	4.30	4.20	4.40	4.00
	% all UK	2.50	2.90	3.00	3.30	3.60
	Location quotient	1.64	1.48	1.40	1.33	1.11
South East	% foreign	41.10	35.30	36.20	36.10	26.90
	% all UK	26.60	25.20	25.90	26.60	23.10
	Location quotient	1.54	1.40	1.40	1.36	1.16
South West	% foreign	2.60	4.30	5.00	5.60	5.40
	% all UK	4.90	5.90	6.50	7.00	7.30
	Location quotient	0.53	0.73	0.77	0.80	0.74
West Midlands	% foreign	9.00	8.00	7.90	7.90	12.10
	% all UK	13.90	13.40	12.80	12.60	13.20
	Location quotient	0.65	0.60	0.62	0.63	0.92
North West	% foreign	13.20	13.80	13.40	13.20	12.50
	% all UK	14.60	13.90	13.50	12.70	12.30
	Location quotient	0.90	0.99	0.99	1.04	1.02
England	% foreign	80.10	81.70	82.30	82.70	80.30
	% all UK	85.40	85.40	85.70	86.10	84.70
	Location quotient	0.94	0.96	0.96	0.96	0.95
Wales	% foreign	4.80	5.50	5.30	5.70	6.50
	% all UK	4.10	4.40	4.10	4.00	4.80
	Location quotient	1.17	1.25	1.29	1.42	1.35
Scotland	% foreign	11.10	9.80	9.50	8.90	10.10
	% all UK	8.30	8.30	8.20	7.80	7.90
	Location quotient	1.34	1.18	1.16	1.14	1.28
UK	Location quotient	1.00	1.00	1.00	1.00	1.00

Source: As for Table A.22.

Note:

1 Share of employment in foreign enterprises in UK private sector manufacturing divided by share of employment in all private sector manufacturing firms

Commentary:

1 Compared to all UK firms, foreign-owned firms tend to favour locations either in South-East England or in the least prosperous areas of the UK, notably Wales and Scotland.

2 Between 1971 and 1992, the location quotient of foreign firms increased most significantly in the South West, Midlands and the North of England, while it fell most sharply in East Anglia and the South East of England.

Table A.24 Acquisitions and mergers of UK companies by US companies, 1987–95
(£ million)

Year	US No. 1	US Value 2.	All foreign No. 3	All foreign Value 4	All A&Ms No. 5	All A&Ms Value 6	% of 1 to 3	% of 3 to 4	% of 1 to 5	% of 2 to 6
1987	22	225	61	2,701	1,589	19,240	36.1	8.3	1.4	1.2
1988	25	872	99	5,690	1,598	28,529	25.3	15.3	1.6	3.1
1989	42	5,475	168	12,130	1,505	39,380	25.0	45.1	2.8	13.9
1990	32	1,785	143	10,958	922	19,287	22.4	16.3	3.5	9.3
1991	39	1,782	146	6,667	652	17,101	26.7	26.7	6.0	10.4
1992	64	1,591	210	4,139	642	10,080	30.5	38.4	10.0	15.8
1993	128	2,764	267	5,187	793	12,270	47.9	53.3	16.1	22.5
1994	93	2,115	202	5,213	876	13,482	46.0	40.6	10.6	15.7
1995	64	4,793	131	12,817	636	45,617	48.9	37.4	10.1	10.5

Source: (UK) Office of National Statistics, *Acquisitions and Mergers Involving UK Companies*, 1997.

Commentary:

1 Data have only recently become available on the acquisitions and mergers (A&Ms) of UK companies by US companies. These, however, suggest that in the last decade US firms have accounted for a larger share of all A&Ms involving foreign firms; and also a larger – and quite significant – proportion of all A&Ms of UK companies.

Notes

PREFACE TO 1998 EDITION

1 For a listing of some of these studies, see John H. Dunning, *Multinational Enterprises and the Global Economy*, Wokingham, Berkshire: Addison Wesley, 1993, and R. E. Caves, *Multinational Enterprises and Economic Analysis*, Cambridge, Mass.: Harvard University Press, 1996.

2 UNCTAD, *World Investment Report 1996: Investment, Trade and International Policy Arrangements*, New York and Geneva: UN, 1996 and J. H. Dunning, The European Internal Market Program and Inbound Foreign Direct Investment', *Journal of Common Market Studies*, March and June 1997, 35, pp. 1–30 and 189–223.

3 US Department of Commerce, *US Direct Investment Abroad, Preliminary 1993 Estimates*, Washington: US Department of Commerce, 1995.

4 Three times the rate in the 1990s. See Dunning, *Multinational Enterprises*, p. 16 and UNCTAD, *World Investment Report 1996*, p. 5.

5 Defined as enterprises which engage in foreign direct investment.

6 In 1995, these sales were valued at $6.0 billion and that of world exports of goods and non-factor services at $4.7 million.

7 UNCTAD, *World Investment Report 1996*.

8 The respective figures for the US alone (i.e. US outbound fdi stock as a proportion of its gdp were 4.6 per cent, 7.1 per cent, 8.1 per cent, 7.9 per cent and 9.1 per cent, for the UK 10.0 per cent, 9.1 per cent, 14.9 per cent, 23.6 per cent and 27.5 per cent (Dunning, *Multinational Enterprises*, p. 17; UNCTAD, *World Investment Report 1996*, pp. 261–2.

9 J. H. Dunning, 'The Geographical Sources of the Competitiveness of Firms'. *Transnational Corporations* 5 (3), December 1996, pp. 1–30.

10 J. H. Dunning, 'Globalization and the New Geography of Foreign Direct Investment', *Oxford Development Studies* 26 (1), 1998, pp. 47–69.

11 US Department of Commerce, *Survey of Current Business, September 1996*, p. 107.

12 For a comparison between a multi-domestic and globally integrated organizational structure of MNEs see M. E. Porter (ed.), *Competition in Global Industries*, Boston: Harvard Business School Press, 1986, especially Chapter 1.

INTRODUCTION

1 Organization for European Economic Co-operation (OEEC), *Private Investment in Europe and the Overseas Territories*, Paris: OEEC, 1954.

2 F. A. Southard, *American Industry in Europe*, Boston: Houghton-Mifflin, 1931.

3 Published by The Brookings Institution (US) 1938.

4 E. R. Barlow, *Management of Foreign Manufacturing Subsidiaries*, Boston: Harvard University Press 1953.

5 See, for example, United States Department of Commerce, 'Foreign Investments of the United States'. Censuses of 1950, 1953, and S. Pizer and F. Cutler, 'Growth of Foreign Investments in the United States and Abroad', *Survey of Current Business* (US Department of Commerce), August 1956, pp. 14ff.

6 Sponsored by the Royal Society of Arts, the British Association for the Advancement of Science and the Nuffield Foundation. For the first results of the work of this committee see C. F. Carter and B. R. Williams *Industry and Technical Progress*, Oxford: Oxford University Press 1957.

7 Subsequent volumes, published by George Duckworth in the later 1950s and early 1960s, and all written by members of the Department of Political Economy of University College London included those on the man-made fibres, radio, building and tin plate industries.

1 THE GROWTH OF US INVESTMENT

1 C. Lewis, *America's Stake in International Investments*, 1938, Chap. 9, pp. 174ff.

2 [M. Wilkins, *The Emergence of Multinational Enterprises: American Business Abroad from the Colonial Period to 1914*, Cambridge, Mass.: Harvard University Press 1970, p. 29.]

3 [Ibid., p. 30. Wilkins drew her material from C. T. Haven and F. A. Belden, *A History of the Colt Revolver*, New York: W. Morrow 1940 (see especially pp. 345–9).]

4 W. Woodruff, 'The American Origin of a Scottish Industry', *Scottish Journal of Political Economy* 2 (1), 1955.

5 [A. Godley, 'The Determinants and Impact of the Pioneering Foreign Direct Investment in British Manufacturing', *Business History Review*, 1998 (forthcoming).]

6 Lewis, *America's Stake*, Washington, DC: The Brookings Institution, Chap. 9 *et seq.*

7 Statistical Abstracts for the United Kingdom; 1903 Cd. 1727, lxxx 1914–16 Cd. 8128, lxxvi.

8 Godley, 'Determinants and Impact'.

9 For further details see M. Plant, *The English Book Trade*, London: Allen & Unwin 1939. Also, R. Hoe, *A Short History of the Printing Press*, New York: R. Hoe 1902.

10 Hoe, *Short History*, p. 37.

11 H. V. Faulkner, *American Economic History*, New York: Harper & Row 1949, pp. 401ff.

12 J. H. Clapham, *An Economic History of Modern Britain* Book III, Cambridge: Cambridge University Press 1938, pp. 43ff.

13 Economic Co-operation Administration (ECA) Mission to the United Kingdom, *Economic Development in the United Kingdom 1850–1950* (n.d.).

14 Electrical Trades Departmental Committee, Report; 1918 Cd. 9072, xiii.

15 A. Cairncross, *Home and Foreign Investment 1870–1913*, Cambridge: Cambridge University Press 1953, p. 4.

16 For the early history of the electric lighting industry see A. A. Bright, *The Electric Lamp Industry: Technological Change and Economic Development from 1800–1947*, New York: Macmillan 1949; also, Edison Swan Electric Co. Ltd, *The Pageant of the Lamp* (n.d.).

17 *The Pageant of the Lamp*, p. 28.

18 H. A. Price-Hughes (comp.), *B.T.H. Reminiscences: Sixty Years of Progress*, London: British Thomson-Houston 1946, pp. 9ff.

19 A. G. Whyte, *The Electric Industry: Lighting, Traction and Power*, London: Methuen 1904.

20 For further details see Bright, *Electric Lamp Industry*

21 Bright, *Electric Lamp Industry*. See also Electrical Trades Departmental Committee, Report; 1918 Cd. 9072, xiii.

22 *B.T.H. Reminiscences*, p. 11.

23 J. Dummilow, *1899–1949*, 1949, p. 29.

24 Ibid., p. 27.
25 Ibid., p. 29.
26 Ibid., p. 3.
27 J. H. Robertson, *The Story of the Telephone: A History of the Telecommunications in Britain*, London: Scientific Book Club 1948, p. 7. Also see A. N. Holcombe, 'The Telephone in Great Britain', *Quarterly Journal of Economics*, 1906–7, pp. 96–135.
28 Holcombe, 'The Telephone in Great Britain'.
29 Telephones Select Committee, Report; 1898 (383) xii.
30 F. A. McKenzie, *The American Invaders*, London: H. W. Bell, 1902. See also, 'Investigation of Prices', Sub-Committee Report, Matches; 1920 Cmd. 924, xxiii. Also, 'Monopolies and Restrictive Practices', Commission Report, 'Supply and Export of Matches and the Supply of Match-making Machinery'; 1952–3 (161) xv.
31 *Financial Times*, 21 September 1901.
32 See, for example, H. W. MacCrosty, *The Trust Movement in British Industry*, London: Longmans, Green, 1907, p. 231.
33 McKenzie, *American Invaders*.
34 J. H. Clapham, *An Economic History of Modern Britain*, Book III, Cambridge: Cambridge University Press, 1938, p. 269.
35 Private letter to writer from British United Shoe Machinery Company. November 1955.
36 McKenzie, *American Invaders*.
37 Boots and Shoes Working Party, Report, pp. 100ff.; 1946 Non-Parl. Board of Trade.
38 R. H. Heindel, *The American Impact on Great Britain, 1898–1914*, Philadelphia: University of Pennsylvania Press 1940, pp. 176ff.
39 W. F. Ford, 'The Limits of the American Invasion', *Contemporary Review*, June 1902.
40 Quoted in Heindel, *American Impact*, p. 176.
41 McKenzie, *American Invaders*, p. 31.
42 Heindel, *American Impact*, pp. 176ff.
43 Patent Medicines Select Committee, Report; 1914 (414) ix.
44 Lewis, *America's Stake*, pp. 311ff.
45 F. A. Southard, *American Industry in Europe*, Boston: Houghton-Mifflin 1931, pp. 115ff.
46 Ibid., p. 119.
47 For further details see Chap. 9.
48 G. C. Allen, *British Industries and Their Organization* (rev. edn), London: Longmans, Green & Co. 1950, pp. 158ff.
49 From interview with Ford Motor Company Ltd.
50 [Or, in the words of the London press quoted in Mira Wilkins's book, to use its 'boundless resources of capital' to snatch away Great Britain's supremacy of the seas (Wilkins, *Emergence of Multinational Enterprise*, p. 70).]
51 Agreement dated 1 August 1903 between the Admiralty and the Board of Trade and the International Mercantile Marine Company and other companies; 1903 Cd. 1704, lxiii, 101.
52 For further details and subsequent history, see F. C. Bowen, *A Century of Atlantic Travel*, Boston: Little, Brown & Co. 1930, and C. R. V. Gibbs, *Passenger Liners of the Western Ocean*, London: Staples Press 1952.
53 Combinations in the Meat Trade. Departmental Committee, Report; 1909 Cd. 4643, xv.
54 Ibid.
55 Heindel, *American Impact*, pp. 190ff.
56 [This figure has been revised upwards since the original edition of this book, primarily because in 1958 I underestimated the employment in Singer at 7,000. It would now seem that in 1914, the Glasgow factories of Singer employed over 14,000 people, compared with 11,000 in 1911 and 7,000 in 1900 (Godley, 'Determinants and Impact').]

57 [These are described by Geoffrey Jones in 'Foreign Multinationals and British Industry before 1945', *Economic History Review* (3), 1988, 429–53.]

58 Heindel (*American Impact*) instances the ice-cream venture of Hortons, New York, failing 'as public demand did not yet exist in the U.K.'.

59 Organization for European Economic Co-operation (OEEC), *Report on International Investment*, 1950, pp. 13ff.

60 Quoted in the English periodical *Anglo-American News*, December 1925.

61 Quoted by Southard, *American Industry*, p. 117.

62 But only until 1922 when production at Cork ended because of lack of demand. The factory production was then switched to cars and trucks and not until 1927 was tractor production re-started.

63 Southard, *American Industry*, p. 77.

64 See, for example, Trusts Sub-Committee, Reports, Electric Lamp Industry; 1920 Cmd. 622, xxiii. Electrical Cable Industry; 1921 Cmd. 1332, xvi. Also, Monopolies and Restrictive Practices Commission, Reports, Supply of Electric Lamps; 1950–1 (287) xvii; Insulated Electric Wires and Cables; 1951–2 (209) xvii.

65 Robertson, *Story of the Telephone*, Chap. 6.

66 The successor of the Western Electric Co., who had acquired the Fowler-Waring Company in 1897.

67 From a letter to the writer from the Central Electricity Authority, November 1955.

68 Southard, *American Industry*, p. 182.

69 Ibid.

70 See *The Economist*, 23 March 1929.

71 *Anglo-American News*, November 1930.

72 For the developments in this field see *Anglo-American News*, January and June 1930. See also Jones, 'Foreign Multinationals'.

73 Among the US companies which first began manufacturing in the UK in these years were International Business Machines (1929) – office equipment, American Timkin (1927) – roller bearings and Otis Elevators (1924) – elevators.

74 From a letter to the writer from the Imperial Chemical Industries, November 1955.

75 F. A. Southard, 'American Industry Abroad since 1929', *Journal of Political Economy*, 41, 1933, pp. 530–47.

76 R. Gelatt, *The Fabulous Phonograph*, Philadelphia: Lippincott 1955, pp. 104ff.

77 *The Economist*, 11 August 1928.

78 United States Department of Commerce, Trade Information Division, *American Direct Investments in Foreign Countries*, No. 731, 1930.

79 United States Department of Commerce, Trade Information Division, *American Direct Investments in Foreign Countries*, No. 731, 1930.

80 'American Branch Factories Abroad', Senate Document 120, 73rd Congress, 2nd Session, 1934.

81 United States Department of Commerce, *American Direct Investments in Foreign Countries*, 1936. Economic Series No. 1, 1938.

82 For further details see G. W. Parker, 'American Branch Plants Meet Foreign Competition', *Anglo American News*, January and February 1933.

83 W. A. Lewis, *Economic Survey*, London: Allen & Unwin 1949, p. 75, and M. F. G. Scott, 'The Problem of Living within Our Foreign Earnings', *Three Banks Review*, June 1955, p. 14.

84 Allen, *British Industries*, pp. 29ff.

85 [F. Bostock and G. Jones, 'Foreign Multinationals in British Manufacturing Activity', *Business History* 36 (1), 1994, 89–126.]

86 United States Department of Commerce, *American Direct Investments in Foreign Countries*, 1940, 1942.

87 United States Treasury Department, *Census of American-Owned Assets in Foreign Countries*, 1947.

88 See United States Department of Commerce, *Establishing a Business in the United Kingdom*, 1956, and 'A Billion Dollars in Britain', *The Economist*, 5 June 1954.

89 For further details see Chap. 10, pp. 224–30.

90 See also Chap. 10, pp. 243ff. For a general discussion see OEEC, 'Private United States Investment in Europe and the Overseas Territories', 1954, pp. 23ff.

91 [The Invest in Britain Bureau, for example, which is now the only development agency handling inward direct investment for the whole of the UK, was not set up until 1977.]

2 THE PRESENT-DAY SCOPE OF AMERICAN PARTICIPATION

1 S. Pizer and F. Cutler, 'Growth of Foreign Investments in the United States and Abroad', *Survey of Current Business* (US Department of Commerce), August 1956, pp. 14ff. Since this chapter was written, the corresponding figures for 1956 have been published. Total US direct investments in the UK now amount to $1,599 million, of which manufacturing interests represent $1,039 million, and petroleum refining and distribution $279 million. See the writer's 'Dollar Investments in Britain Accelerate', *Times Review of Industry*, October 1957.

2 [Central Office of Information, *Britain's International Investment Position*, London: COI 1970.]

3 *Standard Industrial Classification* (reprinted with amendments); 1953 Non-Parl. Central Statistical Office.

4 After making an estimated allowance for investment in non-manufacturing oil companies.

5 For a more precise definition, see United States Department of Commerce, *Foreign Investments of the United States. Census of 1950*, 1953, pp. 36ff.

6 'American Branch Factories Abroad', Senate Document 120, 73rd Congress, 2nd Session, 1934.

7 Pizer and Cutler, 'Growth of Foreign Investments' p. 22.

8 [Between 1943 and end 1956, the figure would have been between 90 and 100. [This figure is broadly in line with estimates made by Frances Bostock and Geoffrey Jones in 1994. See their article, 'Foreign Multinationals in British Manufacturing, 1850–1962' *Business History* 36 (1), pp. 89–126.]]

9 Though in eight cases data had to be collected in a roundabout fashion!

10 It is important to distinguish between these two terms. *Direct* investment includes those cases in which the investor buys stock directly from a foreign company, lends money directly to such a company, builds a factory abroad, etc. *Portfolio* or indirect investments are those in which the investor purchases securities offered (usually publicly) through the intermediary of an investment company. See F. A. Southard, *American Industry in Europe*, Boston: Houghton-Mifflin 1931, pp. 191–2.

11 As an approximation, the corresponding employment and turnover figures for subsequent years would be:

	Employment	Sales turnover
1954	275,000	£740–£780 million
1955	310,000	£775–£825 "
1956	340,000	£825–£870 "

As mentioned earlier in the text, these figures probably underestimate by 5–10 per cent (nearer 10 per cent in 1956) the *total* significance of US-financed firms in British manufacturing industry. By March 1957 the numerical strength of such companies had exceeded the 300 mark.

12 See 'Introductory Notes to Census of Production for 1952 and 1953'; 1956 Non-Parl. Board of Trade.

13 This figure in 1956 was nearer 80 per cent.

14 Accounts relating to Trade and Navigation of the UK, December 1953; 1952–3 (69–XI), xxviii.

15 That is up to 31 December 1953. We make no claim that this represents the total number of firms established during this period as there is no official list: we believe, however, that all important firms have been included.

16 As derived from *Annual Abstract of Statistics*, Nos. 89, 92; 1952, 1955, Non-Parl. Central Statistical Office.

17 See, for example, P. Sargant Florence, *Investment, Location and Size of Plant*, London: Allen & Unwin 1948, Chap. 4, pp. 34ff.

18 Compare, for example, this figure with those given in ibid., pp. 34–7.

19 'Provisional Results of the Census of Production for 1955', *Board of Trade Journal*, 22 December 1956, p. 1321.

20 For further details see J. G. Glover and W. B. Cornell, *The Development of American Industries: Their Economic Significance*, New York: Prentice Hall, 1951.

21 *Board of Trade Journal*, 31 December 1955, p. 1398.

22 For further information see 'The British Petroleum Industry in Great Britain', *Midland Bank Review*, February 1955, and the various oil industry surveys which have been published by the *Financial Times* from time to time in recent years.

23 See, for example, *Financial Times*, 6 April 1956 and 17 July 1956. In addition a £25 million oil refinery for Regent Oil Company, Ltd (joint subsidiary of California Texas Corporation (Caltex) and Trinidad Oil Company) is planned for the UK. Initial throughput is estimated at 5 million tons annually.

24 See pp. 155ff.

25 R. S. Aries and Associates, *Economic Aspects of the Pharmaceutical Industry*, New York [n.p.] 1955.

26 Ibid., p. 7.

27 Estimated from data contained in ibid.

28 Accounts relating to Trade and Navigation of the UK, December 1955; 1954–5 (41–XI), xvii.

29 From information supplied by the Esso Petroleum Co. Ltd.

30 For example the 1907 Census of Production records an output of agricultural machinery worth £1.1 million.

31 For further details see PEP (Political and Economic Planning), *The Agricultural Engineering Industry*, 1949.

32 'Tools on the Land', *The Economist*, 12 July 1952.

33 *Annual Abstract of Statistics*, No. 92, 1955, Table 190; 1956 Non-Parl. Central Statistical Office.

34 From data supplied by Office Appliance and Business Equipment Trades' Association.

35 For further details of the role of US firms in the UK office machinery industry, see 'A Great Anglo-American Venture Pays Off', *Anglo-American News*, March 1957.

36 From data supplied by Council of Petroleum Equipment Manufacturers.

37 Organization for European Economic Co-operation, 'Oil Equipment in Europe', Technical Assistance Mission 121, 1955.

38 As mentioned on p. 35. Blaw Knox is no longer financially associated with Blaw Knox, Pittsburgh. There is, however, still a close technical link between the two companies.

39 [In fact, this did take place in the 1950s, but today (1998) there is no trace of that company.]

40 See, for example, 'British Synthetic Rubber by 1958', *Anglo-American News*, May 1956; '£13 million Expansion at Fawley Refinery', *Financial Times*, 17 July 1956 'Chemicals from Oil', *The Economist*, 23 June 1956.

41 As derived from Census of Production figures for 1935 and Provisional results of Census of Production for 1955 (*Board of Trade Journal*, 22 December 1956).

42 A notable exception is the recent Anglo-American agreement between Mitchell Engineering Ltd, and AMF Atomics Ltd, as a result of which the largest power organization

in the Ruhr is to be supplied with an atomic power station. Mitchell's, the UK concern, is to supply the primary and secondary steam circuits, the reactor vessel and heat-exchange pipes, while AMF Atomics will be responsible for the core, core-control gear and instrumentation. Likewise in the aircraft industry the close association between the Wright Aeronautical Division of Curtiss-Wright (US) and the Bristol Aeroplane Company (UK) has done much to advance jet engine development while in May 1957 it was announced that Armstrong Siddeley Motors of Coventry and the Garrett Corporation of Los Angeles had concluded a licensing agreement covering the manufacturing and selling rights in Britain of the auxiliary power gas turbines and air turbine starters developed by the Air Research manufacturing divisions of the Garrett Corporation.

43 Sir John Cockcroft, 'Science and Technology in Industry', *British Journal of Applied Physics*, May 1955.

3 DISTRIBUTION, SIZE AND OWNERSHIP OF US AFFILIATES

1 In the 1935 Census of Production, for example, there were 41,164 firms and 48,944 plants employing eleven or more workers. See P. Sargant Florence, *The Logic of British and American Industry*, London: Routledge & Kegan Paul 1953, p. 34. [For a more current evaluation of the extent of multi-plant operations of foreign manufacturing subsidiaries in the UK see F. Bostock and G. Jones, 'Foreign Multinationals in British Manufacturing, 1850–1962', *Business History* 36 (1), pp. 89–126. See especially pp. 109ff.]

2 The US firms with the most plants in the UK included Ford, General Motors, United Shoe Machinery, Johnson & Johnson and Monsanto and Hoover.

3 Apart from those in Northern Ireland, and as scheduled in the Distribution of Industries Acts, 1945, 1950. See Distribution of Industry Statement; 1948 Cmd. 7540, ii. In October 1952 North-East Lancashire was also included under these Acts.

4 Including Kraft, Goodyear, Heinz, Caterpillar Tractor, The Prestige Group Ltd.

5 In this instance, obtained by dividing the percentage of workers in US establishments in a particular area by the percentage of total workers found there. See P. Sargant Florence, *Investment Location and Size of Plant*, London: Allen & Unwin 1948, p. 41.

6 Ibid., p. 31. See also footnote to Table 3.1, p. 57.

7 [As indicated in Chapter 1 the actual labour force of Singer in 1914 was nearer 14,000.]

8 In 1932, for example, the average unemployment in the United Kingdom was $22\frac{1}{2}$ per cent of insured persons registered, and in the Development Areas 38 per cent. The corresponding figures for 1937 were 10 per cent and 18 per cent respectively.

9 A. K. Cairncross and R. Meier, 'New Industries and Economic Development in Scotland', *Three Banks Review*, June 1952, pp. 3ff.

10 See, for example, J. H. Dunning, 'The Development Areas: A Further Note', *Manchester School of Economic and Social Studies*, 24, January 1956, pp. 77–95. See also P. Robson, 'Growth of Employment and Diversification of Industry in the Development Areas', *Oxford Economic Papers*, New Series (1) February 1956, pp. 60–77.

11 Including Armstrong Cork, Bakelite, A. J. Siris, Abbott Laboratories, E. R. Squibb and Standard Brands.

12 This, of course, refers to the situation prior to the discovery of North Sea oil and the burgeoning of a major Scottish oil-producing and refining industry.

13 Annual Abstract of Statistics, No. 91, Table 136; 1954 Non-Parl. Central Statistical Office.

4 FINANCIAL AND MANAGERIAL SUPERVISION OF BRANCHES

1 'English Law for Americans', *Anglo-American Year Book*, 1956, pp. 125ff.
2 C. Lewis, *America's Stake in International Investments*, Washington, DC: The Brookings Institution 1938.
3 [And later (1966) that of Ford.]
4 United States Department of Commerce, 'American Direct Investments in Foreign Countries, 1936', *Economic Series*, No. 1, 1938, and Chapter 2, pp. 32ff.
5 US Department of Commerce, *Foreign Investments of the United States*, 1953.
6 See Chapter 1. Also F. A. Southard, *American Industry in Europe*, Boston: Houghton-Mifflin 1931; Organization for European Economic Co-operation, *Private United States Investment in Europe and the Overseas Territories*, Paris 1954.
7 Lewis, *America's Stake*, p. 305.
8 E. R. Barlow, *Management of Foreign Manufacturing Subsidiaries*, Boston: Harvard University 1953, pp. 145, 146.
9 See, for example, 'English Law for Americans', *Anglo-American Year Book*, 1956.
10 Ibid., p. 126. Also see International Bureau of Fiscal Documentation, Amsterdam, *Compilation of the Legal Provisions, Regulations, Circulars and Forms Relating to Double Taxation Relief in the U.K. and Northern Ireland*, 1956.
11 See also Barlow, *Management*, Chap. 3.

5 COMPARATIVE OPERATING METHODS AND PRODUCTIVITY

1 London: Allen & Unwin, 1953.
2 For a bibliography on this subject see Organization for European Economic Co-operation, *Bibliography on Productivity*, Paris: OECC 1956.
3 For a survey of alternative measures see T. E. Easterfield, 'British Managements' Uses of Productivity Indices', *The Manager*, February 1953, and the accompanying bibliography.
4 For instance, some years ago it was reported that the Shredded Wheat subsidiary in England found the centrifugal process used by its American plant to clean the wheat was neither suited to the lighter stones in the Australian wheat used by the English plant nor did it remove the burrs peculiar to that wheat. See F. A. Southard, *American Industry in Europe*, Boston: Houghton-Mifflin 1931, p. 153.
5 For further details see Chap. 10, pp. 224ff.
6 British Productivity Council, *Management Accounting*, 1951, p. 14.
7 United States Treasury Department, *Census of American-Owned Assets – Foreign Countries*, 1947.
8 See Chapter 9 for further details
9 See, for example, P. Sargant Florence, *The Logic of British and American Industry* London: Routledge & Kegan Paul, 1953. For an alternative view on the importance of the market as a determinant of productivity, see E. Rothbarth, 'Causes of the Superior Efficiency of U.S.A. Industry as Compared with British Industry', *Economic Journal*, 56, September 1946, pp. 383–90; M. Frankel, 'Anglo-American Productivity Differences – their Magnitude and Some Causes', *American Economic Review*, 45, Annual Proceedings May 1955, pp. 94–112.
10 For a fuller description of this concept see E. A. G. Robinson, 'The Structure of Competitive Industry', *Cambridge Economic Handbooks*, VII, Cambridge: Cambridge University Press, 1935.
11 Oxford: Basil Blackwell, 1956.
12 See also comments by T. G. Belcher in his article 'American Factory Operation in Scotland Successful', *Foreign Commerce Weekly*, 17 January 1955.
13 This conclusion does not necessarily conflict with Professor Melman's findings. For, first, he was mainly concerned with *changes* in production techniques over a period of time,

and second, his definition of 'materials handling' – which would appear to be the sphere in which the alternative labour and machine hour costs are the most relevant – is considerably wider than our own.

14 We make no judgement about the welfare effects of such a policy!

15 See British Productivity Council, *Production Control*, 1953, pp. 10ff., and pp. 59ff. To quote from this publication: 'The availability of materials in the right place and at the right time is a major factor in determining the efficiency and high productivity of American industry.'

6 THE INFLUENCE OF US FIRMS ON UK DEVELOPMENT

1 See Chap. 1, p. 16.

2 Monopolies and Restrictive Practices Commission, Report, 'Supply of Electronic Valves and Cathode Ray Tubes', 1956–7 (16).

3 See Chap. 1, pp. 16ff.

4 For further details see, for example, R. Evely, 'Monopoly: Good and Bad' *Fabian Research Series*, No. 163, 1954.

5 As, in fact, was concluded by the Monopolies and Restrictive Practices Commission in its report on the 'Supply of Electric Lamps' (1950–1 (287) xvii), 'Supply and Export of Pneumatic Tyres' (1955–6 (133)), 'Supply of Insulin' (1951–2 (296) xvii).

6 *Combinations in the Meat Trade*, Department Committee, Report; 1909 Cd. 4643, xv.

7 For further details see particularly B. Yamey, *Resale Price Maintenance*, London: Allen & Unwin 1953; A. Hunter, 'The Monopolies Commission and Economic Welfare', *Manchester School of Economic and Social Studies*, January 1955; Sir H. Clay, 'The Campaign against Monopoly and Restrictive Practices', *Lloyds Bank Review*, April 1952 – and references cited within these articles.

8 Sir H. Hartley, 'Scientific Research in Britain: Its Structure and Policy', *Progress*, Spring 1955.

9 As derived from 1907 *Census of Production* statistics. See also S. Melman, *Dynamic Factors in Industrial Productivity*, Oxford: Basil Blackwell 1956, Chap. 17

10 National Academy of Sciences – National Research Council, *Applied Research in the U.S.*, edited by E. W. Scott, 1952, p. 5.

11 R. L. Meier, 'The Role of Science in the British Economy', *Research*, May 1951.

12 National Academy of Sciences, *Applied Research*, p. 59.

13 D. W. Hill, 'Man-Made Fibres', *Three Banks Review*, December 1953, p. 33.

14 For further details on comparative sizes of manufacturing establishments in the UK and the US and their average research expenditure, see J. H. Dunning, 'Anglo-American Research Co-operation and Industrial Progress', *District Bank Review*, June 1956, pp. 3–22.

15 S. C. Ogburn, 'Research Management', *Industrial Laboratories*, September 1951.

16 Meier, 'The Role of Science'.

17 National Academy of Sciences, *Applied Research*, p. 1.

18 Ibid., pp. 42ff.

19 Estimated by E. Rudd (DSIR), *Expenditure on Scientific Research and Technical Development in Britain and America*, to be £65 million in 1955. If one includes Government-financed research undertaken by private industry, the relevant US and UK figures are respectively £1,200 million and £185 million. Also see C. F. Carter and B. R. Williams, *Industry and Technical Progress*, London: Oxford University Press, 1957, Chap. 3.

20 For recent US developments see R. Aries and Associates, *Economic Aspects of the Pharmaceutical Industry*, New York [n.p.] 1955.

21 See Chap. 7, pp. 155ff.

22 If the subsidiary is kept informed of preliminary design and development work, a new

technique may be taken up almost immediately, e.g. stereophonic sound came to the UK almost as soon as it was discovered in the US.

23 For further details see Chap. 9, pp. 202ff.

24 Several US-financed firms noted that because of the small demands made of them in the UK, suppliers did not find it economic to install the specialized machinery necessary to manufacture the same materials or parts as were produced in the US. For example, one subsidiary noted that it would like to emulate a type of timing belt which is now an essential part of its parent concern's finished product, but, due to its limited size of orders, has so far found no supplier willing to invest in the necessary equipment to produce the appropriate raw materials.

25 *Anglo-American News*, March 1936.

26 For example, in 1955 that company recorded a trading loss of £27,882 against a profit of £26,576 in the previous year.

27 Which of course, includes the US firms themselves, hence the relevant figures in Table 6.3 tend to overestimate the productivity of the UK firms within the group.

28 Including the agricultural, office, refrigeration, boot and shoe and sewing machinery, domestic electrical appliances, telecommunications equipment and machine tools industries.

29 Published by the National Institute of Economic and Social Research, December 1955.

30 See particularly 'Accounting Ratios', *Accountancy*, July 1956, which discusses the applicability of such ratios in making inter-firm comparisons and F. Sewell Bray, 'Accounting Ratios for Inter-Firm Comparisons', *Times Review of Industry*, November 1956.

7 INFLUENCE ON UK SUPPLIERS

1 A *continuous processing* industry may be defined as one in which the operations to change the raw material into finished goods are performed in a continuous manner on the entire mass of material. The raw materials enter at one end of the plant and pass through various machines and processes without halting at any stage for other finished parts to be brought to them. When such articles thus manufactured are finished, they are completed as a whole and not in sections that must be put together. By contrast, in *assembling* industries, several parts or constituents (or auxiliary appliances) of the product are manufactured simultaneously and then assembled, e.g. as in the manufacture of machinery or motor-cars.

2 A. P. Gray and M. Abrams, 'The Construction of Esso Refinery', *British Institute of Management Occasional Papers, No. 6*, 1954. See also 'Achievement at Fawley', *Petroleum Times*, 30 November 1951; E. M. Hugh-Jones, 'Industrial Productivity: The Lessons of Fawley', *Journal of Industrial Economics*, July 1955.

3 *Purchasing Research*, December 1953, p. 680.

4 Organization for European Economic Co-operation, *Oil Equipment in Europe*, Technical Assistance Mission, No. 121, Paris: OEEC 1955, pp. 13–14.

8 THE PRODUCTS SUPPLIED BY US FIRMS

1 The actual numbers engaged in the production of capital goods would be about three-quarters of this figure.

2 Strictly speaking, one should relate the cost of US-financed firms' products to that of importing from the cheapest comparable source in America and elsewhere.

3 N.B. Our classification of firms in this section has been determined by the *main* products supplied in each instance.

4 *Boots and Shoes*, Working Party Report, pp. 15ff.; 1946 Non-Parl. Board of Trade.

5 R. Hoe, *A Short History of the Printing Press*, New York: R. Hoe, 1902.

6 *Anglo-American News*, November 1935.
7 See, for example, 'Mechanising Flatwork Ironing', *Power Laundry*, 2 September 1950.
8 J. B. Styles, 'Metal Spraying', *Welding*, November 1946.
9 'Mechanised Job Costing', *The Accountant*, 28 May 1955.
10 *Annual Abstract of Statistics, No. 93*, Table 190; 1956 Non-Parl. Central Statistical Office.
11 J. G. Simpson, *Costs of Operating Combine Harvesters*, Leeds: Leeds University Press, 1950.
12 British Productivity Council (BPC) *Review of Productivity in the Agricultural Machinery Industry* London: BPC (n.d.), p. 20.
13 From information supplied by the National Coal Board.
14 For further details in respect of one US subsidiary, see 'Petroleum Refining and Chemical Plant', *Chemical Age*, 21 February 1953.
15 For further details see *Anglo-American News*, November 1956, pp. 489–90.
16 'Towards the Mechanical Kitchen', *Financial Times*, 4 August 1956.
17 See, for example, J. D. McLintock, 'Packaging and Production by Contract', *The Packer and Shipper*, March 1954, and 'A Confidential Processing and Packaging Service', *The British Packer*, April 1954.

9 MANAGERIAL TECHNIQUES

1 All published by the British Productivity Council (formerly Anglo-American Council on Productivity: UK Section) between 1951 and 1953.
2 Anglo-American Productivity Team Report, *Production Control*, 1951, p. 6.
3 R. H. Heindel, *The American Impact on Great Britain 1898–1914*, Philadelphia: University of Pennsylvania Press 1940.
4 *Target* (a monthly publication of the British Productivity Council), March 1953.
5 See 'Vauxhall Go On to Straight Time Basis', *Anglo-American News*, May 1956.
6 Naturally each firm may not confine itself to any *one* of these; however, we have chosen to consider only the main method adopted by the firm.
7 For further details see *Business*, September 1950.
8 'Guaranteed Work in Industry', *Financial Times*, 27 January 1953.
9 By such companies for example as Procter and Gamble, Ford Motor and Quaker Oats. For further details see *Scope*, July 1956.
10 F. A. Southard, *American Industry in Europe*, Boston: Houghton-Mifflin 1931, p. 155.
11 For further particulars see 'Incentive Management in Two Countries', *Business*, March 1953.
12 *Financial Times*, August 1956.
13 *Business*, February 1929.
14 See, for example, cases cited in *Target*, September, December 1948; December 1952. Once again we were impressed by the extent to which the practices of US firms in the UK corresponded to those reported in *Training of Supervisors*, British Productivity Council, 1951, as being commonly adopted in the US.
15 i.e. that introduced by the *News Chronicle* in April 1956.
16 From a speech by Lord (then Sir P.) Perry, quoted in *Business*, November 1931.
17 W. Woodruff, 'The American Origins of a Scottish Industry', *Scottish Journal of Political Economy* 2 (1), February 1955, p. 27.
18 p. 106.
19 *Financial Times*, 13 September 1956.
20 R. Spark, 'How Office Appliance Manufacturers Train Customers' Staff', *Business*, February 1952.
21 Figures derived from *Statistical Review of Press Advertising* 23, January 1955.
22 For a recent discussion on the role of advertising in a competitive economy, see M. Baynes, *Advertising on Trial*, London: The Bow Group, 1956.
23 Much of this case study originally appeared in *Business*, September 1953, under the title,

'From Family Business to Scientific Management'. I am very grateful to the editor of the journal for his permission to incorporate parts of the article in this book.

10 OVERALL EFFECTS AND FUTURE PROSPECTS

1 For the historical background of US corporate investment overseas see C. Lewis, *America's Stake in International Investments*, 1938; Organization for European Economic Co-operation (OEEC), *Report on International Investment*, 1950, and *Private United States Investment in Europe and the Overseas Territories*, 1954; C. R. Carroll, *Private Enterprises Abroad*, New York: American Enterprise Association, 1954; US Department of Commerce, 'Foreign Investment of the United States', *Census of 1950*, 1953.

2 See also A. Cairncross, *Studies in Home and Foreign Investment 1870–1913*, Cambridge: Cambridge University Press 1953, pp. 4ff.

3 F. W. Paish, 'Britain's Foreign Investments: the Post-War Record', *Lloyds Bank Review*, July 1956.

4 For further details see United Nations, *The International Flow of Private Capital, 1946–52*, New York: UN 1954.

5 See R. Nurkse, 'International Investment Today in the Light of Nineteenth Century Experience', *Economic Journal*, December 1954, p. 744. In this article the writer estimates that up to 60 million people emigrated from the British Isles and Continental Europe over the fifty years preceding the outbreak of the First World War.

6 E. Bloch, 'United States Foreign Investment and Dollar Shortage', *Review of Economics and Statistics*, May 1953.

7 See further pp. 243ff.

8 The following section is largely based on two articles by the author, viz. 'U.S. Manufacturing Subsidiaries and Britain's Trade Balance', *District Bank Review*, September 1955, and 'Dollar Exports of U.S. Firms in Britain', *Financial Times*, 10 April 1957. In the light of subsequent information certain of the figures contained in this earlier article have been amended and brought up to date.

9 Defined as those goods and services which first entered into commercial production during the 1930s or subsequently: see the writer's 'Newer British Industries and Increasing Productivity', *District Bank Review*, June 1954. Also, 'Growth of New Export Industries in the UK', *Board of Trade Journal*, 1 May 1954; and 'Progress in New Exports of U.K. Products', *Board of Trade Journal*, 13 October 1956.

10 E. Nevin, 'United States Foreign Investment and Dollar Shortage: A Comment', *Review of Economics and Statistics*, November 1954, p. 428.

11 F. A. Southard, *American Industry in Europe*, Boston: Houghton-Mifflin 1932, p. 163.

12 Quoted in 'U.S. Firms in Britain Set a Faster Pace for an Old Economy', *Business Week*, 29 March 1956.

13 Indeed, there is an added stringency placed on US firms in that they have not been able to obtain credit with the same ease. See 'English Law for Americans', *The Anglo-American Year Book, 1956*, p. 120.

14 This problem has been most acute in the Scottish Development Area. For the experiences of a sample of six post-war established subsidiaries in this connection, see T. G. Belcher, 'American Factory Operation in Scotland Successful', *Foreign Commerce Weekly*, 17 January 1955.

15 Readers who are particularly interested in current developments should consult the *Times Review of Industry* regional reports, published each month by that journal. Other new US subsidiaries or Anglo-American companies who have established manufacturing units in this country within the last few months include: Chemstrand Ltd (synthetic fibres); Rank-Xerox Ltd (xerography products); Cummins Engine Co. Ltd (diesel engines); Cobble Brothers (carpet tufting machinery); Hyster Company (tractor equipment); Ketty Ltd (precision instruments); Du Pont Co. (UK) Ltd (chemical products);

Air Trainers Ltd (air crew training equipment); Cleveland Twist Drill Co. (high speed twist drills); Aircraft Marine Products (solderless electrical terminals); British Oxygen Aro Equipment Ltd (liquid oxygen and nitrogen equipment); West Instrument Ltd (industrial control equipment); Dayton Co. Ltd (rubber and synthetic accessories for the textile trade).

16 *Business*, August 1950.

17 Estimated from an official (US) figure of $1,168 million in 1950 and $1,881 million in 1957.

18 The Fortune Directory of the 500 largest US industrial corporations, *Fortune Supplement*, July 1956.

19 OEEC, *Private U.S. Investment in Europe*, 1954, p. 23.

20 523 H. C. Deb., Ss., 9 February 1954, Cols 101–2.

21 For further details see the writer's 'Dollar Investments in Britain Accelerate', *Times Review of Industry*, October 1957.

22 See also pp. 244ff.

23 See, for example, 'America Buys Foreign', *Investors' Chronicle*, 8 January 1955 and 'America Buys British', *The Economist*, 18 June 1955. Also 'Trinidad Oil Company Proposed Purchase by the Texas Company'; 1955–6 Cmd. 9790, xxxvi.

24 See Southard, *American Industry*, p. 182, also Chap. 1 pp. 21ff.

25 And others cited by E. A. G. Robinson in his *Monopoly*, Cambridge: Cambridge University Press 1941.

26 See *The Chemist and Druggist*, 13 April 1957, p. 394.

27 For further details see J. H. Dunning, 'The Foreign Capital in Britain's Drugs', *Financial Times*, 6 September 1957.

28 S. Pizer and F. Cutler, 'Growth of Foreign Investments in the United States and Abroad', *Survey of Current Business* (US Department of Commerce), August 1956, pp. 21ff. See also Table 10.4, p. 235.

29 Calculated from data contained in 'Progress in New Exports of U.K. Products', *Board of Trade Journal*, 13 October 1956.

30 For a suggestion that larger UK companies should be compelled to publish quarterly financial reports, thereby aiding the quotation of British equities on Wall Street, and for more selling drive by British security holders, see 'Foreign Investment', a letter to *The Economist* by P. J. D. Wiles, 11 June 1955.

31 OEEC, *Private U.S. Investment in Europe*, Paris: OEEC 1954, p. 23.

32 For further details see *The Anglo-American Year Book, 1956*, pp. 9–13.

33 See also Carroll, *Private Enterprises Abroad*, Chap. 3.

34 Published by the American Chamber of Commerce in London, Inc., 1955.

35 *The American Anti-Trust Laws and American Business Abroad*, p. 18.

36 Ibid., p. 19.

37 For comparative details of publicity services offered by individual European countries, see OEEC, *Private U.S. Investment in Europe*, 1954, Appendix I.

38 For a discussion of the experiences of the four US firms already manufacturing in Northern Ireland see G. C. Mitchell, 'U.S. Plants in Northern Ireland', *Anglo-American News*, November 1956.

39 For example, the Netherlands has already attracted more than fifty American subsidiaries in manufacturing industry – most of these since 1945. As is the practice in other Continental countries, but not in Britain, Dutch banks frequently make loans to US plants for the purchase of land or buildings. In a number of cases, particularly in the light engineering industry, US-controlled firms, which chose to establish their factories on the Continent rather than in the UK, are the UK manufacturers' strongest competitors in the overseas markets. Again, at least one American pharmaceutical company abandoned its project of building a plant in Britain because of the difficulties over National Health Service price regulations: it subsequently constructed it in another

European country from which Britain and the Sterling Area as a whole are now compelled to import their requirements.

11 FORTY YEARS ON

1 More specifically, the Marshall Aid Plan.
2 As summarized, for example, by Graham Hutton in *We Too Can Prosper*, London: Allen & Unwin, 1953.
3 E. Rothbarth, 'Cause of the Superior Efficiency of USA Industry as Compared with British Industry', *Economic Journal 56*, September 1946, pp. 383–90, and L. Rostas, 'Comparative Productivity in British and American Industry', *National Institute of Economic and Social Research*, Occasional Papers 13, Cambridge: Cambridge University Press, 1948.
4 Later, these figures were to be confirmed and elaborated on by a US study: M. Frankel, *British and American Manufacturing Productivity*, Urbana, Illinois: University of Illinois Press, 1957.
5 In Chapter 3, I state that 'between 1940 and 1953, US subsidiaries in this area accounted for two-thirds of the increase in the total labour force directed to the (so called) Development Areas of the time'. At the time, I recorded some observations about these phenomena in an article I wrote for the (then) *Annual Survey of the Manchester Guardian* in 1953. See my 'American Factories in Britain', *Manchester Guardian 'Survey of Industry'* 1953, pp. 108/9.
6 As detailed in Chapter 10.
7 See also Table 6.3 (p. 134) and Table 6.6 (p. 139) of this volume.
8 Comparable data are not available on sales.
9 See especially Chapter 1 of this volume (pp. 29–31). This investment today is usually referred to as defensive market-seeking investment.
10 Such fdi is more aggressive market-seeking or is designed to increase the efficiency of existing investment through the rationalization and restructuring in two or more European manufacturing plants.
11 See, for example p. 242.
12 For example, in the 1950s, US manufacturing subsidiaries in the UK probably employed less than 10 per cent of their total labour force on R&D related activities; by 1989 this percentage had increased to 31 per cent. (US Department of Commerce, *US Direct Investments Abroad, Benchmark Survey for 1989*, Washington: US Government Printing Office, 1992.)
13 As described, for example, in R. D. Pearce and S. Singh, *Globalizing Research and Development*, Basingstoke: Macmillan, 1992.
14 J. H. Dunning, 'The Geographical Sources of Competitiveness of Firms: the Results of a New Survey', *Transnational Corporations* 5 (3), December 1996, pp. 1–30.
15 For further details see G. De Long, R. C. Smith and I. Walter, 'Global Merger and Acquisition Tables 1995', New York: Salomon Center (mimeo).
16 See Chapter 10, p. 225.
17 p. 224 of this volume. For estimates in the 1960s see J. H. Dunning, *The Role of American Investment in the United Kingdom Economy*, London: Political and Economic Planning, 1969.
18 UK Census of Production data cited in Table 11.1.
19 See, for example, J. H. Dunning, *Japanese Participation in British Industry*, London: Croom Helm, 1986, and R. Strange, *Japanese Manufacturing Investment in Europe*, London and New York: Routledge, 1993.
20 See particularly Chapter 1 pp. 18–19, for some reasons for US fdi prior to 1914, p. 21 and 26–9 for between 1919 and 1939, and pp. 29–31 for fdi between 1945 and 1953.
21 The first time we used these expressions was in J. H. Dunning, 'The Determinants of International Production', *Oxford Economic Papers*, 25 (3), November 1973, p. 313.

22 The term 'multinational enterprise' had not been coined at this stage.

23 As later detailed by Ray Vernon in his product cycle theory of fdi, see R. Vernon, 'International Investment and International Trade in the Product Cycle', *Quarterly Journal of Economics* 80 (1966), 190–207.

24 See especially Chapters 2, 6, 7, 8 and 9.

25 See, for example, pp. 6, 10, 31, 55, 143, 246.

26 Dunning, 'The Determinants of International Production'.

27 Most recently in J. H. Dunning, *Multinational Enterprises and the Global Economy*, Wokingham, England and Reading, Mass.: Addison Wesley, 1993, and 'Reappraising the Eclectic Paradigm in the Age of Alliance Capitalism', *Journal of International Business Studies*, 26 (3), 1995, 461–91.

28 *Japanese Participation in British Industry.*

29 This last variable is given particular emphasis by scholars such as Frederick Knickerbocker and Raymond Vernon, who argue that much fdi is related to advancing or protecting an oligopolistic market position of the investing firms. See, for example, R. Vernon, 'The Economist's Role in Research on Transnational Corporations: or Why the Dogs Have Barked so Softly', *Transnational Corporations* 3, December 1994, pp. 81–90.

30 In the 1960s, there was some concern lest US firms investing in the pharmaceutical industry, particularly by way of A&Ms, were doing so to gain access to European R&D capabilities. See J. H. Dunning, *Studies in International Investment*, London: Allen & Unwin 1970, Chapter 9.

31 See especially Chapters, 1, 2 and 6.

32 As has been well summarized by Richard Caves, *Multinational Enterprises and Economic Analysis*, Cambridge: Cambridge University Press (2nd edition), 1996, and by a collection of articles in the *Journal of International Business Studies* 29 (1), First Quarter, 1998.

33 e.g. profitability, productivity, market shares and trends in productivity.

34 5 measures × 11 manufacturing sectors = 55.

35 Which was gross output per employee (net selling value).

36 This, in fact, we did in subsequent studies of US affiliates in the UK in the later 1950s and 1960s. See, for example, J. H. Dunning, 'U.S. Subsidiaries and their UK Competitors', *Business Ratios*, 2, Autumn 1966, pp. 5–19, and *US Industry in Britain*, London: Wilton House, 1976. We also compared the rate of return on sales and the sales/net asset ratios of US subsidiaries of UK firms, and found in the 1970s, for example, that these data confirmed our earlier findings.

37 S. Globerman, 'The Structure of US Investment in UK Industry', *Applied Economics*, 11 (1), 1979, 35–41; J. H. Dunning (ed.), *Multinational Enterprises, Economic Structure and International Competitiveness*, Chichester: Wiley, 1985; S. Davies and D. Petts, *The Changing Structure of UK Manufacturing, 1986–1993: Concentration, Diversification and Multinationality*, Norwich, University of East Anglia: The Economics Centre Discussion Research Paper 9702, 1997; M. Blomstrom, *Foreign Investment and Spillovers: A Study of Technology Transfer to Mexico*, London: Routledge, 1989 and UNCTAD (DTCI), *World Investment Report 1995, Transnational Corporations and Competitiveness*, Geneva and New York: UN, 1995.

38 See p. 37 for definition.

39 Dunning, 'The Determinants of International Production'.

40 Standard Industrial Classification.

41 *Multinational Enterprises, Economic Structure and International Competitiveness.*

42 As reviewed, for example, in Dunning, *Multinational Enterprises and the Global Economy.*

43 See particularly the special issue of *Business History* edited by Geoffrey Jones in January 1994 (vol. 36, no. 1) on 'The Making of Global Enterprise'.

44 *Japanese Participation in British Industry.*

45 As set out, for example, in my *JIBS* article, 'Reappraising the Eclectic Paradigm'.

46 Lest I be misunderstood, I am not advocating that the eclectic paradigm is the only – or, indeed, necessarily the best – approach to explaining all aspects of the growth of US

participation in UK industry. But, for evaluating the economic determinants of such participation, I believe it has much to commend it.

47 Perhaps more correctly, these advantages should be called O-specific transaction and co-ordinating net *benefits*. But internalization theory tends to focus on the gains from avoiding the transaction costs of market failure rather than the benefits which arise from co-ordinating activities in hierarchies.

48 The estimation is based on the value of new cross-border A&Ms foreign direct investment flows to developed countries. We have adjusted these percentages to take account of minority A&Ms. UNCTAD-DTCI, *World Investment Report 1996, Transnational Corporations, Investment, Trade and International Arrangements*, New York and Geneva: UN, 1996.

49 Dunning, 'The Geographical Sources of Competitiveness of Firms'.

50 And 19 per cent engaged in some basic research.

51 J. Cantwell and R. Harding, 'The Internationalisation of German Companies R&D', Reading, England: University of Reading, Department of Economics (mimeo), 1997.

52 See, for example, J. Cantwell and U. Kotecha, 'The Internationalisation of Technological Activity: The French Evidence in a Comparative Setting', in J. Howells and J. Michie (eds), *Technology, Innovation and Competitiveness*, Cheltenham: Edward Elgar, 1997, and J. Cantwell and O. Janne, 'The Internationalisation of Technological Activity: The Dutch Case', Reading, England: University of Reading, Department of Economics (mimeo) 1997.

53 In 1994, the sales of the foreign affiliates of US MNEs were 30.7 per cent of their worldwide sales; the corresponding figure for employment was 26.8 per cent (R. Mataloni and M. Fahim Nader, 'Operations of US Multinationals: Results from the 1994 Benchmark Survey', *Survey of Current Business* 76, December 1996, pp. 11–39).

54 The latest comprehensive appraisal of the role of fdi in the British economy dates back to 1988. See S. Young, N. Hood and J. Hamill, *Foreign Multinationals and the British Economy*, London and New York: Croom Helm.

55 Especially those associated with the transfer of relatively standardized and codifiable intangible assets.

56 A unit within the Department of Trade and Industry.

57 For example, even by the 1970s, the profitability gaps between US manufacturing subsidiaries and their UK competitors had been halved since the 1950s. See Dunning, *US Industry in Britain*.

58 These matters are at the cutting edge of contemporary research by industrial geographers, economists and business analysts. In the mid-1950s I observed US firms had had a considerable impact on the development of new industrial clusters in various parts of the UK, notably in the 1930s, in the area around the Great West Road and North Circular Road, and the Slough Industrial Estate, and in the 1950s in the (then) Development Areas of Glamorgan (South Wales) and the Value of Leven (Scotland). I also gave examples of US subsidiaries acting as flagship firms for fostering new industries; these included the Ford Motor Company (around Dagenham in Essex) Vauxhall (General Motors) (around Luton in Bedfordshire) and Briggs Motor Bodies and Esso Petroleum Co. around Southampton in Hampshire. Finally, I noted that in 1953 60 per cent of all US factories (in the UK) were sited within thirty miles of the five major ports of London, Liverpool, Southampton, Glasgow and Cardiff. Later, both in my volume on *Japanese participation in UK industry*, and in the Hood, Young and Hamill volume referred to earlier, more recent examples of clustering of foreign (and particularly Japanese) firms in several regions and districts of the UK (notably in South Wales, mid-Scotland, Sunderland and Derby) were given.

59 'Does Ownership Really Matter in a Globalising Economy?' in D. Woodward and D. Nigh, *Foreign Ownership and US Competitiveness*, Westport, Conn.: Greenwood Publishing, 1998.

60 Around the 30 per cent level. By contrast, the share of global sales of Japanese MNEs

has risen from under 5 per cent in 1985 to 15 per cent in 1990. Bearing in mind that the Japanese home market is half the size of its US counterpart, this would suggest that Japanese firms have a long way to go in their internationalization process.

61 As surveyed by P. Buiges, F. Ilzkovitz and J. Lebrun in 'The Impact of the Internal Market by Industrial Sector: The Challenge of Member States', *European Economy*, special edn 1990, pp. 1–114, and by the author in 'The European Internal Market and Inbound Foreign Direct Investment', *Journal of Common Market Studies* 35, March and June 1997, pp. 1–30 and 189–223.

62 According to one estimate, the IMP may have raised the price stock of UK fdi (at constant prices) in the rest of the EU by 31 per cent (N. Pain and M. Lansbury, 'The Impact of the Internal Market on the Evolution of European Direct Investment', London: NISER (mimeo) 1996).

63 *Vis-à-vis* other countries in the EU.

64 See some statistical details given in Appendix 2.

65 See, for example, UN, *International Investment towards the Year 2001*, Geneva: UNCTAD, 1997.

66 In this respect, to be competitive, countries or regions, like firms, need to develop their core competitive assets which are not easily copied by other countries. At one time, these advantages were based on natural endowments. Today, they must be based on created assets of one kind or another. Since these assets tend to be more mobile across national boundaries, this is a more difficult thing to do.

67 Notably, the Singaporean government and several regional authorities, e.g. Scotland, Alabama, in the US, Bangalore in India and Shanghai in China.

68 *Studies in International Investment*, Chapter 8.

69 Thus the R&D content of US manufacturing subsidiaries has continued to increase over the past thirty or more years. See Appendix 3, Table A.13. For a recent examination of the growth of Japanese-owned innovatory facilities in the UK, see R. Pearce and M. Papanastassiou, *The Technological Competitiveness of Japanese Multinationals*, Ann Arbor: University of Michigan Press, 1996, and L. Turner, D. Ray and T. Hayward, *The British Research of Japanese Companies*, London: Insight Japan, 1997.

70 This assertion seems to us to be as valid in the 1990s as when we first put it forward in the late 1960s. See *Studies in International Investment*, pp. 322ff.

71 At both a national and sub-national level.

72 i.e. gross benefit less gross cost.

APPENDIX 1

1 While this list is as complete and accurate as is known to the author, it makes no claim to be exhaustive.

Index of firms

General index